GENDERED PEACE THROUGH INTERNATIONAL LAW

Two leading feminist lawyers reflect on gender in international law to set out what a gendered peace might look like and its impact on international law in this open access book. In order to challenge orthodoxies, the book takes an unconventional approach, merging personal reflections, expert essays, and interviews. It throws the disciplinary net wide, drawing on international law, gender studies, international relations and history. The authors, undisputed global leaders in the field, challenge the reader to unlearn international law, in order to relearn it in a way that makes it more fit for purpose in the contemporary world. This seminal work is a clarion call to think about international law in a new and transformative way.

For additional material on *Gendered Peace Through International Law* visit https://www.bloomsburyonlineresources.com/gendered-peace-through-international-law.

Gendered Peace Through International Law

Louise Arimatsu
and
Christine Chinkin

·HART·
OXFORD · LONDON · NEW YORK · NEW DELHI · SYDNEY

HART PUBLISHING

Bloomsbury Publishing Plc

Kemp House, Chawley Park, Cumnor Hill, Oxford, OX2 9PH, UK

1385 Broadway, New York, NY 10018, USA

29 Earlsfort Terrace, Dublin 2, Ireland

HART PUBLISHING, the Hart/Stag logo, BLOOMSBURY and the Diana logo are trademarks of Bloomsbury Publishing Plc

First published in Great Britain 2024

Copyright © Louise Arimatsu and Christine Chinkin, 2024

Louise Arimatsu and Christine Chinkin have asserted their right under the Copyright, Designs and Patents Act 1988 to be identified as Authors of this work.

This work is published open access subject to a Creative Commons Attribution-NonCommercial-NoDerivatives 4.0 International licence (CC BY-NC-ND 4.0, https://creativecommons.org/licenses/by-nc-nd/4.0/). You may re-use, distribute, and reproduce this work in any medium for non-commercial purposes, provided you give attribution to the copyright holder and the publisher and provide a link to the Creative Commons licence.

While every care has been taken to ensure the accuracy of this work, no responsibility for loss or damage occasioned to any person acting or refraining from action as a result of any statement in it can be accepted by the authors, editors or publishers.

All UK Government legislation and other public sector information used in the work is Crown Copyright ©. All House of Lords and House of Commons information used in the work is Parliamentary Copyright ©. This information is reused under the terms of the Open Government Licence v3.0 (http://www.nationalarchives.gov.uk/doc/open-government-licence/version/3) except where otherwise stated.

All Eur-lex material used in the work is © European Union, http://eur-lex.europa.eu/, 1998–2024.

A catalogue record for this book is available from the British Library.

Library of Congress Cataloging-in-Publication data.

Names: Chinkin, Christine, author. | Arimatsu, Louise, author.

Title: Gendered peace through international law / Christine Chinkin and Louise Arimatsu.

Description: Oxford [UK] ; New York : Hart Publishing, 2024. | Includes bibliographical references and index. | Summary: "This open access book sets out what gendered peace can look like and how it might impact on international law, drawing on personal reflections, expert essays and empirical research. History, law, international relations and gender studies all merge to support the authors' suggested model for how peace should be considered going forward in international law"— Provided by publisher.

Identifiers: LCCN 2024008000 (print) | LCCN 2024008001 (ebook) | ISBN 9781509970278 (hardback) | ISBN 9781509970247 (paperback) | ISBN 9781509970254 (Epub) | ISBN 9781509970261 (ebook)

Subjects: LCSH: Women (International law) | Women—Violence against—Law and legislation. | Women—Crimes against.

Classification: LCC K644 .C453 2024 (print) | LCC K644 (ebook) | DDC 341.4/858—dc23/eng/20240224

LC record available at https://lccn.loc.gov/2024008000

LC ebook record available at https://lccn.loc.gov/2024008001

ISBN: PB: 978-1-50997-024-7
ePDF: 978-1-50997-026-1
ePub: 978-1-50997-025-4

Typeset by Compuscript Ltd, Shannon
Printed and bound in Great Britain by CPI Group (UK) Ltd, Croydon CR0 4YY

To find out more about our authors and books visit www.hartpublishing.co.uk. Here you will find extracts, author information, details of forthcoming events and the option to sign up for our newsletters.

We dedicate this book to Professor Karen Knop (1960–2022), a very dear friend and inspirational feminist and international lawyer.

Acknowledgements

THIS BOOK IS an output of a European Research Council Advanced Research Grant on 'Gendered Peace' that was awarded under the European Union's Horizon 2020 research and innovation programme. It has been a journey undertaken over four years and there are many people to whom we are indebted and without whom neither the project nor the book would have been completed.

In no particular order we gratefully thank:

The ERC and the reviewers who put their faith in the viability and value of the undertaking.

Dr Kirsten Campbell who with good humour and great care ensured we complied with ethical principles throughout the project. Our publishers, Hart, and the reviewers who also put their faith in us.

Our research officers on the project – Keina Yoshida, Sheri Labenski, Sarah Smith and Elena Stavrevska for their hard work, enthusiasm, ideas, tolerance of our foibles and commitment to gender and peace. We wish them all well in their various new enterprises.

All those who inspired us intellectually, provided ongoing support and encouragement and took part in our events and workshops including but not limited to Madeleine Rees, Dianne Otto, Mohbuba Choudhury, Lisa Gormley, Helen Kezie-Nwoha, Patricia Viseur Sellers, Karen Knop, Gema Fernandez Rodriguez de Lievana, Rasha Obaid, and Mona Siegel. We could not have done what we did without you.

Our colleagues and friends in the LSE, in particular the Centre for Women, Peace and Security and its Advisory Board, the Gender Department, the Law Department, IDEAS and the Conflict Research Programme, especially Mary Kaldor. All those in LSE who provided invaluable administrative support and guidance, especially Jane Ellison and members of the research division.

Special thanks go to the LSE Library and archives staff, and particularly Daniel Payne, for their enthusiasm in including our work into their own programme of events and exhibits and for their patience in answering our many questions.

The many people who participated in various ways in the public events, workshops and seminars that we hosted as part of the project, for sharing their knowledge, insights and understandings of a feminist and gendered peace.

Members of the Committee on the Elimination of Discrimination against Women, UN special rapporteurs, members of the Office of the High Commissioner on Human Rights, the United Nations Institute for Disarmament Research, the International Labour Organisation, archivists in the UN library in Geneva and the ILO library.

The Geneva Graduate Institute; British Academy; the Temple of Peace in Cardiff, especially Craig Owen (Head of Wales for Peace Welsh Centre for International Affairs); the Peace Track Initiative; Gender Action for Peace and Security (GAPS), especially Hannah Bond; Women's International Peace Centre; Women's International League for Peace and Freedom; Peace Brigades International; and CND.

All involved in the documentary, 'The Legacy of the Tokyo Women's Tribunal', and our wonderful director who shared our vision, Sophie Mallett, and the LSE Film and Audio team.

Our families and friends, including those who are no longer with us but whose presence is still so strongly felt within the book and our lives.

Louise Arimatsu and Christine Chinkin
January 2024

Contents

Acknowledgements .... *vii*
Abbreviations and Acronyms .... *xiii*
Table of Treaties .... *xvii*
Table of Non-formally Binding International Instruments .... *xxi*
Table of Jurisprudence .... *xxix*

Conversation between Louise Arimatsu and Christine Chinkin on
   Gendered Peace 1

PART I
INTRODUCTORY CONCEPTS: GENDER AND PEACE

1. Introduction 15

2. Gender 17
    I. Introduction 17
    II. Gender Theory, Gender Analysis, and Feminist Activism 17
    III. Gender in International Fora 20
    IV. Gender in International Human Rights Law 23
    V. Gender in International Criminal Law 25
    VI. State Responsibility and the Gendered State 28
    VII. Gender Matters 30

3. Peace in International Law 34
    I. Introduction 34
    II. Inter-State Peace 34
    III. The Evolution of the Right to Peace in International Law 37
    IV. A Right to Peace? 39
    V. Gender and Peace 44

PART II
GENDERING PEACE THROUGH THE PAST

4. Introduction: Rewriting International Law's Histories 49

5. Peace in the UN Decade for Women 58
    I. Introduction 58

II.　Forerunners of the Decade 59
　　　　　A.　Institutional Forerunners 59
　　　　　B.　Women's Activism Prior to the Decade 60
　　　III.　The UN Decade for Women 1975–1985 62
　　　　　A.　Overview of the Decade 62
　　　　　B.　The Context of the Decade 65
　　　　　C.　Women During the Decade 67
　　　IV.　The Decade and Gendered Peace 70
　　　　　A.　The Politicisation of Peace 70
　　　　　B.　The Conceptualisation of Peace 72
　　　V.　Reflections on the Decade 76

6.　Revisiting the Past: Peace at Beijing and Beyond 79
　　　I.　Introduction 79
　　　II.　The Commission on the Status of Women 1985–1995 80
　　　III.　The Fourth World Conference on Women: Beijing 1995 80
　　　　　A.　The Conference 80
　　　　　B.　Context 82
　　　　　C.　Women at Beijing 83
　　　IV.　Peace in the Beijing Declaration and Platform for Action 90
　　　　　A.　Beijing Declaration 91
　　　　　B.　Women and Armed Conflict 92
　　　V.　Post-Beijing: Women and Peace and Security 94
　　　VI.　Conclusions 97

7.　Women, Disarmament and Peace 100
　　　I.　Introduction 100
　　　II.　Crafting a Different Agenda 101
　　　III.　Seeking Multiple Entry Points for Advancing Disarmament 105
　　　IV.　Disarmament Through a Gender Prism 109
　　　V.　The Past and Future of Disarmament 112

PART III
OBSTACLES TO GENDERED PEACE AND EQUALITY

8.　Introduction to Part III 117

9.　Silence as an Obstacle to Gendered Peace and Equality 126
　　　I.　Introduction 126
　　　II.　Silencing those Protesting War 128
　　　III.　Silence about the Effects of War 129
　　　IV.　Legal Silencing 131

10.　Misogyny and Sexism in the Digital Age 139
　　　I.　Introduction 139
　　　II.　Misogyny and Sexism 140

III.	Obstacles to Addressing Online VAW 144
IV.	Exclusion and Inclusion as Obstacles 150
V.	Final Thoughts 151

11. Crisis and Emergency: Entrenching Gender Systems and Militarism 153
    - I. Introduction 153
    - II. International Law's Crisis Narratives 154
        - A. Arbitrariness of Law's Time 156
        - B. Arbitrariness of Law's Facts 157
    - III. Militarism, Gender and Crises 158
    - IV. Crisis: Entrenchment and Reversal 163

PART IV
STRATEGIC PRACTICE: GENDERING LAW

12. Introduction to Strategic Practices 171

13. Strategic Practice: Peace and Equality Through International Law 176
    - I. Introduction 176
    - II. Foothold into International Law 178
    - III. Making Law Work for Women: Human Rights 180
    - IV. Making Law Work for Women: International Criminal Law 183
    - V. Reflections 186

14. Strategic Practice: Giving Effect to Legal Change 190
    - I. Introduction 190
    - II. Interventions into International Litigation 191
        - A. Jean Paul Akayesu 192
        - B. Hissène Habré 193
        - C. Dominic Ongwen 193
    - III. Interventions into General International Law 197
        - A. State Immunity 198
        - B. Nuclear Weapons 199

15. Strategic Practices: 'Doing Our Own Thing' 204
    - I. Introduction 204
    - II. Peace Processes 204
    - III. Women's Courts and Tribunals 206
    - IV. Subverting Legal Formalism 210

16. Enriching Strategic Practice: Some Reflections 214

PART V
TRANSFORMING INTERNATIONAL LAW

17. Introduction to Part V 221

18. Transformative Reparations and Gendered Peace 229
    I. Introduction 229
    II. Transformative Reparation to Break the Cycle of Gendered Violence 230
    III. Transformative Reparation to Break the Cycle of Gender Injustice 235
    IV. Advancing Gendered Peace Through Reparations 237

19. Searching for Peace in Teaching International Law 244
    I. Introduction 244
    II. The Role of Teachers of Public International Law 246
    III. Peace in Human Rights Courses? 250
    IV. Conversations about Teaching Peace 252
        A. Methodology 252
        B. 'I Don't Teach Peace': Triage in Law School 253
        C. A Preference for Violence and Conflict Over Peace 254
        D. Conceptual Ambiguity: Reclaiming Peace and its Possibilities 255
    V. Compensatory Legal Education 256
    VI. Why Does Teaching Peace and Women's Rights Matter? 257

Index 259

Abbreviations and Acronyms

ASEAN	Association of Southeast Asian Nations
ATT	Arms Trade Treaty
CAT	Committee against Torture
CEDAW	Convention on the Elimination of All Forms of Discrimination against Women
CERD	Committee on the Elimination of Racial Discrimination
CESCR	Committee on Economic, Social and Cultural Rights
CHR	Commission on Human Rights
CND	Campaign for Nuclear Disarmament
CofE	Council of Europe
CRC	Convention on the Rights of the Child
CSW	Commission on the Status of Women
DAWN	Development Alternatives with Women for a New Era
DEDAW	Declaration on the Elimination of Discrimination against Women
ECOSOC	Economic and Social Council
FLS	Forward Looking Strategies for the Advancement of Women
GREVIO	Group of Experts on Action against Violence against Women and Domestic Violence
GSF	Global Survivors Fund
HRC	Human Rights Council
IACommHR	Inter-American Commission on Human Rights
IACtHR	Inter-American Court of Human Rights
ICC	International Criminal Court
ICCPR	International Covenant on Civil and Political Rights
ICESCR	International Covenant on Economic, Social and Cultural Rights

ICJ	International Court of Justice
ICIS	Independent International Commission of Inquiry on the Syrian Arab Republic
ICL	international criminal law
ICTR	International Criminal Tribunal for Rwanda
ICTY	International Criminal Tribunal for the former Yugoslavia
IESOGI	Independent Expert on Protection against Violence and Discrimination Based on Sexual Orientation and Gender Identity
IFIs	international financial institutions
IHL	international humanitarian law
IHRL	international human rights law
ILC	International Law Commission
ILO	International Labour Organisation
IMTFE	International Military Tribunal for the Far East
IWRAW	International Women's Rights Action Watch
IWY	International Women's Year
NAM	Non-Aligned Movement
NGO	non-governmental organisation
NIEO	New International Economic Order
NPT	Treaty on the Non-Proliferation of Nuclear Weapons
NWAC	Native Women's Association of Canada
OHCHR	Office of the United Nations High Commissioner for Human Rights
OTP	Office of the Prosecutor at the International Criminal Court
PCIJ	Permanent Court of International Justice
PFA	Platform for Action
PIL	public international law
REDESCA	Special Rapporteur on Economic, Social, Cultural and Environmental Rights
SC	UN Security Council
SDGs	sustainable development goals
SGBV	sexual and gender-based violence

SR	Special Rapporteur
TERF	trans-exclusionary radical feminism
TFV	Trust Fund for Victims
TPNW	Treaty on the Prohibition of Nuclear Weapons
TWAIL	Third World Approaches to International Law
UDHR	Universal Declaration of Human Rights
UNCED	UN Conference on Environment and Development
UNDRIP	UN Declaration on the Rights of Indigenous Peoples
UNGA	UN General Assembly
UNIFEM	UN Development Fund for Women
UNWCC	UN War Crimes Commission
VAW	violence against women
VAWG	violence against women and girls
WDC	Women's Disarmament Committee
WGDWG	Working Group on Discrimination against Women and Girls
WIDF	Women's International Democratic Federation
WILPF	Women's International League for Peace and Freedom
WPA	World Plan of Action
WPS	women, peace and security
WSP	Women Strike for Peace

Table of Treaties

Treaty of Peace and Amity between the United States and Great
  Britain (Treaty of Ghent) 24 December 1814 240
Final Act of the Vienna Congress, Declaration of the Powers
  on the Abolition of the Slave Trade, 8 February 1815
  (Vienna Declaration, 1815) 240
Convention (I) for the Pacific Settlement of International Disputes,
  The Hague, 29 July 1899 176
Convention (II) with respect to the Laws and Customs of War on Land,
  The Hague, 29 July 1899 213
Convention (I) for the Pacific Settlement of International Disputes,
  The Hague, 18 October 1907 176
Treaty of Peace with Germany (Treaty of Versailles) 28 June 1919;
  Part I: Covenant of the League of Nations; Part XIII:
  Constitution of the International Labour Organisation 52, 103, 229
International Convention to Suppress the Slave Trade and Slavery,
  Geneva, 25 September 1926 240
General Treaty for Renunciation of War as an Instrument of
  National Policy, Paris, 27 August 1928 (Kellogg-Briand Pact) 7, 177
Convention on the Rights and Duties of States, Montevideo,
  26 December 1933 .... 30, 54
Charter of the United Nations, San Francisco, 26 June 1945,
  1 UNTS XVI 35, 59, 96, 178–79,
                                                                                                      201, 245
Statute of the International Court of Justice, San Francisco,
  26 June 1945, 1 UNTS XVI 56, 198, 201, 223
Charter of the International Military Tribunal, London,
  8 August 1945, 82 UNTS 279 .... 37, 132
Charter of the International Military Tribunal for the Far East,
  Proclamation of the Supreme Commander for the Allied
  Powers, Tokyo, 19 January 1946 .... 37, 132, 209, 236
Control Council Law No 10, Punishment of Persons Guilty of War
  Crimes, Crimes against Peace and against Humanity, December 20,
  1945, 3 Official Gazette Control Council for Germany 50–55 (1946) 132, 185
Convention on the Privileges and Immunities of the United Nations,
  New York, 13 February 1946, 1 UNTS 15 137
Convention on the Prevention and Punishment of the Crime of
  Genocide, New York, 9 December 1948, 78 UNTS 277 215

Convention relative to the Protection of Civilian Persons in Time
of War (Fourth Geneva Convention), Geneva, 12 August 1949,
75 UNTS 287 .... 75, 93
Convention for the Protection of Human Rights and Fundamental
Freedoms, Rome, 4 November 1950, CETS 5 135
Convention on the Political Rights of Women, New York, 31 March 1953,
193 UNTS 135 60
Convention on the Nationality of Married Women, New York,
20 February 1957, 309 UNTS 65 60
Convention on the High Seas, Geneva, 29 April, 1958, 450 UNTS 11 107
Vienna Convention on Diplomatic Relations, Vienna, 18 April 1961,
500 UNTS 95 137
Convention on Consent to Marriage, Minimum Age for Marriage and
Registration of Marriages, New York, 10 December 1962,
521 UNTS 231 60
Treaty Banning Nuclear Weapon Tests in the Atmosphere, in Outer
Space and Under Water (Limited Nuclear Test Ban Treaty),
Moscow, 5 August 1963, 480 UNTS 43 107
Protocol No 4 to the Convention for the Protection of Human Rights
and Fundamental Freedoms, Strasbourg, 16 September 1963,
CETS No 46 156
International Convention on the Elimination of All Forms of Racial
Discrimination, New York, 7 March 1966, 660 UNTS 195 146
International Covenant on Civil and Political Rights, New York,
16 December 1966, 999 UNTS 171 .... 23, 38, 65, 146,
156, 223, 250
International Covenant on Economic, Social and Cultural Rights,
New York, 16 December 1966, 993 UNTS 3 .... 38, 65–66, 223, 228
Treaty on Principles Governing the Activities of States in the
Exploration and Use of Outer Space, including the Moon and
Other Celestial Bodies, London, Moscow and Washington DC,
27 January 1967, 610 UNTS 205... 107
Treaty for the Prohibition of Nuclear Weapons in Latin America and
the Caribbean (Treaty of Tlatelolco), Mexico, 14 February 1967,
634 UNTS 281 65
Treaty on the Non-Proliferation of Nuclear Weapons, London,
Moscow, Washington, 1 July 1968, 729 UNTS 161 .... 36, 106, 108, 112,
199, 201–03, 212, 221
Vienna Convention on the Law of Treaties, 23 May 1969,
1155 UNTS 331 .... 121, 201
Convention on the Prohibition of the Development, Production and
Stockpiling of Bacteriological (Biological) and Toxin Weapons and on
their Destruction, London, Moscow and Washington, 10 April 1972,
1823 UNTS 359 (Biological Weapons Treaty) 36, 108
Protocol Additional to the Geneva Conventions of 12 August 1949, and
relating to the Protection of Victims of International Armed Conflicts
(Protocol I), Geneva, 8 June 1977, 1125 UNTS 3 .... 16, 35

Convention on the Elimination of All Forms of Discrimination against
    Women, New York, 18 December 1979 (CEDAW) 1249 UNTS 13 .... 4, 21,
    23–24, 26, 43, 56, 63, 72–74, 76–78, 92, 94, 97–98,
    108, 123–24, 133, 135, 139, 144–46, 148, 157,
    162, 164, 168, 173, 180–84, 191, 200, 204, 209, 212,
    223, 228, 231–32, 236–38, 241–42, 247, 250
African Charter on Human and Peoples' Rights, Banjul, 27 June 1981,
    CAB/LEG/67/3 rev. 5 .... 39, 223
South Pacific Nuclear Free Zone Treaty (Treaty of Rarotonga),
    6 August 1985, 1445 UNTS 177 65
International Labour Organization, Convention (No 169) Concerning
    Indigenous and Tribal Peoples in Independent Countries, adopted
    27 June 1989 by the General Conference of the International Labour
    Organization at its 76th session 224
Convention on the Prohibition of the Development, Production,
    Stockpiling and Use of Chemical Weapons and on their Destruction,
    Geneva, 3 September 1992, 1975 UNTS 45 .... 36, 108
Inter-American Convention on the Prevention, Punishment and
    Eradication of Violence against Women, (Convention of Belém do Pará)
    9 June 1994 .... 86, 148
General Framework Agreement for Peace for Bosnia and Herzegovina,
    Dayton, initialled 21 November 1995, signed Paris, 14 December 1995 122
Comprehensive Nuclear-Test-Ban Treaty, New York, 10/24 September 1996
    (not in force) 36
Convention on the Prohibition of the Use, Stockpiling, Production and
    Transfer of Anti-personnel Mines and on their Destruction, Ottawa,
    18 September 1997, 2056 UNTS 211 (Landmines Convention) 36, 93
Rome Statute of the International Criminal Court, 17 July 1998,
    2187 UNTS 3 .... 21–22, 26–28,
    38, 95, 133–35, 185, 190, 193–96,
    216–17, 234–35, 239
Optional Protocol to the Convention on the Elimination of
    All Forms of Discrimination against Women, 6 October 1999,
    New York, 2131 UNTS 83 182
Council of Europe, Convention on Cybercrime, Budapest,
    23 November 2001, CETS No 185 .... 145–46, 148
Protocol to the African Charter on Human and Peoples' Rights on the
    Rights of Women in Africa (Maputo Protocol), 2nd Ordinary Session
    of the Assembly of the African Union, Maputo, Mozambique,
    11 July 2003 .... 15, 43, 148, 195,
    250–51
International Convention for the Protection of All Persons from Enforced
    Disappearance, New York, 20 December 2006, 2716 UNTS 3 173
Convention on Cluster Munitions, Dublin, 30 May 2008, 2688 UNTS 39 218
Council of Europe Convention on preventing and combating violence
    against women and domestic violence, Istanbul, 11 May 2011,
    CETS No 210 .... 25, 143–45, 148, 195

Agreement between the Government of the Republic of Senegal and the
African Union on the Establishment of Extraordinary African
Chambers within the Senegalese Judicial System, Dakar, Senegal,
22 August 2012 193
Arms Trade Treaty, New York, 2 April 2013, 3013 UNTS 269 .... 22, 36, 218
Treaty on the Prohibition of Nuclear Weapons, New York, 7 July 2017,
3379 UNTS 36, 45, 112–13,
200, 212–13, 218
Agreement for Bringing Peace to Afghanistan between the Islamic
Emirate of Afghanistan which is not recognized by the United States as a
state and is known as the Taliban and the United States of America,
February 29, 2020 which corresponds to Rajab 5, 1441 on the Hijri
Lunar calendar and Hoot 10, 1398 on the Hijri Solar calendar 118
Second Additional Protocol to the Cybercrime Convention on Enhanced
Co-operation and Disclosure of Electronic Evidence, Strasbourg,
12 May 2022, CETS No 224 146

Table of Non-formally Binding International Instruments

Resolution of the Sixth International Conference of American States
   in 1928: Statute of the Inter-American Commission of Women 54
Lima Declaration in Favor of Women's Rights, Eighth International
   Conference of American States, 1938 54
UN ECOSOC Resolution 11 (II), 21 June 1946, Commission on the
   Status of Women 59, 179
UNGAR 95/1, 11 December 1946, Affirmation of the Principles of
   International Law recognized by the Charter of the Nurnberg Tribunal 37
UNGAR 177 (II), 21 November 1947, Formulation of the principles
   recognized in the Charter of the Nurnberg Tribunal and in the judgment
   of the Tribunal 37
UNGAR 217 A (III), 10 December 1948, Universal Declaration of
   Human Rights 38, 91, 179, 228
UNGAR 290 (IV), 1 December 1949, Essentials of peace 38
Final Communiqué of the Asian-African conference of Bandung,
   24 April 1955 .... 42, 58, 106
UNGAR 1378 (XIV), 20 November 1959, General and complete
   disarmament 106
UNGAR 1514 (XV), 14 December 1960, Declaration on the Granting of
   Independence to Colonial Countries and Peoples 43
UNGAR 1777 (XVII), 7 December 1962, United Nations assistance for the
   advancement of women in developing countries 60
UNGAR 1921 (XVIII), 5 December 1963, Draft Declaration on the
   Elimination of Discrimination against Women 60
UNGAR 1962 (XVIII), 13 December 1963, Declaration of Legal
   Principles Governing the Activities of States in the Exploration and
   Use of Outer Space 107
UNGAR 2263 (XXII), 7 November 1967, Declaration on the Elimination
   of Discrimination against Women (DEDAW) 60, 72–73
Final Act of the International Conference on Human Rights,
   Tehran, 22 April – 13 May 1968, A/Conf.32/41 .... 39, 94
Commission on the Status of Women, Resolution 4 (XXII), 27 January –
   12 February 1969, Protection of women and children in emergency
   or war time, fighting for peace, national liberation and independence 90

Table of Non-formally Binding International Instruments

UNGAR 2625 (XXV), 24 October 1970, Annex: Declaration on Principles of International Law concerning Friendly Relations and Cooperation among States in accordance with the Charter of the United Nations 7, 36, 65, 158
UNGAR 2832 (XXVI), 16 December 1971, Declaration of the Indian Ocean as a Zone of Peace 40
UNGAR 3010 (XXVII), 18 December 1972, International Women's Year 62
UNGAR 3281 (XXIX) 12 December 1974, Charter of Economic Rights and Duties of States 66
UNGAR 3314 (XXIX), 14 December 1974, Definition of Aggression 37
UNGAR 3318 (XXIX), Declaration on the Protection of Women and Children in Emergency and Armed Conflict, 14 December 1974 90
World Plan of Action for the Implementation of the Objectives of the International Women's Year, Report of the World Conference of the International Women's Year, Mexico City, 19 June–2 July 1975, E/CONF.66/34 .... 62–63, 79
Conference on Security and Co-operation in Europe, Final Act, Helsinki, 1 August 1975 65
UNGAR 3379, 10 November 1975, Zionism as a form of racism; the Resolution was revoked UNGAR 46/86, 16 December 1991 66
UNGAR 3519 (XXX) 15 December 1975, Women's participation in the strengthening of international peace and security and in the struggle against colonialism, racism, racial discrimination, foreign aggression and occupation and all forms of foreign domination 63
UNGAR 3520 (XXX), 15 December 1975, World Conference of the International Women's Year 63, 73
UNGAR 3521 (XXX), 15 December 1975, Equality between men and women and elimination of discrimination against women 73
Commission on Human Rights, Resolution 5 (XXXII), 27 February 1976, Further promotion and encouragement of human rights and fundamental freedoms, including the question of a long-term programme of work of the Commission, E/CN.4/ RES/5 (XXXII) 39
Commission on the Status of Women, Resolution 7 (XXVII), 20 March–5 April 1978, Protection of women and children in emergency and armed conflict or war time in the struggle for peace, self-determination, national liberation and independence 90
UNGAR 33/73, 15 December 1978, Declaration on the Preparation of Societies for Life in Peace 39, 74
UNGAR 33/185, 29 January 1979, Preparations for the World Conference of the United Nations Decade for Women: Equality, Development and Peace 63
Programme of Action for the Second Half of the United Nations Decade for Women: Equality, Development and Peace, Report of the World Conference of the United Nations Decade for Women: Equality, Development and Peace, Copenhagen, 14–30 July 1980, A/CONF.94/35 63
UNGAR 36/67, 30 November 1981, International Year of Peace and International Day of Peace 77

Table of Non-formally Binding International Instruments xxiii

Human Rights Committee, General Comment 6, Article 6 (Right to Life) (Sixteenth session, 30 April 1982) 39
UNGAR 37/63, 3 December 1982, Annex: Declaration on the Participation of Women in Promoting International Peace and Cooperation........................73
UNGAR 39/11, 12 November 1984, Declaration on the Right of Peoples to Peace..39
Forward-Looking Strategies for the Advancement of Women during the Period from 1986 to the Year 2000, Report of the World Conference to review and appraise the achievements of the United Nations Decade for Women: Equality, Development and Peace, Nairobi, 15–26 July 1985, A/CONF.116/28/Rev.1 .... 20–21, 62–63, 66–67, 70, 72–75, 79–81, 84, 91
UNGAR 40/3, 24 October 1985, International Year of Peace..................................78
UNGAR 40/11, 11 November 1985, Right of peoples to peace................................39
UNGAR 40/153, 16 December 1985, Implementation of the Declaration of the Indian Ocean as a zone of peace...40
UNGAR 41/11, 27 October 1986, Zone of peace and cooperation of the South Atlantic 40
UNGAR 41/109, 4 December 1986, Participation of women in promoting international peace and cooperation...73
UNGAR 44/39, 4 December 1989, International criminal responsibility of individuals and entities engaged in illicit trafficking in narcotic drugs across national frontiers and other transnational criminal activities 38
UNGAR 44/77, 8 December 1989, Implementation of the Nairobi Forward-Looking Strategies for the Advancement of Women 80
UNSCR 678, 29 November 1990, Iraq-Kuwait..159
UNGAR 45/129, 14 December 1990, Implementation of the Nairobi Forward-Looking Strategies for the Advancement of Women 80
UNSCR 687, 3 April 1991, Iraq-Kuwait 159
UNGAR 46/86, 16 December 1991, Elimination of Racism and Racial Discrimination 66
Kari-Oca Declaration and Indigenous Peoples' Earth Charter, World Conference of Indigenous Peoples on Territory, Environment and Development, 25–30 May 1992..89
UN Conference on Environment and Development, Rio de Janeiro, Brazil, 3–14 June 1992, Agenda 21, A/CONF.151/26/Rev. 1 (Vol 1) 77
Committee on the Elimination of Discrimination against Women, General Recommendation 19, 11th session, 1992, Violence against women.. 21, 181, 184
UNGAR 47/95, 16 December 1992, Implementation of the Nairobi Forward-Looking Strategies for the Advancement of Women 80
UNSCR 808, 22 February 1993, International Criminal Tribunal for the former Yugoslavia (ICTY)...25, 157, 184–85, 192
UNSCR 827, 25 May 1993, Statute of the International Tribunal for the Prosecution of the Persons Responsible for Serious Violations of International Humanitarian Law committed in the Territory of the former Yugoslavia since 1991..184

xxiv *Table of Non-formally Binding International Instruments*

World Conference on Human Rights, Vienna Declaration and the
 Programme of Action, Vienna, 14–25 June 1993,
 A/CONF.103/9 ....21, 26–27, 77, 92, 94,
 124, 181, 184
UNGAR 48/104, 20 December 1993, Declaration on the Elimination
 of Violence against Women..21, 75, 179, 251
International Conference on Population and Development (ICPD),
 Cairo, 5–13 September 1994, A/CONF.171/13/Rev.1............................21, 77, 181
UNSCR 955, 8 November 1994, Statute of the International Tribunal
 for the Prosecution of the Persons Responsible for Genocide and
 Serious Violations of International Humanitarian Law committed
 in the Territory of Rwanda and Rwandan Citizens Responsible
 for Genocide and other such Violations in the Territory of
 neighbouring States between 1 January 1994 and 31 December
 1994 (ICTR) 25–26, 185, 192
Fourth World Conference on Women, Beijing Declaration
 and Platform for Action, Beijing 4–15 September 1995,
 A/CONF.177/20/Rev.1 ....21, 55, 78–90,
 108, 171, 181
Beijing Declaration of Indigenous Women, NGO Forum, UN Fourth
 World Conference on Women, Huairou, September 1995........................... 89, 94
UNGAR 50/203, 22 December 1995, Follow-up to the Fourth World
 Conference on Women and full implementation of the Beijing
 Declaration and the Platform for Action..81
UNGAR 51/160, 30 January 1997, Report of the International Law
 Commission on the work of its forty-eighth session...38
Economic and Social Council, Report 1997, chapter IV. A: Agreed
 conclusions, A/52/3, 18 September 1997 (Guidelines on the principles
 and practical implication of mainstreaming a gender perspective
 through proarammes and policy) 22
UNGAR 52/15, 15 January 1998, Proclamation of the year 2000 as the
 International Year for the Culture of Peace.. 99, 216
UNGAR 53/25, 10 November 1998, International Decade for a Culture
 of Peace and Non-violence for the Children of the World 2001–2010................41
UNGAR 53/243, 13 September 1999, Declaration and Programme of
 Action on a Culture of Peace..41
Human Rights Committee, General Comment 28, Equality of rights
 between men and women (article 3), CCPR/C/21/Rev.1/Add.10,
 29 March 2000 23
UNSCR 1308 17 July 2000, HIV/AIDS and Peacekeeping Operations 160
UNSCR 1315, 14 August 2000, Statute of the Special Court for Sierra Leone........... 185
UNSCR 1325, 31 October 2000, Women and peace and security..................... 25, 41,
 44, 95–96, 99, 108–09, 124,
 137, 187, 204, 217, 232

UNGAR 55/282, 7 September 2001, International Day of Peace 77
Report of the World Conference against Racism, Racial Discrimination,
   Xenophobia and Related Intolerance, Durban, South Africa, 2001,
   A/CONF.189/12 238
UNGAR 56/83, 12 December 2001, Annex: Responsibility of states for
   Internationally Wrongful Acts 131, 229
Guidelines on International Protection: Gender-Related Persecution
   Within the Context of Article 1A(2) of the 1951 Convention and/or its
   1967 Protocol Relating to the Status of Refugees, UNHCR,
   HCR/GIP/02/01, 7 May 2002 24
UNSCR 1441, 8 November 2002, situation between Iraq and Kuwait 159
Committee on the Elimination of Discrimination against Women,
   General Recommendation No 25, on article 4, paragraph 1, of the
   Convention on the Elimination of All Forms of Discrimination
   against Women, on temporary special measures, 13th session 2004 23
UN Human Rights Committee, General Comment No 31, the Nature of
   the General Legal Obligation Imposed on States Parties to the Covenant,
   CCPR/C/GC/21/Rev.1/Add. 13, 26 May 2004 135
Committee on Economic, Social and Cultural Rights, General Comment
   No 16, The equal right of men and women to the enjoyment of all
   economic, social and cultural rights (article 3), E/C.12/2005/4,
   11 August 2005 23
UNGAR 60/147, 16 December 2005, Basic Principles and Guidelines on the
   Right to a Remedy and Reparation for Victims of Gross Violations of
   International Human Rights Law and Serious Violations of International
   Humanitarian Law 230
UNGAR 61/295, Declaration on the Rights of Indigenous Peoples,
   13 September 2007 .... 89, 223–26, 238–39
ACHPR, Resolution on the Right to a Remedy and Reparation for
   Women and Girls Victims of Sexual Violence, 42nd Ordinary Session,
   Brazzaville, Republic of Congo, 15–28 November 2007 233
Committee against Torture, General Comment No 2: Implementation
   of article 2 by States parties, CAT/C/GC/2, 24 January 2008 23
UNSCR 1820, 19 June 2008, Women and peace and security 95, 131
Committee on Economic, Social and Cultural Rights, General Comment
   No 20 on non-discrimination pursuant to article 2 of the Covenant,
   E/C.12/GC/20, 2 July 2009 23
UNSCR 1888, 30 September 2009, Women and peace and security 95
UNSCR 1889, 5 October 2009, Women and peace and security 95
Human Rights Council Resolution 14/3, 23 June 2010, Promotion of the
   right of peoples to peace 41
Committee on the Elimination of Discrimination against Women,
   General Recommendation No 28 on the Core Obligations of States
   Parties under Article 2 of the Convention on the Elimination of
   All Forms of Discrimination against Women, CEDAW/C/GC/28,
   16 December 2010 .... 24, 77, 135

xxvi *Table of Non-formally Binding International Instruments*

UNSCR 1960, 16 December 2010, Women and peace and security 95
UNGAR 65/196, 21 December 2010, Proclamation of 24 March as the
   International Day for the Right to the Truth concerning Gross Human
   Rights Violations and for the Dignity of Victims 173
UN SRSG, Guiding Principles on Business and Human Rights:
   Implementing the United Nations 'Protect, Respect and Remedy'
   Framework, A/HRC/17/31, 21 March 2011 149
UNSCR 1983, 7 June 2011, Maintenance of international peace
   and security 160
Human Rights Council resolution S-17/1, 22 August 2011, establishment
   of the Independent International Commission of Inquiry on the
   Syrian Arab Republic 26, 28, 156
Human Rights Committee, General Comment No 34, Article 19:
   Freedoms of opinion and expression, CCPR/C/GC/5, 12 September 2011 151
Committee on the Elimination of Racial Discrimination, General
   Comment No 34, Racial discrimination against people of African
   descent CERD/C/GC/34, 30 September 2011 238
ASEAN Human Rights Declaration, 19 November 2012 42
UN Human Rights Council Working Group on Enforced or Involuntary
   Disappearances, General Comment on women affected by enforced
   disappearances, A/HRC/WGEID/98/2, 14 February 2013 173
G8 Declaration on Preventing Sexual Violence in Conflict, April 2013 98
UNSCR 2106, 24 June 2013, Women, peace and security 95
Declaration of Commitment to End Sexual Violence in Conflict, 2013 98
Committee on the Elimination of Racial Discrimination,
   General Recommendation 35 on Combating racist hate speech,
   CERD/C/GC/35, 26 September 2013 146
Committee on the Elimination of Discrimination against Women, General
   Recommendation No 30 on women in conflict prevention,
   conflict and post-conflict situations, CEDAW/C/GC/30,
   18 October 2013 .... 97, 123, 135,
                                                                                           138, 204, 232
UNSCR 2122, 18 October 2013, Women and peace and security 95
UNGAR 68/165, 18 December 2013, Right to the Truth 173
UNSCR 2177, 18 September 2014, Ebola and its impact in West Africa 160
African Commission on Human and Peoples' Rights, General
   Comment No 2 on Article 14.1(a), (b), (c) and (f) and Article 14.2(a)
   and (c) of the Protocol to the African Charter on Human and
   Peoples' Rights on the Rights of Women in Africa, 28 November 2014 251
UNSCR 2242, 13 October 2015, Women and peace and security 95–96, 187, 218
Committee on the Elimination of Discrimination against Women,
   General Recommendation No 33 on Women's Access to Justice,
   CEDAW/C/GC/33, 23 July 2015 .... 133, 146, 209, 232
UNGAR 70/1, 21 October 2015, Transforming our world: the 2030
   Agenda for Sustainable Development 46, 97

Human Rights Council Resolution 32/28, 1 July 2016, Declaration
 on the Right to Peace 42
UNGAR 71/189, 19 December 2016, Annex: Declaration on the
 Right to Peace.. 42, 244, 250
African Commission on Human and Peoples' Rights, General
 Comment No 4 on the African Charter on Human and Peoples' Rights:
 The Right to Redress for Victims of Torture and Other Cruel, Inhuman or
 Degrading Punishment or Treatment (Article 5), ACPHR 21st
 Extra-Ordinary Session, 23 February to 4 March 2017,
 Banjul, The Gambia 233
African Commission on Human and Peoples' Rights, Resolution
 372 (LX), 22 May 2017, on the Protection of Sacred Natural
 Sites and Territories...226
Committee on the Elimination of Discrimination against Women, General
 Recommendation No 35 on Gender-based Violence against Women
 updating General Recommendation No 19, CEDAW/C/GC/35,
 26 July 2017.. 98, 145, 148, 183
Committee on Economic, Social and Cultural Rights, General
 Comment No 24 on State obligations under the International
 Covenant on Economic, Social and Cultural Rights in the context
 of business activities, E/C.12/GC/24, 10 August 2017 ....135, 138
Committee on the Elimination of Discrimination against Women,
 General Recommendation No 35 on Gender-based Violence against
 Women updating General Recommendation No 19, CEDAW/C/GC/35,
 26 July 2017.. 98, 145, 148, 183
Joint General Comment No 3 (2017) of the Committee on the Protection
 of the Rights of All Migrant Workers and Members of Their Families
 and No 22 (2017) of the Committee on the Rights of the Child on the
 general principles regarding the human rights of children in the
 context of international migration; CMW/C/GC/3-CRC/C/GC/22,
 16 November 2017 135
Committee on the Elimination of Discrimination against Women,
 General Recommendation No 36 (2017) on the right of girls and
 women to education, CEDAW/C/GC/36, 27 November 2017 ....139, 228
Committee on the Elimination of Discrimination against Women,
 General Recommendation No 37 on the gender-related dimensions
 of disaster risk reduction in the context of climate change,
 CEDAW/C/GC/37, 13 March 2018... 124, 164, 166
UNSCR 2439, 30 October 2018, Peace and security in Africa.............................160
UNGAR 73/203, 20 December 2018, Identification of customary law 118
Council of Europe Recommendation CM/Rec(2019)1 to member States
 on preventing and combating sexism adopted by the Committee of
 Ministers of the Council of Europe, 27 March 2019.......................................143
UNSCR 2467, 23 April 2019, Women and peace and security:
 Sexual violence in conflict 95, 138, 187, 198, 232

Human Rights Committee, General Comment 36, on article 6:
Right to Life, CCPR/C/GC/36, 3 September 2019 40
UNSCR 2493, 29 October 2019, Women and peace and security................. 95, 187
UN Human Rights Committee, 'Statement on derogations from the
Covenant in connection with the COVID-19 pandemic',
CCPR/C/128/2, 30 April 2020..156
UNSCR 2535, 1 July 2020, Maintenance of international peace and security............ 160
UNSCR 2565, 26 February 2021, Maintenance of international
peace and security...160
Committee on the Elimination of Discrimination against Women, General
Recommendation No 38, 2020 on trafficking in women and girls in the
context of global migration, CEDAW/C/GC/38, 20 November 2020 183
Human Rights Council resolution 47/16, Promotion, protection and
enjoyment of human rights on the Internet, 13 July 2021,
A/HRC/Res/47/16 151
Council of Europe, GREVIO General Recommendation No 1 on the
digital dimension of violence against women,
20 October 2021 .... 143, 145, 147–48
UNGAR ES-11/1, 2 March 2022, Aggression against Ukraine......................118, 247
Council of Europe, Recommendation CM/Rec (2022)16[1], 20 May 2022
of the Committee of Ministers to member states on combating
hate speech 147
EU Directive to Combat Violence against Women and Domestic Violence,
COM (2022) 150 final, 8 March 2022..144
EU Digital Services Act, Regulation (EU) 2022/2065..144
UNGAR 76/307, 8 September 2022, Modalities for the Summit of the Future............ 45
Regulation (EU) 2022/1925 of the European Parliament and of the Council,
14 September 2022 150
Human Rights Council resolution 51/32, 7 October 2022, from rhetoric to
reality: a global call for concrete action against racism, racial
discrimination, xenophobia and related intolerance..239
Committee on the Elimination of Discrimination against Women, General
Recommendation No 39, Indigenous women and girls, CEDAW/C/GC/39,
26 October 2022 ....182, 238
UNGAR ES-11/5, 14 November 2022, Furtherance of remedy and
reparation for aggression against Ukraine..229
CSW67, Innovation and technological change, and education in the digital age
for achieving gender equality and the empowerment of all women and girls:
Agreed conclusions, 20 March 2023, E/CN.6/2023/L.3 ....140, 150
UNGAR 77/276, 29 March 2023, Request for an advisory opinion of the
International Court of Justice on the obligations of States in respect of
climate change...222
Committee on the Rights of the Child, General Comment No 26 (2023) on
children's rights and the environment, with a special focus on climate
change, CRC/C/GC/26, 22 August 2023 222

Table of Jurisprudence

Permanent Court of International Justice and the International Court of Justice

The Factory at Chorzów (Germany v Poland) Jurisdiction, 26 July 1927,
PCIJ, Ser A, No 9 229
SS Lotus (France v Turkey), 7 September 1927, PCIJ, Ser A,
No 10 .... 8, 120, 158, 211
*Reservations to the Convention on the Prevention and Punishment
of the Crime of Genocide*, Advisory Opinion, 28 May 1951,
1951 ICJ Rep 15 211
Fisheries case (United Kingdom v Norway) 18 December 1951,
1951 ICJ Reports 116 118
Nuclear Weapons (Australia v France) (New Zealand v France)
Jurisdiction and Admissibility, 20 December 1974, 1974 ICJ
Reports, 253, 457 201–02
Military and Paramilitary Activities in and against Nicaragua
(Nicaragua v United States) Provisional Measures, 10 May 1984,
1984 ICJ Reports 169 69
Frontier Dispute (Burkina Faso v Republic of Mali) Judgment
22 December 1986, 1986 ICJ Reports 554 36
Legality of the Threat or Use of Nuclear Weapons, Advisory Opinion,
8 July 1996, 1996 ICJ Reports 226 .... 201–03, 211
*Request for an Examination of the Situation in Accordance with
Paragraph 63 of the Court's Judgment of 20 December 1974 in the
Nuclear Tests (New Zealand v France) Case*, Order 22 September 1995,
1995 ICJ Reports 288 82
*Accordance with international law of the unilateral declaration of
independence in respect of Kosovo*, Advisory Opinion, 22 July 2010,
2010 ICJ Reports 403 211
Jurisdictional Immunities of the State (Germany v Italy: Greece
intervening) Judgment 3 February 2012, 2012 ICJ Reports 99 .... 137, 198, 234
*Application of the Convention on the Prevention and Punishment of
the Crime of Genocide* (Croatia v Serbia) Judgment, 3 February 2015,
2015 ICJ Reports 3 133
*Obligations concerning Negotiations relating to Cessation of the Nuclear
Arms Race and to Nuclear Disarmament* (Marshall Islands v
United Kingdom) Judgment, 5 October 2016, 2016 ICJ Reports 833 201–02

Application of the International Convention for the Suppression of the Financing of Terrorism and of the International Convention on the Elimination of All Forms of Racial Discrimination (Ukraine v Russian Federation), order on provisional measures, 19 April 2017, 2017 ICJ Reports 104 162
Allegations of Genocide under the Convention on the Prevention and Punishment of the Crime of Genocide (Ukraine v Russian Federation: 32 States intervening), order on provisional measures, 16 March 2022, 2022 ICJ Reports 211 162
Application of the Convention on the Prevention and Punishment of the Crime of Genocide (The Gambia v Myanmar) Preliminary Objections, 22 July 2022, 2022 ICJ Reports 1 133
Obligations of States in respect of Climate Change, Request for Advisory Opinion, 12 April 2023 222–23

Human Rights Courts and Tribunals

Bámaca Velásquez v Guatemala, IACtHR, 22 February 2002, Series C No 91 (Reparations and Costs) 242
Caracazo v Venezuela, IACtHR, 29 August 2002, Series C No 95 (Reparations and Costs)...242
Juridical Condition and Rights of Undocumented Migrants, IACtHR, Advisory Opinion, 17 September 2003 29
MC v Bulgaria ECtHR, Appl No 39272/98, 4 December 2003 191
Plan de Sánchez Massacre v Guatemala, IACtHR, Judgment, 19 November 2004, Series C No 105 (Reparations)..173
CEDAW Committee, Report under article 8 of the Optional Protocol to the Convention, and reply from the Government of Mexico, CEDAW/C/2005/OP.8/MEXICO, 27 January 2005 173
Yakye Axa Indigenous Community v Paraguay, IACtHR, Judgment, 17 June 2005, Series C No 125 (Merits, Reparations and Costs).....................224
Miguel Castro Castro Prison v Peru, IACtHR, Judgment 25 November 2006, Series C No 160 (Merits, reparations and costs) 233
Al Skeini v the United Kingdom, ECtHR GC, Appl No 55721/07, 7 July 2011 136
KU v Finland, ECtHR, Appl No 2872/02, 2 March 2009......................................145
Gonzalez, Monreal and Monarrez ('Cotton Field') v Mexico, IACtHR, Judgment, 16 November 2009, Series C No 205 (Preliminary Objection, Merits, Reparations, and Costs) 233
Hirsi Jamaa v Italy, ECtHR GC, Appl No 27765/09, 23 February 2012 136
El Masri v the former Yugoslav Republic of Macedonia, ECtHR GC, Appl No 39630/09, 13 December 2012 138
Janowiec v Russia, ECtHR GC, Appl Nos 55508/07 and 29520/09, 21 October 2013 155
Jones v United Kingdom, ECtHR, Appl No 34356/06 and 40528/06, 14 January 2014..137

Velásquez Paiz v Guatemala, IACtHR, Judgment 19 November 2015,
  Series C No 307 (Preliminary objections, merits, reparations
  and costs) 192
Hacienda Brasil Verde Workers v Brazil, IACtHR, 20 October 2016,
  Series C No 318 (Preliminary objections, merits, reparations
  and costs) 239
The Environment and Human Rights, IACtHR, Advisory Opinion,
  OC-23/17 of 15 November 2017 226
Caso Lopez Soto v Venezuela, IACtHR, Judgment, 26 September 2018,
  Series C No 362 (Merits, reparations and costs) 233
ND and NT v Spain, ECtHR GC, Appl No 8675/15 and 8697/15,
  13 February 2020 136
XYZ v Republic of Benin, AfCtHR, 27 November 2020, 4 AfCLR 83 39
Ukraine v Russia (re Crimea) ECtHR GC, Appl Nos 20958/14 and
  38334/18, (16 December 2020) 162
Georgia v Russia (II), ECtHR GC, Appl No 38263/08, 21 January 2021 136
Terhes v Romania, ECtHR, Appl No 49933/20, 13 April 2021 156
JC and others v Belgium, ECtHR, Appl No 11625/17, 12 October 2021 137
Sacchi et al v Argentina, Brazil, France, Germany and Turkey,
  CRC/C/88/D/104/2019, 11 November 2021 222
Rosanna Flamer-Caldera v Sri Lanka, CEDAW/C/81D/134/2018,
  24 March 2022 191
Ukraine and The Netherlands v Russia, ECtHR GC, Appl Nos 8019/16,
  43800/14 and 28525/20, 30 November 2022 162
Natalie Alfronzo et al v The Philippines, CEDAW/C/84/D/155/2020,
  8 March 2023 .... 236, 241
Semenya v Switzerland, ECtHR, Appl Nos 10934/21, 11 July 2023 168

International Criminal Law

Prosecutor v Washio Awochi, XIII *Law Reports of Trials of War Criminals*
  1 (1946) 132
Prosecutor v Dusko Tadić, IT-94-1, *Decision on the Prosecutor's Motion
  requesting Protective Measures for Victims and Witnesses*,
  10 August 1995 .... 130, 192
Prosecutor v Dusko Tadić, IT-94-1, Decision on the Defence Motion
  for Interlocutory Appeal, 2 October 1995 157
Prosecutor v Jean Paul Akayesu, ICTR-96-04, Judgment,
  2 September 1998 .... 26, 192–193
Prosecutor v Thomas Lubanga Dyilo ICC-01/04 – 01/06-773, Judgment
  on the Appeal against the decision of Pre-Trial Chamber I entitled
  First Decision on the Prosecution Requests and Amended Requests
  for Redactions under Rule 81, 13 December 2006 .... 27, 235
Prosecutor v Brima, Kamara and Kanu, SCSL-2004-16-A, 22 February 2008 196
Prosecutor v Al Hassan Ag Abdoul Aziz Ag Mohamed Ag Mahmoud,
  ICC-01/12-01/18-461-Corr-Red 13 November 2019 27

Decision Pursuant to Article 15 of the Rome Statute on the Authorisation of an Investigation into the Situation in the People's Republic of Bangladesh/Republic of the Union of Myanmar, ICC-01/19-27, 14 November 2019 28
Prosecutor v Dominic Ongwen, ICC-02/04-01/15, Judgment Trial Chamber 4 February 2021; Appeals Chamber, 15 December 2022............194, 216
Prosecutor v Thomas Lubanga Dyilo, 9th Decision on the TFV's administrative decisions on applications for reparations and additional matters, ICC-01/04-01/06, 22 September 2022 235

Domestic Courts

United States v Schwimmer, 279 US 644 (1929) 110
Girouard v US, 328 US 61 (1946)...110
Director of Public Prosecutions v Hutchinson; Director of Public Prosecutions v Smith [1990] 2 AC 783...215
Mutua and others v FCO [2012] EWHC 2678 (QB)..239
Keyu and others v FCO [2015] UKSC 69...239
You v Japan, 150 F Supp 3d 1140 (ND Cal 2015) 137
Kimathi and others v FCO [2018] EWHC 2066 (QB) 239
Leigh and others v The Commissioner of Police of the Metropolis [2022] EWHC 527 (Admin) 163
Kim, Kang-won v State of Japan, Seoul Central District Court, 34th Chamber, Case no: 2016 Ga-Hap 505092 Compensation for Damage, January 2021...199
Kwak Ye-Nam et al v Japan, Seoul Central District Court, 15th Civil Division, Case no: 2016 Ga-Hap 580239 Judgment Summary, 21 April 2021............ 198–99

Conversation between Louise Arimatsu and Christine Chinkin on Gendered Peace

WE HAVE BEEN discussing international law, peace and gender for many years and from many different perspectives; at times it has felt that we never talk about anything else. The conversation below distils just some of the ideas we have been tossing about over coffee, dinner and in more formal settings, and introduces some of the essays in the book.

CC: It's been a long journey since we used to meet for breakfast in the Caffe Amicii (now sadly gone) and talk about how great it would be to have time to break away from the routines of teaching and regular research and do something really different.

LA: The ERC grant[1] (as well as the AHRC grant[2]) gave us this opportunity. We'd worked on quite a few other projects but this was *our* project, and so we were free to do our own thing and to be more creative in how we thought about international law, peace and gender.

CC: I think that that was especially important for you; you were keen on doing some archival work, not just about feminist activism where there's a lot of work being done by some very good historians, but also around the disarmament conferences, to learn more about what was actually going on in the corridors of power in many of the areas we are interested in.

LA: Yes, I've always taken an interest in archival work. I wanted to spend time in the LSE Women's Library – as I know you were – to get a sense of what had been preserved. This quickly led us to working with the LSE's librarians who were very generous and willing to share their time and knowledge with us. We had some excellent exchanges on the challenges of working with archives, on what is retained, by whom, and how it is categorised in both research settings and by the state in national archives and museums, which Benjamin alluded to with the observation that 'there is no document of civilization which is not at the same time a document of barbarism'[3] – only gender wasn't on his horizon. I remember chatting about the parallels between the librarians' work and our own work. How we all stay within our discipline's pre-determined gendered parameters that necessarily restrict our

---

[1] European Research Council Advanced Research Grant on 'Gendered Peace' under the European Union's Horizon 2020 research and innovation programme.
[2] UK Arts and Humanities Research Council research grant on a 'Feminist International Law on Peace and Security'.
[3] Walter Benjamin, 'Theses on the Philosophy of History, VI' *Illuminations* (Pimlico, 1999) 248.

framings and even the questions we ask. Someone else has already chosen the material for archiving, for their own particular reason, and that was generally going to be men, selecting the material to preserve the narrative for mankind. I think in those early days we both wanted to challenge our own preconceptions. This is why we co-hosted that event with the library – Are we asking the right question? – which was also part inspired by Viriginia Woolf's reflections.

CC: And one way to do that was to ask questions about international law through peace, which drew us to the archives at the Temple of Peace in Wales and to the UN and ILO archives in Geneva. At the Temple of Peace we were given boxes and boxes full of materials that hadn't yet been categorised. There was no chronological order and so we were free to engage with these fragments from the past on their own terms and to think about multiple conceptions of peace in time and place. This was exciting. It also led us to think about who else we should be talking to, which was the starting point of our seminar series where we invited experts in feminist architecture, linguistics, development, international relations, history, and peace activists.

LA: One area we focused on was the work and activities of the women from Greenham Common. Listening to their stories against the backdrop of the state's narratives – gleaned from the national archives – gave us a far richer body of material with which to think about law and to juxtapose the gendered regulation of their bodies against the gendered regulation of nuclear weapons.

CC: We also worked closely with women's NGOs, especially the Women's International League for Peace and Freedom (WILPF). Their archives provided us with an alternative history of women's peace activism through international law, prompting us to think about how using doctrinal law helps or interacts with feminist activism. Throughout this project we've both thought about different feminist methodologies and the problems of epistemic violence and practices of exclusion. So we have consciously adopted conversations as a feminist methodology, which also inspired the book on feminist peace conversations.[4] This current book is in some ways a continuation of that earlier publication, although that one had a wider range of conversationalists drawn from across the globe and from different disciplines.

LA: In addition to different disciplinary approaches, we have experimented with different mediums. The paradox is that it was Covid-19 and lockdown that took us in the direction of film. We'd spoken about doing something around the Tokyo Women's Tribunal with Patty [Patricia Viseur Sellers] before lockdown. We'd discussed having an event on the 20th anniversary of the judgment and to think about feminist activism in practice and its impact on international criminal law. But then suddenly we were in lockdown and we weren't able to do that. So we turned to film and ended up making the documentary

---

[4] Sarah Smith and Keina Yoshida (eds), *Feminist Conversations on Peace* (Bristol University Press, 2022), an output of the AHRC-funded project entitled 'A Feminist International Law of Peace and Security'.

	that won the 2022 teaching award.[5] At the same time you were also involved in working with museums – the Imperial War Museum in London and the Kyoto Museum for World Peace …
CC:	That's right. An event at IWM had led me to think about silence[6] while just before lockdown, I'd met Professor Ago Sinichi, Director of the Kyoto Museum and of course we were both in contact with the WAM museum in Tokyo.[7] So those conversations led to thinking about how to bring alive these issues in a way that captures the imagination and is informative. Covid also forced us to rethink the Visions of Feminist Peace Congress we had planned to host in London. Technology enabled us to host it online, which helped to resolve our anxieties about physically locating it in London and reproducing the power dynamics that our project sought to challenge.
LA:	We deliberately staggered the events over three or four days to take account of different time zones, although there was little we could do to address the gendered structural barriers that define the digital space.[8] 'Living a feminist life', to quote Sara Ahmed, does mean 'asking ethical questions about how to live better in an unjust and unequal world' and 'how to create relationships with others that are more equal'.[9]
CC:	We spent a great deal of time reflecting on feminist methodologies which is how the team decided to write the Feminist Peace Letter to UN member states,[10] following their Declaration adopted on Peace Day listing 12 pledges to celebrate the 75th anniversary of the UN.
LA:	Exactly. We had originally toyed with the idea of an alternative UN Security Council resolution – to add to its existing Women, Peace and Security (WPS) agenda – but eventually (after a good deal of debate) concluded that rather than simply asserting a position, we would write a letter which, as a feminist method, invites a response, an exchange, a dialogue. Writing the letter made us think about methodology in a different way[11] from the standard black letter approach that one utilises as a doctrinal lawyer. International law remained central, but what we invited states to do was to adopt a radically different methodology by situating peace and gender as core components in interpreting the scope and content of the law. We then produced a film version, with multiple voices and languages, to showcase at the LSE Festival.[12]

---

[5] 'The Legacy of the Tokyo Women's Tribunal' at https://www.lse.ac.uk/women-peace-security/research/Gendered-Peace-the-legacy-of-the-Tokyo-Womens-Tribunal. The film won first prize in the Educational Film (from a University or College) category of the Learning on Screen awards.
[6] See essay 9 'Silence as an Obstacle to Gendered Peace and Equality'.
[7] Women's Active Museum on War and Peace. The Director, Ms Mina Watanabe, participated in the documentary on the Women's Tribunal.
[8] See essay 10 'Misogyny and Sexism in the Digital Age'.
[9] Sara Ahmed, *Living a Feminist Life* (Duke University Press, 2017) 1.
[10] See https://www.lse.ac.uk/women-peace-security/publications/A-Letter-on-Feminist-Peace.
[11] See https://www.lse.ac.uk/women-peace-security/assets/documents/2020/Method-letter-on-feminist-peace.pdf.
[12] See https://www.lse.ac.uk/research/research-for-the-world/society/reclaiming-the-women-peace-and-society-agenda-a-letter-on-feminist-peace.

CC: Yeah – but no-one ever replied. The letter allowed us to indicate many other areas that we have addressed throughout the project but that we simply can't cover in this book. For example, human trafficking and exploitation,[13] and peace education. Sheri Labenski's work on getting ideas on feminism and gender and peace into school curricula was a very important part of the project.[14]

LA: Yes. All this is about how you take international law and make it work in different environments that haven't necessarily engaged directly with it. That was something that Sheri was beginning to think about when she was taking international law and gender to young people and introducing them to the material that we were dealing with, but also learning from their reactions and ideas, which were so illuminating,

CC: So much of this highlights that when you put peace at the centre, rather than security or conflict, it touches on so many other disciplines and so many – indeed all – branches of international law that we hadn't thought of as being relevant when we started. A difficulty we have struggled with throughout the project is where do we stop. International law creates and maintains boundaries that simply don't exist when you put peace at the centre.

LA: The idea of centring peace led to some enlightening discussions with government officials and those working in the UN system, for instance OHCHR and UNIDIR. We realised that peace is not central to their work and is not talked about. It is not part of the mandates within which they function. It comes back to our earlier point. Just as we are doctrinally constrained by legal reasoning and legal analysis, they are constrained by the terms of the specific treaty that frames the mandate and determines what a particular UN body can do. CEDAW, for instance, does not include a right to peace for women – so peace is not made essential to women's rights. Intellectual boundaries normalise and are co-constituted by the physical boundaries of our lives (in the home, the community, the nation, regional organisations, in refugee camps, gender identities) and which are regulated by law. But what we don't do often enough is question the logic behind the framing, or even reflect on whether we are asking the right question that would allow us to argue for an alternative framing that can better secure the ambitions that drive all we're doing, whether it be law or peace.

CC: This is part of Cynthia Enloe's 'feminist curiosity'. The underlying reason for a feminist methodology is to disrupt and question the patriarchal status quo and in so doing to dismantle gender/sex systems of oppression. We might call this a struggle for equality, or freedom, or dignity, or emancipation, or empowerment, or equity (all useful terms but which also raise some problematic issues).

---

[13] eg Gema Fernández Rodríguez de Liévana and Christine Chinkin, 'Human Trafficking, Human Rights and Women, Peace and Security: The Sound of Silence' in Soumita Basu et al (eds), *New Directions in Women Peace and Security* (Bristol University Press, 2020).

[14] Sheri worked through the ERC project in partnership with the Brilliant Club.

LA: I want to return to something you said earlier, the difference between feminism and gender and how we approach both. This also bring us to the core question of whether we are discussing feminist peace or gendered peace. I guess for us feminism is a political project; we realise of course that there are many feminisms, and we do not seek to put a label on anyone. But for us feminism is about promoting the advancement (primarily although not exclusively) of women and girls[15] through scholarship, activism, and practice. Should we think of feminism not as *who* we are championing but what we are fighting?

CC: And, as we've just said, that framework itself must be challenged and we can't just look at women but also have to challenge other axes of oppression, those based on race, ethnicity, colonialism and neocolonialism, sexuality and gender identity, economic globalisation, militarisation – the mutually reinforcing oppressive and intersecting systems of patriarchy that risk us collapsing under their weight.

LA: We are feminists and that is all part of the politics that we embrace. But as legal academics, we use the term 'gender' as a critical device, an analytic tool, a perspective through which to deconstruct and decode. Gender allows us to see the socially constructed world in a different way and to question why certain things (and people) are privileged and others discounted. It is essential to our feminist politics. Gender bridges our academic work and our feminist politics.

CC: I think it's visible in the opinion we wrote on the legality of the UK government's nuclear review.[16] Our anti-militarist feminist politics is there in the opinion. It frames how we use the law, although I saw that as primarily an academic opinion rather than an expression of my feminist viewpoints.

LA: It's interesting you say that. I have always been suspect of lawyers who claim to take an apolitical position. I don't think there's ever a position one can take that is not political; every position is the outcome of a political choice, even the refusal to take a position is a political choice. I think we are just honest about our politics. Yes we wanted our opinion to be persuasive – as true to the doctrines of law, founded upon recognised sources of international law – and our legal reasoning compelling. But it was also a political gesture.

CC: Accepting to write it was a political statement. It reminds me of a very senior international lawyer who once told me that when I write international law I'm quite good but when I write 'that other (feminist) stuff' that's not the case. To me there is no distinction. But to return to feminist peace and gendered peace; all conflict is gendered, as is all peace. And of course, gender as an analytic tool is not just about the women/men binary; it is about power, about the complexity and fluidity of all social relations, about subverting hierarchies. We have learned a lot from and draw upon queer theory. But nevertheless, the book is primarily about women and women's struggles for equality and peace within the structures of international law.

---

[15] Throughout the book the use of 'women' is not intended to exclude 'girls'.
[16] See essay 15 'Strategic Practices: "Doing Our Own Thing"'.

LA: We've often talked about how as international lawyers we hardly ever seem to speak about peace except as negative peace and when we do talk about a positive peace we assume that it is only relevant to post-conflict situations. And then Covid happened, which brought out the best in many people but also brought to the surface the undercurrents of militarism, sexism, and racism that seem to form the bedrock of all states and highlights just how far we all are from any notion of peace.

CC: Political leaders talked about the pandemic as though it was an enemy: we are going to beat this thing, we are not going to let it defeat us.

LA: The correlation with war really disturbed us. You and Madeleine [Rees] rightly described the militarised rhetoric as dangerous. Dangerous because it normalises violent responses …

CC: Precisely. As does 'securitising' an event or issue. We saw how states securitised and militarised the pandemic to justify increased surveillance, the use of 'robust' policing and in some instances the deployment of the armed forces.

LA: But militarised rhetoric is also dangerous in that militarism always privileges a hegemonic masculinity, accentuating and cementing pre-existing hierarchical gender relations of power that disadvantage women and those who don't fit patriarchy's binaries.

CC: We could see that unfolding in the pandemic. We've written about how pre-existing structural inequalities are exacerbated in times of crisis. But for the most part we've done so in the context of the crises of armed conflict and natural disasters.[17] The global public health crisis was new to us but the patterns it produced were not. It simply reaffirmed the fact that if we're going to make any headway with peace, understanding how systems of power such as gender create and normalise structural inequalities is essential.

LA: Which makes the comment by the senior international lawyer you mentioned earlier so troubling. It seems to me that the potential for law to do justice, let alone deliver on peace, is squandered if you cannot, in the first place, recognise the existing systems of oppression that create injustice, gendered, raced and otherwise. On the other hand, international law is itself a system of power – gendered and raced – that orders and frames …

CC: And it creates silos – there's another war image. Peace in international law is invariably coupled with something else – peacekeeping, peace operations, peace building – that is to be imposed on those who are not at peace, in conflict. It was included as one of the goals of the UN Decade for Women – equality, development and peace – but vanished as a stand-alone critical area of concern in the Beijing Platform for Action.[18] What we are now talking about is women in armed conflict. And in the Security Council's WPS agenda, peace is largely absent. It seems that the only two real concerns are that women should be allowed to participate and that women should be protected from sexual violence.

---

[17] See essay 11 'Crisis and Emergency: Entrenching Gender Systems and Militarism'.
[18] See essay 6 'Revisiting the Past: Peace at Beijing and Beyond'.

LA: I have arrived at pretty much the same conclusions and this also makes me wonder whether we ask too much of the law when we say 'where is the peace?' In search of a positive peace, I recently returned to the Friendly Relations Declaration[19] which was adopted on the 25th anniversary of the UN Charter. I was drawn to the idea of 'friendly relations' as introducing the possibility of a positive rather than negative peace. As I re-read it, it struck me as a bit of a misnomer, although I had to remember its Cold War context. I say misnomer because it reminded me of the 1899 Peace and Disarmament Conference which really has little to do with peace – other than the proposal for arbitration – and certainly not with disarmament. The Declaration recalls the principle of cooperation (as set out in article 1(3) of the UN Charter) which is less than, but necessary to, the idea of 'friendship'. But ultimately cooperation is drowned out by the far stronger language on non-intervention and the protection of the territorially defined autonomous sovereign state. Oddly, I felt that it was law's language that closed down peace. Does that make sense?

CC: Yes it does but I wouldn't go quite that far. Classic international law seeks to regulate interstate relations, preferably through diplomatic means. It gradually came to regulate conflict first in terms of so-called humanising conflicts as well as in trying to promote peaceful dispute settlement through the 1899/1907 Hague Conventions. It was not really until the 1928 Kellogg-Briand Pact that international law renounced conflict and then of course the Charter. But then, and in the context of the Cold War, we have these other concepts like friendly relations, peaceful coexistence, cooperation, good neighbourliness. They're not peace, but they are about a minimal level of stability and non-violence. I'm not saying that's all the peace is …

LA: But insofar as international law is concerned we go back to the negative peace or the absence of conflict.

CC: So then why does international law also have all these conventions on weapons and disarmament?

LA: Perhaps I'm being too cynical, but I don't view the prohibition – and certainly not the limitation – of certain weapons and weapons systems as about promoting peace. Calls for universal disarmament *are* about peace. But states have spent over a century *talking* about it.

CC: But then why does international law also concern itself with human rights?

LA: I did reflect on human rights law, but its primary purpose is to restrict the state's power rather than necessarily promote peace.

CC: That's civil and political rights. Economic and social rights are about what the state should do to ensure that citizens don't necessarily live in peace but at least have the necessities of life – shelter, food, healthcare etc.

---

[19] UNGAR 2625 (XXV), 24 October 1970, Annex: Declaration on Principles of International Law concerning Friendly Relations and Cooperation among States in accordance with the Charter of the United Nations.

LA: You're quite right. In my moments of frustration, I am too dismissive. But I sometimes wonder whether the sidelining that happens with such rights is because they don't sit comfortably within international law's conceptual framework dominated by liberal ideology. But what's your view?

CC: International law in its contemporary framing is essentially derived from Eurocentric thinking around the enlightenment, around the role of the state and individual liberties. The welfarism aspect of the state is a later notion (at least in the UK) that doesn't really emerge until the late nineteenth/early twentieth century with socialism. This didn't fit easily into a positivist international law which was already crafted around state sovereignty (with the exception of the creation of the ILO, which was focused on workers' rights, not peace). Of course, this is an excessively simplistic account of a complex history that discounts many other historiographies of international law. I was thinking of our attempt to rewrite the *Lotus* case as a feminist judgment,[20] where we contrasted the state's right to do whatever it chooses, unless it has voluntarily accepted a prohibition, with a concept of good neighbourliness. International law is clearly formulated in the former mould and largely stays there.

LA: International law assumes a very gendered conception of the state and, that being so, I fear that feminist interventions to date simply tinker with the law from the margins with little scope for transforming it in ways we would like.

CC: I agree. For instance, adding sexual violence as a violation of human rights or forced marriage as an international crime, or prohibiting chemical weapons, landmines, even nuclear weapons (which when it comes down to it actually only impacts upon about nine nuclear weapon states). Maybe where there is a real transformative potential is in an extended idea of gendered persecution: that persecutory behaviour at the core of oppression is targeted around gender relations in this widest possible sense of exercising power. This translates gender persecution of individuals into a broad notion of gender persecution across the entire structure of international law. To put it another way: gender permeates all social structures and relations; it's not just about men and women, and those rejecting the gender binary. It therefore includes all other forms of oppression, and persecution is much wider than targeting individuals. It even includes natural structures so that polluting rivers is a form of gender persecution. Does that make any sense and could it be transformative?

LA: I don't know but it is making me think. So we go from the rights of nature – which is an emerging area of law[21] that seeks to create an alternative entry point to protect the environment, ecosystems and to counter the climate

---

[20] Christine Chinkin et al, '*Bozkurt* Case, aka the *Lotus Case (France v Turkey)*: Ships that Go Bump in the Night' in Loveday Hodson and Troy Lavers (eds), *Feminist Judgments in International Law* (Hart Publishing, 2019).

[21] See essay 17 'Introduction to Transforming International Law'.

emergency[22] – to the idea of gender persecution in the context of the rights of nature. This is precisely why I love working together because we often have exchanges that take us down new paths. But I've also been reflecting on the recent calls to extend the crime against humanity of apartheid to gender.[23] Even if this is achieved, it will still leave us only with individual criminal responsibility. International law seems to have little to say when the entire state machinery is misogynistic, as in Afghanistan under the Taliban or in Iran, which is pursuing a legal and policy agenda where those who do not conform with the determined gender roles are persecuted, oppressed or even executed.

CC: Three things come to mind. First, thinking back on it, it was quite extraordinary in the 60s that the concept of apartheid was criminalised to challenge the entire internal structure of a number of states. It could only flow out of the convulsive transformative moment of decolonisation and the recognition of colonialism as racist. Second, the notion of apartheid was still confused in that on the one hand there was an apartheid state but on the other hand apartheid was deemed an international crime carrying individual criminal responsibility. Third, there has never been a state or group of states to champion the idea of prohibiting gender apartheid as the Group of 77 championed anti-apartheid in the 60s and 70s. I'm becoming convinced that individual criminal law is a major obstacle because it puts responsibility onto individuals not onto the structural formations that uphold power.

LA: Exactly. I sometimes worry that we are overinvested in international criminal law. I hear the abolitionist feminist position and find myself in agreement with them. Carceral feminism is hugely problematic and distracts us from our struggles to be free from structural violence and exploitation by states. But the ILC rejected the provision in the articles on state responsibility for the criminal state. Perhaps we did not pay adequate attention to the gendered ramifications of that decision.

CC: Asserting international criminal jurisdiction over state leaders, people like Bashir or Putin, leaves intact the structures of oppression – patriarchy, capitalism, neoliberalism. Decolonisation transferred power to the local elites but didn't alter the international structures. Indeed *uti possedetis* was written in to prevent changing the territorial structures let alone the infrastructures that sustained power. This is why decoloniality, for instance in law syllabi, is so important.[24] Changing the subject: what do you think peace might look like?

LA: That's a big question and I'm not sure where to begin. If there's one thing we've learned (although I think we both knew this before we even started this

---

[22] But see Helen Kezie-Nwoha et al, *Defending the Future: Gender, Conflict and Environmental Peace* (LSE Centre for WPS, gaps, Women's International Peace Centre, 2021) partly funded by the AHRC-funded project on a Feminist International Law of Peace and Security.

[23] See essay 2 'Gender'.

[24] See essay 19 'Searching for Peace in Teaching International Law'.

project) it's that peace is not singular. It's multiple, fluid, personal and collective, and it's always relational. A friend, Rasha, who I met years ago through the Yemeni feminist Peace Track Initiative, has more recently been spending time working with Yemeni civil society on protecting a threatened species of turtles on the Yemeni coast. I see that as both peace work and peace. We are so wrong to define Yemen exclusively by armed conflict or through the prism of a humanitarian catastrophe. I'm not denying there are huge problems but equally there are pockets of peace in Yemen – and all across the world – that we can learn from. I think we need to find peace in the everyday and protect and nurture it.

CC: This reminds me of a picture I recently saw in *The Guardian* of Gaza City, a place where life is incredibly hard with ongoing violence, uncertainty and being unable to leave.[25] It showed people sitting on the beach at an open-air cinema, a rare event in Gaza City. This too suggests that access to what you and I take for granted as being part of everyday life can constitute a moment of peaceful existence, even if it is temporary.

LA: As you know, I work for a charity supporting Palestinians and recently they shared a video of planting olive trees in Gaza. Planting olive trees is a form of resistance but also exemplifies peace. It is the peace of seeing them grow, of harvesting the crops, of building livelihoods and is another example of everyday peace in the midst of conflict. That's what's so important – protecting spaces for peace – and perhaps this is what international law should be focussed on protecting.

CC: In the book we talk about the importance of recognising everyday crisis[26] and we note, along with our friend and colleague Hilary Charlesworth, that international law tends to focus upon crisis but ignores the everyday crises of poverty and lack of social justice. But what we are saying here is the importance of the everyday to peace.

LA: The project has been hard, harder than we anticipated. There are all sorts of reasons for this. One is the climate we've been doing it in. Obviously, violence and conflict and militarisation are rampant in the world today. Military expenditure is increasing exponentially. Ukraine is getting a very high profile but that deflects attention away from violence in Ethiopia, Sudan, Venezuela, Yemen, Palestine and elsewhere. The growing level of hate directed at asylum seekers and migrants across the world is frightening because it is emblematic of a turn to the right, to a resurgence of fascism, in its twenty-first century guise. One of the reasons for embarking on this project was the hostile political climate being fuelled by leaders across the world towards asylum seekers, towards human rights defenders, environmentalists, women and LGBTQI persons that had angered us. And that prompted our first project report.[27]

---

[25] This conversation took place prior to 7 October 2023.
[26] See essay 11 'Crisis and Emergency: Entrenching Gender Systems and Militarism'.
[27] Elizabeth Rose Donnelly and Vikens Muthiah, *Protecting Women and Girls in Refugee Camps: States' Obligations under International Law* (LSE WPS, 2019).

But we were also motivated by the global backlash that was threatening to undo hard-won feminist work made possible by gender theory. And we wanted to hold on to this anger (I am reminded of Audre Lorde's essay on the uses of anger[28]) and to channel it to constructive ends, although I often think we're losing the fight and wonder why we bother. What difference can our work make?

CC: It's not just why are we bothering but the feeling of guilt that comes from sitting in our privileged university setting in a relatively secure environment while those who are speaking out for women, for gender diversity, for the environment and animal life around the world are being targeted, tortured and killed.

LA: What has also made our task even more difficult is the disavowal of international law itself by states. And the UK has joined the list. International commitments made over 50 years ago – the Refugee Convention, the European Convention on Human Rights, the Nuclear Non-Proliferation Treaty – are being ignored and traduced.

CC: Even at the time of the Iraq war 20 years ago, while we and many – probably most – international lawyers considered it to be illegal under the UN Charter, there were still government attempts at legal justification through the notion of a reviving Security Council resolution and the doctrine of humanitarian intervention. They tried to present themselves as the good guys, whereas now it seems that they don't care about their cruelty and callousness toward those who are seeking peace by fleeing from situations where there is no peace.

LA: It disturbs me that that one of the greatest champions of international law (at least rhetorically) now blatantly admits to acting in breach of long-standing international legal commitments. This is so damaging to the international rule of law; once the law is destroyed or is put to one side then there is no basis upon which to have a conversation framed by law. It is just politics and violence. This is a difficult environment in which to be writing a book on international law, let alone gender and peace.

CC: As we know, contemporary international law was framed to support colonialism and other British interests, notably trading interests. We are witnessing the reaction of a government that is losing power and reputation globally and so is willing to overturn the legal system upon which it relied. What it's doing is tearing away the pillars that protect the most vulnerable – refugees, migrants, those who are harmed in conflict, conflicts in which our successive governments have been complicit. Powerful states are unwilling to conceive of a redrafted international law that provides greater protections for the environment, for the vulnerable, for those that need the protection of the law. This requires putting profit and greed to one side and looking to see how law can be engaged in addressing together the problems facing the planet.

---

[28] Audre Lorde 'The Uses of Anger; Women Responding to Racism' keynote presentation at the National Women's Studies Association Conference, Connecticut (June 1981).

LA: We come back to the notion of gender that reminds us that everything around us is socially constructed, which makes it an easier undertaking to say if these values are socially constructed then they can be socially reconstructed. We can have a different system that values care, sustainability, and diversity.

CC: What we're trying to say in this book is that there are multiple facets to the concept of gendered peace that we have explored through different concepts of international law but that there will never be an end point or a definitive answer. There is so much we have not even begun to cover.

LA: But maybe, as in the peace letter, we have tried to indicate some possible ways forward and so not to be engulfed in the bleak despair of two old Eeyores.

Part I

Introductory Concepts: Gender and Peace

1
Introduction

THIS BOOK IS about gendered peace; the first two essays introduce the two key concepts – gender and peace – how they have been brought into public international law and their place within the discipline. These two concepts have caused us much angst over the four years of the project. Neither is well defined within international law and the meaning to be bestowed upon each is contested in international legal discourse. They are 'ambiguous notions' that 'because of their fluidity of meaning, can be "integrated into widely differing ideological systems"'.[1] For instance, how is gender – a late arrival into international law – to be differentiated from sex? What is meant by the prohibition of discrimination on the grounds of sex or gender? And why does gender provoke so much controversy, violence and hatred? Peace should perhaps be easier to understand, but when we look for it in international law it is rarely found; even the UN Secretary-General's 1992 Agenda for Peace simply assumes its meaning. But is peace only to be understood in opposition to war? What does peace mean in a context where there is no overt conflict but there are tensions, between racial groups, between minorities, and between minorities and the majority population, widespread domestic violence and a rape conviction rate below 10 per cent? And how is peace distinct from freedom[2] or security, or justice? What does it mean to say: 'women have the right to a peaceful existence'?[3] Does this constitute a right to peace and if so who can claim it, where does the obligation to ensure it lie and how can it be made effective? Is it even appropriate to attempt to locate these concepts within the framework of international law?

What is unarguable is that feminists have been at the forefront of struggles for international legal recognition of both peace and gender. In the case of the former, as will be seen in Part II, feminists have been active for well over a century, while gender only entered international discourse comparatively recently, around the mid-1980s. Since that time feminists have been campaigning for recognition that 'gender matters'

---

[1] Wendy B Sharer, 'The Persuasive Work of Organizational Names: The Women's International League for Peace and Freedom and the Struggle for Collective Identification' (2001) 20 *Rhetoric Review* 234, 245 citing Chaim Perelman and L Olbrechts-Tytec.

[2] Delegates at the Second International Women's Congress, Zurich, 1919 debated the name of what became the Women's International League for Peace and Freedom. Inclusion of 'freedom' indicated to some that the organisation would participate in wider activities than peace campaigning such as the labour movement and against racism. One delegate asserted that 'only when freedom is secured is permanent peace possible': cited ibid 245.

[3] Protocol to the African Charter on Human and Peoples' Rights on the Rights of Women in Africa (Maputo Protocol), art 10(1).

and for gender analysis to render visible the social constructions that privilege the powerful, maintain a patriarchal international order and perpetuate oppression, racism, misogyny, homophobia, transphobia, including through the instrumentality of law.

Campaigning and activism have presented feminists with dilemmas, with different views becoming divisive and undermining consistent strategising. This has been particularly the case through the many years of peace campaigning. One such dilemma is the limit of pacifism. As feminists, do we embrace pacifism in all circumstances or do we accept violence as justified, even necessary, in some situations, such as against 'colonial domination, alien occupation or racist regimes',[4] or against aggression? Another is how can women advocate for peace without falling into the essentialist trap, through our own actions reinforcing the gender stereotypes that we seek to erase? And a third is should we join with like-minded or sympathetic men or organise as women-only? Excluded – in many instances by law – from public spaces, women were only allowed to play bit parts in nineteenth century peace movements; women-only spaces allow women to speak but is this at the cost of speaking only to ourselves and losing potential support? And, even in these spaces, which women will be able to speak and which women will be heard?[5] There is concern that Western feminists have constructed 'gender' for their own ends without regard to how the politics of feminism or gender play out for women in the Global South.[6] And in the current environment, the construction of gender identity has caused further deep divisions between feminists while authoritarian and populist right-wing movements adopt an abusive use of gender ideology to oppose women's and trans rights and bodily autonomy.

These are just some of the tensions that are sparked even for those who champion the cause of a peace that takes account of gender. They are further discussed at different points in this book. We acknowledge that there are many others that we do not address; some we feel are already well covered in the literature or we have excluded because they have had little impact on international law. In some cases we have simply had to make the difficult decision to omit them because of space limitations. In the end we must remember always to question: who is making the decisions; who is benefiting; who is being excluded; whose voices are silenced; what assumptions are being built upon; and, importantly, what are the alternatives? In construing gender and peace we must ask ourselves: whose feminism and whose peace?[7]

---

[4] Protocol Additional to the Geneva Conventions of 12 August 1949, and relating to the Protection of Victims of International Armed Conflicts (Protocol I), Geneva, 1977, art 1(4).

[5] 'In contrast to straighter feminisms, they are less concerned with achieving rights for women, more concerned with the cultural politics of opening up and reconfiguring what it means to be a woman, in expanding the possibilities of different ways of being in the world beyond the modes which are currently available': Sasha Roseneil, *Common Women, Uncommon Practices* (Cassell, 2000) (on lesbian feminism at the Greenham Common women's peace camp, which commenced in September 1981).

[6] eg 'Gender is safe. Feminism is threatening. Gender can be accommodated and tolerated by the status quo. Feminism challenges the status quo': Bisi Adeleye-Fayemi Director of Akina Mama wa Afrika (AmwA), 'Creating and Sustaining Feminist Space in Africa: Local-Global Challenges in the 21st Century' at https://www.oise.utoronto.ca/cwse/UserFiles/File/CreatingAndSustaining.pdf.

[7] Nour Abu-Assab et al, 'Feminist Peace Interrupted: A Critical Conversation on Conflict, Violence and Accountability' in Sarah Smith and Keina Yoshida, *Feminist Conversations on Peace* (Bristol University Press, 2022) 19.

2

Gender

I. INTRODUCTION

WE HAD NOT originally planned an essay on gender, although it has shaped our thinking on peace and international law throughout this project. An essay on gender carries enormous risks in what we leave out. Gender has a history and feminists (and others) have spent over five decades writing and thinking about gender in different contexts. Gender carries multiple and varied meanings contingent on place, culture, language, discipline, profession, purpose, and its connotations continue to evolve. Its shape and meaning only become apparent against other words and concepts used by the speaker at a particular moment in a particular context.

International law often insists on definitions to assist in legal interpretation. Meanings of words matter to provide law with clarity. 'Gender' is no exception. In this essay, we trace international law's construction of gender through international human rights law (IHRL) and international criminal law (ICL). These processes have been beset by acrimonious disagreements and have generated in us an unease that law will tame gender and strip it of its political potential and critical edge. We conclude with some thoughts on why gender matters to us and why it should matter to all international lawyers against the backdrop of the global backlash and so-called 'gender wars'.

II. GENDER THEORY, GENDER ANALYSIS, AND FEMINIST ACTIVISM

The term 'gender' was advanced by feminist theorists in the 1970s to subvert established ideas around biological determinism or sex difference (male/female; men/women) which had naturalised inequality, in fact and law.[1] 'Gender' aimed to steer attention to the patriarchal[2] social constructions of difference between women

---

[1] The key contribution of 'gender' is its 'rejection of the biological determinism implicit in the use of such terms as "sex" or "sexual difference"': Joan Wallach Scott, *Gender and the Politics of History* (Columbia University Press, 1988) 2.

[2] 'Patriarchy allows you to talk about the relationship of constructed masculinities and constructed femininities, over time and in relationship to each other and as they relate to structures of power. If you just use "gender" then you can, in fact, never ask about the power relationships that both construct masculinity and femininity and related them to each other unequally': Cynthia Enloe, cited in Carol Cohn, 'Women and Wars: A Conceptual Framework' in Carol Cohn (ed), *Women and Wars: Contested Histories, Uncertain Futures* (Polity Press, 2013) 4; 'When Feminists Look at Masculinity and the Men

and men effected through dominant ideas, norms, customs, and practices around femininity and masculinity that shape lives and disadvantage women. Gender was thus understood as a relational concept – interpersonal and structural – shaping, maintaining, and normalising a patriarchal social and economic order.[3] As 'a constitutive element of social relations based on perceived differences between the sexes' and 'a way of signifying relationships of power', gender provided feminists with a new tool for analysis to 'decode human interaction' and to understand the conditions that give rise to particular social orders and the production of inequalities.[4]

Feminist theorising on gender has become more nuanced and complex, inspired by criticism primarily from within feminist circles. The once single-axis nature of gender is now enriched by intersectionality, a development spearheaded by North American Black feminists who drew attention to the intellectual poverty of the then-dominant one-dimensional conception of gender that obscured the intersectional and interlocking nature of relations of subordination based on race, class, sexuality and gender.[5] Discrimination could not be addressed without understanding the totality of oppressions, systemic, structural, multiple and simultaneous and the conditions that create and sustain them. Nor could discrimination be adequately addressed without appreciating that lived experiences are not static but shift in relation to place and time.[6]

In parallel, feminist anti-essentialist theorists questioned the utility of a universal group called 'women'[7] while others damningly drew attention to homogenisation of women in the so-called Third World by 'mainstream' (Western) feminisms,[8] spawning new insights into the operation of gender in different spaces and times including at the intersection with colonialism.[9] A further critique emanating from post-structuralism and queer theory troubles the duality of gender that obscures its heteronormative assumption[10] and the diversity of gendered power relations.

Who Wage War: A Conversation between Cynthia Enloe and Carol Cohn' in Cynthia Enloe, *The Curious Feminist: Searching for Women in a New Age of Empire* (University of California Press, 2004) 237.

[3] RW Connell, *Masculinities* (Polity Press, 1995) ch 3.

[4] Joan Scott, 'Gender: A Useful Category of Historical Analysis' (1986) 91 *American Historical Review* 1053. Scott identifies four interrelated elements of gender: symbols of representation; normative concepts; social organisations; and subjective identity.

[5] Black feminist thought 'fosters a fundamental paradigmatic shift that rejects additive approaches to oppression' and instead sees distinctive systems of oppression such as class, race, sexual orientation and gender as part of one 'overarching structure of domination', simultaneous and interlocked: Patricia Hill Collins, *Black Feminist Thought*, 2nd edn (Routledge, 2000) 222; bell hooks, *Ain't I a Woman: Black Women and Feminism* (Pluto Press, 1981). On 'intersectionality' and the law, see Kimberly Crenshaw, 'Demarginalizing the Intersection of Race and Sex: A Black Feminist Critique of Antidiscrimination Doctrine, Feminist Theory and Antiracist Politics' (1989) *University of Chicago Legal Forum* 139.

[6] Patricia Hill Collins, ibid 27–28.

[7] Denise Riley, '*Am I That Name?*': *Feminism and the Category of 'Women in History' (Language, Discourse, Society)* (Palgrave Macmillan, 1988).

[8] Chandra Talpade Mohanty, 'Under Western Eyes: Feminist Scholarship and Colonial Discourses' (1984) 12/13 *boundary 2*, 333.

[9] Gayatri Chakravorty Spivak, 'Can the Subaltern Speak?' in Patrick Williams and Laura Chrisman (eds), *Colonial Discourse and Post-Colonial Theory* (Columbia University Press, 1988) 66.

[10] Gayle Rubin, 'The Traffic in Women: Notes on the Political Economy of Sex' in Rayna Reiter (ed), *Toward an Anthropology of Women* (Monthly View Press, 1975); Judith Butler, *Gender Trouble: Feminism and the Subversion of Identity* (Routledge, 1990). Heteronormativity pertains to 'the institutions, structures of understanding, and practical orientations that make heterosexuality seem not only coherent – that is, organized as a sexuality – but also privileged': Lauren Berland and Micael Warner, 'Sex in Public' (1998) 24 *Critical Inquiry* 547, 548.

This scholarship demonstrates how patriarchy's[11] heteronormative binary system not only oppresses women but excludes all non-conforming people, making them vulnerable to multiple vectors of oppression, discrimination, and violence.[12] We are thus urged to understand gender as multiple, performative, fluid[13] *and* to recognise that sex – as with gender – is itself a social construct,[14] discursively produced.[15]

Gender is also understood and used by feminists as a conceptual tool for *analysis*. A gender analysis reveals the work performed by gender in a patriarchal world as 'a way of categorizing, ordering, and symbolizing power, of hierarchically structuring relationships among different categories of people and different human activities symbolically associated with masculinity or femininity'.[16] As a conceptual tool gender is used to deconstruct and decode patterns of power, illuminating the ways in which patriarchy produces hierarchies of binary difference (mind/body; reason/emotion; culture/nature; male/female etc) that ascribe meaning to social categories and thereby perpetuate inequalities. Gender opens avenues to explore, for example, how the male/female dualism associates certain issues and values with femininity and others with masculinity that play out across all social life including through the fabric of the law. Gender analysis provides insights into the social construction of multiple masculinities and femininities,[17] the interrelationship between social identities and norm creation, and helps to account for different manifestations of oppression, discrimination, and violence, including who is made vulnerable, why, and the effects thereof. Gender analysis is thus a tool for prevention of structural violence.

Feminist scholars have interrogated gender as a stratification system symbolising power at the level of the inter-personal, group, the state and on a global scale.[18] Applying a gender perspective to the structural level of the state elaborates the gendered

---

[11] There is a huge literature on patriarchy; see in the context of IHRL Cassandra Mudgway, 'The Elimination of "Patriarchy" under the Convention on the Elimination of All Forms of Discrimination against Women' (2021) 36 *Berkeley Journal of Gender Law and Justice* 79.

[12] 'Identity categories are never merely descriptive, but always normative, and as such exclusionary': Judith Butler, 'Contingent Foundations: Feminism and the Question of "Postmodernism"' in Seyla Benhabib et al, *Feminist Contentions: A Philosophical Exchange* (Routledge, 1995) 50.

[13] Simone de Beauvoir, *The Second Sex* (Vintage Books, 1973) 301. De Beauvoir's insight that gender is not fixed but fluid and acquired over time was further developed by Judith Butler, who argued that biological sex, as with gender, is performative: Judith Butler, 'Sex and Gender in Simone de Beauvoir's *Second Sex*' (1986) 72 *Yale French Studies* 35.

[14] Judith Butler, *Gender Trouble* (n 10) 6–7 (arguing that the distinction between sex as immutable and biological and gender as malleable and socially constructed is false: 'if the immutable character of sex is contested, perhaps this construct called "sex" is as culturally constructed as gender; indeed, perhaps it was always already gender, with the consequence that the distinction between sex and gender turns out to be no distinction at all'. Butler's insight that sex does not exist prior to law and that gender should be seen as 'the very apparatus of production whereby the sexes themselves are established' is echoed by Otto, who urges us to recognise that 'rather than being anchored in biology, sex and gender should both be understood as the effect of performative and reiterative gender norms (legal, social, symbolic ...) which materialise, naturalise, regulate, and discipline sexed bodies and identifications': Dianne Otto, 'Queering Gender [Identity] in International Law' (2015) 33 *Nordic Journal of Human Rights* 299, 301.

[15] Margaret Davies, 'Taking the Inside Out: Sex and Gender in the Legal Subject' in Ngaire Naffine and Rosemary Owens (eds), *Sexing the Subject of Law* (Law Book Co of Australasia, 1997) 42.

[16] Cohn (n 2) 3.

[17] Connell (n 3).

[18] Barbara J Risman, 'Gender as Social Structure: Theory Wrestling with Activism' (2004) 18 *Gender and Society* 429.

logic of protection that is foundational to the construction of state identity;[19] unpacks how gender gives meaning to and organises relationships of domination, intra- and inter-state; and reveals how constructions of gender are core to manufacturing and justifying state violence in its multiple manifestations. Moreover, in understanding gender as a system of power, scholars have traced the mutually constitutive relationship between gender and other vectors of power such as colonialism,[20] the global political economy,[21] capitalism,[22] militarism,[23] international politics,[24] nationalism,[25] self-determination,[26] and international law.[27]

As international lawyers, our concern is with revealing how gender structures our world, our knowledge and our discipline, shaping and determining law's scope and content, its administration and institutions, thereby normalising arrangements of power founded on relationships of subordination, privilege and oppression. We constantly ask ourselves how gender – together with other axes of discrimination – structures international law, its norms, its application, and operation to perpetuate patriarchal domination and how it might be reimagined to secure transformative change.

III. GENDER IN INTERNATIONAL FORA

Gender entered the international arena through the discourse and practice of development[28] and into the lexicon of international law through the efforts of feminist activists who secured its integration into official texts and institutional policies.[29] It first appeared in an international governmental multilateral text in the 1985 Nairobi Forward-Looking Strategies for the Advancement of Women (FLS), a soft law instrument.[30] Although gender was not defined, the FLS provided a framework to eliminate 'gender-based discrimination'[31] and recognised that 'women, by virtue of their

---

[19] The state's role in protection of its citizens derives from its monopoly of legitimate violence, also the basis of militarism and securitisation, both gendered.
[20] Maria Lugones, 'The Coloniality of Gender' in Wendy Harcourt (ed), *The Palgrave Handbook of Gender and Development* (Palgrave, 2016) 13.
[21] Spike Peterson, *A Critical Rewriting of Global Political Economy* (Routledge, 2003).
[22] Maria Mies, *Patriarchy and Accumulation on a Global Scale* (Zed Books, 1986).
[23] Cynthia Enloe, *Bananas, Beaches and Bases* (University of California Press, 1990).
[24] J Ann Tickner, *Gender in International Relations: Feminist Perspectives on Achieving Global Security* (Columbia University Press, 1992); Charlotte Hooper, *Manly States: Masculinities, International Relations and Gender Politics* (Columbia University Press, 1998).
[25] Nira Yuval-Davis, *Gender and Nation* (Sage Publications, 1997).
[26] Glenda Sluga, 'Female and National Self-Determination: A Gender Re-reading of "the Apogee of Nationalism"' (2000) 6 *Nations and Nationalism* 495.
[27] Hilary Charlesworth et al, 'Feminist Approaches to International Law' (1991) 85 *American Journal of International Law* 613.
[28] The classic starting point is Ester Boserup, *Woman's Role in Economic Development* (1970; reissued with new introduction by Nazneen Kanji et al, 2007).
[29] The Working Group on Discrimination against Women and Girls (WGDWG), Gender equality and gender backlash, 2–5 (summarising the evolution of 'gender' in feminism and human rights).
[30] Forward-Looking Strategies for the Advancement of Women during the Period from 1986 to the Year 2000, Report, Nairobi, 1985; see essay 6 'Revisiting the Past: Peace at Beijing and Beyond'.
[31] Nairobi FLS (n 30) para 6.

gender, experience discrimination in terms of denial of equal access to the power structure that controls society'.[32]

'Gender' appears more regularly in soft law instruments in the early 1990s, for instance the Convention on the Elimination of All Forms of Discrimination against Women (CEDAW) Committee's General Recommendation No 19 (1992),[33] United Nations Conference on Environment and Development (UNCED) Agenda 21 (1992),[34] final documents of the Vienna Conference on Human Rights (1993),[35] and the Cairo Conference on Population and Development (1994),[36] as well as in the UN General Assembly's (UNGA) Declaration on the Elimination of Violence against Women (1993),[37] but remained undefined largely due to resistance by the Holy See and its Catholic and Muslim allies.[38] Disagreements over defining 'gender' once again surfaced at the Fourth World Conference on Women in Beijing (1995), polarising states. In particular, the Holy See contributed to the divisiveness over the bracketed language of 'gender', asserting that gender is 'grounded in biological sexual identity, male or female' and excludes 'dubious interpretations based on world views which assert that sexual identity can be adapted indefinitely to suit new and different purposes'.[39] The final compromise was to annex to the Conference Report a statement that throughout the Platform for Action (PFA) the word 'gender' was 'intended to be interpreted and understood as it was in ordinary, generally accepted usage'.[40] While this facilitated the adoption of the PFA, it also presaged further divisions to come around the meaning of 'gender', for instance three years later in Rome at the drafting of the Statute of the ICC.[41]

Given the level of opposition, that gender (even if ill-defined) was included in the PFA was welcomed by feminists as a breakthrough.[42] It provided a solid foundation upon which to press states to eradicate all forms of gender-based discrimination and to address violence against women as gender-based and a form of discrimination rooted in hierarchical relationships. Moreover, it signalled the onset of a commitment by the UN institutions to 'gender mainstreaming'[43] as a strategy for achieving

---

[32] ibid para 46.
[33] CEDAW Committee, General Recommendation No 19, Violence against women, 11th session 1992 ('gender-based violence').
[34] UN Conference on Environment and Development, June 1992, Agenda 21.
[35] Vienna Declaration and the Programme of Action, Vienna, 14–25 June 1993 ('gender-based discrimination'; 'gender-specific data').
[36] Report of the International Conference on Population and Development, Cairo, 5–13 September 1994.
[37] UNGAR 48/104, 20 December 1993.
[38] See essay 6 'Revisiting the Past: Peace at Beijing and Beyond'.
[39] Report of the Fourth World Conference on Women, Beijing, 4–15 September 1995, Written statement by the representative of the Holy See, 162.
[40] ibid 218.
[41] Cate Steains, 'Gender Issues' in Roy S Lee (ed), *The International Criminal Court: The Making of the Rome Statute – Issues, Negotiations, Results* (Kluwer Law International, 1999) 357. See essay 6 'Revisiting the Past: Peace at Beijing and Beyond'.
[42] Dianne Otto, 'International Human Rights Law: Towards Rethinking Sex/Gender Dualism' in Margaret Davies and Vanessa Munro (eds), *A Research Companion to Feminist Legal Theory* (Ashgate Companion Series, 2013) 197.
[43] Beijing Declaration, para 25 and PFA, para 229; CHR, Report of the Expert Group Meeting on the Development of Guidelines for the Integration of Gender Perspectives into United Nations Human Rights Activities and Programme, E/CN.4/1996/105, 20 November 1995, Annex [13]: 'The term "gender" refers

women's equality founded on the social constructionist understanding of gender as elaborated by the Secretary-General in 1998:

> the term 'gender' refers to the socially constructed roles of women and men that are ascribed to them on the basis of their sex, in public and in private life. The term 'sex' refers to the biological and physical characteristics of women and men. Gender roles are contingent on a particular socio-economic, political and cultural context, and are affected by other factors, including age, race, class and ethnicity. Gender roles are learned, and vary widely within and between cultures. As social constructs, they can change. Gender roles shape women's access to rights, resources and opportunities.[44]

Despite this social construction approach, the parallel tendency within some quarters of the UN to use gender synonymously with women remains difficult to dislodge, with knock-on effects. For example, Commissions of Inquiry that treat gender interchangeably with 'women' not only fail to document gender-based violence against men and boys and gender diverse persons but by failing to recognise the gendered nature of harms miss the opportunity to address their structural causes. More broadly, the consequence of this slippage[45] is that gender equality becomes an exercise concerned only with the comparative positions of women and men – so that, for example, parity in representation is understood as equating to gender equality – foreclosing the ability to contest the very values that sustain the male/female dualism.

Bringing gender into international law and institutions has not been smooth sailing. Moreover, attempts to *define* gender in international treaties have generated divisions leaving it either *undefined*, as with the Arms Trade Treaty,[46] or *ill-defined*, as with the Rome Statute of the International Criminal Court (ICC). Multilateral initiatives, such as the UN Sustainable Development Goals (SDGs), have suffered the same fate of non-definition, despite SDG 5 on Gender Equality and the fact that gender equality is one of three identified priorities underpinning all the SDGs. Despite some progress elsewhere, divisions continue, as exemplified by the International Law Commission's (ILC) initial insertion of the Rome Statute definition of gender into its draft articles on Crimes against Humanity[47] and subsequent decision in 2019 to remove it as outdated.[48]

---

to the ways in which roles, attitudes, values and relationships regard women and men are constructed by all societies all over the world ... while the sex of a person is determined by nature, the gender of that person is socially constructed'; Report of the Economic and Social Council for 1997, chapter IV. A, Agreed conclusions; A/52/3 (Guidelines on the principles and practical implication of mainstreaming a gender perspective through programmes and policy). For criticism of the United Nations Economic and Social Council definition see Hilary Charlesworth, 'Not Waving but Drowning: Gender Mainstreaming and Human Rights in the United Nations' (2005) 18 *Harvard Human Rights Journal* 1.

[44] Report by the Secretary-General, Integrating the Gender Perspective into the Work of United Nations Human Rights Treaty Bodies, HRI/MC/1998/6, para 16.

[45] Christine Chinkin, *Women, Peace and Security and International Law* (Cambridge University Press, 2022) 34.

[46] Arms Trade Treaty, 2013, art 7(4) (reference to gender-based violence).

[47] ILC, Crimes against Humanity, Texts and titles of the draft preamble, the draft articles and the draft annex provisionally adopted by the Drafting Committee on first reading, A/CN.4/L.892, 26 May 2017, art 2.3.

[48] ILC, Draft articles on Prevention and Punishment of Crimes against Humanity, with commentaries, 2019, art 2, paras 41–42, A/74/10. The ILC decided against including the definition of 'gender' in art 7(3) of the 1998 Rome Statute 'thereby allowing the term to be applied for the purposes of the present draft articles based on an evolving understanding as to its meaning'. The ILC noted that other terms used in draft art 2(1)(h) are also undefined, such as 'political,' 'racial,' 'national,' 'ethnic,' 'cultural,' or 'religious': ibid.

IV. GENDER IN INTERNATIONAL HUMAN RIGHTS LAW

Since the word 'gender' is not contained in the text of any UN human rights treaty, most of the treaty bodies have elaborated on the term through General Comments or Recommendations, interpreting it as a social construct.[49] For example, the Committee on the Elimination of Racial Discrimination (CERD) General Recommendation No 25 (2000) develops a methodology for 'fully taking into account the gender-related dimensions of racial discrimination' which, in principle, enables it to interrogate the intersecting structures of race and gender that compound inequality. The CESCR's General Comment No 16 on 'the equal right of men and women to the enjoyment of all economic, social and cultural rights' defines gender to refer 'to cultural expectations and assumptions about the behaviour, attitudes, personality traits, and physical and intellectual capacities of men and women, based solely on their identity as men and women'.[50] In the same Comment, the Committee further observes that 'gender-based assumptions and expectations generally place women at a disadvantage with respect to substantive enjoyment of rights' and, echoing the CEDAW Committee,[51] cautions that 'applying a gender-neutral law may leave the existing inequality in place, or exacerbate it'.[52] The UN Committee against Torture (CAT) 2008 General Comment No 2 stresses the need for special attention to be given to protecting marginalised groups or individuals who are 'especially at risk of torture' because of their 'gender, sexual orientation, transgender identity'.[53] Gender, the Committee notes, is 'a key factor' that can intersect with other characteristics to *make* a person more vulnerable to torture or ill-treatment. Moreover, in observing that 'men and women and boys and girls may be subject to violations of the Convention on the basis of their actual or perceived non-conformity with socially determined gender roles', the Committee not only reaffirms its social constructionist conception of gender but disrupts the dominant binary structure.[54]

---

[49] Human Rights Committee, General Comment No 28, Equality of rights between men and women (article 3) CCPR/C/21/Rev.1/Add.10, 2000, does not use the language of gender but 'feminises' each right to take account of women's experiences, enabling the Committee to recognise that domestic violence can constitute a form of torture or cruel, inhuman and degrading treatment contrary to ICCPR, art 7 and the non-provision of safe abortion can constitute a violation of right to life contrary to art 6.

[50] CESCR, General Comment No 16, E/C.12/2005/4, 11 August 2005, para 14.

[51] CEDAW Committee, General Recommendation No 25, on article 4, paragraph 1, of the Convention on the Elimination of All Forms of Discrimination against Women, on temporary special measures, 13th session 2004, fn 1: '[i]ndirect discrimination against women may occur when laws, policies and programmes are based on seemingly gender-neutral criteria which in their actual effect have a detrimental impact on women. [They] may perpetuate the consequences of past discrimination. They may be inadvertently modelled on male lifestyles and thus fail to take into account aspects of women's life experiences which may differ from those of men. These differences may exist because of stereotypical expectations, attitudes and behaviour directed towards women which are based on the biological differences between women and men. They may also exist because of the generally existing subordination of women by men'.

[52] ibid paras 13 and 14. CESCR, General Comment No 20 on non-discrimination pursuant to article 2 of the Covenant, E/C.12/GC/20, 2 July 2009, acknowledges that discrimination on the basis of sex has evolved considerably and covers 'not only physiological characteristics but also the social construction of gender stereotypes, prejudices and expected roles, which have created obstacles to the equal fulfilment of economic, social and cultural rights'. The Committee clarifies that gender identity falls under 'other status' and constitutes a prohibited ground of discrimination.

[53] CAT, General Comment No 2: Implementation of article 2 by States parties, CAT/C/GC/2, 24 January 2008.

[54] ibid paras 21 and 22.

Although CEDAW article 1 adopts the language of sex and sex-based discrimination, the CEDAW Committee's General Recommendation No 25 determined that states' obligation includes addressing 'prevailing gender relations and the persistence of gender-based stereotypes that affect women not only through individual acts by individuals but also in law, and legal and societal structure and institutions' pursuant to Article 5(a)'.[55] In 2010 the Committee clarified that the Convention applies to both sex and gender-based discrimination and defined gender within the context of the Convention as:

> socially constructed identities, attributes and roles for women and men and society's social and cultural meaning for these biological [sex] differences resulting in hierarchical relationships between women and men and in the distribution of power and rights favouring men and disadvantaging women.[56]

Gender is conceived as socially constructed and relational.[57] It operates to shape and produce identities, attributes and roles of *both* women and men in a binary relation to one another justified on the basis of biological difference. Gender founds and normalises a relational binary hierarchy favouring (in a patriarchal gendered world) men and disadvantaging women and this 'social positioning' of women and men is further affected by 'political, economic, cultural, social, religious, ideological and environmental factors that can be changed by culture, society and community'.[58] The Committee also recognises that discrimination on the basis of sex and gender is '*inextricably* linked with other factors that affect women, such as race, ethnicity, religion or belief, health, status, age, class, caste and sexual orientation and gender identity' that 'affect women belonging to such groups to a different degree or in different ways to men'.[59] This understanding of gender as a social construct is firmly embedded not only within the treaty bodies but throughout the international human rights system[60]

---

[55] CEDAW Committee, General Recommendation No 25 (n 51) para 7 cites the 1999 World Survey on the Role of Women in Development: 'gender is defined as the social meanings given to biological sex difference. It is an ideological and cultural construct but is also reproduced within the realm of material practices; in turn it influences the outcomes of such practices. It affects the distribution of resources, wealth, work, decision-making and political power, and enjoyment of rights and entitlements within the family as well as public life. Despite variations across cultures and over time, gender relations throughout the world entail asymmetry of power between men and women as a pervasive trait. Thus, gender is a social stratifier, and in this sense it is similar to other stratifiers such as race, class, ethnicity, sexuality, and age. It helps us understand the social construction of gender identities and the unequal structure of power that underlies the relationship between the sexes'.

[56] CEDAW Committee, General Recommendation No 28 on the core obligations of States parties under article 2 of the Convention on the Elimination of All Forms of Discrimination against Women, CEDAW/C/GC/28, 16 December 2010, para 5.

[57] CEDAW, arts 2(f) and 5(a) recognise that women's equality with men will not be achieved without changes in the social and cultural production of stereotypes 'based on the idea of the inferiority or the superiority of either of the sexes'. Article 5 'reflects central elements in the concept of gender as an expression of socially and culturally entrenched gender-based expectations and attributions': 'Introduction' in Patricia Shulz et al (eds), *The UN Convention on the Elimination of All Forms of Discrimination against Women and its Optional Protocol: A Commentary*, 2nd edn (Oxford University Press, 2022) 24.

[58] General Recommendation No 28 (n 56) para 4.

[59] ibid para 18.

[60] eg *Guidelines on International Protection: Gender-Related Persecution Within the Context of Article 1A(2) of the 1951 Convention and/or its 1967 Protocol Relating to the Status of Refugees*, UNHCR, HCR/GIP/02/01 (2002) defined gender as 'the relationship between women and men based on socially or

including the Office of the United Nations High Commissioner for Human Rights and Special Procedures of the Human Rights Council.[61]

The regional Inter-American, African, and European human rights systems have likewise treated gender as a social construct in their reports and jurisprudence. The 2011 Council of Europe Convention on Preventing and Combating Violence against Women and Domestic Violence (the Istanbul Convention) is the first multilateral treaty (thereby creating legally binding obligations for states parties) to embrace prevailing feminist theorising and gender as advanced in international human rights law. 'Gender' is defined as 'the socially constructed roles, behaviours, activities and attributes that a given society considers appropriate for women and men'.[62] The preamble recognises 'the structural nature of violence against women as gender-based violence, and that violence against women is one of the crucial social mechanisms by which women are forced into a subordinate position compared with men'. Although it is a Council of Europe Convention, article 76 allows accession by any state.

V. GENDER IN INTERNATIONAL CRIMINAL LAW

Within the practice and discipline of ICL, gender is typically associated with the body of jurisprudence on sexual and gender-based violence (SGBV) generated by the International Criminal Tribunal for the former Yugoslavia and the International Criminal Tribunal for Rwanda, although the Statute of neither Tribunal uses the term. This jurisprudence was furthered by prosecution policy, informed by feminist theorising and activism that drew attention to the gendered dimensions of armed conflict:[63] that women and men experience conflict in different and particular ways due to their gender and sex and that law's androcentricity had historically silenced the different and particular harms and violence experienced by women in war.[64] For feminists, a gender perspective and gender analyses of human behaviour in

---

culturally constructed and defined identities, status, roles and responsibilities that are assigned to one sex or another, while sex is a biological determination. Gender is not static or innate but acquires socially and culturally constructed meaning over time.'

[61] eg Special Rapporteur on extrajudicial, summary or arbitrary executions, A gender-sensitive approach to arbitrary killings, A/HRC/35/23, 6 June 2017, para 16; Independent Expert on protection against violence and discrimination based on sexual orientation and gender identity (IESOGI), A/HRC/47/27, 3 June 2021, para 13 (gender describes 'the sociocultural constructs that assign roles, behaviours, forms of expression, activities and attributes according to the meaning given to biological sex characteristics'); letter dated 30 November 2018 to the ILC from 24 UN Special Rapporteurs and other UN experts, at https://www.ohchr.org/sites/default/files/Documents/Issues/Executions/LetterGender.pdf.

[62] Istanbul Convention, art 3(c). The Convention 'thoroughly integrates gender theory, and contains a progressive definitional framework that includes sex, gender, gender identity, gender expression and sexual orientation': IESOGI report (n 61) para 18.

[63] See essay 13 'Strategic Practice: Peace and Equality through International Law'.

[64] The UN commissioned two reports following the adoption of UNSCR 1325, 31 October 2000: *Women, Peace and Security* (UN October 2002); Elisabeth Rehn and Ellen Johnson Sirleaf, *Women, War, Peace: The Independent Experts' Assessment on the Impact of Armed Conflict on Women and Women's Role in Peace-building* (UNIFEM, 2002). There is an enormous body of feminist research on the gendered dimensions and effects of war and war as a gendered practice in general and in specific contexts. See eg Cohn (n 2); ICRC, *Gendered Impacts of Armed Conflict and Implications for the Application of International Humanitarian Law* June 2022.

armed conflict[65] and of crimes such as genocide[66] help to explain who is targeted, by whom, when, why, and how, as necessary steps toward *registering*, *preventing* and *addressing* serious human rights violations. Recognising the gendered dimensions of violations acknowledged their roots in socially constructed systems that could be changed. Ensuring that gender was understood as a social construct in ICL was thus critical to securing gender justice and transformative change.[67]

In the negotiations for the ICC, states determined that a definition of gender was required given its inclusion in the Rome Statute including in the crime against humanity of persecution.[68] The 'definition' reads:

> For the purposes of this Statute, it is understood that the term 'gender' refers to the two sexes, male and female, within the context of society. The term 'gender' does not indicate any meaning different from the above.[69]

Valerie Oosterveld described this wording as a form of 'constructive ambiguity'[70] and as 'intentionally opaque' to satisfy opposing views.[71] The phrase 'two sexes' was a nod to the reactionaries while 'within the context of society' provided a lifeline to the social constructionists, enabling the ICC Prosecutor's Office (OTP), the Office of Public Counsel for Victims, and the Trust Fund for Victims to integrate a social constructionist approach in discharging their work. For example, the 2014 OTP Policy Paper on Sexual and Gender-Based Crimes cites article 7(3), adding that the 'definition acknowledges the social construction of gender, and the accompanying roles, behaviours, activities and attributes assigned to women and men, and girls and boys'.[72] In support, the paper refers to article 21(3) of the Rome Statute, which mandates that its application and interpretation 'be consistent with internationally recognised human rights, and be without any adverse distinction founded on grounds such as gender ... or other status'. The OTP concludes that 'it will take into account the evolution of internationally recognised human rights ... including those relating to women's human rights and gender equality', footnoting CEDAW, the 1993

---

[65] eg for a gender analysis of the crimes perpetrated in Syria between 2011 and 2018, see Conference room paper of the Independent International Commission of Inquiry on the Syrian Arab Republic (ICIS), '"I Lost My Dignity": Sexual and Gender-based Violence in the Syrian Arab Republic', A/HRC/37/CRP.3.

[66] *Prosecutor v Akayesu*, ICTR-96-4-T, Judgment, 2 September 1998 (determining that rape and sexual violence could be constitutive acts of genocide; see essay 14 'Strategic Practice: Giving Effect to Legal Change'). A gender perspective enabled the Tribunal to uncover how gender determines the ways in which victims were persecuted and that rape and sexual violence formed a continuum of the genocidal violence disproportionately directed at female members of the protected group, the Tutsis. See 'Beyond Killing: Gender, Genocide Obligations under International Law' (Global Justice Center, December 2018).

[67] See essay 14 'Strategic Practice: Giving Effect to Legal Change'.

[68] While some maintained that legal certainty required a definition, 'gender' remains the only protected class of persecution to be defined; other protected grounds – political, racial, national, ethnic, cultural and religious – are undefined.

[69] Rome Statute of the ICC, art 7(3); see also arts 21(3) (no discrimination including on the ground of gender); 42(9) (prosecutor to appoint advisers with expertise in sexual and gender violence); 54(1)(b) (protect victims and witnesses having regard to their gender).

[70] Valerie Oosterveld, 'Constructive Ambiguity and the Meaning of "Gender" for the International Criminal Court' (2014) 16 *International Feminist Journal of Politics* 563.

[71] ibid 564. Catholic and Islamic states fought to ensure that gender should not be construed to include homosexuality.

[72] OTP Policy Paper on Sexual and Gender-Based Crimes (June 2014) Key terms, 3 and para 15.

Vienna Declaration and Programme of Action and the 1995 Beijing Declaration and PFA.[73] The ICC's Appeal Chamber has likewise emphasised that the 'provisions [of the Statute] must be interpreted and more importantly applied in accordance with internationally recognized human rights', indicating that the Court too understands gender as a social construct.[74] For the OTP, gender-based crimes are 'those committed against persons, whether male or female, because of their sex and/or socially constructed gender roles' and do not always manifest in sexual violence.[75]

The OTP builds on the gendered analyses of international crimes developed by the ad hoc international criminal tribunals, understanding gender as an analytic tool shaping and linking its methodology to its strategic goals that will enable it to contribute to the deterrence and prevention of crimes within its mandate.[76] A gender perspective will enable it to better investigate and prosecute SGBV, not least by interrogating how the construction of gendered identities and gendered patterns of power that create gendered inequalities in a specific context give rise to the commission of international crimes with gendered dimensions and gendered effects.

In 2022, the OTP released its 'Policy on the Crime of Gender Persecution' in which it further expands on its social constructionist interpretation of gender to clarify the contours and scope of the offence.[77] Drawing on post-structuralist feminist and queer theory, the OTP notes that gender 'varies within societies and from society to society and can change over time' and that it 'refers to sex characteristics and social constructs and criteria used to define maleness and femaleness, including roles, behaviours, activities and attributes'.[78] Thus, while persecution refers 'to the intentional and severe deprivation of fundamental rights contrary to international law by reason of the identity of a group or collectivity',[79] *gender* persecution is the crime against humanity of persecution 'committed against persons because of sex characteristics and/or because of the social constructs and criteria used to define gender'.[80] Pushing back against the tendency to equate gender with women and in order to disrupt the gender binary, the OTP's paper further observes that 'all persons can be subjected to gender persecution because all persons have gender identities' and specifically that 'targeted groups may include women, girls, men, boys and LGBTQI+ persons'.[81] Elaborating on the intention of perpetrators of gender-based crimes, the

---

[73] ibid paras 26 and 27.
[74] *Prosecutor v Thomas Lubanga Dyilo* (AC) [2006] ICC- 01/ 04- 01/ 06 para 37.
[75] OTP Policy Paper on Sexual and Gender-Based Crimes (n 72) para 16.
[76] To 'gain a better understanding of the crimes, as well as the experiences of individuals and communities in a particular society' the OTP is committed to applying a 'gender perspective' understood as 'an understanding of differences in status, power, roles, and needs between males and females, and the impact of gender on people's opportunities and interactions': ibid 3.
[77] The OTP, Policy on the Crime of Gender Persecution, 7 December 2022, 3: 'just as social constructs and criteria used to define the understanding of race, ethnicity or culture [as per the ICC's jurisprudence] so are social constructs and criteria [including for example, sexual orientation, gender identity and gender expression] used to define the understanding of gender'.
[78] ibid Use of key terms, 3.
[79] Rome Statute of the ICC, art 7(2)(g).
[80] OTP, Policy on the Crime of Gender Persecution (n 77) para 4. See *The Prosecutor v Al Hassan Ag Abdoul Aziz Ag Mohamed Ag Mahmoud* ICC-01/12-01/18-461-Corr-Red 13 November 2019 (confirming the charge of gender-based persecution the ICC Pre-Trial Chamber appears to recognise that the victims were targeted on the basis of their gender rather than sex).
[81] OTP, Policy on the Crime of Gender Persecution (n 77) para 45.

OTP notes that such crimes are used 'to regulate or punish those who are perceived to transgress gender criteria that define "accepted" forms of gender expression manifest in, for example, roles, behaviors, activities, or attributes'.[82]

To date, gender persecution as a crime against humanity has received little attention by prosecuting authorities.[83] By developing its gender analysis of the crime, the OTP's paper enables us to recognise the prevalence of the crime across the world and to see the commonalities between the conduct of ISIS in Iraq[84] and Syria[85] and other parties to the conflicts in Syria;[86] the Houthis (among other armed actors) in Yemen;[87] the armed actors in Myanmar;[88] the Taliban in Afghanistan;[89] the state authorities in Iran,[90] to list but some situations. A gender perspective provides us with the insight that these instances of persecution are not anomalies but rather are structurally linked to patriarchal gender systems founded on and nurturing discrimination. As the OTP paper states:

> as with all forms of persecution, accountability for gender persecution requires recognition and understanding of the discrimination that underlies the crime. It is insufficient to only hold perpetrators accountable for crimes that take place during atrocities. Justice also requires a holistic understanding as to why perpetrators committed such acts, if we are to eliminate discrimination and break cycles of violence.[91]

VI. STATE RESPONSIBILITY AND THE GENDERED STATE

Gender theory has enabled feminists to make significant progress in advancing the primary rules of international law in specialist regimes such as IHRL and ICL,

---

[82] ibid 4.

[83] But see Susann Aboueldahab, 'Gender-based Persecution as a Crime against Humanity: A Milestone for LGBTI Rights before the Colombian Special Jurisdiction for Peace' *EJIL:Talk!*, 4 May 2021 (recognising five LGBTI persons as victims of the Colombian armed conflict and that their gender-based persecution might have amounted to a crime against humanity).

[84] ISIS ideology was described as 'grounded on a systematic discrimination against persons on the basis of gender and gender expression, which has included torturing and killing those deemed not to be in conformity with their understanding of gender roles'; Special Rapporteur on Extrajudicial, Summary or Arbitrary Executions (n 61) para 47.

[85] ICIS, '"They Came to Destroy": ISIS Crimes against the Yazidis', A/HRC/32/CRP.2, 15 June 2016.

[86] 'I Lost My Dignity' (n 65) 3; Christine Chinkin and Madeleine Rees, 'Commentary: "I Lost My Dignity": Sexual and Gender-based Violence in the Syrian Arab Republic', WILPF/LSE 2019.

[87] Group of Eminent International and Regional Experts on Yemen, Situation of Human Rights in Yemen, including violations and abuses since September 2014, A/HRC/45/CRP.7, 29 September 2020, paras 196–234.

[88] *Decision Pursuant to Article 15 of the Rome Statute on the Authorisation of an Investigation into the Situation in the People's Republic of Bangladesh/Republic of the Union of Myanmar*, 14 November 2019, ICC-01/19-27, para 86.

[89] 'The Taliban is punishing those who transgress its rights-violating edict, enforcing severe deprivation of fundamental rights through acts or crimes of violence, such as arbitrary detention, torture, or inhuman or degrading treatment. ...[W]omen and girls are being targeted for gender persecution because of their sex characteristics and because of the social constructs and criteria used to define gender roles, behaviour, activities and attributes': Special Rapporteur on the situation of human rights in Afghanistan and the WGDWG, 'Situation of women and girls in Afghanistan', A/HRC/53/21, 20 June 2023, para 92.

[90] Repressive enforcement of Iranian hijab laws symbolises gender-based persecution: UN experts, 14 April 2023.

[91] OTP, Policy on the Crime of Gender Persecution (n 77) 4.

including especially legal recognition of gender-based violence against women and girls in both regimes. A gender perspective has also helped to expose the public/private bias upon which international law is founded, prompting a re-reading of existing norms *to register in law* the experiences of women linked to their gender/sex. Nevertheless, the foundational secondary rules of international law, namely, 'the core structures and process of international law-making, principles of state responsibility and treaty law remain largely intact'[92] and impervious to feminist critique. The consequence is that international law can be the obstacle to gender justice and peace,[93] most clearly demonstrated by the fact that the law provides few, if any, meaningful options for dealing with the misogynistic state, such as the extreme examples Afghanistan and Iran.[94]

To address this normative gap, there have been proposals to extend the definition of the crime against humanity of apartheid in the ILC Draft Convention on Crimes against Humanity,[95] to include gender. While this still situates the remedy within ICL, it may provide an entry point giving rise to third state responsibility, a 'duty to take effective action to end the practice'[96] and prompt stronger political action on the part of states, as it did in respect of South Africa.[97] The element of an 'institutionalised regime' in the crime against humanity of apartheid accurately describes the situation in Afghanistan where 'systematic discrimination against women and girls is at the heart of Taliban ideology and rule'.[98] Yet, attempts to extend the crime to gender are likely to meet stiff resistance, since both apartheid and racial discrimination (upon which apartheid rests) are accepted norms of *jus cogens* giving rise to obligations owed *erga omnes*. In contrast, states and mainstream international lawyers reject the same status being accorded to gender/sex discrimination;[99] their rejection is justified on the basis of convoluted and self-referential arguments around the lack of state practice and *opinio juris*, revealing the intransigent androcentric obstacles that feminists regularly encounter in international legal argument.[100]

---

[92] Hilary Charlesworth and Christine Chinkin, *The Boundaries of International Law: A Feminist Analysis*, rvsd edn (Manchester University Press, 2022) Introduction, xlviii.
[93] See essay 9 'Silence as an Obstacle to Gendered Peace and Equality'.
[94] See essay 10 'Misogyny and Sexism in the Digital Age'.
[95] ILC (n 48), art 2(2)(h). The definition replicates that in the Rome Statute, art 7(2)(h): 'The crime of apartheid means inhumane acts of a character … committed in the context of an institutionalized regime of systematic oppression and domination by one racial group over any other racial group or groups and committed with the intention of maintaining that regime.'
[96] Karima Bennoune, 'The International Obligation to Counter Gender Apartheid in Afghanistan' (2022) 54 *Columbia Human Rights Law Review* 1.
[97] A gender apartheid approach 'not only implicates the perpetrators of apartheid, but as was the case with racial apartheid in South Africa, it means that no Member State can be complicit in or normalize the Taliban's illegal actions, and that States must take effective action to end the situation … there can be no recognition of the Taliban and certainly no place for them at the United Nations, at least as long as their system of gender apartheid persists': Karima Bennoune, statement to the UN Security Council, S/PV.9423, 26 September 2023.
[98] Special Rapporteur on the situation of human rights in Afghanistan (n 89) para 95.
[99] ILC, Draft conclusions on identification and legal consequences of peremptory norms of international law (*jus cogens*) with commentaries, 2022 YBILC vol II, part 2. See, however, *Juridical Condition and Rights of Undocumented Migrants*, IACtHR, Advisory Opinion, 17 September 2003, para 101 (sex discrimination as constituting *jus cogens*).
[100] These arguments are critiqued in Patricia Viseur Sellers, 'Jus Cogens: Redux' (2022) 116 *AJIL Unbound* 281; see essay 9 'Silence as an Obstacle to Gendered Peace and Equality'.

International law is ill-equipped to deal with the misogynistic state in that it constructs the state as independent and autonomous, entitled to be free from external intervention, a sovereign right derived from statehood. The principles of non-intervention and non-interference in the domestic affairs of states[101] mean that once statehood is recognised and the criteria (though gendered) are satisfied,[102] international law takes little interest in the internal governance structures and policies pursued by state authorities unless viewed as a threat to the maintenance of peace and security of the existing statist system. The structure of international law is such that there are few options for addressing even the most egregious human rights abuses and only in a handful of instances does the law give rise to third state responsibility, introducing obligations that are typically framed in the negative rather than as positive duties.

VII. GENDER MATTERS

Gender matters. It matters in the part it plays in the incidence of so-called 'new wars'[103] that are fought to further the power of essentialist identities, nationalist, ethnic, religious, or tribal. Without an understanding of how gender intersects to normalise and perpetuate different forms of violence, we are consigned to developing solutions that are, by definition, inadequate. For example, in formerly colonised territories, contradictory principles of international law relating on the one hand to the sanctity of international boundaries (set by the colonial powers) and, on the other, the right to self-determination of peoples fuelled new wars, characterised in some cases by ethnic cleansing and genocide. Despite women's active participation in earlier nationalist struggles for independence, women seeking roads to peace across identity lines or national borders can be cast as betraying the national, religious or ethnic group to which they 'belong' as well as subverting associated gender roles. Nationalist, religious or ethnic identities are rendered inflexible by conflict and prevail over gender, which is itself constructed to support the relevant ideology. Nationalism, for instance typically presents women as the 'mother' of the nation, the inherent carrier and preserver of the national culture, and as child-bearers responsible for its continuity. These mark women's bodies for 'protection' by men of their own national or ethnic identity, thereby restricting their choices, and for targeted gendered violence by the 'other', hitting through the women at the male protagonists. Those that reject the gender binary are also vilified. In the context of the conflict in Croatia:

> Sexism and homophobia are correlates of this national chauvinism .... In such a climate, any fluidity of identity becomes impossible: you must be a Croat before all else or you will

---

[101] UN Charter, art 2(7) and reiterated in the Declaration on Friendly Relations.
[102] The accepted criteria for statehood remain those in the Convention on the Rights and Duties of States, Montevideo, 26 December 1933; James Crawford, *Creation of States in International Law* (Oxford University Press, 2007); for a feminist analysis see Hilary Charlesworth and Christine Chinkin (n 92) ch 5.
[103] Mary Kaldor, *New and Old Wars: Organised Violence in a Global Era*, 3rd edn (Polity Press, 2012); Christine Chinkin and Mary Kaldor, 'Gender and New Wars' (2013) 67 *Journal of International Affairs* 167.

find yourself excluded. By a strange logic of reversal, feminists are accused of rape and homosexuals are transformed into Serbian aggressors.[104]

Gender matters as a tool of analysis. It provides a deeper, nuanced understanding of social axes of power and of how patterns of subordination are produced and reproduced. It has helped concerned policymakers and lawyers to understand who is made vulnerable and the causes of that vulnerability and to craft legal principles and norms more receptive to these issues. Gender reveals how and why resources are distributed in a manner to perpetuate inequalities or what measures states should take in a humanitarian emergency so as to not entrench existing inequalities.[105] Naming a harm as gendered and establishing its roots in structural discrimination and inequalities experienced by different groups can disrupt the normalisation and institutionalisation of discrimination and violence to help 'contribute to sustainable peace'.[106] Feminists have long been aware of the threat presented by those opposed to the social construction of gender and have accordingly organised transnationally to protect the gains made, at least at the level of the international.[107] But the global backlash has been swelling and progress secured over the years is being rolled back by states, causing significant anxiety among progressive feminists and those within the international human rights community.[108]

Uniting against what they describe as 'gender ideology' and 'human rights fundamentalism', conservative social movements across the world present the emancipatory projects of gender and rights as ideological threats to societal wellbeing.[109] The origins of contemporary anti-gender movements did not 'gestate at the ground level' but rather date to the 1990s and the international conferences that brought together the Vatican and its allies, a relationship cemented by a common purpose that has evolved and expanded over time.[110] What has been a game changer is the global ascendency of right-wing politics, the re-entry of a 'respectable' fascist ideology into mainstream politics, and the rise in autocratic populist political elites that have fuelled and consolidated their political power base through a rhetoric that plays to the prejudices of disparate right-wing nationalist, transphobic, misogynist and homophobic collectives within and between states. The common strategies of centring of 'family values' and the demonisation of certain bodies to stoke societal insecurities has enabled power holders to reverse domestic laws protecting women's rights, most notably reproductive rights; curtail the rights of LGBTQI people; withdraw public

---

[104] Tatjana Pavlovic, 'Women in Croatia: Feminists, Nationalists and Homosexuals' in Sabrina P Ramet (ed), *Gender Politics in the Western Balkans: Women and Society in Yugoslavia and the Yugoslav Successor States* (Pennsylvania University Press, 1999) 152.

[105] An intersectional gender analysis reduces the likelihood that state interventions will result in direct and/or indirect discrimination, immediate, medium and long-term.

[106] Lisa Davis, 'Dusting off the Law Books on the Crime of Gender Persecution' *Just Security*, 30 May 2023.

[107] Doris Buss, 'Robes, Relics and Rights: The Vatican and the Beijing Conference on Women' (1998) 7 *Social & Legal Studies* 339.

[108] WGDWG (n 29).

[109] See essay 11 'Crisis and Emergency: Entrenching Gender Systems and Militarism'. The incoherence of claims does not make them any less dangerous.

[110] On the history of the Vatican's pivotal role in opposing 'gender ideology', see Mary Anne Case, 'Trans Formations in the Vatican's War on "Gender Ideology"' (2019) 44 *Signs* 639; Sonia Correa, 'Gender Ideology: Tracking its Origins and Meanings in Current Gender Politics' *LSE Blog*, 11 December 2017.

funding for education programmes on gender, post-colonial and critical race studies; and attempt to redefine gender as 'a biological, immutable condition' in domestic legislation.[111] At the international level, states have systematically cut back on development aid supporting women's healthcare, withdrawn from treaty regimes protecting women from gender-based violence, and sought to replace the language of gender with 'women and girls' in international fora, such as the Commission on the Status of Women[112] and UNGA Third Committee.[113]

The assault on gender theory is not confined to the anti-gender movement that aims to reassert patriarchal rule by reversing progressive legislation won by both LGBTQI and feminist movements.[114] In parallel with the anti-gender movement, gender theory has also been attacked by 'gender-critical feminists'[115] who, in opposing trans women's and non-binary people's inclusion in women's spaces and services, also reject gender theory as an ideological tool of deflection to argue for 'women's sex-based rights' on the grounds that 'biological sex' is an essential and immutable condition of femaleness.[116] Although gender-critical feminists may represent a minority view within the broader feminist movement, their ideas have travelled globally through online spaces and are providing the basis for normalising discrimination in all walks of life.[117] Moreover, by fuelling insecurities through pathologising those who do not fall within the binary[118] and in urging for the denaturalisation of the heteronormative sexual order, gender-critical feminists help the cause of the anti-gender movements to uphold patriarchy's coercive dichotomised sex-gender regimes and its 'protection racket',[119] violently erasing the harms that the trans community face daily and across the world.[120]

---

[111] See essay 11 'Crisis and Emergency: Entrenching Gender Systems and Militarism'; Andrea Peto, 'Three Readings of One Law: Reregulating Sexuality in Hungary' *LSE Blog*, 6 July 2021.

[112] eg Concluding Statement on the CSW 2019 Agreed Conclusions, 22 March 2019, US Mission to the UN. The US asserted its preference for 'the use of the tern "women and girls" where it provided greater clarity and focus in the document' and that it 'strongly supports the irreplaceable primacy of parents and the family they create, which is the foundational institution of society, vital to the health of a nation and human flourishing'.

[113] Julian Borger 'Trump Administration Wants to Remove "Gender" from UN Human Rights Documents' *The Guardian*, 25 October 2018.

[114] Judith Butler, 'Why is the Idea of "Gender" Provoking Backlash the World Over?' *The Guardian*, 23 October 2021.

[115] 'Trans-exclusionary radical feminism' (or TERF) is often interchangeably used with 'gender-critical feminism' although some argue that all TERFs are gender-critical but not all gender-critical people are TERFs.

[116] eg 'Declaration of Women's Sex-Based Rights' an initiative launched in 2019 by a group of women activists and academics, https://www.womensdeclaration.com/en/. For an incisive and compelling critique on how the Declaration puts forward a case for the elimination of 'gender identity' and the removal of legal protections for trans people, see Sandra Duffy, 'An International Human Rights Law Analysis of the WHRC Declaration' *sandraduffy.blog*, 26 October 2021.

[117] Ideas have been coopted by sports governing bodies to restrict or ban trans and intersex women's participation on the grounds that they are 'biological males' who are unfairly advantaged and present a danger to women.

[118] In that process, claims of white cis womanhood vulnerability/victimhood play into ideas on white supremacy.

[119] Ali Phipps, 'From "Sex-based Right" to "Become Ungovernable": from Supremacy to Solidarity' 12 May 2022, at https://phipps.space/2022/05/12/sex-based-rights/.

[120] Sophie Lewis and Asa Seresin, 'Fascist Feminism: A Dialogue' (2022) 9 *Transgender Studies Quarterly* 463. Contemporary disagreements within feminism over trans people's rights are sadly all too evocative of a history of reactionary feminist activism that has served to justify racial eugenics, segregation, lynching, settler-genocide, labour exploitation, imperialism, fascism and militarism.

The anti-gender crusaders recognise that gender matters. They are not wrong in depicting gender theory as dangerous. After all, the eradication of the binary structure of sexual difference upon which social hierarchies are founded would overturn dominant modes of social organisation from the family unit to the international ordering of states, calling into question its very foundations.

3

Peace in International Law

I. INTRODUCTION

THE RELATIONSHIP BETWEEN international law and peace altered dramatically over the course of the twentieth century. Law evolved from its earlier acceptance of war between states, preceded by a formal declaration of war and involving complex rules relating to neutrality, through the inauguration of institutional mechanisms for resolving inter-state disputes without recourse to war, to the gradual erosion of states' right to wage war. War not peace has been the primary focus of the political (male) elites who, at the end of the nineteenth century, preferred to attempt to humanise war rather than to abolish the weapons with which they fought each other.[1] Meanwhile, peace activists sought a peaceful world through various means, including law as an alternative to resolving inter-state disputes. Despite the objective of saving succeeding generations from the scourge of war, conceptions of peace in international law remain anchored to a particular world view, militarised and gendered, cemented by the post-World War II international legal and institutional order of the UN Charter. This essay reflects on two strands of international law: attempts at promoting inter-state (negative) peace and at establishing a separate individual and collective right to (positive) peace. Both remain chained to this history, preventing a non-militarised, gendered conception of peace through law.[2]

II. INTER-STATE PEACE

There is a common assumption that the primary purpose of contemporary international law is to maintain inter-state peace and international security. This assumption not only imagines law in contradistinction to violence occluding its own violence[3]

---

[1] See essay 7 'Women, Disarmament and Peace'.
[2] Christine Chinkin, 'From the Spectacular to the Everyday: International Law, Violence and the Agenda for Women Peace and Security' in *Experiencing Violence* (British Academy, 2021).
[3] While law provides an alternative method to violence for resolving conflict, this ignores law's own violence. Legal theorists and philosophers have interrogated the problematic relationship between law, violence and justice: eg Walter Benjamin, 'Critique of Violence' in Marcus Bullock and Michael Jennings (eds), *Walter Benjamin Selected Writings vol 1 1913–1926* (Belknap Press, 1921); Robert M Cover, 'Violence and the Word', in Bruce B Lawrence and Aisha Karim (eds), *On Violence: A Reader* (Duke University Press, 2007) 295. International law's enforceability is often contingent on military power, accentuating its violence.

but has tended to privilege a restrictive and negative conception of peace, namely the prevention of inter-state war, that is also deeply gendered.[4] The role of international law in the post-World War II architecture was originally contested.[5] Exchanges within and between the allied political classes during the war years were dominated by how (if at all) to craft a post-war international order that would best maintain inter-state peace and security. It was only after considerable lobbying[6] that the phrase 'in conformity with the principles of justice and international law'[7] was included and enshrined as one of the foundational pillars of the UN Charter. The prevention of inter-state conflict (negative peace) is now seen as the driving force behind the work of the UN[8] and the underlying raison d'etre for the principles set out in article 2 of the Charter including the prohibition of the use of force in international relations[9] and the obligation to settle disputes by peaceful means.[10] Collective security is envisaged through the UN Security Council's primary responsibility for the maintenance of international peace and security,[11] establishing an institutional hierarchy[12] grounded in militarism despite the language of sovereign equality of states. The onset of armed conflict was nevertheless assumed and legitimated by the 1949 Geneva Conventions.[13] The further expansion of the laws of war in 1977 legitimated violence against colonial domination, alien occupation and racist regimes by designating them as international armed conflict.[14]

Peace is ill-defined in international law. It is murky, fragmented through a slew of specialist regimes, doctrines, and principles that perform different functions directed principally at minimising inter-state conflict and its consequences. It underpins: weapons law that encompasses the multiple conventions that regulate the transfer

---

[4] A negative peace – absence of conflict – is problematic on multiple levels. It assumes a distinction between peace and war; is blind to the continuum of violence; privileges the public/spectacular violence of military hostilities and obscures the violence of the everyday, all of which are gendered.

[5] During the war opinion diverged within and between the Allied Powers as to the need for a post-war international institutional framework, its purpose (promoting security or economic interests), its structure and management: Ruth Russell, *A History of the United Nations Charter: The Role of the United States, 1940–1945* (Brookings Institution, 1958).

[6] The Chinese delegation, supported by less powerful states, successfully fought for the inclusion of a reference to the 'principles of justice and international law'. Their amendment to add 'justice and international law' as criteria for the Security Council in maintaining peace was not adopted: ibid 656.

[7] UN Charter, 1945, art 1(1). 'It was not by chance that international law was mentioned both in the Preamble and in Article 1 of the Charter': opening remarks by Mr Kerno, Assistant Secretary-General in charge of Legal Affairs, 1st session of the ILC; 1949 YBILC, vol 1, 9.

[8] 'Launching New Agenda for Peace Policy Brief, Secretary-General Urges States to "Preserve Our Universal Institution" amid Highest Level of Geopolitical Tension in Decades' SG/SM/21885, 20 July 2023.

[9] UN Charter, art 2(4).

[10] ibid arts 2(3) and 33.

[11] ibid art 24 and chapter VII.

[12] The hierarchy is reinforced by Security Council permanent membership for China, France, the Russian Federation, the UK and the USA (UN Charter, art 23(1)) and the veto (ibid art 27(3)).

[13] Chris Jochnick and Roger Normand, 'The Legitimation of Violence: a Critical History of the Laws of War' (1994) 35 *Harvard International Law Journal* 49; David Kennedy, 'Lawfare and Warfare' in James Crawford and Martii Koskenniemi (eds), *The Cambridge Companion to International Law* (Cambridge University Press, 2012) ch 7.

[14] Protocol Additional to the Geneva Conventions of 12 August 1949, and relating to the Protection of Victims of International Armed Conflicts (Protocol I), Geneva, 1977, art 1(4).

of weapons,[15] prohibit the use or possession of certain weapons,[16] prohibit testing of weapons,[17] or establish regional nuclear-free zones; the *jus in bello* (international humanitarian law) that aims to minimise the adverse effects of war and may also facilitate processes for peace; international criminal law, which determines individual criminal responsibility for those who commit acts that undermine peace, most particularly the crime of aggression.

The sovereign equality of states, the doctrine of state consent, and the principle of non-intervention, aim to reinforce 'peaceful' co-existence among states and deter conflict.[18] Conceptual developments have sought to enhance stability and reduce inter-state rivalry through, for instance, the sanctity of boundaries,[19] principles of common heritage and global commons, the designation of areas beyond national jurisdiction, shared management of rivers, although these have the capacity to provoke as well as to reduce conflict. Underpinning each of these normative developments is the autonomous, independent sovereign state situated in a hostile Hobbesian environment and attentive to the ever-present risk that its security, indeed its very existence, must be protected by force, which is upheld by the exception to the prohibition of the use of force – the inherent right to individual and collective self-defence.[20]

International law's peace is not entirely negative. The principle of co-operation,[21] codified in the UN Charter, seeks to bridge the gap between a negative and positive conception of peace, as do the references to 'friendly relations', and 'harmonizing the actions of nations'.[22] The commitment to 'promoting and encouraging respect for human rights and for fundamental freedoms for all without distinction as to race, sex, language, or religion' is now a peace project in its own right. International law has been invoked in seeking peace within states, justifying, for instance, intervention into a state's domestic affairs and thereby reducing the space ring-fenced by UN Charter, article 2(7).[23] In more recent times, there have been steps to integrate the concepts

---

[15] Arms Trade Treaty, 2013; Treaty on the Non-Proliferation of Nuclear Weapons, 1968.

[16] Biological Weapons Convention, 1972; Chemical Weapons Convention, 1992; Landmines Convention, 1997; Cluster Munitions Convention, 2008; Treaty on the Prohibition of Nuclear Weapons, 2017.

[17] Comprehensive Nuclear-Test-Ban Treaty, 1996 (not in force).

[18] Cecilia Baillet, 'Normative Evolution of the International Law of Peace in a Post-Western Age' in Cecilia Baillet (ed), *Research Handbook on International Law and Peace* (Edward Elgar, 2019); ch 3 recounts the concept of peaceful co-existence through international peace theorists, the Non-Aligned Movement and Soviet ideology.

[19] The principle of *uti possidetis* as a general principle of customary international law 'to prevent the independence and stability of new States being endangered by fratricidal struggles provoked by the challenging of frontiers': *Frontier Dispute (Burkina Faso v Republic of Mali)* Judgment, 1986 ICJ Reports 554, para 20.

[20] UN Charter, art 51; see Gina Heathcote, *The Law on the Use of Force: A Feminist Analysis* (Routledge, 2013).

[21] Art 1(3): 'to achieve international co-operation in solving international problems of an economic, social, cultural, or humanitarian character'.

[22] UN Charter, arts 1(2) and (4). These concepts are repeated in the Cold War inspired UNGAR 2625, 24 October 1970, Declaration on Principles of International Law concerning Friendly Relations and Cooperation among States in accordance with the Charter of the United Nations. See essay 5 'Peace in the UN Decade for Women'.

[23] 'Nothing contained in the present Charter shall authorize the United Nations to intervene in matters which are essentially within the domestic jurisdiction of any state'.

of human security, responsibility to protect and humanitarian intervention into its fabric[24] in furtherance of a positive peace, albeit with consequences that have too often been catastrophic.

Amidst this plethora of legal norm formation and theorising around inter-state peace, there is another body of work that explicitly addresses peace as a free-standing good for the benefit of all humanity. Since at least the creation of the UN, states have sought to define peace as a positive right, individual and collective and, in parallel, to advance individual criminal responsibility for a breach of the peace under international law. These efforts have had mixed results, not least for being gender-blind and consequently impoverished.

III. THE EVOLUTION OF THE RIGHT TO PEACE IN INTERNATIONAL LAW

Peace as a stand-alone condition is absent from the UN Charter. It has subsequently been articulated in numerous soft law instruments – resolutions, declarations, programmes of action.[25] The concept of a right to peace has had a complex history within UN bodies. It has been integrated as a component of many policy agendas without the necessary joining up that would provide coherence and minimise ambiguity as to both its substantive content and legal status.

Peace was seen in 1945 as the basis for the emerging international criminal and human rights law. In 1946, the UN General Assembly (UNGA) affirmed the Nuremburg Charter and judgment as principles of international law,[26] including the 'planning, preparation, initiation or waging of a war of aggression' as constituting a crime against peace, thereby pronouncing individual not state responsibility.[27] The Assembly sought further legal clarification, directing the Committee on the Codification of International Law to work on the Nuremburg Principles by developing either a general codification of offences against the peace and security of mankind or an International Criminal Code.[28] The newly-established International Law Commission (ILC) adopted a draft Code of Offences against the Peace and Security of Mankind in 1954.[29] The work remained largely in limbo[30] until it was resumed at the

---

[24] Christine Chinkin and Mary Kaldor, *International Law and New Wars* (Cambridge University Press, 2017) chs 5 and 11.

[25] See Liva Diacoba Tehindrazanarivelo and Robert Kolb, 'Peace, Right to, International Protection', *Max Planck Encyclopaedia of Public International Law* (arguing that the implicit place of peace in the UN Charter bestows that instrument's authority on soft law articulations) at https://opil.ouplaw.com/display/10.1093/law:epil/9780199231690/law-9780199231690-e858?rskey=Z02m4T&result=1&prd=MPIL.

[26] UNGAR 95/1, 11 December 1946, Affirmation of the Principles of International Law recognized by the Charter of the Nurnberg Tribunal.

[27] As in Charter of the International Military Tribunal, London, 8 August 1945, art 6(a); Charter of the International Military Tribunal for the Far East, Tokyo, 19 January 1946, art 5(a).

[28] UNGAR 177 (II), 21 November 1947 directed the ILC to prepare a draft code of offences against the peace and security of mankind.

[29] Draft Code of Offences against the Peace and Security of Mankind with commentaries, Text adopted by the ILC, 2 YBILC 1954.

[30] In 1974 the UNGA reaffirmed that a 'war of aggression is a crime against international peace': UNGAR 3314 (XXIX), definition of aggression.

request of the UNGA in the 1980s and in the post-Cold War environment[31] when a further draft was adopted by the ILC in 1996.[32] However, since then, there has been no additional progress.

In 1989 the UNGA asked the ILC to consider, in conjunction with the Draft Code on Crimes against Peace and Security, the question of an international criminal court.[33] The ILC developed a draft statute but in 1994 the UNGA effectively moved the process away from the ILC to states through the Preparatory Commission for the International Criminal Court.[34] The Rome Statute acknowledges its genealogy with peace only in the preamble by 'recognizing that such grave crimes threaten the peace, security and well-being of the world' and in inclusion of the crime of aggression.[35] Ironically, given that the impetus in 1989 for renewal of interest in a permanent international criminal court lay in 'illicit trafficking in narcotic drugs across national frontiers and other transnational criminal activities', such crimes are not included in the ICC's jurisdiction, which is limited to aggression, genocide, crimes against humanity and war crimes. The ILC discussed a wider range of crimes against peace and security, including drug trafficking and wilful damage to the environment. Twelve categories of crime were reduced to five in the draft as adopted,[36] a stance that was regretted by some ILC members.[37] This narrowing is further cemented by international criminal law, with its focus on individual accountability for aggression and conflict-related crimes.

Peace was a motivating factor in the early days of human rights law. There is no right to peace in the Universal Declaration of Human Rights (UDHR), although the preamble asserts 'the inherent dignity and ... equal and inalienable rights of all members of the human family' to be the 'foundation of freedom, justice and peace in the world'. This assertion is reiterated in the preamble of both UN Covenants.[38] Additionally, the right to a 'social and international order' for the realisation of all human rights[39] encapsulates a vision of peace that is not limited to absence of inter-state conflict and violence. By 1949 the UNGA was expressing the 'urgent necessity' for its members to act in accordance with Charter principles for 'enduring' peace.[40] Freedom of 'peaceful expression of political opposition, full opportunity for the exercise of religious freedom and full respect for all the other fundamental rights' in the UDHR were spelled out as 'essentials of peace', as was the removal of 'barriers which deny to peoples the free exchange of information and ideas essential to international understanding and peace'.

---

[31] Katerina Tomasevski, 'The Right to Peace after the Cold War' (1991) 3 *Peace Review* 14.
[32] Draft Code of Offences against the Peace and Security of Mankind with commentaries, Text adopted by the ILC 2 YBILC 1996 (part two).
[33] UNGAR 44/39, 4 December 1989.
[34] UNGAR 51/160, 30 January 1997, Report of the ILC on the work of its forty-eighth session, para 2.
[35] Rome Statute of the ICC, 1998, art 8*bis*.
[36] Draft Code 1996 (n 32) (aggression, genocide, crimes against humanity, war crimes and crimes against UN personnel).
[37] 1996 2 YBILC (part 2) paras 40–46.
[38] International Covenant on Civil and Political Rights (ICCPR) and International Covenant on Economic, Social and Cultural Rights (ICESCR), 16 December 1966.
[39] UNGAR 217A, 10 December 1948, Universal Declaration of Human Rights, art 28.
[40] UNGAR 290 (IV), 1 December 1949, Essentials of peace.

IV. A RIGHT TO PEACE?

In 1968 peace was recognised as a 'universal aspiration' that was essential for the realisation of human rights[41] rather than as a right itself. A change of direction and enhanced institutional activity ensued in the 10-year period from 1976, the year that the UN Covenants came into force. Following appeals by the UNGA for 'initiatives intended to contribute to the peace, security and economic and social progress of all mankind'[42] resolutions were adopted by the Commission on Human Rights[43] and the UNGA. On the one hand, this was viewed in the West as a politicisation of peace by the Soviet bloc states[44] which instigated the resolutions, and, on the other hand, peace was conceptualised as a third generation, solidarity right. The language also shifted. In 1978 the right was declared to be that of 'individuals, States and all mankind [sic] to life in peace';[45] in 1984 'the people of our planet' were declared to 'have a sacred right to peace'[46] with states bearing the corollary 'fundamental' obligation to promote its implementation;[47] and in 1985 peace as 'an inalienable right of every human being'[48] was reiterated. Commentators debated – and continue to debate[49] – its justiciability and whether peace can be designated or protected as an individual or collective right. Absence from the human rights treaties weighed against acceptance of a right to peace, although this was changed by its inclusion in the 1981 Banjul Charter as a collective (peoples') right.[50] The African Court of Human Rights has observed that peace under the Banjul Charter symbolises 'the absence of worry, turmoil, conflict or violence. Its symbiosis with security contributes to social well-being'.[51] Further, human rights as a tool for peace requires taking into account the full range of rights, not just civil and political rights. The UN Human Rights Committee spelled out that peace is inherent to the (individual) right to life.[52]

---

[41] Final Act of the International Conference on Human Rights, Proclamation of Tehran, 22 April–13 May 1968.

[42] CHR Resolution 5 (XXII), Further promotion and encouragement of human rights and fundamental freedoms, including the question of a long-term programme of work of the Commission, E/CN.4/ RES/5 (XXXII), 27 February 1976, preamble.

[43] ibid: 'Everyone has the right to live in conditions of international peace and security and fully to enjoy economic, social and cultural rights, and civil and political rights.'

[44] See essay 5 'Peace in the UN Decade for Women'.

[45] UNGAR 33/73, 15 December 1978.

[46] UNGAR 39/11, 12 November 1984. This is 'extraordinarily elevated language for an assemblage of government representatives, many of whom are jurists, who in the tradition of the Enlightenment, usually avoid entering the realm of the sacred': John Fried, 'The United Nations' Effort to Establish a Right of the Peoples to Peace' (1990) 2 *Pace International Law Review* 21, 31.

[47] This is a dangerous idea for states, as it implies a basis for challenging state action.

[48] UNGAR 40/11, 11 November 1985, Right of peoples to peace.

[49] See the different views expressed in OHCHR, Report on the outcome of the expert workshop on the right of peoples to peace, A/HRC/14/38, 17 March 2010.

[50] African Charter on Human and Peoples' Rights, Banjul, 1981, art 23: 'All peoples shall have the right to national and international peace and security'.

[51] *XYZ v Republic of Benin*, AfCtHR, 27 November 2020, 4 AfCLR 83, paras 132–36. The judgment suggests peace as a collective right as 'presenting and adopting a revision of the fundamental law of Benin without a national consensus, ... poses a threat to the peace and stability of Benin and the security of Benin citizens'.

[52] Human Rights Committee, General Comment 6, art 6 (Sixteenth session, 1982), HRI\GEN\1\Rev.1 at 6 (1994), para 2: 'States have the supreme duty to prevent wars, acts of genocide and other acts of

In addition, 'zones of peace' were introduced or reactivated[53] and 1986 was proclaimed the International Year of Peace, an opportunity for setting in motion the preparation of societies for life in peace. NGOs too were active in proclamations of peace.[54]

This period also constituted the UN Decade for Women, with its objectives of equality, development and peace.[55] But there seem to have been two parallel tracks of peace resolutions and resolutions pertaining to women; the UNGA resolutions on peace make no reference to women or to the importance of their participation in activities for peace,[56] in averting the nuclear threat and in educating young people for peace that were all emphasised in the documents adopted by the Decade's women's conferences and endorsed by the Assembly.[57] Nor was the significance for women of an International Year of Peace, or that the Mexico City Women's conference had called for such a year, acknowledged.

Discussing a right to peace in 1980, Philip Alston concluded that such a right existed[58] but that its parameters were ill-defined (as is also true of many first and second generation rights).[59] He stressed the complementarity of the various solidarity rights, giving as an example that proposals to promote realisation of the right to peace must take into account inequalities and inequities in inter-state relations, the gross imbalances in resource distribution and consumption, and the many forms of domination and exploitation. Accordingly, Alston argued, promotion of the right to development and of other solidarity rights such as the right to benefit from the common heritage of mankind, must go hand in hand as part of an integrated approach to the promotion of human rights. 'The creation of a new international economic order based upon a true community of interests and guided by a spirit of solidarity and designed to achieve equity, social justice and respect for human rights for all peoples, is thus a prerequisite for realization of the right to peace.'[60]

---

mass violence .... Every effort they make to avert the danger of war, especially thermonuclear war, and to strengthen international peace and security would constitute the most important condition and guarantee for the safeguarding of the right to life.' In 2019 the Committee stated: 'Efforts to avert the risks of war and any other armed conflict, and to strengthen international peace and security, are among the most important safeguards of the right to life': Human Rights Committee, General Comment 36, CCPR/C/GC/36, 3 September 2019, para 69.

[53] eg UNGAR 2832 (XXVI), 16 December 1971, Declaration of the Indian Ocean as a zone of peace; UNGAR 40/153, 16 December 1985, Implementation of the Declaration of the Indian Ocean as a zone of peace; UNGAR 41/11, 27 October 1986, Zone of peace and cooperation of the South Atlantic; key features of a zone of peace include preservation from militarisation, the arms race, military bases and nuclear weapons, and social and economic development, environmental protection and conservation of living resources.

[54] eg Conference on Peace and Human Rights = Human Rights and Peace, International Peace Research Institute, Oslo and International Institute of Human Rights, Strasbourg, December 1978: 'The right to peace is one of the fundamental human rights. Every nation and every human being without distinction ... sex, possess the inherent right to live in peace.'

[55] See essay 5 'Peace in the UN Decade for Women'.

[56] Although the UNGA adopted separate resolutions on women's participation in peace: see essay 5 'Peace in the UN Decade for Women' fn 132.

[57] See essay 5 'Peace in the UN Decade for Women'.

[58] This view is not necessarily shared – eg Vera Gowlland-Debbas in 2010 concluded that the right had not yet crystallised in human rights law: Report of the OHCHR (n 49) para 14.

[59] Philip Alston, 'Peace as a Human Right' (1980) 11 *Bulletin of Peace Proposals* 319.

[60] ibid.

Alston does not mention the Mexico City, Copenhagen and Nairobi conferences,[61] but these would have provided him with concrete examples of how development, equality and peace are mutually reinforcing in ways that are absent from the UNGA resolutions on peace.

Following the break-up of the USSR there were no further resolutions on a right to peace until 2001.[62] UN attention turned to institutional peace operations – peacemaking, peacekeeping and peacebuilding – processes for guiding states (usually non-Western) experiencing or emerging from conflict toward peace.[63] In 2010[64] the Human Rights Council recalled UN history with respect to a right to peace, reaffirmed that the 'peoples of our planet have a sacred right to peace' and requested its Advisory Committee to prepare a draft declaration on the right of peoples to peace.[65] The topic remained divisive and contested. The report of the Advisory Committee,[66] comprising independent experts, drew on wide ranging sources for the more than 40 standards it envisaged for a far-reaching declaration.[67] These included core dimensions such as: the right to full disarmament; human security; freedom from fear and want; the right to resist and oppose oppression; peacekeeping; the right to conscientious objection and freedom of religion. Additional dimensions included a commitment to professional peace education that looks to diminish racist, aggressive, discriminatory and violent attitudes; the right to development; the environment and climate change as crucial aspects of the right to peace. The Committee identified groups with specific vulnerabilities who need protection, including 'women in particular [unidentified] situations'. It referenced Security Council Resolution 1325, focusing on women's equal participation in efforts to maintain and promote a just peace and protection from rape and sexual violence. The Committee observed that the Security Council had introduced 'new approaches' for the integration of gender into issues of peace and security but did not expand on what these entailed. It recognised that people who are vulnerable in conflict have often previously experienced discrimination and oppression, the importance of this continuum and that addressing discrimination is a preventive measure against violence and conflict. Its Draft Declaration published two years later incorporated these commitments in 14 articles broken down in 57 sub-paragraphs.[68]

---

[61] See essay 5 'Peace in the UN Decade for Women'.
[62] Liva Diacoba Tehindrazanarivelo and Robert Kolb (n 25).
[63] Report of the Secretary-General, An Agenda for Peace Preventive diplomacy, peacemaking and peace-keeping, A/47/277–S/24111, 17 June 1992; Supplement to an Agenda for Peace: position paper of the Secretary-General on the occasion of the 50th anniversary of the United Nations, A/50/60, S/1995/1, 25 January 1995.
[64] 2010 was the final year of the International Decade for a Culture of Peace and Non-Violence for the Children of the World declared by UNGAR 53/25, 10 November 1998; see Declaration and Programme of Action on a Culture of Peace, UNGAR 53/243, 13 September 1999; UNESCO, Mainstreaming the culture of peace (2002) describes the evolution of the concept of a culture of peace.
[65] Human Rights Council Resolution 14/3, 23 June 2010, Promotion of the right of peoples to peace.
[66] Progress report of the Human Rights Council Advisory Committee on the right of peoples to peace, A/HRC/17/39, 1 April 2011.
[67] eg NGO reports on peace, for instance the Santiago Declaration on the Human Right to Peace (2011) 28 *International Journal on World Peace* 94. This Declaration resulted from a four-year campaign that collected materials worldwide and local and international law from Western and non-Western traditions: ibid para 12.
[68] Report of the Human Rights Council Advisory Committee on the right of peoples to peace, A/HRC/20/31, 16 April 2012.

The Declaration as adopted – four years later – first by the state-based Human Rights Council[69] and then the UNGA is a much-reduced version of the earlier draft and fails to include the fuller set of commitments identified by the Committee.[70] Even this shortened text was not acceptable to many European states, nor to Australia, Canada, UK and the US.[71] It has a lengthy preamble (36 paragraphs) and a main body comprising a mere five articles. The preamble recognises that peace is more than an absence of conflict; it is a 'positive, dynamic participatory process where dialogue is encouraged and conflicts are solved in a spirit of mutual understanding and cooperation, and socioeconomic development is ensured'. It is heavily imbued with the traditional international legal concerns for the maintenance of international peace and security – state sovereignty, the prohibition of the use of force in international relations, non-intervention, self-determination, an end to foreign occupation and alien domination, and, reflecting the contemporary geo-political landscape, the fight against terrorism. Values such as tolerance, dialogue, cooperation and solidarity among all human beings, peoples and nations are extolled as means of fostering peace and preventing the scourge of war.

In the operative paragraphs language has shifted from that of the UNGA resolutions of the 1970s and 80s. It does not unequivocally declare a right to peace but rather that of 'everyone to enjoy peace such that all human rights are promoted and protected and development is fully realized'.[72] This is expressed as an individual ('everyone') not a collective (peoples') right, although mention of development recalls the collective right to development. The almost contemporaneous ASEAN Human Rights Declaration[73] similarly frames a right to 'enjoy peace' individually ('every person') and collectively (the 'peoples of ASEAN') within the framework of security and stability, neutrality and freedom of ASEAN for the realisation of rights. Evoking the language of the 1955 Bandung Communique it states that 'ASEAN Member States should continue to enhance friendship and cooperation in the furtherance of peace, harmony and stability in the region.'[74] The UNGA Declaration on Peace, on the other hand, recalls the Cold War resolutions on peace and details its 1970 Declaration on Friendly Relations, but 'friendship' is noted only in the context of minority rights.

States struggle with formulating the corollary obligation to the right to peace, apparently unwilling to accept accountability. In an echo of the human rights typology of states' obligation to respect, protect and fulfil human rights, the UNGA Declaration requires that states 'should respect, implement and promote equality and non-discrimination, justice and the rule of law and guarantee freedom from fear and want'[75]

---

[69] HRC Resolution 32/28, 1 July 2016.
[70] UNGAR 71/189, 19 December 2016, Annex, Declaration on the Right to Peace; Tuba Turan, 'The 2016 UN General Assembly Declaration on the Right to Peace: a Step towards Sustainable Positive Peace within Societies?' (2023) 23 *Human Rights Law Review* 1.
[71] 131 in favour, 34 against, and 19 abstentions.
[72] Declaration on the Right to Peace, art 1.
[73] ASEAN Human Rights Declaration, 19 November 2012, para 38.
[74] Final Communiqué of the Asian-African conference of Bandung, 24 April 1955, G, Declaration on the promotion of world peace and co-operation: 'nations should practise tolerance and live together in peace with one another as good neighbours and develop friendly co-operation'.
[75] Declaration on the Right to Peace, art 2.

as ways to build peace within and between societies. Other actors, the UN and specialised agencies, are brought into this exhortatory, not mandatory, language for implementation; in any case, as an UNGA resolution, the Declaration is soft law. The dilution of state responsibility weakens the supposed entitlement to enjoy peace. Institutions of peace education are promoted for their role in strengthening the values of tolerance, dialogue, cooperation and solidarity.

The Declaration omits dimensions of peace identified by the Human Rights Council's Advisory Committee, such as disarmament and the environment, the last an astounding omission when there is no graver threat to peace and security than effects of climate change and destruction of ecosystems.[76] The continuing threat of nuclear weapons is also astonishingly absent. The Declaration fails to take account of the violence of borders and that those who seek a more peaceful existence by moving away from situations of violence are met with constructed borders that 'organise the distribution of the means of survival and flourishing and structure our relations with one another'.[77] The assertion that 'everyone' has the right to enjoy even negative peace for the realisation of their rights is hollow for the millions of migrants: we might ask '[a]re we now at war again … ? Not between armies or states but between those who flee their homes and those who fortify them.'[78] In the pre-Covid world of 2016, pandemics and inequalities in their prevention and treatment have no place. Coloniality has not moved beyond the 1960 Declaration on the Granting of Independence to Colonial Countries and Peoples[79] and there is no challenge to the prevailing neoliberal economic ideology that fosters greed, exploitation and violence. Earlier Cold War articulations of the right of peoples to peace were associated with inequalities between states and the New International Economic Order;[80] with the acceptance of the neoliberal globalised economic order, which demands inequalities, can there be any realistic vision of peace?

And women too are largely absent. While some human rights instruments are listed, those explicitly for the advancement of women's rights are not. Instrumental language from the preamble to CEDAW is repeated, recalling that the development of a country, the welfare of the world, and the cause of peace require the maximum participation of women[81] and there is a general assertion of non-discrimination. The explicit assertion of women's right to peace in the Maputo Protocol[82] is not recalled. The linkage – at least rhetorical – between Women and Peace and Security

---

[76] Carol Cohn and Claire Duncanson, 'Re-arranging the Deckchairs on the Titanic? The UK Government and the WPS Agenda in a Time of Climate Crisis' *LSE Blog*, 21 October 2022.

[77] Hannah Wright, 'There Are No Feminist Borders' *LSE Blog*, 28 October 2022.

[78] Rebecca Lowe, *Slow Road to Tehran* (September Publishing, 2022) 48.

[79] UNGAR 1514 (XV), 14 December 1960.

[80] See essay 5 'Peace in the UN Decade for Women'.

[81] CEDAW's language repeats International Conference on Human Rights, Tehran, 1968, Resolution IX, Measures to promote women's rights in the modern world including a unified long-term United Nations programme for the advancement of women. It seems extraordinary that in 2017 there was no further advance.

[82] Protocol to the African Charter on Human and Peoples' Rights on the Rights of Women in Africa, 2003, art 10(1): 'Women have the right to a peaceful existence and the right to participate in the promotion and maintenance of peace.' See essay 19 'Searching for Peace in Teaching International Law'.

made by Security Council Resolution 1325 (2000)[83] and the succession of following resolutions finds no place in the UNGA's Declaration on the Right to Peace, underlining the siloed thinking between UN institutions. Racism and racial discrimination are spelled out as obstacles to 'friendly and peaceful relations', but sexism and sex/gender discrimination are not. Nor is there any attempt to define what peace might mean for women and gender diverse people: freedom from the violence and exploitation of sexism, misogyny, homophobia and transphobia. '[T]olerance, dialogue, and cooperation ... are [undoubtedly] among the best guarantees of international peace and security'[84] but these values must not be misused so as to maintain an unequal and oppressive status quo. Women and gender diverse persons should not tolerate the abuses they endure, even if their anger causes social disruption and threatens the extant order. Dialogue is meaningless unless it is inclusive. Despite consistent calls for their participation,[85] women's place in dialogue remains irregularly implemented at national and international levels and agendas are invariably determined by those holding more powerful positions, usually men. Cooperation is only possible from a starting point of equality. The gender 'neutrality' of the Declaration conceals the gender-specific obstacles to peace and security for women and those who reject the gender binary. The Declaration is static. It pays lip service to cultural diversity but offers no feminist or queer curiosity to interrogate the masculine heteronormative world of the UN Charter: despite asserting a process of peace, it remains rooted in the negative peace of 'sparing future generations the scourge of war'.

V. GENDER AND PEACE

'Peace remains an elusive promise for many around the world.'[86] New initiatives are emerging and voices calling for change, although the principles they urge have been around for a long time. Successive holders of the UN Human Rights Council (HRC) mandate on human rights and international solidarity seek to reinvigorate the principle of international solidarity,[87] seeing it as 'based on, and in accordance with: (a) Justice, equity, peace, non-interference, self-determination, mutual respect and accountability in international relations'.[88] Its objective is to 'create an enabling environment' for removing structural obstacles to inequalities and poverty eradication, to engender trust between states and non-states 'to foster peace and security, development and human rights'. To this end states should undertake a human rights-based approach to international cooperation in matters appertaining to 'peace and security, global governance, environmental protection and climate justice,

---

[83] See essay 6 'Revisiting the Past: Peace at Beijing and Beyond'.
[84] Declaration on the Right to Peace, preamble.
[85] See essay 5 'Peace in the UN Decade for Women', essay 6 'Revisiting the Past: Peace at Beijing and Beyond' and essay 15 'Strategic Practices: "Doing Our Own Thing"'.
[86] Our Common Agenda: Policy Brief 9, A New Agenda for Peace (UN, July 2023) 3.
[87] 'The concept of solidarity is embedded in the work of the United Nations. ... the General Assembly recognized solidarity as one of the essential values for the twenty-first century': ibid at 9.
[88] Independent Expert on human rights and international solidarity, Virginia Dandan, A/HRC/35/35, 25 April 2017, Annex: Draft declaration on the right to international solidarity, art 1(3).

humanitarian relief and assistance, trade, foreign debt, official development assistance, social protection, education, health, and food and nutritional security'.[89] In 2023 the current Independent Expert revised a draft declaration on human rights and international solidarity, proposed by his predecessor.[90] He questions why some states find it difficult to accept a right to international solidarity.[91] He points out that almost the same states that reject some form of such a right favour the responsibility to protect:

> [a]lmost all of these actors support this claim as inclusive of the legal authority to intervene militarily and economically around the world to protect human rights (a right or responsibility that only more powerful States and peoples can enjoy and only weaker States can suffer or benefit from).

He deplores the inconsistency of a position that accepts 'allegedly pro-human rights great power interventions in weaker States' but then rejects the concept of a global community 'when it comes to the people of those other lands sharing in the COVID-19 vaccines produced by the great powers. In both cases, lives are threatened and human rights are at stake.'[92] The same double standards and denial of responsibility are at play with the right to peace.

Similar calls continue from others of the UN HRC special procedures, the treaty bodies, environmental groups and civil society. For some the language is shifting from that of peace to that of survival: 'International solidarity is a foundational principle underpinning contemporary international law in order to preserve the international order and to ensure the survival of international society'[93] and 'the catastrophic consequences of nuclear weapons cannot be adequately addressed, transcend national borders, pose grave implications for human survival'.[94] They are confronted by resistance from the powerful, who resort to domestic power to deny the right to protest and are closing space to civil society.[95] The powerful within the state-based international legal order remain immune to attitudinal change[96] and through threats, intimidation and violence deny peace and equality.[97]

It is in this context and that of extreme challenge to the multilateral order that the New Agenda for Peace[98] is evolving. The Secretary-General has called for a holistic

---

[89] ibid.
[90] Independent Expert on human rights and international solidarity, Obiora Chinedu Okafor, Revised draft declaration on human rights and international solidarity, A/HRC/53/32, 2 May 2023.
[91] ibid paras 14–24.
[92] ibid para 24.
[93] ibid.
[94] Treaty on the Prohibition of Nuclear Weapons, 2017, preamble.
[95] Many have commented on the closing space for civil society action deliberately constraining activism for equality, peace and security: eg '5 Examples of Closing Space for Civil Society and What We Can Do about It' *IWRAW Asia Pacific Blog*.
[96] eg no nuclear weapons state has signed the Treaty on the Prohibition of Nuclear Weapons.
[97] Report of Secretary-General, Twentieth anniversary of the Declaration on the Right and Responsibility of Individuals, Groups and Organs of Society to Promote and Protect Universally Recognized Human Rights and Fundamental Freedoms, A/73/230, 27 September 2018.
[98] A 'Summit of the Future: multilateral solutions for a better tomorrow' is planned for September 2024; UNGAR 76/307, Modalities for the Summit of the Future, 8 September 2022. The Secretary-General's report on 'Our Common Agenda' is part of the preparation for this.

approach to peace,[99] linking actions for peace with the Sustainable Development Goals.[100] We applaud many of the obstacles to peace he has identified, including the impact of misogyny in justifying violence, the urgent need to 'dismantle patriarchal power structures' and transform gender norms.[101] But he is apparently unwilling to address the failure of the WPS agenda to achieve its transformative potential. He attributes this not to the reality that the agenda in its current form is flawed but that 'incrementalism has not worked'.[102] We agree with the Secretary-General's solution – political will, precipitating women's meaningful participation in all decision-making, eradicating all forms of violence against women, and upholding women's rights – but they must be integral to the many other issues he raises throughout his policy for a New Agenda for Peace. Nor do they go far enough. They do not challenge the structures of the international legal order based on patriarchy, imperialism and militarism. Nor is 'general and complete disarmament' mentioned as the ultimate objective of the UN in the field of disarmament, and critical to both a negative and positive peace.[103] As the Secretary-General acknowledges, risk reduction does not suffice when the survival of humanity is at stake.[104] Addressing peace through a gender lens has the potential to disrupt the existing order, making a gender perspective critical for an effective international legal order that places inter-state and inter-personal peace at its centre.

---

[99] Our Common Agenda: Policy Brief 9 (n 86).
[100] UNGAR 70/1, Transforming our world: the 2030 Agenda for Sustainable Development.
[101] Our Common Agenda: Policy Brief 9 (n 86).
[102] ibid 20.
[103] Securing Our Common Future: An Agenda for Disarmament (UNODA, 2018).
[104] ibid 16.

Part II

Gendering Peace Through the Past

4

Introduction: Rewriting International Law's Histories

WOMEN HISTORIANS HAVE revealed the richness of feminist activity, especially in the late nineteenth and early twentieth centuries as women forged what has become understood as a transnational feminist movement,[1] pursuing women's advancement through suffrage, political rights, social justice and workers' rights. Women also joined the peace societies that had flourished in Europe and the US from the early nineteenth century, although they were not entitled to participate on an equal basis with men and were, as a rule, barred from speaking in public meetings. Nevertheless, by the second half of the century women 'somehow found ways to organize, publish and speak' about peace.[2] Some key personalities came to the fore – Bertha von Suttner, Jane Addams, Carrie Catt, Rosika Schwimmer, Lady Aberdeen, Aletta Jacobs, Sophia Duleep Singh,[3] Mary Church Terrell – but their contributions rested upon the efforts of thousands of other women who participated in their own ways. Their activities ranged widely, including from becoming an officer or member of an international, regional, or local organisation, to joining a protest, march or demonstration, to adding their name to the millions of women who signed petitions – for instance urging disarmament[4] or against war.[5]

Despite claims to universality, the international feminist movement was dominated by white middle- and upper-class women from Europe and the US. But feminist activism flourished elsewhere, in every region moulded by their own history and context. Feminists within the Soviet Union and its subsequent satellite states had to navigate their way through communist ideology and state control; Black women in the US their way through the Jim Crow laws;[6] women in Latin America, released

---

[1] Leila J Rupp, *Worlds of Women: The Making of an International Women's Movement* (Princeton University Press, 1997).
[2] Cynthia Cockburn, *Anti MILITARISM: Political and Gender Dynamics of Peace Movements* (Palgrave MacMillan, 2012) 25–27: the 'transparently conservative gender attitudes' of male members of British peace societies meant female membership was low. Cockburn discusses in detail how women both interacted with 'mainstream' peace activism and travelled their own paths.
[3] Sumita Mukherjee, *Indian Suffragettes: Female Identities and Transnational Networks* (Oxford University Press, 2018).
[4] eg petition presented in 1932 to the President of the League of Nations Disarmament Conference.
[5] eg petition from the women of Wales to women in America asking them to use their influence to persuade their government to join the League of Nations so as to avoid the horror of another world war: https://www.peoplescollection.wales/collections/1778851.
[6] Margaret Murray Washington, 'Account of the Origins of International Council for Women of Darker Races', 10 November 1924 (Alexander Street Archive).

earlier from the yoke of colonialism, had to avoid US domination and express their own priorities, while those in what were still colonised territories devised their own strategies within the overriding goal of national liberation.⁷ No single narrative can capture the many ways in which women across time and space have sought to challenge the structural subordination of patriarchy, a goal intensified by the further divisions of, inter alia, ethnicities, class, and national origin. This book does not seek to add to the historical excavation of feminist movements but rather to explore one aspect – the interaction between international law and feminist demands for equality and peace.

Feminist activism has multiple layers, one of which is women's grasp at opportunities offered by the growth of international law and institutions from the Hague Peace conferences of 1899 and 1907 onwards,⁸ through the creation and operations of the League of Nations and subsequently the United Nations. From the earliest days of international institution building, women peace activists embraced a more expansive and progressive understanding of both international law and peace than their male counterparts. Their perception of the potential of international law as a site for advancing their interests differed from that of its male custodians, who viewed it as regulating inter-state behaviour within the framework of state sovereignty and legal positivism, leaving domestic affairs strictly untouched. In contrast, women campaigners sought normative change at the international level as a tool for challenging domestic resistance to their demands for social justice, equality, and disarmament as necessary preconditions to peace, within and between states.⁹

The outbreak of World War I caused divisions between women, who struggled to determine their stance between supporting the war effort and decrying war. In Washington DC a women's conference for peace was held in early 1915 followed by the 1915 International Congress of Women in The Hague, chaired by Jane Addams, the second woman recipient of the Nobel Peace Prize.¹⁰ Women peace activists from belligerent and neutral states joined together to protest the war and to adopt resolutions on a pathway to peace for the ongoing war and on the conditions necessary for a permanent peace.¹¹ A lasting peace settlement had to be based on the 'principles of justice', while a permanent peace was contingent on respect for nationality, a commitment to arbitration to settle disputes between states, democratic control of foreign policy, and women's equality with men, including their participation in

---

⁷ eg in 'an iconic moment in Egyptian history' in 1922, Huda Shaarawi, returning from a meeting of the Women's Suffrage Alliance in Rome, removed her veil at the railway station. Others followed and the Egyptian Feminist Union was founded in 1923: Kenzy Fahmy, 'Huda Shaarawi and the Feminists that Paved the Road to Reform in Egypt', https://csa-living.org/oasis-blog/huda-shaarawi-and-the-feminists-that-paved-the-road-to-reform-in-egypt.

⁸ see essay 7 'Women, Disarmament and Peace'.

⁹ This should not be over-stated; European women's hope in international law for achieving political and social emancipation did not generally extend to women in the colonies.

¹⁰ Jane Addams, *Newer Ideals of Peace* (MacMillan, 1907) 7 introduced the term 'negative peace', which some 60 years later was mainstreamed by Johan Galtung. Jane Addams sought an enriched understanding of [positive] peace, as a radical break from the inadequate 'old dogmatic peace', understood as an absence of war. On the difficulties of remaining a pacifist in the midst of war, see Jane Addams, *Peace and Bread* (Macmillan, 1922) ch VII.

¹¹ BS Chimni, 'Peace through Law: Lessons from 1914' (2015) 3 *London Review of International Law* 245.

the post-war peace settlement.¹² The resolutions also called for 'a permanent International Conference' to develop 'practical proposals for further international co-operation'; the establishment of a permanent international court; a treaty on universal disarmament; and the recognition of women's civil and political rights on an equal basis with men at national and international levels. Inter-state peace was radically bonded to equality, without which there could not be peace.

Figure 1 International Congress of Women 1915
Source: LSE Library.

The Women's Congress (subsequently named the Women's International League for Peace and Freedom, WILPF) reconvened in Zurich in parallel to the 1919 Paris Peace Conference from which they were excluded.¹³ The year 1919 saw an 'explosion of global women's activism', with women from across the world championing a very different type of peace settlement from that adopted by the 'peacemakers' at Paris.¹⁴ For example, the Zurich Congress was not only highly critical of the peace settlement that 'so seriously violate[d] the principles upon which alone a just and lasting peace [could] be secured'¹⁵ but signalled the many ways in which attending to women's needs and recognising their activities would contribute to world peace.

---

¹² Report of the International Congress of Women, The Hague, 1915.
¹³ The 1915 Hague Congress resolved that 'an international meeting of women shall be held in the same place at the same time as the Conference of the Powers which shall frame the terms of the peace settlement after the war for the purpose of presenting practical proposals to that Conference': ibid.
¹⁴ Mona Siegel, 'Peacemaking and Women's Rights ... A Century in the Making' *LSE Blog*, 18 November 2019.
¹⁵ WILPF Resolutions, 2nd Congress, Zurich, 1919.

The Congress urged that a Women's Charter[16] be inserted in the Peace Treaty, setting out a range of principles for promoting women's equality in the workplace, in the family and in political life that would 'confer lasting benefits upon the whole world' as well as emphasising that women's service to others, as wage earners, mothers and homemakers comprises 'an essential factor in the building up of the world's peace'.[17] The Zurich Congress also adopted resolutions on race equality[18] and the civil and political rights of Jews.[19]

The Versailles Treaty contained no commitment to 'the status of women' nor did it recognise their political, economic, and social standing to be of 'supreme international importance'.[20] Instead, the Treaty and the other international agreements stemming from the post-World War I peace negotiations 'represented a concerted defence by Western statesmen of a patriarchal political and social order'[21] that was also anchored to the racial order of colonialism and militarism.

Despite opposition at the international level,[22] women secured a foothold through provision for representation into the League of Nations and the International Labour Organisation (ILO) that was also created in 1919.[23] Although only a handful of (elite) women ever attained significant positions in these early international bodies,[24] women continued to campaign individually and through their organisations for legal change on issues of concern to them,[25] fashioning an alternative vision of peace.

---

[16] Earlier Women's Charters were: Olympe de Gouges, Declaration of the Rights of Woman and of the Female Citizen (1791) (art 1: 'woman is born free and remains equal to man in rights'); Mary Wollstonecraft, *A Vindication of the Rights of Woman* (1792) ('I do earnestly wish to see the distinction of sex confounded in society'). Olympe de Gouges was executed in 1793 and Mary Wollstonecraft's reputation was tainted by her 'unconventional' personal relationships.
[17] WILPF Resolutions, Zurich (n 15).
[18] ibid resolution 32. This was proposed by Mary Church Terrell; on the challenges facing Black women in the evolving transnational feminist movement see Noaquia Callahan Banks, 'Mary Church Terrell, The Women's International League for Peace and Freedom, and Germany's "schwarze Schmach" Campaign, 1918–1922' (2023) 14 *Journal of Transnational American Studies* 5 ('practicing international sisterhood proved to be difficult, particularly when it came to matters involving race. African American women's participation in the early transnational women's movement often challenged white leaders to live up to the great principles the ICW and WILPF claimed to uphold': ibid 7).
[19] WILPF Resolutions, Zurich (n 15) resolution 33.
[20] ibid Women's Charter.
[21] Mona Siegel (n 14).
[22] eg in 1919 the Supreme War Council refused to act on a proposal received by President Woodrow Wilson from 'a group of ladies representing the Suffrage Associations of the Allied Countries' to establish a Commission to report to the Peace Congress 'on the condition and legislation concerning women and children worldwide'. Prime Minister Clemenceau indicated that he had no objections to an enquiry into female and child labour but would 'strongly object' to any consideration of women's political status: Records of the Supreme War Council, January–February 1919.
[23] Covenant of the League of Nations, art 7; Treaty of Versailles, 1919, arts 389, 395.
[24] Dame Rachel Crowdy was the only woman appointed head of a League section in the Geneva Secretariat; two Scandinavian women served on the Permanent Mandates Commission, Anna Bugge-Wicksell and Valentine Dannevig: Susan Pedersen, 'Metaphors of the Schoolroom: Women Working the Mandates System of the League of Nations' (2008) 66 *History Workshop Journal* 188.
[25] There is a growing literature on women's activism throughout the League of Nations; eg, Carol Miller, '"Geneva – the Key to Equality": Inter-war Feminists and the League of Nations' (1994) 3 *Women's History Review* 219; Mona Siegel, *Peace on Our Terms: The Global Battle for Women's Rights after the First World War* (Columbia University Press, 2021); Caitriona Beaumont, 'Women's Organisations, Active Citizenship, and the Peace Movement: New Perspectives on Female Activism in Britain, 1918–1939' (2020) 31 *Diplomacy and Statecraft* 697.

In 1924, for example, WILPF adopted a manifesto urging for a 'New International Order' founded on the principles of international justice and international cooperation.[26] The Congress urged new thinking to address the causes of war, which were 'most commonly the direct consequence of social injustices', and accordingly believed that there was a need to 'bring about the organization of economic life, not for individual or class profit, but for the highest possible development of every human being'.[27] But these calls were in vain, as was equality. It would take another World War before non-discrimination on the basis of sex was brought into a world constitution.[28] Nor was a Bill of Rights integrated into the UN Charter, but in contradistinction to what women peace activists had urged in 1915, was developed as a separate agenda through the UN General Assembly (UNGA), the UN Economic and Social Council and the Commission on Human Rights. The institutional binary this created (replicated in the location of security in New York and human rights in Geneva), reinforced for women through the separate Commission on Human Rights and Commission on the Status of Women, has inhibited joined-up thinking on gender and peace.

Feminist histories reveal shared purposes and friendships throughout the lifetime of the League but also rivalries and variance as to priorities, strategies and tactics both within and outside the institution. There were opposing views, for instance, between those who sought equality and those who apprehended that this would detract from securing protective measures within the workplace.[29] Some women favoured institutional intervention solely to further an agenda for women's advancement while others were determined that they should not be consigned to 'women's issues' but that they should be heard on matters of broader 'political' concern,[30] notably on disarmament.[31] There were also disagreements around how best to pursue peace. These encompassed such issues as whether to harness the role of motherhood and women's 'natural' affinity with peace or to reject this essentialist stereotyping[32] and the advantages and drawbacks of 'women only' organising. With the rise of fascism in the increasingly troubled 1930s, there were divisions around the meaning and limits of pacifism and anti-militarism necessitating hard decisions about support for predominantly male conscientious objectors,[33] and, continuing, around the discourse and practice of motherhood and peace. There were also uneasy alliances. In the UK, for instance, women supporters

---

[26] Sheri Labenski, '"The World is Not Organized for Peace": Feminist Manifestos and Utopias in the Making of International Law' (2022) *Global Constitutionalism* 1.
[27] 'Manifesto', Report of the Fourth Congress of WILPF, Washington, May 1924, 141–43.
[28] See essay 13 'Strategic Practice: Peace and Equality through International Law'.
[29] See Hilary Charlesworth and Christine Chinkin, *The Boundaries of International Law: A Feminist Analysis* (Manchester University Press, 2022) introduction.
[30] WILPF, for instance, refused to be sidelined away from significant issues of international politics: Jo Vellacott, 'A Place for Pacifism and Transnationalism in Feminist Theory: the Early Work of the Women's International League for Peace and Freedom' (1993) 2 *Women's History Review* 23.
[31] See essay 7 'Women, Disarmament and Peace'.
[32] For discussion of the literature around 'maternalist pacifism' see Caitriona Beaumont (n 25).
[33] In 1919 WILPF recognised the devotion of those who refused to take part in the war; it fortified their 'faith in the achievement of permanent peace to know that ... thousands of young men have ... counted it worth the cost to bear the loss of health, fortune and friends and to face imprisonment, obloquy and death': WILPF Resolutions, Zurich (n 15). See Cynthia Cockburn (n 2).

of Oswald Mosely campaigned for peace with Hitler,[34] while from the opposite end of the political spectrum WILPF's pacifist stance led to members having to determine their positions.[35] These events raised troubling questions: what were the appropriate feminist responses to peace campaigns by right wing women who rejected war against Hitler? Should all violence be condemned or was the war against fascism an exception? Should a commitment to pacifism be upheld even if it meant decreasing membership in women's organisations for peace?[36] In the aftermath of World War II women delegates to the 1946 WILPF Congress from occupied countries, who had participated in armed resistance and considered peace without freedom to be meaningless, caused soul-searching about whether WILPF still had a purpose and, indeed, whether women had any role in the pursuit of peace.[37] And, as national liberation movements gained further prominence, the question remained as to whether social justice and equality can ever be achieved through peaceful, non-violent resistance.[38] The dilemma remains for those opposed to violent and repressive regimes.[39]

The impact on international law of feminist activity in the inter-war years was limited, apart from within the Americas where the first intergovernmental body committed to women's advancement was created in 1928[40] and the first treaty directly on the status of women was adopted.[41] The language of human rights entered the Americas through the Equal Rights Treaty signed by four states in Montevideo in 1933 and the Declaration of Lima in 1938.[42] Efforts to secure an international legal commitment to women's equality were thwarted by the outbreak of World War II and the demise of the League.[43]

---

[34] eg British Union of Fascists and National Socialists' women called for a negotiated peace and organised a Women's Peace campaign against World War II. They were heavily racialised: Julie Gottlieb, 'Gender and the "Jews' War": Women, Antisemitism, and Anti-War Campaigns in Britain, 1938–1940' (2020) 31 *Diplomacy and Statecraft* 745.

[35] WILPF condemned imperial police violence (and supported independence for Europe's colonies) and fascist brutality, aggression and antisemitism but was divided over how to respond – whether peace could be achieved through the appeasement or overthrow of fascist regimes: Laura Beers, 'Feminism, Internationalism and the Women's International League for Peace and Freedom', at https://www.historyandpolicy.org/dialogues/discussions/women-peace-andtransnational-activism-a-century-on.

[36] eg a policy of absolute pacifism during World War II contributed to large-scale reduction in membership of the Women's Co-operative Guild: Gill Scott, 'Darkness at the End of the Tunnel: Pacifism, Democracy, and the Women's Co-operative Guild in England in the 1930s' in Joy Emmanuel and Ian MacPherson (eds), *Co-operatives and the Pursuit of Peace* (New Rochdale Press, 2007).

[37] Catia Cecilia Confortini, *Intelligent Compassion: The Women's International League for Peace and Freedom and Feminist Peace* (Oxford University Press, 2012).

[38] In 1971, while still asserting its 'duty' to engage in non-violent movements for change, WILPF controversially recognised 'the inevitability of violent resistance by the oppressed when other alternatives have failed': WILPF Resolutions, 18th Congress, New Delhi, 28 December 1970–2 January 1971.

[39] See essay 12 'Introduction to Strategic Practices' on the dilemma for Ukrainian women today.

[40] 'The Inter-American Commission of Women was established by way of resolution of the Sixth International Conference of American States in 1928'; Statute of the Inter-American Commission of Women, art 1. The resolution assigned the first commissioners to prepare juridical material for consideration by the 7th conference on the 'civil and political equality' of women: JB Scott, 'Inter-American Commission of Women' (1930) 24 *American Journal of International Law* 757.

[41] Treaty on the Nationality of Married Women, 1933.

[42] The Lima Declaration in Favor of Women's Rights, Eighth International Conference of American States, 1938 declared women's right to political equality, equality in civil status, labour rights and protection as mothers.

[43] The League set up an expert Committee to study women's status worldwide; its work provided the basis for the early activities of the UN Commission on the Status of Women: Carol Miller (n 25).

The first two essays in this section concentrate on a later period of institutional activity, when the UN turned its attention directly to women's advancement – the UN Decade for Women 1975–1985 – with its mantra 'Equality, Development and Peace'. The Decade brought women's activism directly into the UN system through the NGO fora held alongside each of the three global summits on women convened in 1975, 1980 and 1985. Much of women's organising, lobbying and campaigning was channelled through these events, which produced governmental plans of action and forward-looking strategies for action supplemented by a wealth of NGO 'grey' literature – research, theoretical analysis, case studies, critiques and manifestos for change. Ten years after the end of the Decade, in 1995, the Fourth World Conference on Women adopted the Beijing Declaration and Platform for Action (PFA). The UNGA adopted resolutions endorsing the final documents negotiated by the global conferences.

By 1995 the post-1945 international institutional architecture had produced detailed roadmaps for women's advancement that built on women's historical action, including for the attainment of peace. But unveiling the historical account also reveals its continued paucity with respect to histories of international law – and indeed its substantive content. The same is true of histories of peace movements where mainstream accounts frequently discount, or refer only at the margins, to women's peace activism.[44] The turn to history in contemporary public international law research and writing takes little – or no – account of women's activity in the international realm.[45] Contextual and historical analyses of international legal development have examined how the complex interplay of geo-politics, interests (personal, state and non-state, imperial) and power dynamics have fashioned the agendas of international institutions, including law. These have recognised how imperialism, religions, nationalisms, race, and economics have impacted on the evolution of the international legal order, but the tight grip of patriarchy in all such structures is rarely mentioned. Nor are the contributions of women – as individuals or acting collectively – credited in mainstream historiographies of international law,[46] omissions that normalise the discipline's androcentric biases.[47]

---

[44] eg for a brief overview of mainstream accounts see Charles Howlett, 'Peace History: The Field and the Sources' (1994) 8 *Organization American Historians Magazine of History* 26; John Gittings, *The Glorious Art of Peace from the Iliad to Iraq* (Oxford University Press, 2012). Martin Ceadel's two volumes on the British Peace Movement are the exception: *The Origins of War Prevention: The British Peace Movement and International Relations 1730–1854* (Clarendon Press, 1996); and *Semi-detached Idealists: The British Peace Movement and International Relations 1854–1945* (Oxford University Press, 2000). For women's activism around the 1919 peace process see Mona Siegel (n 25); Glenda Sluga, 'Female and National Self-Determination: A Gender Re-reading of the "Apogee of Nationalism"' (2000) 6 *Nations and Nationalism* 495.

[45] eg the UN Decade for Women receives no mention in Martti Koskenniemi, 'History of International Law since World War II' *Max Planck Encyclopaedia of International Law* (2011), at https://opil.ouplaw.com/view/10.1093/law:epil/9780199231690/law-9780199231690-e714.

[46] Recent writings have exposed some of these silences: eg Rebecca Adami and Dan Plesch, *Women and the UN: A New History of Women's Human Rights* (Routledge 2022); Jeremy Levitt (ed), *Black Women and International Law* (Cambridge University Press, 2015); Immi Tallgren, *Portraits of Women in International Law: New Names and Forgotten Faces?* (Oxford University Press, 2023).

[47] Hilary Charlesworth and Christine Chinkin (n 29); Gina Heathcote, *Feminist Dialogues on International Law* (Oxford University Press, 2019).

The histories of events and processes of paramount concern to women are similarly excluded from, or given little shrift, in even critical accounts of the development of international law. In this vein the Decade is entirely absent from even the most recent account of international law in this period of the Cold War.[48] Beijing too remains largely invisible in conventional accounts of international law. The final documents of global summit meetings do not come within the formal sources of international law as set out in article 38(1) of the Statute of the International Court of Justice; they are in formal terms political – not legal – commitments, at best a form of soft law without mechanisms for implementation or enforcement. Accordingly, except for the 1979 Convention on the Elimination of All Forms of Discrimination against Women (CEDAW), a legally binding treaty, these documents are rarely included in any table of international instruments in leading international law texts. Neither the Nairobi Forward-looking Strategies nor the Beijing Declaration and PFA for instance are entered in core university textbooks such as those by James Crawford[49] or Malcolm Shaw.[50] Nor is 'Beijing' an index entry in either book. It seems extraordinary that such key instruments, incorporating a vast body of principles for the advancement of the world's women and for peace, negotiated by states over four world conferences, should be deemed of no relevance for students and practitioners of international law.

We believe the history of women's activity through international institutions and law throughout the twentieth century and into the twenty-first for their own advancement and for peace is important as we think about peace through a feminist lens today. This is for two reasons. First, many of the quandaries faced by women throughout this history continue to resonate in contemporary situations. The dilemma facing pacifists in the 1930s was echoed in debates around NATO's action in 1999 in Serbia and Kosovo; was this a good or bad war?[51] Can military action for what are said to be humanitarian goals, including seeking an end to women's oppression – as in Afghanistan in 2001 – ever be legitimate, or are such claims simply an attempt to co-opt women into support for men's wars? What is clear is that 'there is no neat blueprint for practising [feminist] ethical politics'.[52] In 2023, Ukrainian feminists and their supporters (including Russian feminists) speak of their anguish: 'it is not an abstract ethical question of supporting militarisation. It is a question of life or death, of allowing people on the ground to defend themselves and defend civilians from constant shelling by Russia.'[53] They have urged 'an empathetic and involved response to the unjustly treated people, a response that pulses with rage

---

[48] Matthew Craven et al (eds), *International Law and the Cold War* (Cambridge University Press, 2019); Upendra Baxi, '"The Dust of Empire": The Dialectic of Self-Determination and Re-colonisation in the First Phase of the Cold War' notes that feminist perspectives on the Cold War are missing: ibid 397.
[49] James Crawford, *Brownlie's Principles of Public International Law*, 9th edn (Oxford University Press, 2019).
[50] Malcolm Shaw, *International Law*, 9th edn (Cambridge University Press, 2021).
[51] Christine Chinkin, 'Kosovo: A Good or Bad War?' (1999) 93 *American Journal of International Law* 841.
[52] Darya Tsymbalyuk and Iryna Zamuruieva, 'Why We As Feminists Must Lobby for Air Defence for Ukraine' *Open Democracy*, 16 March 2022.
[53] ibid.

and solidarity. Hesitating to support more weapons for Ukraine means supporting the perpetuation of war crimes from the privilege of one's safety.'[54] There may be some comfort in hearing the echoes from history. Second, there are dangers in forgetting or ignoring the past, in not realising that we are still pursuing the 'unfinished business' of those who have gone before us. This is so particularly in the context of women's activism in the field of disarmament, the topic of the third essay.

Understanding this 'helps us grasp the subjugated histories, their temporality, and unsettle the linearity of past and present'.[55] Excavating the genealogies of past movements enables us to begin to make connections with our own continuing struggles 'with power, with authoritarian regimes, with colonialism, poverty, capitalism, and systems of oppression'[56] and the structures that maintain them that we still have not been able to dismantle. The writings in this section of the book explore in greater detail how, despite over 100 years of feminist activism within first the League and subsequently the United Nations, the institutions of international law remain far from embracing any concept of peace, let alone a gendered peace.

---

[54] ibid. See also Kateryna Semchuk, 'Right to Resist: How War Changed Ukraine's Feminist Movement' *Open Democracy*, 23 February 2023.
[55] Itziar Mujika Chao and Linda Gusia, 'Unfinished Activism: Genealogies of Women's Movements and Re-imagining of Feminist Peace and Resistance' in Sarah Smith and Keina Yoshida (eds), *Feminist Conversations on Peace* (Bristol University Press, 2022) 47, 55.
[56] ibid.

5

Peace in the UN Decade for Women

I. INTRODUCTION

THE TURN TO history in contemporary public international law research and writing has engendered reconsideration of how key events were shaped by the applicable legal regimes and in turn shaped the evolution of international law. Strikingly omitted from such accounts and from the narratives of international law and peace is the UN Decade for Women 1975–1985, a significant period in women's struggle for an international legal norm of sex and gender equality and for world peace. The Decade saw women convene in unprecedented numbers across Cold War and North/South divides to participate in three global conferences in Mexico City (1975), Copenhagen (1980) and Nairobi (1985). The conferences concluded with significant statements and strategies for the advancement of women that resonate today.

The Decade can be compared with another visionary moment – the 1955 Bandung conference – where representatives from previously and still colonised territories whose voices were routinely discounted by the international lawmakers joined together to challenge the bipolar Cold War power structures in a configuration of non-alignment. Bandung has been temporalised 'as a moment or an event … given direction concretely as an agenda and abstractly as a spirit. It lives through its lineages and survives in the play of analogies'.[1] Like the Non-Aligned Movement (NAM),[2] the transnational feminist movement was about resistance to colonial domination, imperialism and racism, but, unlike Bandung, also to patriarchy. It too was forward-looking, with an 'almost utopian dimension with an unprecedented number of peoples across the world actively reimagining, changing, and prefiguring the rules of the global order'[3] to promote equalities and peace.[4]

This essay revisits the Decade and seeks to redress its omission from accounts of international law and from peace studies. The next section outlines forerunners

---

[1] Luis Eslava et al, 'The Spirit of Bandung' in Luis Eslava et al, *Bandung, Global History and International Law Critical Pasts and Pending Futures* (Cambridge University Press, 2017).
[2] NAM was formed in Belgrade in 1961.
[3] Luis Eslava et al (n 1).
[4] 'The Asian-African Conference gave anxious thought to the question of world peace and co-operation … Freedom and peace are interdependent. … Free from mistrust and fear, and with confidence and goodwill towards each other, nations should practice tolerance and live together in peace … and develop friendly cooperation': Final Communique of the Asian/African Conference, Bandung, 24 April 1955, G: Declaration on the Promotion of World Peace and Cooperation.

to the Decade; the following sections some of its highlights, its context and the different situations of the women who participated. The essay then focuses on peace within the Decade's documents. It concludes with some reflections about the Decade's contribution to international law.

II. FORERUNNERS OF THE DECADE

A. Institutional Forerunners

From the outset of the League of Nations and the ILO women activists saw the international arena as a useful site for their campaigns,[5] seeking a political space for intervention and progress that was denied to them by socially conservative national governments.[6] In turn, the League recognised women as a valuable support group and some initiatives on their behalf were introduced.[7] The Americas saw the first intergovernmental organisation on the status of women, an omission from even a 'Hidden History of International Law in the Americas'[8] and human rights language entered Latin American discourse.[9] The small number of women present at the negotiations for the UN[10] succeeded in including in the Charter the beginnings of a commitment to equality and a positive concept of peace through reaffirmation of 'fundamental human rights', 'equal rights of men and women' and for 'conditions under which justice and respect for ... international law can be maintained, and to promote social progress and better standards of life in larger freedom'.[11] Machinery for the furtherance of these lofty words was also secured through provision for setting up a commission for the promotion of human rights and other functional commissions as required.[12] The Commission on the Status of Women (CSW) was originally a sub-commission of the Commission on Human Rights but its first chair, Bodil Begtrup from Denmark, argued convincingly that 'women's problems' should be addressed by a full Commission of the UN Economic and Social Council (ECOSOC). This status was secured in 1946 and CSW tasked with promoting women's rights in the 'political, economic, social and educational fields'.[13] Working with limited resources, CSW prioritised the preparation of

---

[5] Jacqui True and J Ann Tickner, 'A Century of International Relations Feminism: from World War One Women's Peace Pragmatism to the Women, Peace and Security Agenda' (2018) 62 *International Studies Quarterly* 221.

[6] Glenda Sluga, 'Women, Feminisms and Twentieth-Century Internationalisms' in Glenda Sluga and Patricia Clavin, *Internationalisms: A Twentieth Century History* (Cambridge University Press, 2017) ch 4.

[7] Torild Skard, 'Getting our History Right: How Were the Equal Rights of Women and Men Included in the Charter of the United Nations?' (2008) 1 *Forum for Development Studies* 37.

[8] Juan Pablo Scarfi, *The Hidden History of International Law in the Americas* (Oxford University Press, 2017).

[9] See essay 1 'Introduction'.

[10] See essay 13 'Strategic Practice: Peace and Equality through International Law'.

[11] Charter of the United Nations, 1945, preamble.

[12] ibid art 68.

[13] UN ECOSOC Resolution 11(II), 21 June 1946, Commission on the Status of Women, section I, Functions.

treaties focusing on specific areas of women's disadvantage in political life[14] and marriage[15] but did not locate these in the wider context of structural inequalities and patriarchy. Mandating a particular body with women's advancement freed others from addressing 'women's issues', marginalising them within the UN system.

Women's advancement was not a UN priority[16] until the 1960s, when there was a burst of activity around socio-economic development[17] in light of growing inequalities in the wake of political independence for colonial territories. The General Assembly (UNGA) requested that the Secretary-General study the possibilities for a 'unified long-term United Nations programme for the advancement of women'.[18] The ensuing study set out objectives: promotion of the equal rights of women and men; enabling women's participation in the development of society; and to stimulate awareness among women and men of women's full potential.[19] Meanwhile, in a somewhat self-satisfied resolution in 1963,[20] the UNGA requested that ECOSOC invite CSW to prepare a Declaration on the Elimination of Discrimination against Women (DEDAW). The non-binding Declaration was adopted in 1967.[21] In 1968 the Tehran Human Rights Conference reflected on the continued 'considerable discrimination against women in the political, legal, economic, social and educational fields' and endorsed the initiation of a unified programme for their advancement.[22] The stage was set for the UN to bring women out from the wings of CSW to the forefront of its activities.

B. Women's Activism Prior to the Decade

Alongside the rebirth of global institutionalisation, in 1945 women's NGOs had to adjust to the changed political environment.[23] Two examples are illustrative. First, the Women's International League for Peace and Freedom (WILPF) that had been

---

[14] Convention on the Political Rights of Women, 1953.
[15] Convention on the Nationality of Married Women, 1957; Convention on Consent to Marriage, Minimum Age for Marriage and Registration of Marriages, 1962.
[16] Judith Zinsser, 'From Mexico to Copenhagen to Nairobi: The United Nations Decade for Women, 1975–1985' (2002) 13 *Journal of World History* 139.
[17] The 1960s were designated the First Development Decade and the 1970s the Second Development Decade. For their relevance to the UN Decade for Women see Peggy Antrobus, *The Global Women's Movement Origins, Issues and Strategies* (Zed Books, 2004).
[18] UNGAR 1777 (XVII), 7 December 1962, United Nations assistance for the advancement of women in developing countries.
[19] Report of the Secretary-General, *United Nations Assistance for the Advancement of Women*, 1967, E/CN.6/467, 67.
[20] UNGAR 1921 (XVIII), 5 December 1963: 'Noting with satisfaction … the progress made in the field of equal rights; noting also with satisfaction the efforts made by the United Nations and the specialised agencies in achieving that progress'.
[21] UNGAR 2263 (XXII), 7 November 1967.
[22] International Conference on Human Rights, Tehran, 12 May 1968, Resolution IX, Measures to promote women's rights in the modern world including a unified long-term United Nations programme for the advancement of women.
[23] Ironically. as women's equality is brought into international law through the UN Charter, western organised feminism goes silent until its 'second wave' in the 1970s: Celia Donert, 'Women's Rights in Cold War Europe: Disentangling Feminist Histories' (2013) 218 *Past and Present* 180.

established in the throes of World War I had to rebuild following the suspension of its Triennial Congresses during the war and internal divisions over whether pacifism could be maintained in the face of fascism.[24] At its 1946 Congress WILPF affirmed 'its adherence to the necessity of firmly maintaining respect for the human rights of each individual friend or ex-enemy alike' and expressed its desire that 'good will' should govern the national sections.[25] WILPF continued to oppose warfare, to advocate for disarmament and to 'secure prohibition of preparation of all means of mass devastation'.[26]

Another continuing divisive issue was the future of Europe's colonies; some European women assumed the continuation of colonial rule, while others actively resisted colonial policies, for instance by obstructing arms shipments for use by colonial forces to suppress insurrections.[27] In colonial territories women had long assumed leadership roles in struggles for liberation from colonial rule and peasant reform.[28] Many were prepared to use violence in the cause of national liberation, which was not 'additional to the struggle for women's rights' but rather a 'necessary cornerstone' for women's access to political and economic rights.[29] In this context the second example is of a new NGO – the Women's International Democratic Federation (WIDF) – that was inaugurated in 1945[30] to promote world peace, women's rights, anti-fascism, and children's welfare.[31] Associated with the socialist bloc,[32] it also drew membership from Africa, Asia and Latin America and in the 1950s claimed to speak for 91 million women worldwide. In 1949 – six years before Bandung[33] – WIDF hosted the Asia Women's Conference in Beijing, which brought together anti-colonial, socialist women to strategise against imperialism.[34] WIDF's goals for the Conference included to 'fight for peace' and for the rights of women and children. Peace was understood in the framework of Moscow's foreign policy and in the wake of the Communist success in China. While 'peace' was not necessarily a synonym for socialism, it contrasted with American imperialism and European violence in resisting decolonisation: it was 'both a project of uniting a

---

[24] See essay 4 'Introduction: Rewriting International Law's Histories'.
[25] WILPF Resolutions, 10th Congress, Luxemburg August 4th–9th, 1946, preliminary statement.
[26] WILPF Resolutions, 11th Congress, Copenhagen August 15th–19th, 1949, para XI.
[27] Elisabeth Armstrong, *Bury the Corpse of Colonialism: The Revolutionary Feminist Conference of 1949* (University of California Press, 2023) 61.
[28] African diaspora women participated in the organisation of pan-African Congresses in Europe and the US, although this was scarcely recorded: Sylvia Tamale, *Decolonization and Afro-Feminism* (Daraja Press, 2020) 348–49.
[29] Elisabeth Armstrong (n 27) 46.
[30] In 1945 WIDF was the only 'transnational women's organization that explicitly condemned colonialism': ibid at 28.
[31] WIDF saw these objectives as inherently linked: Yulia Gradskova, *The Women's International Democratic Federation, the Global South and the Cold War* (Routledge, 2021) 65.
[32] WIDF's membership and actions in the socialist bloc, for instance support for North Vietnam, aroused US hostility. In 1954 it lost ECOSOC consultative status, which was reinstated in 1967. WILPF too aroused US suspicions for its meetings with Soviet women and sending delegates to Hanoi in 1973.
[33] The Bandung Communique made no reference to the 1949 Asia Women's Conference. Women speakers participated at the second conference of leaders of colonised or newly independent states in Cairo in 1964 and the Afro-Asian Federation for Women was created: Vijay Prashad and Howard Zinn, *A Peoples History of the Third World* (The New Press, 2007).
[34] The Pan-Asian Women's Conference assembled 367 women from 37 countries in Asia and Africa.

range of political forces across the world and an ideological way to show the political dangers of capitalism'.[35] With the virulent anti-communism in the US from the late 1940s, women in both the West and the Soviet bloc had to navigate ideology in pursuing internationalism on behalf of women's rights.[36]

III. THE UN DECADE FOR WOMEN 1975–1985

A. Overview of the Decade

In 1972 on CSW's recommendation, the UNGA proclaimed 1975 as International Women's Year (IWY),[37] expressing CSW's 25th anniversary as a moment to take stock 'of the positive results achieved'.[38] The IWY objectives were: 'to promote equality between men and women'; 'to ensure the full integration of women in the total development effort'; and 'to recognise the importance of women's increasing contribution to the development of friendly relations and cooperation among states and to the strengthening of world peace'. These themes to some extent represented the priorities of three political blocs: equality (the US and its allies); development (the non-aligned states, then generally referred to as the Third World); and peace (the socialist bloc). Although the thematic objectives were lauded as denoting unity and interdependence in the advancement of women,[39] the reality was political disagreement and contested priorities.

CSW recommended an international conference[40] as a 'focal point' for IWY's activities.[41] The ensuing World Conference in Mexico City[42] was a world first – the first ever conference devoted to women and where women formed part of 'virtually every delegation'.[43] It was heralded by delegates as the beginning of a new era of greater participation by women and girls in all aspects of social progress, development and the search for peace.[44] It nevertheless took place within and offered no resistance to the pre-existing patriarchal framework of social, national and international relations:[45] women were invited to join (to a limited extent) men's worlds.

---

[35] Elisabeth Armstrong (n 27) 21; peace was 'a process of social organization sustained by cultures and ideologies of mutually beneficial coexistence', with women's rights and freedom from exploitation requiring a world at peace: ibid 45.
[36] Celia Donert (n 23).
[37] UNGAR 3010 (XXVII), 18 December 1972. See Jocelyn Olcott, *International Women's Year: The Greatest Consciousness-raising Event in History* (Oxford University Press, 2017).
[38] UNGAR 3010 (XXVII), 18 December 1972.
[39] The Forward-looking Strategies for the Advancement of Women during the Period from 1986 to the Year 2000, para 37 (Nairobi FLS).
[40] CSW, Report on the Twenty-fifth Session, 1974, E/CN.6/L.658.
[41] Report of the World Conference of the International Women's Year, Mexico City, 19 June–2 July 1975, (Mexico City Report).
[42] The choice of Mexico City 'outraged' Mexican feminists because of the government's bloody suppression of student protests in 1968: Olcott (n 37) 57.
[43] President of the Conference, Mr Pedro Ojeda Pauilada, Attorney-General of Mexico, Mexico City Report (n 41) 125. Women delegates could be (and were) replaced by male delegates when wider political issues were at stake – a 'problem that would continue up to Beijing': John R Mathiason, *The Long March to Beijing: the United Nations and the Women's Revolution Vol 1: The Vienna Period* (New York, 2001).
[44] General Debate, Mexico City Report (n 41).
[45] Zinsser (n 16) 143–44.

Following Mexico City, the UNGA proclaimed 1976 to 1985 as the 'United Nations Decade for Women: Equality, Development and Peace'.[46] The Decade was devoted to 'effective and sustained action at national, regional and international levels' to implement the recommendations adopted in the World Plan of Action (WPA) and the objectives of IWY.[47] In a separate resolution, the UNGA affirmed the Mexico Declaration that promulgated key principles[48] and called upon governments, INGOs and NGOs 'to intensify their efforts to strengthen peace', to make détente irreversible and to eliminate all forms of colonialism, racism and racial discrimination, alien domination, foreign aggression and occupation – issues that had bedevilled the conference as well as the divided UNGA.[49] After the hotly contested Mexico Declaration no further holistic statement of values was adopted throughout the Decade. The subsequent conferences focused on strategic blueprints for action rather than far-reaching but ideologically divisive assertions of principle.[50]

The objective of the Copenhagen conference[51] was to review and evaluate progress in advancing the Mexico City WPA. Employment, Health and Education[52] were added as substantive sub-themes to the more abstract themes of Equality, Development and Peace. The conference adopted the Programme of Action for the Second Half of the United Nations Decade for Women and 40 related resolutions.[53] For lawyers, the high spot was the opening of the Convention on Elimination of All Forms of Discrimination against Women (CEDAW) for signature. The Decade's final UN conference was held in Nairobi. It reviewed the Decade's achievements, identified obstacles to their fulfilment and, recognising the need for further action, adopted the Forward-looking Strategies for the advancement of women for the years 1996–2000 (Nairobi FLS).

Alongside each of the government conferences was an NGO parallel proceeding, the NGO tribune, subsequently called the NGO forum. This echoed the long tradition of women's congresses: that where women are excluded from formal decision-making processes and from determining agendas or priorities, they forge their own paths. This autonomy was reflected by Mildred Persinger, chair of the Mexico City tribune organising committee, who envisaged 'an open forum for

---

[46] UNGAR 3520 (XXX), 15 December 1975.

[47] UNGAR 3520 (XXX), 15 December 1975; 107 in favour; 1 against; 26 abstentions. The US abstained because of the 'blanket endorsement' of all resolutions adopted in Mexico City and the ambiguity of the call to implement the WPA and all resolutions; *Digest of United States Practice in International Law, 1975* (Dept of State, 1976) 211.

[48] Declaration of Mexico on the Equality of Women and their Contribution to Development and Peace, 1975; 89 votes in favour; 3 against; 18 abstentions.

[49] UNGAR 3519 (XXX) 15 December 1975; 90 in favour (USSR and non-aligned states); 21 against; 22 abstentions (opposed by the US and its allies).

[50] At Nairobi time constraints prevented consideration of a Draft Declaration proposed by over 30 states from the Soviet bloc and the Global South. It was included in Annex I of the Conference Report, along with Draft Resolutions which were not discussed.

[51] Tehran was the original choice for the midway conference, but the 1979 Iranian revolution, seizure of the American hostages and the Soviet invasion of Afghanistan necessitated a change of venue.

[52] UNGAR 33/185, 29 January 1979, Preparations for the World Conference of the United Nations Decade for Women: Equality, Development and Peace, including the adoption of the subtheme 'Employment, Health and Education'.

[53] Report of the World Conference of the United Nations Decade for Women: Equality, Development and Peace, Copenhagen, 14–30 July 1980 (Copenhagen Report).

private citizens' that was 'open to all interested persons'.[54] The Nairobi NGO forum was the first organised under UN auspices with participants registered as representatives of NGOs with ECOSOC consultative status. Thousands of women attended the NGO fora, forming and renewing alliances and networks.[55] They engaged in debates, often heated confrontations and in informal (often spontaneous) side events – panels, workshops, theatre, dance, art and protests – that took place alongside, and sometimes disrupted, scheduled sessions. The mountains of distributed materials must be differentiated from official conference documents.

Women attended the conferences as government delegates and, individually or through women's organisations, the NGO fora. Attendances dramatically increased over the Decade: 133 governments participated at Mexico City, with approximately 6,000 attending the NGO tribune; 145 governments attended Copenhagen, with approximately 8,000 at the NGO tribune; and 157 governments attended Nairobi, with some 12,000 participants at the NGO forum.

Numerous other global, regional and national events – some state initiated and others organised for and by civil society – were held during the Decade. For some women the IWY represented the UN's bureaucratisation and raised fears of co-option. For instance, an International Tribunal on Crimes against Women held in Brussels in 1976 was described as 'a feminist event, organised by and for women', unlike the events of IWY.[56] Simone de Beauvoir compared the Tribunal with Mexico City where, she said, women were 'directed by their political parties, by their nations [that] were only seeking to integrate Woman into a male society'. In contrast, the Tribunal brought women together 'to denounce the oppression to which women are subjected'.[57]

Another example is the World Congress organised by WIDF in East Berlin in the autumn of 1975, in coalition with other NGOs, including WILPF and the Pan-African Women's Organization.[58] WIDF was instrumental in instigating CSW's recommendation to the UNGA for an IWY and participated in the Mexico City conference (and the other Decade conferences, with UN support[59]). It held another Congress in Prague in 1981. Apprehension about the symbolism of a successful IWY congress in socialist East Berlin motivated the US to engage seriously with planning for the UN conference and its late change of location to Mexico City 'seemed to mark a victory for the US over the Soviets'.[60]

---

[54] Cited in Olcott (n 37) 64.

[55] 'Networking became the modus operandi worldwide. Even the major media began reporting on the worst situations for women in the world such as bride burning, female genital mutilation, poverty, and illiteracy as well as the work of the new groups at national and international levels': Arvonne Fraser, 'Making History Word by Word' (2012) 24 *Journal of Women's History* 193.

[56] Diana Russell, 'Report of the International Tribunal on Crimes against Women' (1977) 2 *Frontiers: A Journal of Women Studies* 1.

[57] Diana EH Russell and Nicole Van de Ven (eds), *Crimes Against Women: Proceedings of the International Tribunal*, 3rd edn (1990).

[58] WIDF support for Korean and Vietnamese communists led to its headquarters moving from Paris to East Berlin in 1951: Yulia Gradskova (n 31).

[59] Lisa Milner, '"The Most Important Event in IWY": Freda Brown and the World Congress for International Women's Year' (2020) 17 *History Australia* 172.

[60] Olcott (n 37) 61.

B. The Context of the Decade

The Decade's geopolitical context was dominated by Cold War ideologies and the impact of the political self-determination of formerly colonised states, the backdrop for the interlocking contestations between, on the one hand, the socialist bloc and the West and, on the other, between what were then termed the First and Third Worlds. These divisions were accentuated as the US and the USSR each sought to extend its influence, and colonial legacies continued to generate violence, for instance the civil wars in Angola and Mozambique, the 1975 invasion of East Timor by Indonesia, of Western Sahara by Morocco, the 1982 Falklands/Malvinas war and continuing violence in the Middle East.

Despite communist victories in Vietnam, Laos and Cambodia in 1975, détente between the US and USSR in the 1970s allowed some global cooperation for example the 1970 Declaration on Friendly Relations,[61] the 1975 Helsinki Accords,[62] and a slew of UN global conferences.[63] Détente lasted until around 1980, when the elections of Ronald Reagan in the US and Margaret Thatcher in the UK brought it to end. Superpower rivalry manifested through proxy conflicts, through policies toward the apparently entrenched apartheid system in southern Africa, and in Central and South America, where the USSR backed revolutionary resistance to right-wing dictatorships, which were in turn covertly supported by the US. The arms race and the nuclear threat cast their shadow, despite continuing talks on nuclear weapons control through SALT II (1972–1979) and START (commenced 1982, abandoned 1983 and resumed 1985). Disarmament of both nuclear and conventional weapons was a key objective of the NAM,[64] as well as the formation of legally defined nuclear-free zones.[65] Anti-nuclear peace camps and civil society protests occurred throughout Europe, North America and Australasia.

Delegates negotiated language that promoted their governments' ideological stance, and women delegates were not necessarily able to share views across political divides.[66] The coming into force of the two UN human rights Covenants[67] in 1976 epitomised the respective ideologies, with the US emphasising the ICCPR's 'freedom from' stance and the USSR the social and economic 'welfarism' of the

---

[61] UNGAR 2625, 24 October 1970, adopted without vote.
[62] Conference on Security and Cooperation in Europe, Final Act.
[63] eg UN Conference on the Human Environment, Stockholm, 1972; Third UN Conference on the Law of the Sea, Montego Bay, 1973–82; World Population Conference, Bucharest, 1974; World Food Conference, Rome, 1974; UN Conference on Human Settlement, Vancouver, 1976; UN Water Conference, Mar del Plata, 1977.
[64] The 7th Summit Conference of Heads of State or Government of the NAM, 1983, UN Doc A/38/132 S/15675, 8 April 1983; paras 28–38 seek pursuit of nuclear and conventional disarmament.
[65] eg Treaty for the Prohibition of Nuclear Weapons in Latin America and the Caribbean (Treaty of Tlatelolco) 1967; South Pacific Nuclear Free Zone Treaty (Treaty of Rarotonga), 6 August 1985.
[66] Arvonne Fraser recalled that US women delegates were forbidden to speak to women from socialist countries, 'even informally in the hallways or in the women's restroom' cited in Kristen Ghodsee, 'Revisiting the United Nations Decade for Women: Brief Reflections on Feminism, Capitalism and Cold War Politics in the Early Years of the International Women's Movement' (2010) 33 *Women's Studies International Forum* 3.
[67] International Covenant on Civil and Political Rights, (ICCPR) and International Covenant on Economic, Social and Cultural Rights (ICESCR), 16 December 1966.

ICESCR. Tension between the Western 'equality' (freedom) agenda and the Soviet 'peace' agenda spilled over into opposing views on the controversial political issues of the day (notably apartheid, racism, Palestine,[68] Zionism[69]) and the appropriateness of their inclusion in conferences for women's advancement. At Mexico City and Copenhagen both the conferences and NGO tribunes were marred by heated politicisation across these fault lines,[70] frustrating those who saw such confrontations as deflecting attention away from women's priorities.[71] Anti-Zionist language caused the US not to accept either the Mexico Declaration (with the UK and the Federal Republic of Germany) or the Copenhagen Plan of Action (with Australia, Canada and Israel). Antagonisms spilled over into process. Apprehension at Nairobi that the FLS might not be accepted led to paragraphs being adopted by consensus (or after a vote if requested), enabling a state to reserve specific paragraphs without rejecting the entire text. The US was thus able to disassociate itself from provisions it had challenged throughout the Decade, correlating women's inequality and poverty with imperialism, colonialism, neocolonialism, apartheid, racism, racial discrimination and unjust economic relations[72] while accepting the final document.[73]

The second of the Decade's objectives – development – was prioritised by delegations from the Global South. By 1975 the Group of 77 dominated voting in the UNGA (often in conjunction with the Soviet bloc) and much language in the Decade documents echoes that of contemporaneous UNGA debates and resolutions, including demands for a New International Economic Order (NIEO). The Charter of Economic Rights and Duties of States was adopted immediately prior to the Decade, over strong opposition from the US and several European states.[74] It was initially proposed by President Luis Echeverría, host of the Mexico City conference, and who, unsurprisingly, saw vital linkages between the NIEO and 'social change in the situation of women'.[75] The Decade provided an opportunity for the feminisation of the NIEO's objective of securing a 'just and equitable economic and social order'.[76] At Mexico City and Copenhagen, politicisation around the NIEO pitted

---

[68] The Palestinian Liberation Organisation had UNGA permanent observer status and attended the Decade conferences in that capacity.

[69] The notorious UNGAR 3379 (XXX), 10 November 1975, on Zionism as a form of racism replicated language from the Mexico Declaration, repealed by UNGAR 46/86, 16 December 1991.

[70] The Copenhagen conference has been described as the 'most conflictive' of the Decade, with many leaving 'convinced that the international women's movement had been irreversibly damaged': Jane Jaquette, 'Losing the Battle/Winning the War: International Politics, Women's Issues, and the 1980 Mid-Decade Conference' in Anne Winslow (ed), *Women, Politics and the United Nations* (Greenwood Press, 1995) 45.

[71] Martha Alter Chen, 'Engendering World Conferences: The International Women's Movement and the United Nations' (1995) 16 *Third World Quarterly* 477.

[72] Nairobi FLS (n 39) para 44; see also the US' reservation to para 95.

[73] The US accepted the FLS as a 'milestone' in reaffirming women's right to full equality but could not agree with political positions which had only nominal relevance to women's situation: Nairobi Report, 145–46.

[74] UNGAR 3281 (XXIX) 12 December 1974; 120 in favour; 6 against (Belgium. Denmark, Federal Republic of Germany, Luxembourg, UK and US); 10 abstentions.

[75] Mexico City Report (n 41) 124.

[76] '[E]fforts to promote the economic and social status of women should rely in particular on the development strategies that stem from the goal and objectives of the International Development Strategy and the principles of a new international economic order': Nairobi FLS (n 39) para 26.

the Global South against the North with opponents considering it a distraction from progressing women's equality.[77]

The economic climate, as well as the geopolitical environment shifted over the Decade. Early optimism 'that accelerated economic growth, sustained by growing international trade, financial flows and technological developments' would foster women's increased participation in economic and social development[78] were dashed by the Decade's end. The severe economic downturn of the 1980s impacted developing countries especially severely. Debt, debt servicing and structural imbalance widened the gap between the developed and developing countries. Neoliberal economic reforms imposed by the international financial institutions and the weakening of state regulation reduced possibilities for women's empowerment. There were renewed calls at Nairobi for pursuit 'with all vigour' of a NIEO 'founded on equity, sovereign equality, interdependence and common interest'.[79] But the neoliberal economic orthodoxy, as espoused through the policies of Ronald Reagan and Margaret Thatcher, made this a vain hope.

C. Women During the Decade

International law histories of the Cold War fail to take adequate account of either the role of civil society in challenging superpower hegemony or the advance in legal recognition of women's rights throughout the Decade. On the one hand, focus upon these aspects 'question[s] the unified narrative that has long predominated'[80] of Cold War history while on the other it conceals divisions between women, between different concepts of feminism and between different understandings of 'women's issues'. Conflicting perspectives were apparent among the civil society participants at the NGO fora, where heated exchanges broke out over ideologies, priorities, strategies and between women from opposing sides in specific conflicts. Class and economic privilege created further obstacles to mutual understanding. Alliances formed around identities or life experiences such as lesbianism,[81] prostitution, unionism. Competing caucuses formed and no one group represented the NGO perspective, although at times media prominence given to 'celebrity' feminists from the West[82] suggested otherwise. Forum participants sought various means to influence states' delegates, who differed in the attention they gave to the concerns expressed through NGO avenues.

---

[77] Roland Burke, 'Competing for the Last Utopia? The NIEO, Human Rights, and the World Conference for the International Women's Year, Mexico City, June 1975' (2015) 6 *Humanity: International Journal of Human Rights, Humanitarianism, and Development* 47.
[78] Nairobi FLS (n 39) para 7.
[79] ibid paras 7–8.
[80] Etienne Peyrat, 'International Law and the Cold War' (2021) 23 *Journal of the History of International Law / Revue d'histoire du droit international* 501, 505.
[81] Lesbian attendance was controversial: Mandana Hendessi, 'Fourteen Thousand Women Meet: Report from Nairobi, July 1985' (1986) 23 *Feminist Review* 147, n 2.
[82] eg Betty Friedan, 'Scary Doings in Mexico City' in Betty Friedan, *It Changed My Life, Writings on the Women's Movement* (Harvard University Press, 1998) 440.

The thumbnail sketch of the women who joined the Decade conferences recognises that their numbers, diversity and experiences make generalisations dangerous.[83]

One divide was the Cold War rivalry[84] between Northern, especially American, women who in feminism's 'second wave' perceived themselves as world leaders in setting feminist agendas, and those from socialist countries where, at least formally, they held more legally guaranteed equality rights.[85] Neither cohort was homogenous. One internal disagreement among American attendees was between those who confined their campaigning to 'women's issues' – primarily equality between women and men – and those who sought full participation in public affairs, including foreign policy.[86] Another was with African-American women whose feminist agenda differed from that of white women of European descent.[87] Critical race writings emphasised the 'whiteness' of 1970s 'second wave feminism' and its exclusion of women of African descent.[88] Nor could commonality between Black American women and women from Africa be assumed, given the gulf in lived experience.[89] For Eastern bloc women 'social rights were understood as the embodiment of state policies, realized through material guarantees, rather than justiciable claims against the state'.[90] While women from socialist countries held diverse views,[91] supporting equality as well as the peace agenda, they ensured that a 'vocal critique of capitalism' was expressed and that other bases of oppression – class, colonialism and violence in pursuit of wealth accumulation – figured in all three conferences.[92]

---

[83] '[N]o study exists of the women and men who lobbied for the Decade, who organized the hundreds of NGO sessions, wrote the Conference documents, who argued and maneuvered the Plans, Programmes, and Strategies through to final acceptance': Zinsser (n 16) 167–68.

[84] '[T]he cold war enveloped the world of international women's organisations, although rivalry between the two camps led to increased global organising' especially as more countries gained independence: Leila J Rupp, *Worlds of Women: The Making of an International Women's Movement* (Princeton University Press, 1997) 47.

[85] 'Both camps used the supposed emancipation and independence of women in their rhetoric as symbols of their respective ideological superiority': Helen Pankhurst, 'Commentary' to 'Women, Peace and Transnational Activism, a Century On', 30 March 2015, https://www.historyandpolicy.org/dialogues/discussions/women-peace-and-transnational-activism-a-century-on#pankhurst.

[86] 'That the limitation of women's role to domestic issues, even when they enter the public sphere, may be congenial to men in power is borne out by the 1979 firing of Bella Abzug as Co-Chair of the United States special presidential National Advisory Commission for Women because the women insisted on using that platform to talk about war and the economy': Jo Vellacott 'A Place for Pacifism and Transnationalism in Feminist Theory: The Early Work of the Women's International League for Peace and Freedom' (1993) 2 *Women's History Review* 23, 25.

[87] There were protests at the American embassy in Mexico City that the composition of the US delegation was 'insufficiently representative': Olcott (n 37) Scene 8, 'This is an Illegitimate Delegation'.

[88] eg bell hooks, *Ain't I a Woman Black Women and Feminism*, 2nd edn (Routledge, 2014); bell hooks, *Feminist Theory: from Margin to Center* (South End Press, 1984).

[89] Mandana Hendessi (n 81) 147.

[90] Celia Donert (n 23) 180.

[91] For a perspective from Bulgarian women, see Kristen Ghodsee, 'Rethinking State Socialist Mass Women's Organizations: The Committee of the Bulgarian Women's Movement and the United Nations Decade for Women, 1975–1985' (2012) 24 *Journal of Women's History* 49; for Poland, Magdalena Grabowska, 'Bringing the Second World In: Conservative Revolution(s), Socialist Legacies, and Transnational Silences in the Trajectories of Polish Feminism' (2012) 37 *Signs* 385; for the former Yugoslavia, Chiara Bonfiglioli, 'The First UN World Conference on Women (1975) as a Cold War Encounter: Recovering Anti-Imperialist, Non-Aligned and Socialist Genealogies' (2016) 27 *Filozofija Drustvo* 521.

[92] Kristen Ghodsee (n 66) 3.

Third World women's feminisms were rooted in their experiences of colonisation and nationalist independence movements, either in the recent past, or more distantly for women from Central and South America. There are long histories of women's organisation nationally and regionally throughout the Americas as well as of tensions between US feminists and their Latin counterparts. The superiority assumed by some of the former was resented by the latter in their opposition to US hegemony, ongoing support for right-wing military regimes[93] and racism. Priorities also differed. US feminists perceived equality in civil and political affairs as feminism's primary goal while the Latin Americans sought a broader social justice agenda encompassing economic and welfare rights, the status of indigenous women and rural and urban poverty.[94] At Mexico City the Coalition of Latin American women formed in opposition to the US dominated and misleadingly named United Women of the Tribune.[95]

Feminisms across Africa and Asia were similarly shaped by local contexts and social realities, rooted in historical specificities – notably colonisation and the trajectory to independence.[96] In many parts of Asia, Japanese occupation also moulded women's experience. Religious differences additionally played their part. Continental diversity makes generalisations unwise but one commonality was the complexity of negotiation of the relationship with Western feminisms: 'African feminisms have always stood between the hard rock of Western influence and domination and African relativism and disparagement.'[97] Feminism in Africa is generally anti-imperialist, socialist-oriented and anti-racist, grounded in their history of domination through slavery, colonialism, racism and neocolonialism.[98] Similar threads constitute Asian feminisms.[99] Before decolonisation, women participated in national and transnational gatherings as well as international activities, for instance those hosted by WIDF.[100]

More women from Africa and Asia came to Nairobi than to the earlier Decade conferences, with Third World women comprising a majority of attendees.[101] Their divisions with women from developed states were less pronounced than earlier in

---

[93] eg the 1973 overthrow of the democratically elected Allende government in Chile by Pinochet with CIA assistance; proceedings by Nicaragua in the International Court of Justice; *Military and Paramilitary Activities in and against Nicaragua* (Nicaragua v United States) Provisional Measures 1984 ICJ Reports 169.
[94] Latin American women before World War II 'broadened the meanings of international women's rights and global feminism': Katherine M Marino, *Feminism for the Americas: The Making of an International Human Rights Movement* (University of North Carolina Press, 2019) 168.
[95] Olcott (n 37) Scene 11, 165–73.
[96] Elisabeth Armstrong (n 27) 56, 88.
[97] Sylvia Tamale (n 28) 40.
[98] Jeremy Levitt, 'Law, Peace-Construction and Women's Rights in Africa: Who will Safeguard Abeena and Afia?' in Jeremy Levitt (ed), *Black Women and International Law: Deliberate Interactions, Movements and Actions* (Cambridge University Press, 2015).
[99] Mina Roces and Louise Edwards (eds), *Women's Movements in Asia: Feminisms and Transnational Activism* (Routledge, 2010).
[100] Bisi Adeleye-Fayemi, Director of Akina Mama wa Afrika (AmwA), 'Creating and Sustaining Feminist Space in Africa: Local-Global Challenges in the 21st Century' (4th Annual Dame Nita Barrow Lecture, Toronto, November 2000).
[101] Women from the Pacific were barely involved in the Decade conferences: International Women's Development Agency, 'Beneath Paradise: The Pacific Women's Documentation Project', 1995.

the Decade. One view is that the 1980s economic downturn and the predominance of neoliberal economic policies sensitised Northern women to the nexus between inequalities, poverty and social oppression. They had also learned to cede space and not to assume their representation of the lived experiences of all women.[102] There was a growing consolidation of Third World feminisms through networking, sharing strategies and the emergence of new NGOs to combat the patriarchal structures that were perpetuating women's subordination.[103] It was becoming possible for women from across the globe to share 'different, but often converging, perspectives' on common issues without the divisiveness of the early conferences.[104] The FLS recognised the intersections of race, class and gender[105] and provided a lengthy list of women made especially vulnerable.[106] Differences still divided women, but the connections, extended networks and friendships forged throughout the Decade opened the way for new local, national, regional and international alliances.[107] Women had changed the discourse since Mexico City, and Nairobi marked a turning point in women's understanding of their relationship to the twin issues of equality and development: fighting for stand-alone gender equality or integrating women into an unjust economic order would not achieve either of these Decade goals,[108] or peace.

IV. THE DECADE AND GENDERED PEACE

A. The Politicisation of Peace

Peace was regarded by some as of lesser significance to women's advancement than the objectives of equality and development and was largely omitted from the UN Secretariat's first draft for the Mexico City conference.[109] The diverse ideological agendas of the Decade politicised peace. The USSR asserted women's equality (constitutionally accorded at home) as part of the peace agenda[110] it promoted abroad.[111]

---

[102] Aoife O'Donoghue and Adam Rowe, 'Feminism, Global Inequality, and the 1975 Mexico City Conference' in Jeremy Levitt (ed) (n 98).

[103] eg Development Alternatives with Women for a New Era (DAWN), a network of scholars and activists in the South was established shortly before Nairobi. Significant Global South networks shifted leadership 'perceptibly although not entirely from North to South': Martha Alter Chen (n 71) 480. See essay 6 'Revisiting the Past: Peace at Beijing and Beyond'.

[104] Nilüfer Çağatay et al, 'The Nairobi Women's Conference: Toward a Global Feminism?' (1986) 12 *Feminist Studies* 401.

[105] eg Nairobi FLS (n 39) para 23: 'Women, subject to compound discrimination on the basis of race, colour, ethnicity and national origin, in addition to sex, could be even more adversely affected by deteriorating economic conditions.' See also para 46.

[106] ibid para 41.

[107] Bisi Adeleye-Fayemi (n 100).

[108] Gita Sen, *Neo-libs, Neo-cons and Gender Justice: Lessons from Global Negotiations*, UNRISD Occasional Paper 9 (Geneva, 2005).

[109] Olcott (n 37) 75.

[110] The Cold War saw women's rights 'embedded in Soviet and East European cultural diplomacy "in defence of peace"': Celia Donert (n 23) 190.

[111] At the Nairobi NGO forum the 'peace contingent' was led by women from the USSR and Eastern Europe, supported by NGOs affiliated to communist-backed parties: Mandana Hendessi (n 81) 155.

The US government[112] suspected the Soviets of using peace 'as a 'front' to influence and infiltrate non-communist organizations'[113] and as a distraction from the advancement of 'women's issues'. The assertion in the Mexico Declaration that peace requires rejection of foreign intervention into the domestic affairs of other states and respect for all states' sovereign right to establish their own economic, political and social system[114] was perceived as an attack on US foreign policy, especially in 1975, the year of the fall of Saigon.[115] At the outset of the Decade, representatives of military dictatorships from South and Central America argued that the stability imposed by military regimes guaranteed equality, development and peace.[116] Neither the Soviet nor right-wing authoritarian positions on peace offered any gendered analysis. In stark contrast was women's peace activism, opposing the placing of cruise missiles in Europe, the reignited arms race and the threat of nuclear war. Women's peace camps proliferated, including at Greenham Common[117] (commenced September 1981), at La Ragnatela (commenced March 1983) and the Women's Encampment for a Future of Peace and Justice at Seneca Falls in 1983. Civil society peace activists worked across the East/West divide,[118] challenging the arms race and demanding disarmament.[119]

As chair of programme development for the Copenhagen NGO forum and of the planning committee for the Nairobi forum, Edith Ballantyne, Secretary-General of WILPF,[120] ensured a strong emphasis on peace and disarmament in those fora. She pressed for a space at the Nairobi forum where views about peace could be aired – the Peace Tent that was pitched on the University of Nairobi campus.[121] It provided an arena 'for the resolution of conflicts and tensions [through] productive and peaceful dialogue, even on issues that have historically divided [women] by nationality, class, or race'.[122] Despite differences, the level of participation showed peace to be a shared concern and underscored the linkages between peace, combating violence, poverty alleviation, economic justice, national liberation, and development. WILPF, for instance, saw peace hindered by injustices to Third World women attributable to First World attitudes that manifested in forms of violence such as sex tourism,

---

[112] Samuel Moyn, *Humane: How the United States Abandoned Peace and Reinvented War* (Verso, 2022) suggests that the Cold War led the US to abandon its immediate post-World War II policy of advancing peace for one of freedom.
[113] Olcott (n 37) 157.
[114] Mexico Declaration (n 48) para 29.
[115] Jennifer Klot, 'The United Nations Security Council's Agenda on Women, Peace and Security: Bureaucratic Pathologies and Unrealised Potential' (LSE, Doctoral thesis, 2015) ch 3.
[116] Olcott (n 37) 151.
[117] There is a vast literature on Greenham: eg Jill Liddington, *The Road to Greenham Common: Feminism and Anti-Militarism in Britain since 1820* (Virago Press, 1989); Sasha Roseneil, *Common Women, Uncommon Practices* (Cassell, 2000).
[118] Mary Kaldor (ed), *Europe from Below: An East West Dialogue* (Verso, 1991).
[119] See essay 7 'Women, Disarmament and Peace'.
[120] WILPF has a long history of challenging militarisation and urging disarmament. During the Decade its 'Stop the Arms Race' gathered signatures worldwide seeking cancellation by NATO of its decision to deploy Pershing missiles. The campaign concluded with a mass rally in Brussels and presentation of petition signatures to NATO leadership.
[121] This was initiated by the Feminist International for Peace and Food and funded by an American feminist: Genevieve Vaughan, 'The Nairobi Peace Tent' (1984).
[122] Nilüfer Çağatay et al (n 104) 409.

prostitution, pornography and exploitation.[123] The vitality of the NGO discourse around peace is not captured in the outcome documents of the Decade conferences that are outlined in the next section.

B. The Conceptualisation of Peace

There is greater concentration on peace in the Nairobi FLS than in the earlier conference documents. The FLS sets out a lengthy list of threats to peace, to human progress and to women's advancement that includes imperialism, apartheid, racism, colonialism, neocolonialism, foreign domination, human rights violations, sex-based discrimination[124] and the unabated arms race.[125] These reinforce and are reinforced by historic hostile attitudes and bigotry. It brings together two strands of international law that contribute to the construction of peace: prohibition of the use of force and intervention into the internal affairs of states;[126] and protection of human rights and fundamental freedoms. Peace accordingly encompasses not only negative peace – 'the absence of war, violence and hostilities – but also the enjoyment of economic and social justice, equality and the entire range of human rights and fundamental freedoms within society'.[127] It goes beyond positive intentional law through embracing mutual cooperation, trust and goodwill between nations, social groups and individuals. It cannot be achieved amidst economic and sexual inequalities, deliberate exploitation of peoples and exploitative economic relations.[128] CEDAW, adopted at the mid-point of the Decade, requires states parties to take appropriate measures to ensure equality in the workplace, in access to education, healthcare and cultural activities. These are not identified as pertaining to peace but are core to a peaceful existence. Peace thus enfolds aspects of human security (physical security, food security, health security, economic security).

Three themes recur throughout the provisions on peace. First is the importance of women's participation in activities for peace. Women have long demanded access to decision-making about peace[129] and before the Decade this demand was given rhetorical, albeit instrumental, support. The 1967 DEDAW saw women's 'maximum participation' as necessary for 'the full and complete development of a country, the welfare of the world and the cause of peace',[130] wording that was repeated at the Tehran Conference on Human Rights.[131] Women's participation was made an explicit

---

[123] WILPF Resolutions, 23rd Congress, Gothenburg, Sweden, 1983.
[124] Nairobi FLS (n 39) para 232.
[125] ibid para 233.
[126] Mexico Declaration (n 48) para 29: 'Peace requires that women as well as men should reject any type of intervention in the domestic affairs of States, whether it be openly or covertly carried on by other States or by transnational corporations.' This last is a radical linkage between peace and corporate activity.
[127] Nairobi FLS (n 39) para 13. See essay 3 'Peace in International Law'.
[128] ibid.
[129] See essay 4 'Introduction: Rewriting International Law's Histories'.
[130] UNGAR 2263 (XXII), DEDAW, preamble. CSW's draft Declaration submitted to ECOSOC was silent on peace; CSW Report on the nineteenth session, 21 February–11 March, 1966, 1966 ECOSOC OR, 42nd session, supp 7, E/CN.6/454, 103.
[131] Resolution IX (n 22) preamble.

objective of the Decade.¹³² The Mexico City conference declared that 'women have vital role to play in the promotion of peace ...: in the family, the community, the nation and the world'.¹³³ The language of DEDAW and Tehran was again replicated in CEDAW's preamble and, following the adoption of CEDAW, the UNGA proclaimed its detailed Declaration on the Participation of Women in Promoting International Peace and Cooperation.¹³⁴ The FLS avows that '[u]niversal and durable peace cannot be attained without the full and equal participation of women'.¹³⁵ Women's participation is also promoted for its own value, since peace cannot be lasting without the elimination of discrimination and inequalities.¹³⁶ Women's equal participation in decision-making about peace is asserted as a right.¹³⁷ It is women's responsibility to participate in activities to secure peace,¹³⁸ albeit a responsibility sometimes shared with men.¹³⁹ This denotes providing support and encouragement to each other in peace initiatives at the universal level and in specific local contexts.¹⁴⁰ Women's responsibility is to be proactive in promoting peace, while governments should eliminate obstacles to enable women's participation, which remains limited¹⁴¹ and an underutilised resource. To this end, unspecified 'special national and international measures' are needed.¹⁴² Resources should be made available for women's participation in their country's political life and hence in international affairs.¹⁴³ Introduction of training and educational opportunities at all levels through institutional programmes, lectures and other events on international affairs is a priority.¹⁴⁴ There are, however, no provisions around relieving women of their domestic and caring burdens or of the need for an equitable distribution of workloads between women and men¹⁴⁵ that would facilitate realisation of the right.¹⁴⁶

---

[132] UNGAR 3520 (XXX) proclaiming the Decade: 'women must play an important part in the promotion, achievement and maintenance of international peace'. UNGAR 3521 (XXX) requested that CSW complete the draft of CEDAW, calling upon all states to 'promote vigorously wider participation of women in the strengthening of international peace'.
[133] Mexico Declaration (n 48) para 25.
[134] UNGAR 37/63, Annex, 3 December 1982, integrated into Nairobi FLS (n 39) by para 239; see also UNGAR 41/109, Participation of women in promoting international peace and cooperation, 4 December 1986.
[135] Nairobi FLS (n 39) para 235.
[136] Copenhagen Programme of Action (n 53) para 5.
[137] Nairobi FLS (n 39) para 253: women's 'equal role in participation in decision-making should be seen as a basic human right', reinforcing CEDAW, arts 7 and 8.
[138] Copenhagen Programme of Action (n 53) para 76: 'Women in the entire world should participate in the broadest way in the struggle to strengthen international peace and security'.
[139] Mexico Declaration (n 48) para 30: women (with men) 'must maintain their vigilance and do their utmost to achieve and maintain international peace'.
[140] Nairobi FLS (n 39) para 241.
[141] ibid para 234.
[142] UNGAR 37/63 (n 134) annex, art 5.
[143] Mexico Declaration (n 48) para 9.
[144] Copenhagen Programme of Action (n 53) para 76; Nairobi FLS (n 39) para 266.
[145] UNGAR 37/63 (n 134) annex, art 2 recognises the importance of a 'balanced and equitable distribution of roles between men and women in the family and in society as a whole'.
[146] Nairobi FLS (n 39) para 101 acknowledges the increased burden on women as an obstacle to development.

74 *Peace in the UN Decade for Women*

The second recurring theme is apprehension of nuclear war or catastrophe and the arms race, seen unsurprisingly as the greatest threat to peace.[147] The 1968 World Conference on Human Rights had appealed for states to cooperate toward 'immediate conclusion of an agreement on general and complete disarmament'[148] and nuclear disarmament, which would contribute to women's equality. This is repeatedly demanded throughout the Decade.[149] How women might perform their allocated 'essential role'[150] – even 'responsibility'[151] – in avoiding nuclear catastrophe is not elucidated. The 1968 Conference had noted the potential for accelerated economic and social progress and human rights implementation through the release of economic resources that would follow disarmament.[152] The FLS represents the global expenditures on arms as a waste of resources which could be used for furthering wellbeing through their redistribution to enhance social and economic conditions in developing countries.[153] The third theme is peace education, or education for peace, with women – and men – playing a special role in educating young people toward engendering 'compassion, tolerance, mutual concern and trust'.[154]

The 'special', 'important' or 'vital' contribution of women to the pursuit of peace, that women are inherently 'peace loving or 'good at peace' are reiterated without evidence or justification. Women's love of peace is also noted,[155] presumably in an oblique reference to their peace activism. This essentialising stereotype has been much critiqued, as it fails to take account of the many roles women play in supporting and participating in conflict. A nexus between gender relationships and peace is hinted at in the assertion that the 'meaning of peace for women cannot be separated from the broader question of relationships between women and men in all spheres of life and in the family', followed by recognition of the need to change 'traditional gender norms' to enhance women's participation in peace.[156] The language lacks gender analysis; like the UNGA resolutions on peace[157] of the same era, there is little attention to the role of gender, gender roles, or constructions of masculinity and femininity in the conceptualisation of peace.

It is ambiguous whether there is an individual or collective right to peace, or whether the right is to live in peace as declared by the UNGA in 1978.[158]

---

[147] See essay 7 'Women, Disarmament and Peace'.
[148] Tehran Conference on Human Rights (n 131) Resolution XVI, Disarmament.
[149] Mexico Declaration (n 48) para 30; CEDAW, preamble; Nairobi FLS (n 39) para 254.
[150] Nairobi FLS (n 39) para 250.
[151] WIDF had similarly argued that 'the responsibility of women for preventing this catastrophe is as high as never before': cited in Yulia Gradskova (n 31) 69.
[152] Tehran Conference on Human Rights (n 131) Resolution XVI, Disarmament.
[153] Nairobi FLS (n 39) para 254. In 1985, WILPF published its first women's budget, showing a 50 per cent cut in military spending that could be redirected to development, education, peace and security for all of humanity.
[154] Nairobi FLS (n 39) paras 252, 256.
[155] ibid para 237: 'It is evident that women all over the world have manifested their love for peace and their wish to play a greater role in international co-operation, amity and peace among different nations.' The FLS also repeats much of the Cold War language of 'friendly relations'.
[156] Nairobi FLS (n 39) paras 253 and 275 reflect states' obligations under CEDAW, arts 2(f) and 5(1). See essay 10 'Misogyny and Sexism in the Digital Age'.
[157] See essay 3 'Peace in International Law'.
[158] UNGAR 33/73, 15 December 1978, Declaration on the Preparation of Societies for Life in Peace.

The Copenhagen Conference adopted a similar resolution but brought women into the frame by recognising that impediments to women's participation militate against preparing for a life in peace.[159] Such preparation begins in the family, through instilling values of tolerance and mutual respect in children. Women artists, writers, journalists, educators and civic leaders are especially asked to persevere in preparing societies for a life in peace, including eliminating biases and stereotypes; the resolution is apparently oblivious to the stereotype it perpetuates of women as peaceful.

Violence against women is absent from understandings of peace in the early Decade documents. The Mexico Declaration, paragraph 28 urges women to unite against human rights violations, listing 'rape, prostitution, physical assault, mental cruelty, child marriage, forced marriage and marriage as a commercial transaction'. This progressive language recognises violence against women as a human rights violation, including prostitution (not 'forced' prostitution[160]), mental cruelty and marriage as a commercial transaction, all contested manifestations of gender-based violence. But this language vanishes from the WPA. At Copenhagen, national legislation was called for to prevent 'domestic and sexual violence against women'[161] and for policies to protect women from the resulting physical and mental abuse.[162] The conference adopted a resolution on 'Battered Women and Violence in the Family' in which violence was seen as a grave problem for the physical and mental health of the family and society. By Nairobi, violence against women that 'exists in various forms in everyday life in all societies' was recognised as a major obstacle to peace that necessitates special attention.[163] The FLS documents that 'a peaceful social environment compatible with human dignity' must be sought in the family and the community, foreshadowing the soon to be widely adopted conceptualisation of gender-based violence as occurring in the family, community and the state.[164] Despite acknowledging women as one of the 'most vulnerable groups' in armed conflict, the focus in 1985 was on the violence of conflict, not the violence that is perpetrated against women (and others targeted because of their gender) and which prevents their living in peace.

The limited attention to violence against women in the conference documents contrasts with the International Women's Tribunal held in Brussels in 1976.[165] Powerful personal testimonies from diverse women (including Australian indigenous, Native American, Black South African, lesbians, women political prisoners) from over 40 countries exposed the realities and ubiquity of the different forms of violence experienced by women. This opened the way for future events where survivors of

---

[159] Copenhagen Report (n 53) resolution VII, The role of women in the preparation of societies for life in peace.
[160] As for instance in Convention relative to the Protection of Civilian Persons in Time of War, Geneva, 12 August 1949, art 27.
[161] Copenhagen Report (n 53) para 65.
[162] ibid para 141(f)f) under the heading of 'Health'.
[163] Nairobi FLS (n 39) para 258.
[164] eg UNGAR 48/104, 20 December 1993, Declaration on the Elimination of Violence against Women, art 3: 'violence against women is an obstacle to the achievement of equality, development and peace.'
[165] Diana Russell (n 56).

violence could speak out and for women's global networking around the imperative to combat gender-based violence. Following Nairobi, women's organisations coalesced successfully around efforts to have such violence understood as structural and as a human rights violation incurring state responsibility for failure to exercise due diligence for its prevention, prosecution and punishment.[166]

V. REFLECTIONS ON THE DECADE

Much has been written about the lasting legacies of the Decade, primarily from the perspective of its contribution to a global feminist movement,[167] with Nairobi as the 'Bandung' moment, ushering in the 'era of the international women's movement, with its multitude of diverse regional and global manifestations'.[168] The seeds for this growth were planted at Mexico City and fertilised in Copenhagen.[169] The Decade was focused on the position of women vis-à-vis men; the goal was women's equality with men; 'gender' had not yet entered the lexicon of international law.[170]

Less has been written about the Decade's impact on international legal guarantees for women's rights and promotion of peace.[171] This is unsurprising for two reasons. First, the Decade for Women overlapped with the designated decades for development, which were bestowed with special significance, especially for the newly independent Group of 77 states. Second, final conference documents are legally non-binding. Helvi Sipila, the Secretary-General of IWY, reminded the Mexico City tribune that UN documents are only binding 'to the extent that they [NGOs] could hold their governments accountable'.[172] The exception was CEDAW, which came into force in 1981.[173] The preamble – admittedly not part of the legally binding text – recognises that equality is necessary to development and peace, thereby reinforcing the linkages with the two other Decade themes. CEDAW – like all Decade documents – echoes the political and economic concerns of the day, so that equality is framed as contingent on addressing, inter alia, racism, ending alien and colonial domination, advancing nuclear and general disarmament and a commitment to a new economic model founded on equity and justice. Although it received little attention at the time, as a legally binding treaty CEDAW became available for dissemination as the UN's blueprint for women's human rights,[174] albeit diluted by reservations and indeterminate language. On the one hand, putting

---

[166] See essay 6 'Revisiting the Past: Peace at Beijing and Beyond'.
[167] Peggy Antrobus (n 17).
[168] Charlotte Bunch, 'Women and Gender: The Evolution of Women Specific Institutions and Gender Integration at the United Nations' in Thomas G Weiss and Sam Daws (eds), *Oxford Handbook on the United Nations* (Oxford University Press, 2007).
[169] The metaphor is Olcott's (n 37) 242.
[170] See essay 2 'Gender'.
[171] Zinsser notes writings about the Decade by journalists, political scientists, development specialists, women scholars and activists. Law – international law – is strikingly absent: Zinsser (n 16) fn 8.
[172] Cited in Olcott (n 37) 189.
[173] The CEDAW Committee held its first session between 18 and 22 October 1982.
[174] Arvonne Fraser (n 55).

sex – and later gender-based[175] – discrimination on a formal legal footing was a significant outcome of the Decade. On the other hand, despite near universal ratification (189 states parties in 2023) and determined efforts by the CEDAW Committee to strengthen and update the scope of the Convention through a succession of general recommendations, the Convention remains widely disregarded by mainstream international lawyers and sex and gender-based discrimination ignored as candidates for peremptory norm status.[176]

Dismissing the other conference documents as legally non-binding soft law fails, however, to capture their importance for the advancement of women. State delegates made determined efforts to excise unacceptable language and entered reservations where they could not prevent its inclusion, while NGOs strived for input into the texts, actions suggesting the wording could not be dismissed as of no normative value. Subsequently NGOs did not just seek to hold governments to account. Strengthened by the learning processes of the Decade and through the networks and coalitions formed, they organised and engaged systematically at the global conferences convened during the 1990s on topics that were not directly 'women's issues', but into which women sought successfully inclusion of their agendas.[177] Women campaigners pursued international legal change, building on ideas generated throughout the Decade, achieving, inter alia, recognition of 'women's rights as human rights' and gender-based violence against women as a human rights violation.[178] NGO campaigns, state initiatives, and recommendations of the CEDAW Committee contributed to a plethora of changed state and institutional practice through, among others, adoption of domestic legislation and jurisprudence, creation of national women's institutions, statements at the UNGA and international human rights bodies that are all pertinent to the evolution of customary international law[179] relating to gender equality, non-discrimination and violence against women.

Recognition of women's rights and tackling gender-based violence are components of a broad understanding of peace but legal recognition of women's input to peace – or indeed of state commitment to peace – was less forthcoming. Despite lip service paid to women's peace activism, peace was not feminised, as demonstrated by the UNGA's designation in 1981 of an annual day of peace.[180] The UNGA

---

[175] CEDAW Committee, General Recommendation No 28 on the core obligations of States parties under article 2 of the Convention on the Elimination of All Forms of Discrimination against Women, CEDAW/C/GC/28, 2010, para 5 asserts that although the Convention only refers to sex-based discrimination, it also covers gender-based discrimination against women.

[176] See essay 2 'Gender'.

[177] eg UN Conference on Environment and Development, Rio de Janeiro, 1992; World Conference on Human Rights, Vienna, 1993; International Conference on Population and Development, Cairo, 1994.

[178] World Conference on Human Rights, Vienna Declaration and Programme of Action, 25 June 1993, I, 18.

[179] The ILC listed 'conduct in connection with resolutions adopted ... at an intergovernmental conference' as state activity relevant for identifying evidence of state practice, one of the two required elements for determining customary international law: ILC, Draft conclusions on identification of customary international law, with commentaries, A/73/10, 2018, Conclusion 6.2.

[180] UNGAR 36/67, 30 November 1981; supplemented by UNGAR 55/282, 7 September 2001: the 'International Day of Peace shall henceforth be observed as a day of global ceasefire and non-violence, an invitation to all nations and people to honour a cessation of hostilities for the duration of the Day'.

made no reference to a similar proposal in the Mexico Plan of Action, nor to the Decade, nor to women's long advocacy for peace. The chosen year was 1986, with efforts concentrated on the 'promotion and achievement of the ideals of peace by all possible means'.[181] Peace was denoted as a universal ideal requiring: prevention of war and removal of threats to peace; upholding UN Charter principles relating to the prohibition of the use of force and the peaceful settlement of disputes; confidence building measures; disarmament; human rights and fundamental freedoms; decolonisation; elimination of apartheid and racial discrimination; 'enhancement of the quality of life, the satisfaction of human needs, and the protection of the environment'.[182] Even immediately after the Decade, elimination of sex discrimination is conspicuously absent from this vision of peace. The CEDAW Committee at its next session adopted its Resolution on the International Year of Peace.[183] It pointed to the preamble of CEDAW which asserts 'that the cause of peace requires the maximum participation of women' and to women's longstanding history in pursuit of peace. It called for states to demonstrate their commitment to peace by ensuring the equal participation of women in all bodies with decision-making power with respect to 'peace, war and disarmament'.

The Decade was followed by the changed geopolitical climate of the end of the Cold War. Peace processes in conflict zones that had engendered much discussion during the Decade conferences sought to bring stability in accordance with the post-Cold War mantra of 'democracy, human rights and the rule of law'. The vision of the NIEO was lost in this 'liberal peace agenda' that furthered neoliberal economic globalisation, amplifying inequalities between and within countries, including between women and men, and proving antithetical to social or gendered peace. Nor were women present in these processes. Ten years later, as women again gathered at the Fourth World Conference on Women, it was admitted that 'most of the goals set out in the Nairobi Forward-looking Strategies for the Advancement of Women have not been achieved'.[184] And this time around peace slipped even further off the agenda.[185]

---

[181] UNGAR 40/3, 24 October 1985, International Year of Peace.
[182] ibid.
[183] Report of the Committee on the Elimination of Discrimination against Women (Fifth Session), UN GAOR, 41st Session, Supp No 45, UN Doc A/41/45, 51.
[184] Beijing Platform for Action, Report on the Fourth World Conference on Women, Beijing, 4–15 September 1995, para 42.
[185] See essay 6 'Revisiting the Past: Peace at Beijing and Beyond'.

6

Revisiting the Past: Peace at Beijing and Beyond

I. INTRODUCTION

THIS ESSAY RE-EXAMINES the significance of the 1995 Fourth World Conference on Women in Beijing for international law concepts of peace and equality. It first outlines how the UN Commission on the Status of Women (CSW) approached its task of review and appraisal of implementation of the commitments made at the three preceding global conferences on women that took place during the UN Decade for Women 1975–1985.[1] It discusses the changes in the geopolitical landscape since 1985 as well as the different priorities of and tensions between women at Beijing. It shows how the commitment to peace, expressed by so many women over decades of activism and resistance, was splintered at Beijing. Despite commitment to '[achieving] the full and effective implementation of the Nairobi Forward- looking Strategies for the Advancement of Women',[2] peace was not a 'critical area of concern' at Beijing. It was instead brought within other critical areas of concern, notably those of women in armed conflict and violence against women. This sidelining of peace[3] has continued through the shift from the Decade's (and Beijing's) objectives of 'equality, development and peace' to 'women, peace and security' (WPS) in the UN Security Council (SC). The essay concludes with an assessment of the place of peace in international law and questions whether it could be a unifying concept across distinct special regimes.

---

[1] CSW's responsibility for implementing the Decade's outputs was repeated: World Plan of Action for the Implementation of the Objectives of the International Women's Year, Report, Mexico City, 1975, para 45; Programme of Action for the Second Half of the United Nations Decade for Women: Equality, Development and Peace, Report, Copenhagen, 1980, para 273; Forward-looking Strategies for the Advancement of Women during the Period from 1986 to the Year 2000, Report, Nairobi, 1985, para 319 (Nairobi FLS).
[2] Beijing Declaration and Platform for Action, Report on the Fourth World Conference on Women, Beijing 1995 (Beijing Report, Beijing Declaration and PFA): Beijing Declaration, para 11.
[3] In his opening statement, UN Secretary-General Boutros Boutros-Ghali recognised 'the role of women in peace' as a conference theme, noted that in 'United Nations peace missions, women remain a largely untapped resource', that '[v]iolence against women seems to be increasing' and that '[m]ore women are today suffering directly from the effects of war and conflict than ever before in history'. He then moved on from the theme of peace: Beijing Report (n 2) 187.

II. THE COMMISSION ON THE STATUS OF WOMEN 1985–1995

The Nairobi FLS gave CSW oversight of progress toward achievement of its goals.[4] CSW consequently proposed to the UN Economic and Social Council (ECOSOC) resolutions with respect to ensuring women's active participation in the promotion of international peace. It recommended regular follow-ups to the global women's conferences (initially envisaged at five-year intervals) and the identification of priority themes within the Decade's overall objectives, to be taken up in consecutive annual sessions of the Commission. The 1988–92 priority themes for peace were: access to information, education for peace, and efforts to eradicate violence against women within the family and society; women's full participation in the construction of their countries and in the creation of just social and political systems; women in areas affected by armed conflicts, foreign intervention, alien and colonial domination, foreign occupation and threats to peace; refugee and displaced women and children; equal participation in all efforts to promote international co-operation. In 1990 the UN General Assembly (UNGA) decided to convene a world conference on women in 1995[5] and subsequently accepted the Chinese government's offer for it to be held in Beijing.[6] New CSW priority themes for 1993–96 were identified: women and the peace process; measures to eradicate violence against women in the family and society; women in international decision-making and education for peace. These themes merged in CSW's annual discussions, with ever increasing focus on violence against women, violence against women in armed conflict and women's participation in peace processes, specifically with respect to the end of apartheid, the Middle East and Central America. The end of the Cold War shifted the discourse towards, for instance, democracy and human rights, women in absolute poverty, and, with reports from Bosnia-Herzegovina and elsewhere of its incidence, sexual violence against women in armed conflict. In preparation for the scheduled global conference, 12 critical areas of concern for consideration at Beijing were identified, with peace no longer explicitly included.[7]

III. THE FOURTH WORLD CONFERENCE ON WOMEN: BEIJING 1995

A. The Conference

The Beijing conference started from the premise that the Decade goals had not been met[8] and that more was needed to fulfil the Nairobi FLS. Continuity was maintained

---

[4] Nairobi FLS (n 1) para 319 provided that CSW should consider, on a regular basis, progress made and concrete measures adopted for their achievement.

[5] UNGAR 44/77, Implementation of the Nairobi FLS, 8 December 1989, para 8 requests that CSW consider holding a world conference on women in 1995 'at the lowest possible cost'; UNGAR 45/129, Implementation of the Nairobi FLS, 14 December 1990, para 8 endorses ECOSOC resolution 1990/12 recommending a conference on women in 1995.

[6] UNGAR 47/95, Implementation of the Nairobi FLS, 16 December 1992, para 8 expresses appreciation for the Chinese government's offer to host the conference in Beijing in September 1995.

[7] Some CSW representatives had earlier observed that the priority theme of peace was neglected and that it should receive more attention in UN activities; CSW, Report on the 32nd Session (14–23 March 1988) ECOSOC OR 1988, Supp 5, E/1988/15/Rev 1 E/CN.6/1988/11/Rev.1, para 189.

through the espousal of the Decade's objectives: equality, development and peace. Conference facts have been much repeated: it was at the time the most widely attended event in UN history, with some 6,000 government delegates in the formal negotiations, more than 4,000 accredited representatives from international governmental organisations and NGOs and around 4,000 media personnel. It remains the largest gathering of women in history. Drafts agreed at regional preparatory meetings (prepcoms) as well as numerous other submissions were fed into CSW's detailed preliminary text, which at the commencement of the conference contained around 40 per cent in square brackets,[9] including all references to gender and gender equality.[10] Intense negotiations resulted in the adoption of two instruments: the Declaration – the first agreed statement of core values since the Mexico Declaration 20 years earlier[11] – and the Platform for Action (PFA). Unlike the Nairobi FLS, which was adopted by consensus, the more conservative PFA was adopted with reservations and interpretive declarations.[12]

The Beijing Declaration and PFA set out the strategic objectives and actions to be taken by governments and other bodies, including UN bodies, international financial institutions (IFIs) and the private sector in 12 critical areas of concern, providing a roadmap for women's empowerment. The UNGA endorsed the Declaration and PFA and charged CSW with a 'central role' in monitoring implementation.[13]

The parallel NGO forum was held some 50 kilometres outside Beijing, necessitating over an hour's traveling in dilapidated buses to a location that resembled a building site.[14] A further 30,000, mainly women, attended[15] the forum. The distance from Beijing made liaison between the conference delegates and the NGO forum difficult, but the Women's Caucus worked assiduously to monitor all amendments, rewrite drafts and lobby on a daily basis. The Women's Caucus is a misnomer: no single caucus – of which there were many including a peace caucus – spoke for all participants, and separate statements were put out by forum attendees who felt that their interests were marginalised or that the PFA did not challenge the colonial and racist structures that sustain women's continued inequality.

---

[8] Beijing PFA (n 2) para 42: 'Most of the goals set out in the Nairobi Forward-looking Strategies for the Advancement of Women have not been achieved.'
[9] Contested text is placed in square brackets, meaning that most conference time is spent on seeking compromise on controversial wording.
[10] References to 'gender' and 'gender equality' were square bracketed at the behest of Honduras, joined by the Holy See, Catholic and Muslim states; see essay 2 'Gender'.
[11] A Draft Declaration on the Achievements of the United Nations Decade for Women – Equality, Development and Peace, proposed by socialist and African countries was not considered at Nairobi but included as Annex I of the conference report.
[12] Beijing Report (n 2) 154–75. Reservations and declaratory statements related primarily to women's reproductive and sexual rights, 'gender' and sexuality.
[13] UNGAR 50/203, Follow-up to the Fourth World Conference on Women and full implementation of the Beijing Declaration and the Platform for Action, 22 December 1995.
[14] The NGO forum was scheduled for the Workers Stadium, close to the governmental conference, but, apparently apprehensive about the presence of thousands of women activists, the Chinese government declared this site unsafe and reallocated it to Huairou: Ruth Dawson, 'When Women Gather: The NGO Forum of the Fourth World Conference on Women, Beijing 1995' (1996) 10 *International Journal of Politics, Culture, and Society* 7.
[15] UN Women, *World Conferences on Women* at https://www.unwomen.org/en/how-we-work/intergovernmental-support/world-conferences-on-women#beijing.

B. Context

The Beijing conference took place in a different context from those of the Decade – the aftermath of the Cold War and collapse of the USSR that gave rise to US hegemony and the consolidation of neoliberal economic globalisation. The PFA sought new processes of global governance, with women participating equally in the 'decision-making process and access to power'[16] in the 'New World Order'[17] – a triumphalist moment for the West and one of transition from socialism for Eastern Europe. Some long-running conflicts came to an end, as did apartheid in South Africa. The UN sought in this opportune moment to enhance preventive diplomacy, peace-making, peacekeeping and post-conflict peace-building.[18] Attention turned to devising mechanisms for delivering what became termed 'transitional justice'.[19]

There was another side to the post-Cold War context, that is the extreme violence, displacement and organised crime of the 'new wars'[20] in, inter alia, Bosnia-Herzegovina, Somalia, Sierra Leone, Liberia and Haiti, as well as genocide in Rwanda. These saw targeted violence against civilians, including sexual violence used deliberately as a weapon and tactic of war. Institutional responses included increased policing through UN or regionally mandated peacekeeping operations, the creation of the ad hoc international criminal tribunals and post-conflict peace settlements in accordance with the liberal peace model of democratisation, human rights and the rule of law.[21] These responses allowed the West to advance its 'civilising' mission while disregarding its own complicity in violence through the legacies of colonialism and Cold War proxy conflicts, as well as contemporary policies relating to military security, free market neoliberalism and closed borders.

The threat posed by nuclear weapons continued despite the end of the Cold War. Nuclear testing was carried out by France[22] and by China. At the 1995 Review Conference of the Nuclear Non-Proliferation Treaty, non-nuclear weapon states criticised the lack of progress toward implementation of article VI – the commitment 'to pursue negotiations in good faith on effective measures relating to cessation of the nuclear arms race … and to nuclear disarmament, and on a treaty on general and complete disarmament under strict and effective international control'.[23] In accordance with article X.2, the Non-Proliferation Treaty was renewed.

---

[16] Beijing Declaration (n 2) para 13.
[17] President George Bush declared 'a new world order', a 'new era – freer from the threat of terror, stronger in the pursuit of justice and more secure in the quest for peace. An era in which the nations of the world, east and west, north and south, can prosper and live in harmony': *Washington Post*, 12 September 1990.
[18] Report of the Secretary-General, An Agenda for Peace Preventive diplomacy, peacemaking and peace-keeping, A/47/277 – S/24111, 17 June 1992; Supplement to an Agenda for Peace: position paper of the Secretary-General on the occasion of the 50th anniversary of the United Nations, A/50/60, S/1995/1, 25 January 1995.
[19] Ruti Teitel, *Transitional Justice* (Oxford University Press, 2000).
[20] Mary Kaldor, *New and Old Wars: Organised Violence in a Global Era*, 3rd edn (Polity Press, 2012).
[21] Christine Chinkin and Mary Kaldor, *International Law and New Wars* (Cambridge University Press, 2017) ch 9.
[22] New Zealand attempted unsuccessfully to reopen its case against France with respect to nuclear testing; *Request for an Examination of the Situation in Accordance with Paragraph 63 of the Court's Judgment of 20 December 1974 in the Nuclear Tests (New Zealand v. France) Case*, 1995 ICJ Reports, 288.
[23] See essay 7 'Women, Disarmament and Peace'.

The years following the Decade saw feminist interventions into international agendas through the networks and alliances that had been built and sustained since the Nairobi conference. The Decade had imparted important lessons for those seeking women's advancement through international institutions: that preparation is vital including familiarisation with UN processes; that high levels of organisation produce success; that preparatory meetings are the best time to influence outcomes; and that coalitions are needed to develop the consensus necessary to bridge divides.[24] By the early 1990s women's groups were developing strategies for negotiating gender relations within the framework of other global agendas.[25] They were supported in articulating priorities and in advocacy at regional prepcoms and global conferences, including Beijing, by the UN Development Fund for Women (UNIFEM) which had been established following the Decade. Feminist interventions in successive global conferences secured progressive language for women through recognition of: 'the crucial role of women in sustainable development and protecting the environment'; 'the human rights of women as an inalienable, integral and indivisible part of universal human rights'; 'violence against women as an intolerable violation of these rights'; and 'health, maternal care and family planning facilities, and of access to education and information, as essential to the exercise by women of their fundamental rights'.[26] By the time of the Beijing conference, there was sufficient agreement between women around some core issues (in particular violence) to allow for concerted campaigning and a growing consensus that social and economic justice and gender justice need to go hand in hand.[27] Despite these successes and the apparently progressive momentum, both the Beijing governmental conference and the NGO forum were sites of struggle and contestation, as well as compromise, between women from different geographic, socioeconomic and ideological conditions.

C. Women at Beijing

The end of the Cold War saw the rivalry between the Soviet bloc and the US diminished. Women from the US were no longer directly challenged as to feminist priorities by women from Eastern and Central Europe as they had been throughout the Decade, although tensions continued as each sought to navigate the changed context.[28] Women from the former Soviet bloc did not form a homogenous group – their histories under communism varied greatly – but they shared transitioning from socialism within changed and diverse contexts. At home women had to stand up against allegations that feminism was a 'leftover' from communism, explaining it as

---

[24] Martha Alter Chen, 'Engendering World Conferences: The International Women's Movement and the United Nations' (1995) 16 *Third World Quarterly* 477.

[25] 'These conferences – on environment, human rights, population, social development, women, habitat, children, HIV/AIDS, small island states, food security, racism – and their five- and 10-year reviews have provided a unique opportunity for negotiating a progressive social agenda in a systematic and ongoing way': Gita Sen, 'Neolibs, Neocons and Gender Justice: Lessons from Global Negotiations' UNRISD, Occasional Paper 9, 2005.

[26] Boutros Boutros-Ghali, closing statement: Beijing Report (n 2) 208–209.

[27] Gita Sen (n 25).

[28] Laura Busheikin, 'Is Sisterhood Really Global? Western Feminism in Eastern Europe' in Tanya Renne (ed), *Ana's Land: Sisterhood in Eastern Europe* (Westview Press, 1997).

an evolving and mobilising response to the ambivalent effects of the new regimes on women's lives. They were simultaneously being accused of being co-opted by Western feminism and seeking to resist Western feminists' attempts to define feminism for them.[29] Women's NGOs were flourishing but women were excluded from renewed political life, their part in overturning the previous regimes was discounted and a return to the public/private divide imposed.[30] A related tenson in some countries was what the revival of both religion and nationalism meant for women. Polish feminists for instance, challenged their government's conformity with the views of the Catholic church and depiction of women as primarily located within the family.[31] Women from many areas within the region feared curtailment of sexual and reproductive rights, including access to abortion.

Women from Eastern and Central Europe were unable to prepare a draft regional PFA as theirs was a UN spatial 'non-region',[32] albeit one that was seen as 'becoming' Western through democratisation and free market economics in a post-Cold War replay of the 'civilising mission'. Women from these regions felt displaced, not fitting easily with the objectives of either the Global North or South[33] and excluded from the global conversation on women's human rights.[34] They prepared a 'Statement from a Non-Region' in which they declared their most serious problem to be 'the consistent and drastic decline in the status of women'.[35]

The end of super-power rivalry shifted the transnational feminist dialogue to that between women from the Global South and those from the Global North, with diverse priorities and agendas within all such groupings. The African women's movement had built upon the lessons learned and networking achieved since Nairobi, as well as responding to conflicts and violence in many parts of the continent. Gaps in the FLS and critical areas of concern, identified at national and regional levels, constituted the core of the African PFA:[36] women's poverty, food insecurity and lack of economic empowerment; inadequate access to education, training, and technology; women's role in culture, family, and socialisation; programmes for improvement in health; women's relationship to the environment; involvement in peace processes; political empowerment; legal and human rights; mainstreaming of gender-disaggregated data; communication, information, and the arts; and the girl child were core areas of concern.[37]

---

[29] ibid.

[30] Magdalena Grabowska, 'Bringing the Second World In: Conservative Revolution(s), Socialist Legacies, and Transnational Silences in the Trajectories of Polish Feminism Author(s)' (2012) 37 *Signs* 385.

[31] Jennifer Ramme, 'Exclusion through Inclusion. Struggles over the Scalar Regimes of Belonging Europe and the Family at the 1995 Fourth UN World Conference on Women and the Agency of (Polish) Women' (2019) 4 *Frontiers in Sociology* 1.

[32] Regional platforms for Beijing were prepared in Asia and the Pacific, Latin America and the Caribbean, North America and Europe, Western Asia, and Africa.

[33] One participant at Beijing explained: 'We were nobody, we were not identified, nobody, nobody knew at that time who we are, even we didn't know who we are', cited in Jennifer Ramme (n 31).

[34] Jennifer Suchland, 'Is Post-colonialism Transnational?' (2011) 36 *Signs* 837.

[35] Magdalena Grabowska (n 30) 408.

[36] Preparation for and Follow-Up to Regional and International Conferences and Programmes of Action [I]E/ECA/CM.21/6 (Part I), 15 March 1995.

[37] African states made the girl child a critical area of concern: Nomtuse Mbere, 'The Beijing Conference: a South African Perspective' (1996) 16 *SAIS Review of International Affairs* 167.

There was significant political, economic, social and cultural change in the Asia-Pacific region since 1985,[38] but also considerable diversity. There were both democratic and authoritarian governments. Some countries were in transition from centrally planned to market economies (the 'Stans'); some had high economic growth while others were undertaking far-reaching economic restructuring and structural adjustment programmes. In the Pacific region[39] there was continued anger over the effects of nuclear testing.[40] Despite the conclusion of some intra- and inter-state conflicts, there was continuing violence in, inter alia, Tajikistan, East Timor, Aceh, the Chittagong Hill Tracts, and Bougainville with women frequently the targets of violence. HIV/AIDS was an issue of particular concern to women with sex tourism, migration and a growing international sex and drug trade fuelling commercialisation of prostitution in the region. The conference location in China created challenges for women and their supporters from other Asian regions, especially Tibet and Taiwan, many of whom were denied visas or approval for attendance by ECOSOC, apparently influenced by the Chinese government. Critical areas of concern for women across Asia and the Pacific were:[41] feminisation of poverty; economic inequalities; inadequate recognition of women's role in environmental and natural resource management; inequitable access to power and decision-making; women's human rights; health; education. Attention was also directed towards women's participation in peace-building, peace education and research.[42]

Women from Central and South America and the Caribbean reflect the region's historical, social and economic complexity and diversity.[43] In 1985 the region was suffering the adverse impacts of structural adjustment programmes and debt but by Beijing recovery was underway. Transition to democracy following the end of military and authoritarian regimes in many countries generated optimism for reform, with women exploring the 'potential and limits of post-authoritarian democracies as vehicles for the promotion of greater gender justice'.[44] Poverty and inequalities persisted, especially among indigenous and rural women, as well as ongoing conflict in some areas.

---

[38] ESCAP, Jakarta Declaration for the Advancement of Women in Asia and the Pacific, Second Asian and Pacific Ministerial Conference on Women in Development, 7–14 June 1994, para 1.
[39] Women from Pacific countries prepared extensive documentation for the NGO forum, telling their stories and articulating their concerns to enable them to use the outcomes to improve their lives: International Women's Development Agency, 'Beneath Paradise: The Pacific Women's Documentation Project' 1995.
[40] 'Nuclear radiation and the incineration of stockpiles of chemical weapons have also had an adverse impact on the environment, particularly in the Pacific': ibid para 10.
[41] ESCAP, Jakarta Declaration (n 38).
[42] ibid 46–47.
[43] The Coordinator of the Latin American and Caribbean NGO Forum, Virginia Vargas, described the 'concrete face' of diversity in the region as 'black women, lesbian women, indigenous women, disabled women, refugee women, displaced women, persecuted women, young women, old women, imprisoned women, women of occupied and dependent territories, and women living under economic blockade mobilize ... and demand of the world their right to have rights' at https://www.un.org/esa/gopher-data/conf/fwcw/conf/ngo/14123221.txt.
[44] Maxine Molyneux and Nikki Craske, 'The Local, the Regional and the Global: Transforming the Politics of Rights!' in Nikki Craske and Maxine Molyneux (eds), *Gender and the Politics of Rights and Democracy in Latin America* (Palgrave, 2002) 1.

Work on women's human rights and democracy flourished within national and regional institutions[45] and, as elsewhere, civil society groups increased post-Nairobi.[46] A distinctive feature of the regional landscape was the regular meetings of women and women's NGOs in what are termed '*encuentros*', described as 'highlighting the key strategic, organizational, and theoretical debates that have characterized the political trajectory of contemporary Latin American feminisms'.[47] Participants gathered from diverse public spaces – 'lesbian-feminist collectives to trade unions, landless movements, research and service nongovernmental organizations (NGOs), university women's studies programs, revolutionary organizations, main-stream political parties, and state institutions'. The 1993 *encuentro* saw disagreements about the desirability of NGO participation in Beijing: concerns were expressed about how this might threaten the independence of the feminist movement, especially since the United States Agency for International Development was funding NGO participation at Beijing. This fuelled deep-rooted antagonisms about American interventions in the region and raised apprehension that such funding 'might politically compromise, or worse, come to control, the feminist agenda'.[48]

Preparations for Beijing did go ahead across the region under the auspices of UNIFEM, with numerous meetings at local, national and regional levels. The Inter-American Commission of Women prepared the Strategic Plan of Action which was adopted by the Assembly of Delegates in 1994 for presentation at Beijing. Four topics were prioritised: women's participation in power and decision-making structures; education; elimination of violence; and eradication of poverty. The region adopted the first treaty on the eradication of violence against women,[49] recognising 'the critical link between women's access to adequate judicial protection when denouncing acts of violence, and the elimination of the problem of violence and the discrimination that perpetuates it'.[50]

Women across the Global South met within their own regional networks and held inter-regional workshops before Beijing. For example the delegate from one such organisation, GROOTS (Grassroots Organisations Operating Together in Sisterhood) told the government conference that they had held 70 grassroots forum meetings around the world and through focal points across continents.[51] She argued

---

[45] The Organization of American States continued to pioneer combating discrimination against women and VAWG. In 1994 the Inter-American Commission on Human Rights (IACommHR) decided to prepare a report on *de jure* and *de facto* discrimination against women within member state legal systems: Annual Report of the IACommHR 1995, OEA/Ser.L./V/II.91 Doc 7 rev, 28 February 1996, ch 5.

[46] eg CLADEM, a feminist campaigning NGO established in 1987 to promote women's access to rights and bring women's human rights onto the agendas of political institutions. CLADEM works in 16 of the region's countries as well as within communities and with social movement organisations.

[47] Sonia E Alvarez et al, 'Encountering Latin American and Caribbean Feminisms' (2003) 28 *Signs* 537, 539.

[48] ibid 552.

[49] Inter-American Convention on the Prevention, Punishment and Eradication of Violence against Women, 1994 (Convention of Belém do Pará).

[50] IACommHR, Rapporteurship on the Rights of Women, Access to Justice for Women Victims of Violence in the Americas, para 33.

[51] Dr Nandini Azad, Chairperson, GROOTS Delegation at https://www.un.org/esa/gopher-data/conf/fwcw/conf/ngo/14120137.txt.

for strategies 'to radically transform structures that ... favour markets over people, the rich over the poor, men over women, short term advantage over sustainable development, and commodities over communities'. GROOTS' priorities were to hold macro institutions accountable and to address poverty through empowered participation and to make micro institutions – the family and community – democratic, gender equitable and sustainable. DAWN,[52] another NGO active in South-South dialogue, sought new alternatives to global capitalism through 'the development of a holistic human potential' as the goal of economic growth.[53] Despite the complexities of the changed (and changing) economic and political environment, DAWN saw optimism in the prolific, better organised women's movements that had become more skilled in challenging governments and international agencies. Its Beijing manifesto argued for an engendered human development, with social movements and women's organisations playing the role of 'autonomous watchdogs' over governments and public and private international agencies 'to provide alternative models of development organizations that work for women, and to catalyse and challenge other movements to address issues of patriarchy and gender power'.

Despite unifying activities by NGOs such as DAWN, solidarity between women in the Global South was not stable amidst growing economic disparities. Regional inequalities lessened the capacity and political will for effective joint negotiations. Other actors sought to exploit these differences. Just as the USSR and the US had each sought to assert its influence in the then-Third World during the Decade, at Beijing religious conservatives sought to champion the South by working with them against what was perceived as a Northern feminist agenda. Hardline economic positions taken by some Northern states on issues such as the right to development, debt reduction, trade and financing allowed for apparent common cause on economic and social justice between actors with otherwise seemingly disparate interests.[54] The Holy See, for instance, sought alignment with Global South women through its endorsement of economic justice, women's workplace rights, healthcare needs and eradication of violence against women.[55] Its assertion of 'family values' confronted Northern-based feminists,[56] although it also received support from Northern pro-family and parental rights organisations.[57] It reiterated its position from the Cairo Conference on Population and Development (and from throughout the Decade) that abortion services are not part of reproductive health or reproductive

---

[52] See essay 5 'Peace in the UN Decade for Women'.
[53] *Markers on the Way: The DAWN Debates on Alternative Development DAWN's Platform for the Fourth World Conference on Women* (Beijing, September 1995).
[54] Gita Sen (n 25).
[55] Written statement by the representative of the Holy See, Beijing Report (n 2) 158–62; see also statement to the Beijing conference by Jeanne Head, representative of the International Right to Life Federation, who emphasised women's need for 'basic security such as housing, medical care before and after pregnancy', educational opportunities, protection from physical or mental abuse, and societal respect' while speaking out against abortion: https://www.un.org/esa/gopher-data/conf/fwcw/conf/ngo/11174846.txt.
[56] Naila Kabeer, 'Tracking the Gender Politics of the Millennium Development Goals: Struggles for Interpretive Power in the International Development Agenda' (2015) 36 *Third World Quarterly* 377.
[57] eg International Coordinator of Associations in Beijing, 'Betrayal in Beijing', 1995, Wendy Thomas, Papers from the Fourth World Conference on Women; 2003-M118, carton 1, folder 'Family, Motherhood, Conservative Women', Schlesinger Library, Radcliffe Institute, Harvard University, Cambridge, Mass.

health services, and its 'well-known position … concerning family planning services that do not respect the liberty of spouses, the human dignity or the human rights of those concerned'.[58] The Holy See associated itself with the preferred language of 'reproductive health' of feminists from the Global South over that of 'reproductive rights' of Northern-based feminists.[59] It lobbied the UN to deny accreditation to Catholic NGOs that opposed its position on contraception and abortion[60] and rejected language relating to gender.[61]

Regional affiliations and broad coalitions were not the only factors that brought women together, or divided them, at Beijing. Multiple other alliances and networks that cut across spatial lines – such as rural women, peasant women, women with disabilities,[62] co-religionists – formed, re-formed and shifted. American women of African descent from the US, South America and the Caribbean prepared for Beijing through their own networks to ensure recognition of the intersection of race and gender. A representative told the governmental conference that a global strategy for women must include the 'expertise, knowledge and strength of African American Women and women of color' to eradicate the racism and discrimination that 'permeate the development of global society'.[63] Building upon the long history of Black women's activism in the US and internationally,[64] African-American women formed their own caucus and aligned in some ways more with women from the Global South than with other Americans. Circumstantial differences between the lived experiences of women in the US and those of women in Africa meant that such alignment was not necessarily reciprocated. Black women from Latin America and the Caribbean sought to share their own experiences within the wider regional feminist movement and in 1992 convened their own *encuentro* in the Dominican Republic, for dialogue, strategising, and celebration.[65]

Indigenous women similarly felt marginalised in feminist movements. In Latin America the Beijing preparatory process provided the catalyst for sustained regionwide meetings of Indigenous women[66] and for seeking their own space at Beijing, a position shared by Indigenous women from other regions.[67] In their Beijing Declaration, Indigenous women identified themselves as 'Daughters of Mother Earth' as well as 'citizens of colonial and neo-colonial countries, as women and as members of the

---

[58] Written statement, Holy See (n 55) 158–62.
[59] Naila Kabeer (n 56).
[60] Yasmin Abdullah, 'The Holy See at United Nations Conferences: State or Church?' (1996) 96 *Columbia Law Review* 1835.
[61] See essay 2 'Gender'.
[62] Maria Rantho, Deputy Chairperson Disabled Peoples' International at https://www.un.org/esa/gopher-data/conf/fwcw/conf/ngo/11175142.txt. Accounts describe the difficulties faced by women in wheelchairs in the mud and uneven ground at Huairou.
[63] Statement to the Fourth World Conference on Women Document Submitted by National Council of Negro Women at https://www.un.org/esa/gopher-data/conf/fwcw/conf/ngo/14170040.txt.
[64] Linda Sheryl Greene, 'African-American Women on the World Stage: The Fourth World Conference on Women in Beijing' in Jeremy Levitt, *Black Women and International Law: Deliberate Interactions, Movements and Actions* (Cambridge University Press, 2015).
[65] Sonia E Alvarez et al (n 47) 565.
[66] ibid.
[67] Rauna Kuokkanen, 'Self-Determination and Indigenous Women's Rights at the Intersection of International Human Rights' (2012) 34 *Human Rights Quarterly* 225.

poorer classes of society'.[68] They explained how they continue to protect and transmit their own indigenous cosmovision, science and technologies, arts and culture and socio-political economic systems that exist 'in harmony with the natural laws of mother earth'. They rejected the 'new world order' which was being viciously forced upon them at the instance of rich industrialised states, transnational corporations and the IFIs. The Declaration of Indigenous Women criticises the PFA[69] for its failure to identify where policies and practices of these entities were responsible for the harms inflicted and for the 'overemphasis on gender discrimination and gender equality which depoliticizes issues confronting Indigenous women'.[70] The Declaration backs its detailed critique of the PFA with a series of demands, including for political, economic and cultural self-determination, respect for human and territorial rights, an end to violence against women, and participation.[71]

Another grouping that spanned regions and geopolitical interests was that of lesbians. Sexual orientation and gender identity remained divisive within UN fora before, at Beijing,[72] and subsequently. Homosexuality was criminalised in China and the Chinese government withheld visas from some lesbian groups and harassed others who came to Beijing.[73] A lesbian caucus hosted workshops, film screenings and discussions. Lesbians lobbied the official conference,[74] where a young South African spoke of the violence, harassment and discrimination experienced by lesbians because of their sexual orientation. She explained that free determination of sexuality is essential to women's self-determination and to 'address the concerns of all women' the conference must 'recognize that discrimination based on sexual orientation is a violation of basic human rights'.[75] Several governments proposed inclusion of sexual orientation in the forms of prohibited discrimination in the PFA. Ultimately – following acrimonious discussion on the final day – sexual orientation

---

[68] Beijing Declaration of Indigenous Women, NGO Forum, UN Fourth World Conference on Women, Huairou, http://www.ipcb.org/resolutions/htmls/dec_beijing.html (Beijing Declaration of Indigenous Women). See also Declaration of the Second International Indigenous Women's Conference, 1990; Kari-Oca Declaration and Indigenous Peoples' Earth Charter, World Conference of Indigenous Peoples on Territory, Environment and Development, 1992, para 29 ('Indigenous women's rights must be respected. Women must be included in all local, national, regional and international organizations').

[69] eg Beijing Declaration of Indigenous Women (n 68) paras 10–16, Critique of the Beijing Draft Platform for Action: it fails to 'present a coherent analysis of why it is that the goals of "equality development and peace" become more elusive to women each day in spite of three UN conferences on women since 1975'.

[70] ibid para 16.

[71] The draft Declaration on the Rights of Indigenous Peoples was approved in 1994 by the Sub-Commission on the Prevention of Discrimination and Protection of Minorities and adopted by the UNGA in 2007: UNGAR 61/295, 13 September 2007. Art 22 seeks 'particular attention … to the rights and special needs of indigenous elders, women, youth, children and persons with disabilities' and requires states to 'take measures, in conjunction with indigenous peoples, to ensure that indigenous women and children enjoy the full protection and guarantees against all forms of violence and discrimination'.

[72] Charlotte Bunch, 'Opening Doors for Feminism: UN World Conferences on Women' (2012) 24 *Journal of Women's History* 213.

[73] Tingting Wei, 'A Look at the Beijing Conference through Lesbian Eyes' (2015) 21 *Asian Journal of Women's Studies* 316.

[74] Lesbian Caucus Recommendations, 'Sexual Orientation in the Platform for Action', 4 September 1995.

[75] Palesa Beverley Ditsie, International Gay and Lesbian Human Rights Commission, United Nations Fourth World Conference on Women, Beijing, 13 September 1995 at https://www.un.org/esa/gopher-data/conf/fwcw/conf/ngo/13123944.txt.

was not included,[76] although paragraph 96 states that the 'human rights of women include their right to have control over and decide freely and responsibly on matters related to their sexuality, including sexual and reproductive health, free of coercion, discrimination and violence'. While less than had been hoped for, it was 'another milestone in the journey for recognition of sexual rights'.[77]

IV. PEACE IN THE BEIJING DECLARATION AND PLATFORM FOR ACTION

In 1969, CSW moved from considering women only in peacetime conditions[78] to taking up their situation in times of emergency and war. It expressed the hope that the International Committee of the Red Cross would include more women in missions to war torn or occupied territories and appealed to women everywhere 'to make every effort to contribute, in their families and in their communities, to the establishment of peace and justice and towards finding a just solution to armed conflicts'.[79] The resolution was described as 'strictly humanitarian', a compromise response to CSW's aspiration to provide safeguards for women in occupied or war torn territories.[80] On CSW's recommendation the UNGA adopted its 1974 Declaration on the Protection of Women and Children in Emergency and Armed Conflict.[81] The Declaration conveyed awareness of the suffering of women and children in armed conflict, describing them as the 'most vulnerable members of the population'. It sought greater protection for women without specifying any gendered harms. In line with other Cold War instruments, the context was colonial and racist domination, a perspective repeated in a 1978 CSW resolution,[82] without reference to gender.

As the third of the objectives of the UN Decade for Women, peace was addressed in a separate section in the final documents of each of the three Decade conferences. During the Cold War peace was politicised, associated with and claimed by the USSR as core to its foreign policy, supporting those seeking self-determination from Western imperialism.[83] The demise of the USSR provided the 'opportunity … to achieve the great objectives of the Charter', taken up by the UN Secretary-General in his Agenda for Peace.[84] Although he acknowledged the forthcoming conference

---

[76] On the final day, at the instance of the Chair of the main working group, the four references to sexual orientation in the PFA were 'deleted in a "trade" with another unresolved issue: whether cultural relativity would be allowed to modify the universality of the application of human rights standards': Dianne Otto, 'Lesbians? Not in My Country' (1995) 20 *Alternative Law Journal* 288.

[77] Charlotte Bunch, 'Opening Doors for Feminism' (n 72).

[78] CSW noted that the Tehran World Conference on Human Rights, 1968, Resolution I was on human rights in occupied territories and Resolution XXIII on human rights in armed conflicts: CSW, Report on the 22nd Session, 27 January–12 February 1969, E/4619 E/CN.6/527, 16.

[79] Resolution 4 (XXII), Protection of women and children in emergency or war time, fighting for peace, national liberation and independence, CSW, Report on the 22nd Session: ibid 66.

[80] ibid para 47.

[81] UNGAR 3318 (XXIX), 14 December 1974.

[82] Resolution 7 (XXVII) Protection of women and children in emergency and armed conflict or war time in the struggle for peace, self-determination, national liberation and independence; CSW, Report on the 27th Session, 20 March–5 April 1978, E/1978/32/Rev.1; E/CN.6/620/Rev. 1, 58.

[83] See essay 3 'Peace in International Law' and essay 5 'Peace in the UN Decade for Women'.

[84] An Agenda for Peace (n 18) para 3.

on women,[85] neither the Agenda for Peace nor its 1995 Supplement[86] discuss the gendered nature of conflict and offer no gendered analysis of the concept or practice of peace.

Peace remained within the articulated objectives of the Beijing conference – equality, development and peace – but unlike the Nairobi FLS[87] the PFA has no heading 'Peace', which was now fragmented across women in armed conflict[88] and less explicitly in those relating to violence against women[89] and human rights.[90] Peace was seen as devalued by governments.[91] At the NGO forum, women's peace organisations, notably WILPF, ensured a 'peace caucus'[92] and followed the 1985 Nairobi NGO forum in organising a peace tent where issues such as demilitarisation and disarmament and their direct relevance to women's lives were the subject of workshops and other activities.[93] Unlike NGOs, it seems that 'governments never intended to seriously open issues of peace for discussion at a "women's" conference'[94] and the contestations over gender and sexuality in the PFA excluded any concept of a gendered peace. But in terms of achieving internal and external peace for all women, commitment to and implementation of the entire PFA is essential.

A. Beijing Declaration

The Beijing Declaration is an aspirational expression of key commitments for the realisation of equality, development and peace. It optimistically asserts the attainability of '[l]ocal, national, regional and global peace' that is 'inextricably linked' with women's advancement. Women have agency in that they are 'a fundamental force for … promotion of lasting peace at all levels',[95] while states are determined to 'take positive steps to ensure peace for the advancement of women'.[96] Recognising

---

[85] ibid para 5.
[86] Supplement to an Agenda for Peace (n 18).
[87] The FLS has 44 paragraphs (232–76) on peace, comprising obstacles, strategies, women living under apartheid, Palestinian women, women in conflict zones, intervention and threats to peace, and measures for implementation of strategies for peace at the national level.
[88] Beijing PFA (n 2) paras 131–49.
[89] 'Violence against women is an obstacle to the achievement of the objectives of equality, development and peace': ibid para 112.
[90] 'Whereas recognition of the inherent dignity and of the equal and inalienable rights of all members of the human family is the foundation of freedom, justice and peace in the world': UNGAR 217 A, 10 December 1948, Universal Declaration of Human Rights.
[91] 'We are concerned that the Platform for Action undervalues the role of peace in advancing equality and development': Statement to the United Nations Fourth World Conference on Women by WILPF on Behalf of the NGO Peace Caucus at https://www.un.org/esa/gopher-data/conf/fwcw/conf/ngo/12140933.txt.
[92] WILPF defined peace as 'an environment within which every individual can realize her or his fullest creative potential, within which technological achievements are balanced by complementary, moral and ethical advancements': ibid.
[93] Catia Cecilia Confortini, *Intelligent Compassion: The Women's International League for Peace and Freedom and Feminist Peace* (Oxford University Press, 2012).
[94] Dianne Otto, 'Holding up Half the Sky, but for Whose Benefit: Critical Analysis of the Fourth World Conference on Women' (1996) 6 *Australian Feminist Law Journal* 7, 24.
[95] Beijing Declaration (n 2) para 18.
[96] ibid para 28.

women's 'leading role'[97] in the peace movement, states' resolve extends to working actively towards 'general and complete disarmament under strict and effective international control' and supporting negotiations for a 'universal and multilaterally and effectively verifiable comprehensive nuclear-test-ban treaty' contributing long-term to nuclear disarmament and non-proliferation of nuclear weapons.[98] The Declaration then turns to prevention and elimination of violence against women without reference to armed conflict other than to ensuring 'respect for international humanitarian law to protect women and girls in particular'.[99]

B. Women and Armed Conflict

Peace in the PFA is brought within critical area of concern E: women and armed conflict – an implicit assumption of the inevitability of conflict and of women as targeted victims of violence and needing protection. The widespread and systematic sexual violence perpetrated in the 'new wars' of the 1990s made the prevention of and protection against such violence the priority of women activists,[100] not permanent peace as was the case for the women at the Hague. The section nevertheless commences with an expansive understanding of world peace and its inextricable linkage with equality between women and men. It provides a wide-ranging sweep of the obstacles to human rights attainment worldwide – economic and social as well as civil and political.[101] As at the Vienna World Conference on Human Rights, it collapses the boundary between the legal regimes of international humanitarian law (IHL) and international human rights law[102] and notes how the former is at times systematically ignored and the latter violated in armed conflict. It condemns the 'abhorrent practices' inflicted on women in conflict and insists that perpetrators be punished.

The first recommendation to governments and international and regional institutions is again for increased participation of women in conflict resolution. Women have demanded equal participation in political life for well over a century; this was repeated, and acknowledged, throughout the Decade[103] and confirmed for states parties in CEDAW, articles 7 and 8. Strategic objective E.1 addresses gender balance (increased numbers of women participants and appointments in international bodies) and the inclusion of a gender perspective in all such processes. No explanation is offered for why women's 'full involvement' in conflict prevention and resolution processes is deemed essential for the maintenance of international peace and security; the inherent association of women with peace is again simply

---

[97] ibid.
[98] See essay 7 'Women, Disarmament and Peace'.
[99] Beijing Declaration (n 2) para 33.
[100] See essay 13 'Strategic Practice: Peace and Equality through International Law'.
[101] Beijing PFA (n 2) para 131.
[102] ibid para 132: 'The Vienna Declaration and Programme of Action, adopted by the World Conference on Human Rights, states that "violations of the human rights of women in situations of armed conflict are violations of the fundamental principles of international human rights and humanitarian law"'.
[103] See essay 5 'Peace in the UN Decade for Women'.

assumed and promoted.[104] There is no road map for its achievement or any challenge to existing structural inequalities; women are to be accorded 'equal access and full participation ... in [existing] power structures'.[105]

Strategic objective E.2 reiterates another long-held demand of women's peace activism: reduction in military expenditures. The 1915 Women's Congress had observed that 'private profits accruing from the great armament factories' constituted a powerful hindrance to the abolition of war. Women have sought diversion of military budgets to economic and social needs. In the PFA this objective is weakened by qualifying 'weasel' words.[106] Released monies may allow for the 'possible allocation of additional funds for social and economic development, in particular for the advancement of women'. With a nod to the 'the leading role that women have played in the peace movement', the PFA calls for governments to 'work actively towards general and complete disarmament under strict and effective international control'. The continued existence of nuclear weapons is, however, assumed through the call to support negotiations for a verifiable comprehensive nuclear test ban treaty and for restraint in nuclear testing. Wording in the Draft PFA calling for states to commit to promoting the 'elimination of all weapons of mass destruction, especially nuclear weapons' did not make the final document. Several paragraphs address the deleterious effect on women and children of the indiscriminate use of landmines.[107] And, somewhat strangely placed between two paragraphs addressing military expenditures, is the requirement to investigate and punish perpetrators of acts of violence – in particular rape and other forms of sexual violence – against women in armed conflict.

Strategic objective E.3 focuses on non-violent forms of conflict resolution – the peaceful settlement of disputes – and on reducing human rights violations in conflict. It reaffirms principles of IHL and human rights law appertaining to crimes of sexual violence and for the protection of women against such crimes. Much of the language derives from article 27 of the Fourth Geneva Convention ('rape, forced prostitution and any other form of indecent assault') and reaffirms rape as a war crime, crime against humanity and genocidal, where the other conditions for these crimes are satisfied. The need for 'assistance' to and 'redress' for victims of such abuse is specified.

The PFA implicitly feminises the Secretary-General's Agenda for Peace through its calls for women's representation in decision-making with respect to 'peace-keeping, preventive diplomacy and related activities'. The political tensions that resonated throughout the Decade are recalled through the inclusion of matters of general concern without expressly relating them to women, for instance self-determination of all peoples and manifestations of terrorism. The adoption of unilateral measures

---

[104] Charlesworth notes the ambivalent approach between women's difference (women as 'good at peace') and women's right to equality in participation: Hilary Charlesworth, 'Are Women Peaceful? Reflections on the Role of Women in Peace-Building' (2008) 16 *Feminist Legal Studies* (2008) 347.
[105] Inclusion of women in existing political and social structures of power rather than challenging those structures is a recurring theme throughout the PFA; eg, critical area of concern G, women in power and decision-making; strategic objective J1 seeking to increase women's participation in decision-making in and through the media.
[106] See essay 7 'Women, Disarmament and Peace'.
[107] The Landmines Convention was concluded on 18 September 1997.

(sanctions) that undermine the right to an adequate standard of living for women and children is rejected as 'food and medicine must not be used as a tool for political pressure'.[108] Women's contribution to fostering a culture of peace is promoted through encouragement of education and training, peace research and identification of innovative mechanisms for containing violence and for conflict resolution.[109]

Neither peace nor a culture of peace[110] is defined in the PFA, although placing them within the rubric of women and armed conflict implicates a narrow understanding of negative peace – absence of conflict. It acknowledges that 'some situations of armed conflict' originate in colonialism and its perpetuation through 'state and military repression'[111] but does not locate violence and conflict in the history of Western (or Soviet) imperialism or in ongoing aggressive actions on indigenous land by transnational corporations and governments.[112] No measures are recommended for addressing violations of and obstacles to enjoyment of human rights that constitute obstacles to peace. Indeed, once peace is no longer accorded its own heading there seems to be ambivalence as to where it belongs: at Vienna it was addressed primarily in the context of human rights education[113] but at Beijing there is no explicit cross-reference to peace within critical area of concern I on 'Human rights of women'. Disarmament – a component of peace throughout the Decade – was brought within human rights discourse at the Tehran World Conference on Human Rights[114] and through its inclusion in CEDAW, but at Beijing was subsumed within women and armed conflict. And although violence against women is recognised as instilling 'fear and insecurity in women's lives' and as an 'obstacle to the achievement of equality and for development and peace',[115] it is not spelled out that there can be no peace for women while gender-based violence continues in all societies. Rather than providing a tool to wage against patriarchy, the PFA was less ambitiously a roadmap for how to live within patriarchy without subverting its structures and forms of power: militarism; the arms trade; and nuclear policies.

V. POST-BEIJING: WOMEN AND PEACE AND SECURITY

Following Beijing there were some concrete steps at the national and institutional level. For instance, between 1995 and 2000 18 states became parties to CEDAW and the Optional Protocol to CEDAW[116] was completed.[117] In 1997 UN Secretary-General,

---

[108] Beijing PFA (n 2) para 145(h). See also CESCR, General Comment No 8 (1997), The relationship between economic sanctions and respect for economic, social and cultural rights, E/C.12/1997/8, 12 December 1997.
[109] Beijing PFA (n 2) para 146.
[110] See essay 3 'Peace in International Law'.
[111] Beijing PFA (n 2) para 131.
[112] Beijing Declaration of Indigenous Women (n 68).
[113] Vienna Declaration and Programme of Action (n 102) para 80: 'Human rights education should include peace, democracy, development and social justice'.
[114] Final Act of the International Conference on Human Rights, Tehran, Resolution XVI: Disarmament.
[115] Beijing PFA (n 2) paras 112, 117.
[116] Beijing PFA (n 2) para 230(k) urges support for an optional protocol to CEDAW.
[117] Rebecca Cook, 'Effectiveness of the Beijing Conference Advancing International Law Regarding Women' (1997) 91 *Proceedings American Society of International Law* 310.

Kofi Annan, appointed Angela King to the new position of Special Adviser on Gender Issues and Advancement of Women, at the level of Assistant Secretary-General. She became the leading advocate for gender equality and promotion of gender mainstreaming throughout the UN system.[118] Other signifiers of progress were the evolving jurisprudence of the ad hoc international criminal tribunals and the adoption of the Rome Statute of the International Criminal Court in 1998 with its listing of specific forms of sexual violence as war crimes and crimes against humanity when other requirements of those crimes are satisfied.[119]

Despite such 'significant positive developments', the UNGA's five-year review acknowledged that 'barriers remain and that the goals set and commitments made in Beijing need to [be] implemented'.[120] Peace remained subsumed within 'women and armed conflict' and all forms of conflict recognised as 'serious obstacles to women's advancement'.[121] Violence against women in armed conflict had increased, displacement 'compounded by loss of home and property, poverty, family disintegration and separation' was severely affecting women and girls; abduction or recruitment of girls as combatants, sexual slaves and/or domestic servants was continuing and women remained underrepresented in decision-making.[122] The concept of women's empowerment had been 'transformed from its original political understanding based on collective action, solidarity, agency and decolonial development models into an individualised, depoliticised and westernised concept'.[123]

Dismay at the absence of women from the Dayton peace process in November 1995 (formally ending the war in Bosnia-Herzegovina two months after Beijing) contributed to NGOs seeking further ways of bringing the gendered dimensions of conflict into international law and institutions.[124] The process leading to the adoption by the SC of Resolution 1325 on Women and Peace and Security (WPS), followed by nine further resolutions,[125] and their content has been described elsewhere.[126] Lobbying for Resolution 1325 was simultaneously an expression of frustration at inadequate implementation of the PFA and of optimism about bringing its strategic objectives relating to women and armed conflict within the authority of the SC. The operative paragraphs of Resolution 1325 reiterate PFA recommendation

---

[118] Mainstreaming is urged throughout the PFA, eg para 231(c): 'Develop a comprehensive policy programme for mainstreaming the human rights of women throughout the United Nations system'; see essay 2 'Gender'.
[119] See essay 13 'Strategic Practice: Peace and Equality through International Law'.
[120] Five-year Review of the implementation of the Beijing Declaration and Platform for Action (Beijing + 5). Outcome of the twenty-third special session of the General Assembly, 'Women 2000: gender equality, development and peace for the twenty-first century', 2000, para 6.
[121] ibid para 16.
[122] ibid para 19.
[123] Farah Daibes, 'How Women in the Global South Reclaim Feminism', *Friedrich Ebert Stiftung blog*, 8 March 2022, https://feminism-mena.fes.de/e/how-women-in-the-global-south-reclaim-feminism.
[124] The omission of gender analysis from the Brahimi report was another indication that the PFA was not being acted upon: Report of the Panel on United Nations Peace Operations, A/55/305–S/2000/809, 21 August 2000.
[125] UNSCR 1820, 19 June 2008; 1888, 30 September 2009; 1889, 5 October 2009; 1960, 16 December 2010; 2106, 24 June 2013; 2122, 18 October 2013; 2242, 13 October 2015; 2467, 23 April 2019; 2493, 29 October 2019.
[126] eg Christine Chinkin, *Women Peace and Security and International Law* (Cambridge University Press, 2022).

E1 – the importance of women's enhanced participation in conflict prevention, management and resolution, call for the integration of a gender perspective into negotiation and implementation of peace processes, and for respect for international law provisions relating to the protection of women and girls in armed conflict – international humanitarian law, human rights law, international criminal law and refugee law. The following nine WPS resolutions supplement the so-called participation pillar, with other pillars for prevention of and protection against rape and sexual violence when 'used or commissioned as a tactic of war' against the civilian population, and for relief and recovery in post-conflict situations. The gender binary is maintained. Gendered stereotypes of women as peace-loving and as victims in need of protection and men as both women's protectors and protagonists of violence are continued without challenge. Women's empowerment is integrated into WPS but is not given substantive content. The WPS resolutions make little concessions to conflict-affected violence against men and boys and none explicitly at the targeting of LGBTQI persons.

WILPF and the Hague Appeal for Peace sought WPS as a feminist peace agenda and women's human rights agenda. WILPF advocated that international actors 'shift how they approach the question of what keeps people safe, requiring re-evaluation and reprioritisation from militarised security to human security'.[127] The PFA's more political provisions that suggested a form of human security – disbursement of military expenditures, disarmament and peaceful dispute settlement – were omitted from Resolution 1325 as compromises were made to secure the SC as a site of engagement for women.[128] But turning to it necessarily entailed its responsibility for the maintenance of international peace and security,[129] understood as militarised security for national defence and peacekeeping operations. Peace is only indirectly addressed in the WPS resolutions, through urging women's participation in conflict prevention.

Resolution 1325 was widely welcomed by feminist scholars and activists but it does not represent feminist peace mainly because its 'dual position of being both an agenda for feminist women and for the UN Security Council', creates a – possibly unresolvable – tension between 'existing international power structures and normative frameworks and the desire to eliminate, or at least reduce, gender inequalities and include women in peacebuilding'.[130] The SC ignored the cry of 'No to militarization; yes to prevention' from the world's women in 2015,[131] instead linking WPS to its militaristic measures for countering terrorism and violent extremism.[132]

---

[127] WILPF, 'UNSCR 1325 at 20 Years: Perspectives from Feminist Peace Activists and Civil Society' (2020).
[128] The NGO Working Group on WPS headed lobbying for Resolution 1325; involved NGOs were not primarily feminist or human rights bodies, although some of the leading individuals were: Jennifer Klot, 'The United Nations Security Council's Agenda on Women, Peace and Security: Bureaucratic Pathologies and Unrealised Potential' (LSE, Doctoral thesis, 2015).
[129] UN Charter, 1945, art 24.
[130] Zeynep Kaya, 'Feminist Peace and Security in the Middle East and North Africa' in *Transforming Power to Put Women at the Heart of Peacebuilding: A Collection of Regional-Focused Essays on Feminist Peace and Security* (Oxfam, 2020) https://oxfamilibrary.openrepository.com/bitstream/handle/10546/621051/dp-feminist-peace-security-essay-collection-210920-en.pdf.
[131] Radhika Coomaraswamy et al, *Preventing Conflict, Transforming Justice, Securing the Peace: A Global Study on the Implementation of Security Council Resolution 1325* (United Nations, 2015) 394.
[132] UNSCR 2242, 13 October 2015.

Institutional divides further the problem. Gender inequality and women's empowerment lie within the remit of the UNGA, its global summits on women and the human rights bodies; security is within that of the SC. The CEDAW Committee has attempted to bridge the two through its recommendation that states implement WPS in accordance with their obligations under CEDAW,[133] but there is no reciprocal bridging by the Council.

Another potential bridge is the UNGA's Sustainable Development Agenda that explicitly reaffirms the Beijing PFA.[134] The UNGA lists peace as an area of critical importance and records states' determination to 'foster peaceful, just and inclusive societies which are free from fear and violence'.[135] The Sustainable Development Goals' emphasis on poverty reduction, gender equality and empowerment within a human rights framework (economic, social and cultural rights as well as civil and political) resonate with a vision of peace freed from the constraints of 'women and armed conflict'. In contrast, the SC's objective appears to be limited to calling for women's participation in conflict prevention, resolution and management and making conflict safer for women and girls through condemning sexual and gender-based violence and requiring reparation. It does not prioritise preventing conflict, advancing women's rights or securing peace.

VI. CONCLUSIONS

The Beijing Declaration and PFA, endorsed by UNGA resolution, form an ambitious blueprint for the empowerment of women worldwide. But this is empowerment within a neoliberal economic framework shorn of a transformative vision. From an international law perspective, these, in common with the final documents of the Decade conferences, are non-legally binding instruments, 'soft law', generating not legal obligation but only political commitment and expectations of compliance. Nor is the WPS agenda in legally binding form; SC resolutions adopted under UN Charter chapter VI are not legally binding on member states under UN Charter article 25.[136] The key principles are not routinely integrated into SC resolutions that mandate specific actions of member states.[137] It seems that states regard soft law forms as most appropriate (or least demanding) for advancing women's claims for equality. For feminist activists, the value of settling for expressions of soft law is debatable. On the one hand, governments can dismiss demands for accountability on the basis of their non-legal status but they are more politically achievable than formal treaty making and are not subject to ratification. States

---

[133] CEDAW Committee, General Recommendation No 30 on women in conflict prevention, conflict and post-conflict situations, CEDAW/C/GC/30, 18 October 2013, paras 25–28.
[134] UNGAR 70/1, Transforming Our World: the 2030 Agenda for Sustainable Development, 21 October 2015, para 11.
[135] ibid.
[136] See Christine Chinkin (n 126) for analysis of the legal significance of the WPS agenda.
[137] Sarah Kenny Werner and Elena Stavrevska, 'Where are the Words? The Disappearance of the Women, Peace and Security Agenda in the Language of Country-Specific UN Security Council Resolutions' (WILPF and LSE Centre for WPS, 2020).

nevertheless still seek to have it both ways by fiercely negotiating text and inserting reservations to non-binding conference documents, as they did with the Beijing PFA, hedging their bets against claims for implementation and accountability for non-implementation.

Soft law may potentially crystallise into customary international law binding on all states through the generation of the two requirements – consistent state practice and *opinio juris*.[138] Certain UNGA resolutions are deemed to carry greater legal weight and the ILC has recognised that conduct generated in accordance with the resolutions of inter-governmental conferences may constitute evidence of state practice or *opinio juris*.[139] The WPS resolutions have spawned institutional practices, over 100 National Action Plans setting out governments' assurances of domestic implementation and further political declarations,[140] which are all relevant for determining the evolution of a rule customary international law.[141] But this is a slow, uncertain and in many ways unsatisfactory process.[142]

Despite over 100 years of feminist activism within first the League and subsequently the UN, instruments relating to women's interests are largely in legally non-binding form[143] – resolutions, declarations, plans and programmes for action, commitments – all of which are readily disregarded when other imperatives prevail. Regardless of legal form, neither the Beijing conference – a global summit that resulted in significant documentation on a range of contemporary issues – nor the substantive influence on the lives of half the world's population have been considered worthy of legal analysis by mainstream international lawyers. It seems extraordinary that such a vast body of principles negotiated by states over four world conferences and their preparatory proceedings should be deemed to carry no legal weight and only limited expectations of compliance. The contemporary abusive use of gender ideology that is fuelling backlash against human rights and women's rights[144] makes it even more important that Beijing and its follow-up in the form of the WPS agenda are recognised for their place in entrenching women's entitlement to equality under international law.

Any legal commitment to the tools for peace – so long the focus of women's activism – was diluted through Beijing where we took our fingers off 'peace' and instead focused on the specificities of violence against women and 'women and armed conflict'. Attention then turned to the SC, seeking to engage that body's authority,

---

[138] ILC, Draft conclusions on identification of customary international law, 2 YBILC (2018) Pt II, Conclusion 2.
[139] ibid Conclusions 6 and 10.
[140] eg G8 Declaration on Preventing Sexual Violence in Conflict, April 2013; Declaration of Commitment to End Sexual Violence in Conflict, 2013; Preventing sexual violence in conflict (PSVI) conference 2022: a political declaration on conflict-related sexual violence.
[141] For a fuller analysis see Christine Chinkin (n 126) ch 2.
[142] This is accepted as having occurred with the prohibition of gender-based violence against women: CEDAW Committee, General Recommendation No 35 on gender-based violence against women, updating General Recommendation No 19, CEDAW/C/GC/35, 26 July 2017, para 2.
[143] CEDAW is of course a legally binding treaty but, despite its near universal acceptance, sex and gender-based discrimination are denied peremptory norm status; essay 5 'Peace in the UN Decade for Women' and essay 2 'Gender'.
[144] See essay 2 'Gender'.

Conclusions 99

but the shift from 'equality, development and peace' to 'women and peace and security' displaced the centrality of both women's rights and peace. Disarmament, another repeated demand of women activists including throughout the four world conferences on women, has no place in the agenda of a SC dominated by the five permanent members, nuclear weapon states and leading participants in the arms trade.

Linkages between peace and women, peace and gender, are piecemeal throughout international law and institutions, reduced at best to stereotypical binaries about women and men: civilians and combatants; protected and protectors; victims and perpetrators. The gender binary is not challenged; queer analysis to break that first binary would undercut these others, opening the way for changing mindsets and reimagining peace.[145]

Peace is not a stand-alone concept in international law. In the UN Charter it is referenced solely in conjunction with security, as is also the case in the SC's WPS agenda. Despite being ostensibly about peace as well as security, SC Resolution 1325 fails to acknowledge that 2000, the year of its adoption, had been proclaimed by the UNGA as the International Year for the Culture of Peace.[146] The ensuing Declaration and Programme of Action on a Culture of Peace presents peace as a 'positive, dynamic participatory process where dialogue is encouraged and conflicts are solved in a spirit of mutual understanding'.[147] The 'culture of peace' is based on and integrally linked to equality between women and men and eliminating discrimination against women. Implementation of the Beijing PFA 'with adequate resources and political will' is sought but the fuller enunciation of peace made throughout the UN Decade for Women is not drawn upon. And when the UNGA eventually adopted its Declaration on the Right to Peace[148] it failed to make a gendered analysis or envisage what peace might mean for women or for non-binary persons. Peace is fragmented across international law and its institutions that fail to join the dots across legal regimes. Through the various instruments there is the material to understand peace through a feminist lens as more than absence of conflict, or even combating conflict-related sexual and gender-based violence and (at least in theory) allowing women to be at the table. But this is not done and peace remains decontextualised, detached from the structural violence of the international legal order. The institutions of international law remain far from embracing any concept of gender equality and thus a gendered, decolonial or anti-racist peace.

---

[145] Dianne Otto (ed), *Queering International Law: Possibilities, Alliances, Complicities, Risks* (Routledge, 2019).
[146] See essay 3 'Peace in International Law'.
[147] UNGAR 53/243, 6 October 1999, Declaration and Programme of Action on a Culture of Peace.
[148] See essay 3 'Peace in International Law'.

7
Women, Disarmament and Peace

I. INTRODUCTION

DISARMAMENT HAS BEEN a core objective of women's peace activism for over a century. Although women have often been at the forefront of progressive change, this history is one that rarely appears in mainstream literature, an absence that is in part explained by the fact that disarmament histories are typically centred on the state, a political space from which women were originally excluded by law. Yet, notwithstanding *de jure* equality, the absence of women in this field persists, a pattern that cannot be explained other than through the prism of gender. Gender systems still operate to nurture the belief that matters pertaining to weapons and – by implication – disarmament, are the preserve of men. The coding of the field as masculine continues to present obstacles to women's equal participation, including in UN multi-lateral disarmament fora.[1] Women's erasure is redoubled by the state-centric bias of disarmament histories, including by international law's histories, that feed into the marginalisation and devaluing of the activities of those engaged in disarmament work *outside* the official parameters of the state, a space typically occupied by women, by necessity and choice.

Women's absence from these histories reflects a broader problem, namely women's absence from historical narratives more generally. Feminist historians have made significant inroads uncovering and producing a wealth of new knowledge that critically engages with mainstream and women's histories, while remaining attentive to the dangers of universalism and exclusion.[2] However, what cannot be undone are the gendered decisions of the past as to what knowledge merited preservation. The non-retention of records pertaining to women's transnational peace activism – such as the eight million signatures collected by women peace activists from across the world and which were presented to the delegates to the 1932 World Disarmament Conference as evidence of women's support for universal and complete disarmament – stands as a reminder of the particular gendered histories

---

[1] Renata Hessmann Dalaqua et al, *Still Behind the Curve: Gender Balance in Arms Control, Nonproliferation and Disarmament Diplomacy* (UNIDIR, 2019).

[2] But 'feminisms are also implicated in and non-innocent in the (failure of) transmission of feminism. Feminists produce some memories and not others, some archives and not others': Niamh Moore, 'Remembering an Eco-feminist Peace Camp' in Catherine Eschle and Alison Bartlett (eds), *Feminisms and Protest Camps: Entanglements, Critiques and Re-imaginings* (Bristol University Press, 2023) 235, 240.

that have been preserved and the functions they perform in shaping contemporary collective identities that feed into the future.[3]

In this essay we retrace women's activism in the field of inter-state disarmament and reflect on how women have engaged with international law to further that agenda. We first outline women's transnational peace activism, from the final years of the nineteenth century until the outbreak of World War II, to uncover the emergence of a distinctive 'feminist' agenda on disarmament as integral to peace and equality. We then turn to women's post-war disarmament activism against the backdrop of the Cold War nuclear arms race, a period that saw women from disparate backgrounds and political traditions unite – domestically and in transnational fora – to oppose nuclear weapons and testing. This period is marked by efforts on the part of women to advance disarmament through international law and its institutions, with mixed results. In the penultimate section we reflect on disarmament through the prism of gender and the implications for feminist activism. Finally, we ask what we can take from 125 years of women's struggles for disarmament in light of the rising trend in global military expenditure and arms sales and the reignited prospect of nuclear war.

II. CRAFTING A DIFFERENT AGENDA

Disarmament strategies adopted by women peace activists at national and international levels have evolved considerably over the last 125 years, as has their engagement with international law as a tool for securing change. The first generation of women peace activists placed enormous faith in international law, regarding it as means by which domestic political resistance to disarmament could be overcome in the interests of inter-state peace. The idea of the international as a site for advancing consensual inter-state disarmament, first proposed by Czar Nicholas II in 1898, was welcomed by women peace activists as a significant breakthrough. Their jubilation was short lived. As is well documented, by the opening of the 1899 Hague Peace (and Disarmament) Conference the revised agenda was dominated by proposals for an international arbitration mechanism and for 'humanising' or regulating warfare, representing, in the words of peace activist Bertha von Suttner, a 'wedge … calculated to rob [the Conference] of its individual character' namely, disarmament.[4]

The 1899 Conference was a turning point for women's transnational peace activism. The decision by the male-led peace movements *not* to focus their efforts on disarmament, but rather to fall in behind states to support an international arbitration mechanism, came as a bitter blow. An arbitration mechanism, the women reasoned, was essential[5] but not at the expense of delaying disarmament. The rise in weapons expenditure, justified by states as advancing security, did not

---

[3] What remains are a handful of photographs, fragments of film footage and an original copy of the petition in the archives of the People's History Museum, Manchester: https://www.lse.ac.uk/women-peace-security/research/Disarmament-Exhibition/Homepage-Women-Weapons-and-Disarmament.

[4] Bertha von Suttner, *Memoires of Bertha Von Suttner: The Records of an Eventful Life* (Ginn and Company, 1910) 228. In 1905 von Suttner became the first woman to be awarded the Nobel Peace Prize.

[5] See essay 13 'Strategic Practice: Peace and Equality through International Law' for a discussion of women's support for arbitration.

reflect women's lived experience. For many, the primary sources of insecurity were their daily economic and social insecurities. The permanent war economy and the diversion of resources from human needs to unproductive military purposes was not only an anathema but founded on a fiction that did not correspond to their reality.

These irreconcilable differences account, at least in part, for the rise in separate women-led peace organisations, enabling them to shape their own distinctive feminist agenda, including over disarmament.[6] In addition to urging for greater attention to be paid to the gendered social cost of the arms race, progressive feminists developed sophisticated critiques of imperialism and militarism that were fuelling the arms race and of the interlinkages with women's oppression. Women were more outspoken in their criticism of governments than their male counterparts and embraced a broader internationalist agenda – often more radical – through cross-border feminist alliances that in some cases bonded them even in war. For example, in April 1915, undeterred by the outbreak of World War I, over a thousand women peace activists from belligerent and neutral states gathered in The Hague despite official resistance and at enormous personal cost.[7] On their return, the delegates from one German city were prosecuted and imprisoned for treason, while very many others were publicly ridiculed in the popular press and castigated and shunned by their fellow citizens not only for their pacifist ideals but as women for failing to conform to dominant gender expectations and stereotypes.[8]

Many women who gathered in The Hague had met before through the International Women's Suffrage Alliance (the primary sponsors of the conference) and recognised the strategic value of co-ordinating transnationally.[9] The resolutions adopted by the women after four days of deliberation were 'visionary' not least for their appeal to international law, which foreshadowed the normative and institutional developments embraced by states over the following century including, for example, the respect for the territorial integrity of states; the right to self-determination; the creation of a permanent international conference and a permanent International Court of Justice; a system of pacific settlement of disputes; and the enfranchisement of women.[10] A permanent international peace required 'the substitution of [international] law for war'.[11] The 'Women and War' resolution, the first of many on the topic that would subsequently be adopted by what became the Women's International

---

[6] Cynthia Cockburn, *Anti MILITARISM: Political and Gender Dynamics of Peace Movements* (Palgrave MacMillan, 2012) 25–27. The creation of women-led collectives as a direct consequence of marginalisation within male-dominated organisations is a pattern that is frequently repeated in time and space: eg Anais Duong-Pedica et al, 'Tracing Kanak Feminist Earthly and Oceanic Paths' 14 December 2021, https://thefunambulist.net/magazine/the-ocean/tracing-kanak-feminist-earthly-and-oceanic-paths.
[7] On other aspects of The Hague Congress see essay 9 'Silence as an Obstacle to Gendered Peace and Equality'; essay 4 'Introduction: Rewriting International Law's Histories'.
[8] See essay 9 'Silence as an Obstacle to Gendered Peace and Equality'.
[9] The Congress was chaired by Jane Addams of the US-based Women's Peace Party, established in early 1915 in response to an appeal by peace activists Emmeline Pethick-Lawrence, from the UK, and Rosika Schwimmer, from Hungary, who had called on US women to protest against the war in Europe. Addams would subsequently co-found the American Civil Liberties Union and the National Association for the Advancement of Colored People.
[10] WILPF, First Congress, The Hague, 1915, 11–16.
[11] Dorothy Hutchinson, 'Political Settlements' WILPF 14th Congress, Stockholm, 1959, 31.

League for Peace and Freedom (WILPF), drew attention to the different and disproportionate impact of conflict on women, thereby laying the conceptual foundations for a gendered understanding of war and peace.[12] The delegates were unambiguous in advocating for 'universal and complete disarmament' as a means to ensure that 'nations would settle their inevitable disputes peaceably' through 'negotiation, mediation, conciliation and judicial settlement'.[13]

Many of WILPF's proposals were subsequently integrated into US President Woodrow Wilson's Fourteen Points,[14] bar equality which was deemed a matter for domestic law. As for disarmament, Wilson proposed a reduction in national armaments 'to the lowest point consistent with domestic safety'. Although less than what WILPF had urged, disarmament was again placed squarely on the international agenda reinforced by the popular belief that the arms race had *created* insecurity, thereby making war inevitable. This reasoning was incorporated into the Covenant of the League of Nations established by the Treaty of Versailles. Article 8 of the Covenant, the first operative article, expressly recognised that 'the maintenance of peace requires the reduction of national armaments to the lowest point consistent with national safety and the enforcement by common action of international obligations'. The League was tasked with advancing international disarmament as its principal aim and was also charged with addressing the regulation of the private sector in the manufacture of arms.[15] While WILPF welcomed these steps, it was hugely critical of the differentiated approach to disarmament adopted in the Treaty of Versailles. Enforced and immediate for the vanquished and consensual and prospective for the victors[16] was not, they argued, conducive to securing a sustainable peace. Instead, activists called for an 'immediate reduction of armaments on the same terms for all member-states' and urged states to go beyond the terms of the Covenant and commit to 'total disarmament (land, sea, air)'.[17]

The inter-war years saw women peace activists coalesce around two objectives: universal disarmament and the regulation of the private arms trade. To more effectively lobby governments the women developed their technical and

---

[12] Recognition that women experienced war differently and were often disproportionally adversely affected was vividly captured in Emily Hobhouse, *The Brunt of War and Where it Fell* (Methuen and Company, 1902).

[13] Gladys Walser, 'World Disarmament and World Development' WILPF 14th Congress, Stockholm, 1959, 34–35; Marie Lous-Mohr, WILPF Chairman, Opening Speech, 12th Congress, Paris, 1953, 11: '[W]e always have worked for total and universal disarmament, because when conflicts are solved through arbitration and law there will be no need for military forces'.

[14] President Wilson praised the resolutions adopted at The Hague 'as by far the best formulation which ... has been put out by anybody': Jo Vellacott, 'A Place for Pacifism and Transnationalism in Feminist Theory: The Early Work of the Women's International League for Peace and Freedom' (1993) 2 *Women's History Review* 23, 28.

[15] Covenant of the League of Nations, art 8: 'The Members of the League agree that the manufacture by private enterprise of munitions and implements of war is open to grave objections. The Council shall advise how the evil effects attendant upon such manufacture can be prevented, due regard being had to the necessities of those Members of the League which are not able to manufacture the munitions and implements of war necessary for their safety.'

[16] Treaty of Peace with Germany (Treaty of Versailles), June 28, 1919, Part V: requiring, as a first step, the disarmament of Germany 'to render possible the initiation of a general limitation of armaments of all nations'.

[17] WILPF, 2nd Congress, Zurich, 1919, 245.

scientific knowledge of weapons and their understanding of international law; organised campaigns to garner public support for disarmament; actively grew their global networks; produced petitions gathering signatures to present to delegates at multilateral disarmament conferences; and organised marches on an unprecedented scale to press for disarmament.[18] As with the 1899 Peace Conference, the League's 1932 World Disarmament Conference represented a turning point in women's disarmament activism. For the first time in history, several states appointed women as official delegates, disrupting entrenched prejudices that had barred women's participation in an area regarded as the exclusive realm of men. Proactive steps were taken by a handful of states to include women's voices into the formal proceedings by extending special status to the Women's Disarmament Committee (WDC), a collective founded by women peace activists comprising 14 women's international organisations and five national organisations, representing over 40 million women from 56 states across the world.[19]

Progress was slow, and by 1935 it was clear to many, including the WDC, that there would be no meaningful agreement on disarmament. Militarism and nationalism were on the rise and fascism and nazism taking root across Europe: the arms race was back on track. That same year the WDC changed its name to the Peace and Disarmament Committee, a gesture that spoke to the frustration with the lack of progress and a rejection of the siloed and decontextualised approach to disarmament prevailing at the time. The recoupling of peace and disarmament opened the way for activists to better interrogate the links between conflict and structural oppressions, develop analyses that sought to address the causes of conflict, and to advance holistic strategies in pursuit of peace, integral to which was disarmament. Universal and total disarmament could not be divorced from the private trade in arms but nor could it be divorced from the forces of militarism, colonialism, and patriarchy, each of which operated to normalise inequalities between and within states, making conflict that much more likely.

Women's transnational peace activism was suspended for much of the war years but was reawakened following the bombings of Hiroshima and Nagasaki in 1945 and the near instant massacre of over 100,000 civilians. For many Western feminist peace activists, achieving world disarmament became more than a matter of peace: it was 'human survival'.[20] Nonetheless, it would be some years before there was a recognition among even the most ardent that 1945 marked the beginning of nuclear warfare, unconstrained by law and directed at those least able to be heard, destroying their bodies, their lands, their way of existence and making spaces uninhabitable for all sentient beings, the effects of which continue to be felt today.[21]

---

[18] See Exhibition at https://bloomsbury.pub/gendered-peace; Louise Arimatsu, 'Transformative Disarmament: Crafting a Roadmap for Peace' (2021) 97 *International Law Studies* 833, 851–54.

[19] The Disarmament Committee of the Women's International Organisation, The Women's Library, LSE, Corbett Ashby archives 7MCA/C/08-09, Box FL484, 1934–1942; Denise Ireton, 'Fighting for Peace in an International City: The Disarmament Committee of the Women's International Organizations in Geneva, 1931–1939' (Alexander Street Archive, 2012).

[20] Cynthia Cockburn, *Anti MILITARISM* (n 6) 49.

[21] In 1986 Maori activist Titewhai Harawira, speaking on behalf of a Pacific women's collective, described the nuclear testing in the Pacific as an undeclared 'nuclear war that we've been forced to live

III. SEEKING MULTIPLE ENTRY POINTS FOR ADVANCING DISARMAMENT

In the immediate aftermath of World War II women's groups made certain that the institutional gains they had secured in the League were not lost with the creation of the United Nations. Several women's organisations, including WILPF, were among the first NGOs to acquire consultative status to the ECOSOC, thereby giving them access to the UNGA and Commission on Human Rights. These institutional footholds, together with the UN Commission on the Status of Women (CSW),[22] provided valuable international platforms to further women's particular concerns. NGOs were however accorded no defined role within the UN's disarmament architecture, meaning that WILPF was unable to advance the case for disarmament within the UN, a shortcoming made even more difficult by Cold War rivalry and the nuclear arms race. The gendered structure of the post-war settlement had thus excluded women from areas coded masculine: institutional inclusion into patriarchy's world was conditional. Unwilling to 'wait idly on the side-lines'[23] women peace activists sought out alternative entry-points to advance disarmament. They would maximise the opportunities presented by the growth of the international – institutional and normative – and would seek to influence public opinion, local and global.

For peace activists, the most difficult obstacle to dislodge has been the revival of the now dominant claim that weapons, including nuclear, are an effective means of guaranteeing peace, as well captured by Winston Churchill's warning to a Joint Session of the US Congress in January 1952 to 'be careful above all things not to let go of the atomic weapon until you are sure, and more than sure, that other means of preserving peace are in your hands'.[24] The UN Charter offers little in support to counter this rationale. Although it is not entirely silent on disarmament,[25] the normative structure of the Charter rests on the competing rationale that it was insecurity between states that fuelled the arms race, and ultimately war, rather than that the growing arms race caused insecurity, leading to war.[26] Accordingly, the Charter centres the prohibition of the use of force and respect for the territorial integrity and sovereignty of states as its two interlinking core values to 'maintain international peace and security'. This has enabled states – and especially those most invested in weapons proliferation – to insist on security as the precondition to disarmament.

---

in for forty years': cited in Catherine Eschle, 'Why Haven't You Known? Transoceanic Solidarity and the Politics of Knowledge in Feminist Anti-nuclear Activism' (2023), https://link.springer.com/article/10.1007/s42597-023-00091-1. Since 1945, at least eight states have detonated over 2,000 nuclear devices at dozens of test sites in lands occupied by indigenous peoples, minorities, and nomadic communities, including the Pacific atolls, the Sahara desert in Algeria, Australia, the South Atlantic, Nevada, Lop Nor in China, Semipalatinsk in Kazakhstan, across Russia and elsewhere.

[22] See essay 5 'Peace in the UN Decade for Women'.
[23] Adelaide Nichols Baker, 'Work with the United Nations at UN Headquarters, New York', WILPF 14th Congress, Stockholm, 1959, 59.
[24] Winston Churchill, British Prime Minister, Address to the US Congress, 17 January 1952.
[25] UN Charter, art 11 grants the UNGA authority to 'consider the general principles of co-operation in the maintenance of international peace and security, including the principles governing disarmament and the regulation of armaments' and to make recommendations; art 26 extends to the SC the responsibility 'for formulating … plans to be submitted to the Members of the United Nations for the establishment of a system for the regulation of armaments'. The P5 states are the world's most weaponised.
[26] In contrast to the League Covenant, art 8 (n 15).

This rationale was challenged, as for instance by the UNGA resolution on 'general and complete disarmament'.[27] The resolution was welcomed by WILPF for reinstating 'general and complete disarmament' as a substantive goal of the international community; for recognising the question of disarmament as 'the most important one facing the world', echoing WILPF's plea to the UNGA to 'consider disarmament as its most pressing task'[28] adopted earlier in the year; and for recognising disarmament as a *means* for achieving 'trust and peaceful co-operation between states', thereby disrupting the Charter's rationale.

For much of the second half of the century, women's activism was shaped by Cold War geopolitics and the schism between nuclear weapons states and those that sought a world free of nuclear weapons.[29] The course of inter-state disarmament was dictated by a narrow class of political elites within the US and USSR (themselves accorded elite status as permanent members of the SC) to the exclusion of most states and, for the most part, women and those directly impacted by nuclear weapon testing. Confronted by the fact that equality in law had done little to unsettle the gendered space of disarmament (nor had it delivered the equal distribution of political power), women sought out allies among some new and emerging states, including those within the Non-Aligned Movement (NAM) which, at the Bandung conference in 1955, had declared that 'universal disarmament is an absolute necessity for the preservation of peace'.[30] In addition to urging for 'disarmament and the prohibition of the production, experimentation and use of nuclear and thermo-nuclear weapons', NAM called on the UN 'to continue its efforts' and for 'all concerned speedily to bring about the regulation, limitation, control and reduction of all armed forces and armaments, including the prohibition of the production, experimentation and use of all weapons of mass destruction, and to establish effective international control to this end'. The inclusion of the Global South into the world of disarmament has fostered regional nuclear free zones,[31] but done little to progress general and complete disarmament or the inclusion of women.[32]

The 1950s rise in nuclear weapons testing by the US, USSR and UK spurred WILPF to seek alternative conduits to press for a ban, including, for example, appealing to the then fledging World Health Organization (WHO) to consider the public health

---

[27] UNGAR 1378 (XIV), 20 November 1959, on general and complete disarmament.

[28] WILPF, 14th Congress, Stockholm, 1959, 92 (reiterating 'that only total and universal disarmament can free the world from war' and urging the UNGA to 'consider disarmament as its most pressing task'). WILPF had been urging the UNGA to prioritise disarmament since at least 1949 and had called for a special session of the GA on disarmament: 11th Congress, Copenhagen, 1949, 'Disarmament' resolution. In 1961 NAM also called for a special session of the UNGA on Disarmament: UNGA, Existing Principles and Proposals for the Conduct of Disarmament Negotiations, A/AC.187/30 and Corr.1, 2 May 1977, 1. The first UNGA Special Session on Disarmament was held in 1978.

[29] The divide was effectively legalised by the Treaty on the Non-proliferation of Nuclear Weapons (NPT), 1968.

[30] Final Communique of the Asian-African Conference of Bandung (1955) 6.

[31] For treaties establishing nuclear weapon free zones, see https://www.armscontrol.org/factsheets/nwfz. See essay 6 'Revisiting the Past: Peace at Beijing and Beyond'.

[32] On the marginalisation of women within the Pacific anti-nuclear movement, notwithstanding their pivotal part in securing the 1985 Rarotonga Treaty for a Nuclear Free Zone in the Pacific, see Rebecca Hogue and Anais Maurer, 'Pacific Women's Anti-nuclear Poetry: Centring Indigenous Knowledges' (2022) 98 *International Affairs* 1267, 1270. Women's anti-nuclear activism increased post-1985 as Pacific women turned their attention to the devastating health and environmental effects of the testing programmes.

implications of nuclear weapons testing. WHO rejected its plea on the grounds that the 'issue of experiments with nuclear weapons is a political issue ... and we at WHO must, of course, abstain from any discussion of political questions'.[33] It would be another two decades before the WHO would adopt a resolution 'deploring all nuclear weapons testing' and urge for an 'immediate cessation'.[34] In 1955 WILPF saw an opportunity to lobby states to extend the provision on preventing pollution in the ILC's draft Convention on the Freedom of the High Seas – intended to address oil spillages – to radioactive waste, thereby indirectly prohibiting testing.[35] By the time the final text was being negotiated in 1958, an express reference to radioactive waste had been included in the draft treaty, prompting considerable debate among states as to its legal effect in respect of nuclear weapons testing on the high seas. On adoption,[36] some states understood the treaty as banning nuclear testing on the high seas but, paradoxically, the very absence of an express prohibition was interpreted by nuclear weapons states as *permitting* testing, much to the dismay of activists.

By the early 1960s, the level of testing had reached a shocking level worldwide. The resumption of testing at the Nevada site galvanised US women to join mainstream anti-nuclear movements to protest, only to experience marginalisation within those male-dominated movements. Women began to establish parallel organisations (as they did in 1915) exemplified by the formation of the Women Strike for Peace initiative (WSP). The WSP garnered significant public support, leading to one of the largest women's protests of the twentieth century when, on 1 November 1961, 50,000 women marched in 60 cities in the US to demonstrate their opposition. The women capitalised on popular support and thereby exerted influence over the Kennedy administration's decision to adopt the Limited Test Ban Treaty in 1963.[37] While the political influence of the WSP should not be over-stated – the US and USSR were already in discussions over a test ban treaty, although progress had been halted in 1962 over the Cuban missile crisis – it cannot be entirely dismissed.

At the international level, WILPF used its own platform to advance thinking on disarmament. For example, in 1962 a resolution was adopted urging states to prohibit the use of outer space for nuclear testing,[38] pre-empting the adoption of an UNGA resolution in 1962 on the Legal Principles Governing Outer Space,[39] which became the basis for the 1966 Outer Space Treaty prohibiting the placement of nuclear weapons or other weapons of mass destruction in orbit or on celestial bodies.[40]

---

[33] WILPF, 13th International Congress, Birmingham, England, 1956, 24.
[34] WHO, 26th World Health Assembly, 1973, Pt II, 386, 393.
[35] WILPF, 14th Congress, Stockholm, 1959, 49–50.
[36] Convention on the High Seas, Geneva, 1958, art 25.
[37] Limited Test Ban Treaty, 5 August 1963 (signed by the US, USSR, and Great Britain).
[38] WILPF, 15th Congress, San Francisco, July 1962, Resolution 7: Prevention of the Use of Outer Space and the High Seas for Activities Endangering Mankind. The Congress viewed 'with alarm the attempts being made deliberately to underestimate the dangers of nuclear testing, and to prepare the people of the world for nuclear war, rather than strengthen the policies by which it can be avoided': ibid resolution 8.
[39] UNGAR 1962 (XVIII), Declaration of Legal Principles Governing the Activities of States in the Exploration and Use of Outer Space.
[40] Treaty on Principles Governing the Activities of States in the Exploration and Use of Outer Space, including the Moon and Other Celestial Bodies, 27 January 1967.

This was followed in 1966 by WILPF resolutions calling for agreement on a comprehensive test ban and non-proliferation of nuclear weapons together with a 'proposed treaty on nuclear non-proliferation'.[41] Although WILPF welcomed the 1968 NPT, it was nevertheless critical of the failure to include a provision prohibiting nuclear weapon states from using or threatening the use of nuclear weapons against non-nuclear weapon states (as it had done) and for containing no obligation on nuclear weapon states to take 'speedy measures of effective disarmament', failings that remain relevant to this day.[42] In addition to addressing nuclear weapons, in 1966 WILPF also urged the adoption of a UN convention prohibiting biological and chemical weapons; it was not until 1972 and 1992 that the Biological Weapons and the Chemical Weapons conventions were adopted by states. In parallel to these specific calls for action, WILPF sought to link disarmament – nuclear and conventional – with both development[43] and women's equality and in doing so establish a more holistic understanding of peace or positive peace, resisting the dominant trend among states to treat each of these areas as separate.

The UNGA's designation of 1975 as International Women's Year and 1975–85 as the Women's Decade,[44] provided peace activists with the opportunity to ensure that 'general and complete disarmament' was made a core priority, interlinking it with the three objectives: equality; development; and peace.[45] Largely due to WILPF's efforts, disarmament was incorporated into the main agenda at the conferences in Copenhagen and Nairobi,[46] and into the text of the Beijing Declaration and PFA, although the agreed language was less than activists had called for. The goal of reducing 'excessive' military expenditure is qualified by being made subject to 'national security considerations'[47] or 'legitimate national defence needs',[48] while the commitment to 'promote the elimination of all weapons of mass destruction, especially nuclear weapons' was deleted. Nonetheless, inclusion of disarmament in the PFA reaffirmed what had already been expressly recognised in CEDAW, that general and complete disarmament was inextricably linked to and a means for securing women's de facto equality with men.[49]

Twenty-five years after Beijing, the Declaration issued by states to commemorate its anniversary is silent on disarmament, reproducing the silence in SC Resolution 1325

---

[41] WILPF, 16th Congress, The Hague, July 1966, Resolution 1 (Comprehensive Test Ban Treaty); 2 (World Disarmament Conference); and 4 (Proposed Treaty on the Non-Proliferation of Nuclear Weapons).
[42] WILPF, 17th Congress, Denmark, Nyborg, 1968, 74.
[43] WILPF, 12th Congress, Paris 1953, 281 called on states to convene a world conference to further total and universal disarmament and to 'develop a plan for using the resources in money, manpower and the treasures of the earth released through the lifting of the crushing burden of armaments, to attack the social and economic problems created by large scale hunger, disease and illiteracy which have been among the prime causes of war.'
[44] See essay 5 'Peace in the UN Decade for Women'.
[45] ibid, and see also essay 6 'Revisiting the Past: Peace at Beijing and Beyond'.
[46] See essay 5 'Peace in the UN Decade for Women'.
[47] Beijing Platform for Action, Report on the Fourth World Conference on Women, Beijing 1995, para 143(a).
[48] ibid para 143(d).
[49] CEDAW, preamble: 'Affirming that the strengthening of international peace and security, ... general and complete disarmament, in particular nuclear disarmament under strict and effective international control, ... will promote social progress and development and as a consequence will contribute to the attainment of full equality between men and women.'

on WPS (2000).⁵⁰ The decision not to pursue the inclusion of disarmament in WPS was a high price to pay for women's admission into the realms of SC decision-making. In retrospect, the deal struck was a regressive compromise that, in effect, reinscribed the gendered boundaries that feminist peace activists had fought against throughout the UN Decade for Women and that had birthed the women's peace movement a century earlier.⁵¹

IV. DISARMAMENT THROUGH A GENDER PRISM

Over the years, women peace activists have frequently found themselves under attack for being utopian and pressured to defend their call for general and complete disarmament. Few, if any, would suggest that disarmament alone would prevent inter-state war, although it would make warfare that much more unfeasible. Most, on the other hand, subscribe to the position that redirecting public resources away from the production and maintenance of the tools of warfare to public interest projects is more likely to advance peace both within and between states. This latter position is usually countered by the all too familiar assertion that peace is conditioned on the state's ability and capacity to resort to force (if and when needed) to maintain the stability of the international order. Weapons, it is thus reasoned, are *necessary* to maintaining order and security, to enable the state to defend itself against threats, and, at times, may be the *only* way to secure peace.⁵² Advocates of this stance concede (albeit reluctantly and only occasionally) that the proliferation of weapons can lead to escalating levels of violence in armed conflict and perpetuate war rather than ending it. They are less keen to admit that the proliferation of weapons in peacetime can intensify insecurity, lead to arms races, and outbreaks of violence and war.

Although women peace activists have engaged in these somewhat polarised exchanges, they have also sought to carve out a different entry point utilising gender as an analytic tool to unpack state resistance to disarmament. Economic and financial motivations aside, the reluctance by most states to advance general and complete disarmament is difficult to fathom without peeling back the layers to see how gender systems operate to reinforce the insatiable appeal for weapons and the logic of arms accumulation. Feminist scholars have pointed to the history of disarmament as one

---

⁵⁰ Political declaration on the occasion of the twenty-fifth anniversary of the Fourth World Conference on Women, 2 March 2020, E/CN/6/2020/L.1. This contrasts with discussions at the 23rd special session of the UNGA on Follow-up to the PFA in 2000. The Outcome Document identified 'actions to be taken' including to 'Strengthen efforts toward general and complete disarmament under strict and effective international control, based on the priorities established by the United Nations in the field of disarmament, so that the released resources could be used for, inter alia, social and economic programmes which benefit women and girls': A/S-23/10/Rev.1, para 98(k).

⁵¹ Attempts to debate inter-state disarmament using the SC's WPS agenda tend to be channelled to women's participation in the field. Although the agenda urges incorporation of gender perspectives in all areas of peace support operations including disarmament, demobilisation and rehabilitation initiatives, states have interpreted these narrowly to post-conflict situations and primarily in respect to non-state actors. On the fragmented approach, see Henri Myrttinen, 'Connecting the Dots: Arms Control, Disarmament and the Women Peace and Security Agenda' (UNIDIR, 2020). See essay 3 'Peace in International Law'.

⁵² UK Secretary of State for Defence, James Cleverly, asserted '[g]iving the Ukrainians the [weapons] they need to finish the job is the swiftest – indeed the only – path to peace': *Times of Malta*, 5 February 2023.

that has often entailed the *forced* disarming of a belligerent state and consequently is associated with capitulation, defeat, lack of power and weakness, characteristics that are deeply gendered and typically coded female. In contrast, 'to arm' or 'to be armed' conjures up imageries of power and strength, attributes coded male. Full citizenship, including the right to engage in public life, was often attached to military service and the duty to bear arms, typically coded male, although not exclusively so.[53] The contemporary landscape is more complex.[54] Nonetheless, gender binaries continue to operate, saturating popular culture and all other spheres of social interaction, shaping norms and identities. Notwithstanding critical feminist scholarship, the gendered and often sexualised symbolism that attaches to weapons remains prevalent from the inter-personal to the level of states.[55] Weapons define – and are defined by – hegemonic masculinities,[56] from the possession of a 'bigger nuclear button' that 'works'[57] to the pressure exerted on Germany to arm Ukraine with Leopard 2 tanks being presented as an act of *courage* meriting respect.[58] Moreover, attacks on states that are highly invested in weapons production, possession and cutting edge technologies of warfare are more likely to resort to disproportionate uses of force in response, precisely because their masculinities have been publicly undermined. To *voluntarily* disarm is consequently deeply unsettling to the gendered binary logic that sustains the weapons discourse. For hegemonic masculinities, it represents a dangerous act precisely because it risks disrupting the gender hierarchies upon which political, economic, social, and cultural orders are founded.

Gender has also shaped women's own struggles for disarmament and the responses of states to women's activism. Activists have divided, fluctuating between a politics of maternalism that risks biological determinism versus an anti-essentialist politics. On occasion, women have consciously adopted strategies to conform to dominant gender norms and identities as a means by which to be heard. For example,

---

[53] eg although women were excluded from military service in the US, when Rosika Schwimmer, the prominent Hungarian peace activist, fled Hungary in 1921 and applied for US citizenship, she was rejected by the Supreme Court on the grounds that she would not take up arms: *United States v Schwimmer*, 279 US 644 (1929). The appeal court had granted Schwimmer citizenship reasoning 'women are considered incapable of bearing arms', an equally troubling decision. Seventeen years later, in *Girouard v US*, 328 US 61 (1946) the Supreme Court overruled *Schwimmer*, holding that 'refusal to bear arms is not necessarily a sign of disloyalty or a lack of attachment to our institutions', enabling conscientious objectors to acquire US citizenship: Susan N Herman, 'Rosika Schwimmer, Woman Without a Country', *ACLU blog*, 20 November 2020, https://www.aclu.org/issues/rosika-schwimmer-woman-without-country.

[54] On evolving state discourses on nuclear weapons, see Claire Duncanson and Catherine Eschle, 'Gender and the Nuclear Weapons State: A Feminist Critique of the UK Government's White Paper on Trident' (2008) 30 *New Political Science* 545.

[55] Carol Cohn, 'Sex and Death in the Rational World of Defense Intellectuals' (1987) 12 *Signs* 687. The atomic bomb used in Hiroshima was named 'Little Boy' while the one in Nagasaki was 'Fat Man'.

[56] 'Hegemonic masculinity' describes a model of masculinity which is 'constructed in relation to women and subordinated masculinities' and defines what counts as manly behaviour: RW Connell and James W Messerschmidt, 'Hegemonic Masculinity: Rethinking the Concept' (2005) 19 *Gender and Society* 829. It is an analytic concept that is context specific and cannot be assumed to equate to violent and/or militarised masculinities: Henri Myrttinen et al, 'Re-thinking Hegemonic Masculinities in Conflict-affected Contexts' (2017) 3 *Critical Military Studies* 103.

[57] Lauren Gambino, 'Donald Trump Boasts that His Nuclear Button is Bigger than Kim Jong-un's', *The Guardian*, 3 January 2018.

[58] Timothy Garton Ash, 'If Germany Has Truly Learned from its History it Will Send Tanks to Defend Ukraine', *The Guardian*, 18 January 2023.

by emphasising their role as mothers[59] concerned with protecting their children's future, the WSP garnered significant public support for their anti-nuclear testing campaign. This strategy alienated the more progressive generation of feminists, who viewed it as counter-productive to the fight for gender equality.[60] Moreover, the cost of the strategy became all too apparent when the WSP expanded its activities to protest the war in Vietnam, a move that exposed the women to widespread criticism for being 'too militant' – for failing to conform to dominant gender norms – and lost them public support.[61]

States have used gendered norms to undermine women's activism. Not only do the disarmament activities of women peace activists appear in official national records only occasionally (marginalisation is a display of patriarchal power) but their appearance is presented as a security risk, a 'major problem', annoyance or embarrassment, as per the women who gathered at RAF Greenham Common to protest against the deployment of US nuclear cruise missiles in the early 1980s.[62] From exchanges among state officials, we learn of their priority: to remove the women and their 'peace camps', to protect and make space for the unimpeded movement of the missiles, the instruments of war.[63] The records also expose the level of hostility directed at the women not only for their anti-nuclear stance but for refusing to conform to prevailing gendered norms and social expectations. Official reports describe the women as 'dirty and scruffy', doing 'no useful work while living off social security benefits': it is the women who present a drain on the state, not the weapons. The peace camp is described as 'an environmental health hazard', occluding the environmental and health hazards presented by the nuclear missiles.[64]

The 1990s saw women peace activists embrace two new complementary strategies that have delivered some measure of success. The first involved drawing attention to international law's blind spots through the prism of gender to expose how weapons law had singularly failed to register the different and disproportionate impact of their use on women and girls, due to their sex and gender. At around the same time, the possibilities presented by working in collaboration with a growing constituency of transnational organisations, international bodies, and 'like-minded' states to shape the content and trajectory of international weapons law became apparent, as demonstrated by the adoption of the 1997 Landmines Treaty. The emergence of the concept of 'humanitarian disarmament' which directs attention to the impact of weapons including their gendered [and intersectional] effects, has paid dividends

---

[59] Jane Wong, 'The Anti-essentialism v Essentialism Debate in Feminist Legal Theory: The Debate and Beyond' (1999) 5 *William and Mary Journal of Women and the Law* 273.
[60] The paradox of taking a position against testing is to divert attention from the weapons per se. See essay 12 'Introduction to Strategic Practices'.
[61] Louise Arimatsu, Transformative Disarmament (n 18) 870–72.
[62] Letter from Michael McNair-Wilson, MP for Newbury to the Prime Minister, Margaret Thatcher, 16 September 1982, UK National Archives, HO 287/3094.
[63] Letter from Gareth Gimblett, Leader of the Conservative Group, to Secretary of State for Defence, Michael Heseltine, 14 March 1983, UK National Archives, DEFE 24/3020.
[64] Meeting among officials from the Ministry of Defence, Home Office and Thames Valley Police to determine the strategy for 'solving' the Greenham Common 'problem', 1983, UK National Archives HO 325/566.

with adoption of the 2008 Cluster Munitions Convention and the 2017 Treaty on the Prohibition of Nuclear Weapons (TPNW).[65] Women peace activists have continued to work with and through international law at the intersection of gender to press for the prohibition of certain weapons and, at a minimum, to ensure that states are required by law to consider the gendered impact of weapons as exemplified by the 2014 Arms Trade Treaty (ATT).[66]

These successes notwithstanding, global military expenditure continues to increase as do arms sales.[67] Overwhelming evidence of IHL and IHRL violations has done little to dent the level of arms exports to belligerent states, despite legal obligations not to do so by states parties to the ATT. Meanwhile, the growing number of states parties to the TPNW stands in stark contrast to the current trajectory adopted by nuclear weapons states.[68] The prospect of nuclear conflict is once again part of the public discourse[69] and as we become acclimatised to the language of nuclear weapons, their use – including against non-nuclear weapon states – is once more becoming thinkable. Meanwhile, there is growing anxiety that the technologies of today are producing ever more new means and methods of war-fighting that exceed the pace (and structures) of international law. The weaponisation of artificial intelligence, quantum technology, robotics, autonomous systems, biotechnology, and digital technologies is growing, as is the development of hypersonic and directed energy weapons, some of which are being trialled in war zones. Women peace activists have been here before. The weaponisation of emerging technologies in the inter-war years, coupled with the diversion of state resources to the ever-growing stockpiles of weapons, had galvanised them to demand that states advance general and complete disarmament as necessary to peace.

V. THE PAST AND FUTURE OF DISARMAMENT

If anything can be gleaned from over a century of women's peace activism, it is that accepting the status quo has never been an option. Today, the challenges seem more daunting than ever, whether in the shape of meaningful participation or countering

---

[65] The TPNW is the first treaty to acknowledge the gendered impacts of nuclear weapons and the racialised histories of their use. It requires states parties to 'adequately provide age- and gender-sensitive assistance, without discrimination' to those affected by the use or testing of nuclear weapons 'including medical care, rehabilitation and psychological support, as well as provide for their social and economic inclusion': Preamble and art 6(1).

[66] ATT, art 7 makes it illegal to transfer weapons if there is a risk that the weapon will be used to facilitate gender-based violence. ATT is the first treaty to recognise the link between gender-based violence and the international arms trade.

[67] Global military expenditure rose for the eighth consecutive year in 2022 to reach an estimated US$2240 billion, the highest level ever recorded by the Stockholm International Peace Research Institute; arms sales of the 100 largest arms-producing companies continue to increase despite the effects of the pandemic, including the disruption in supply chains and labour shortages: https://www.sipri.org/yearbook/2023/05.

[68] The NPT is being eroded and a qualitative race in nuclear armaments is gathering momentum: United Nations Disarmament Yearbook 2021: Part II, 5-9. See essay 14 'Strategic Practice: Giving Effect to Legal Change', section III.

[69] UN Secretary-General, 'A New Agenda for Peace' Our Common Agenda: Policy Brief 9, July 2023, 4.

cultures of militarism and patriarchal gender systems that sustain the demand for weapons. As feminist international lawyers, we are not sanguine about the potential for international law to deliver radical change without addressing the drivers of weapons proliferation. Feminist critical engagements provide valuable insights into the workings of patriarchy and militarism through gender regimes and into the complex ways in which gender functions to ascribe meaning to weapons beyond their material form which, in turn, fuels demand. Meaningful progress on general and complete disarmament cannot be achieved without demystifying the symbolic value attached to all weapons and eliminating the gender regimes that create and sustain the demand and proliferation of all weapons, in particular nuclear. The bonds of patriarchy and militarism that materialise in the shape of weapons transcend inter-state conflict.[70] And this is precisely why we constantly draw attention to the insidious language of militarism and binary gender identities and norms that are relentlessly invoked by political figures that pollute popular culture and consciousness.

In parallel, women peace activists have expended considerable energy countering false narratives that equate weapons with security, not least the claim repetitively voiced by nuclear weapon states that such weapons *contribute* to peace and security.[71] Exposing myths, false narratives and false distinctions are undertakings that demand constant commitment, as is the task of revealing the silences. Over the last two decades, general and complete disarmament has been disappeared not only from multilateral normative initiatives involving women's rights but from the UNGA Declaration on the Right to Peace.[72] It does not feature in the Sustainable Development Goals, including in Goal 16 on Peace, Justice and Strong Institutions.[73] The UN Secretary-General's disarmament initiative, launched in 2018,[74] mentions it once – acknowledging that it 'remains the ultimate objective of the United Nations in the field of disarmament' – but has all but vanished from his 2023 'A New Agenda for Peace' released in preparation for the 2024 Summit of the Future. Each of these developments has effectively closed down the spaces for dialogue and progress and together they represent a trend that calls for a strong response from women peace activists across the world.

---

[70] Joint Statement of the Leaders of the Five Nuclear-Weapon States on Preventing Nuclear War and Avoiding Arms Races, 3 January 2022, https://www.whitehouse.gov/briefing-room/statements-releases/2022/01/03/p5-statement-on-preventing-nuclear-war-and-avoiding-arms-races/. This statement must be read in conjunction with the joint statement released in 2018 reiterating their opposition to the TPNW: https://www.gov.uk/government/news/p5-joint-statement-on-the-treaty-on-the-non-proliferation-of-nuclear-weapons.
[71] UK Government, Integrated Review on Security, Defence, Development and Foreign Policy, 2021, 76: 'The fundamental purpose of our nuclear weapons is to preserve peace, prevent coercion and deter aggression.' See essay 14 'Strategic Practice: Giving Effect to Legal Change'.
[72] References to disarmament in the original draft are missing in the final agreed text. See essay 3 'Peace in International Law'.
[73] Efforts on the part of the UN Office of Disarmament Affairs (UNODA) to link its work to Goal 16, 'to promote peaceful and inclusive societies for sustainable development, provide access to justice for all and build effective, accountable and inclusive institutions at all levels' draws attention to the fact that disarmament is missing from the SDGs: Izumi Nakamitsu, UN High Representative for Disarmament Affairs, 'Advancing Disarmament within the 2030 Agenda for Sustainable Development' (August 2018) 55 UN Chronicle 15.
[74] UNODA, Securing Our Common Future: an Agenda for Disarmament, 2018.

Our focus in this essay has been on inter-state disarmament rather than on the disarmament of armed groups such as the police, security sector (public and private), gangs, 'rebels', 'freedom fighters', 'terrorists' and individuals. This does not mean that we view the disarmament of these actors as any less important to facilitating peaceful societies. Most of these actors, an overwhelming majority of whom are men and boys, are armed with small arms and light weapons.[75] While men and boys are the main victims of such weapons, the prevalence and proliferation of small arms is shown to contribute to femicide and gender-based violence and heightens insecurity for women and girls and non-binary people, increasing gender inequalities. Global and regional normative frameworks to counter the proliferation of small arms and light weapons tend to assume multiple binary separations including between war/peace, national/international, state/non-state actors, with little attention directed to the gendered dimensions of small arms violence that cut across each domain. Women peace activists are at the forefront of projects to counter patriarchal gender systems that shape contemporary masculinities that intersect with the lucrative trade in weapons and thus perpetuate the desire and demand for small arms and light weapons and their normalisation in the hands of paternalist officials.

---

[75] 'Men and Masculinities in Gender Responsive Small Arms Control' (Pathfinders, WILPF and GENSAC briefing paper, 2022) 6.

Part III

Obstacles to Gendered Peace and Equality

8

Introduction to Part III

Women's struggle for peace and for political, economic and social rights is paralleled by a history of opposition in the shape of the gendered state that remains committed to violence to resolve inter-state disputes and hostile to ensuring women's rights on an equal basis with men. Part of women's struggles have been to identify and understand the gendered obstacles – structural and systemic – that impede peace and gender justice, including international law's role as structural obstructer and facilitator of those ambitions. Although this labour has resulted in some progress (with some shift in the law's content, interpretation, and application) the question of how to surmount the structural obstacles that form the very edifice of law remains largely unanswered.[1] In the following essays we (re)interrogate some of the structural and systemic impediments that operate with and through international law. The obstacles identified – primarily vectors of power – are neither free-standing nor static but are mutually reinforcing, intermeshed, dynamic, and context dependent. But first, a word of caution.

There is nothing intrinsically novel in what we write: the tragedy is that we have been here before. Repeating and naming, repeating and naming, again and again. Within and outside our discipline we are heard (if we are heard at all) 'as the ones repeating ourselves, a broken record, stuck on the same point. We don't even have to say it before eyes start rolling'.[2] But if we remain silent, nothing changes. In the spirit of feminist resistance, we continue to repeat and name.

The first essay surveys the multiple manifestations of silence of the gendered state, of what and who are silenced, including through international law's norms, doctrines and its institutions. Feminists have frequently reflected on silence,[3] both the silences imposed upon women and the silence with which their actions and claims are frequently met. Silence operates as an instrument of patriarchal power at all levels, from the international to the domestic. Law accords silence meaning and legitimacy. It is a well-used diplomatic tool with legal implications under international law; for instance, failure to protest may be relevant to determination that a practice is

---

[1] To strip international law of its heteropatriarchal underpinnings or to decolonise it is nothing short of dismantling its entire architecture, leaving it in its current form unrecognisable. See essay 17 'Introduction to Part V'.
[2] Sara Ahmed, 'In Conversation with Judith Butler' *Feminist killjoys*, 26 July 2023.
[3] Tillie Olsen, *Silences* (Dell Publishing, 1965) is a classic collection of essays about silences and creativity relating to sex, class, race, and historical contingency.

opposable to another state⁴ or to the evolution of a principle of customary international law.⁵ Institutionally, abstention from a vote is never neutral; it may denote acquiescence or opposition depending on context. Abstaining from a resolution condemning a use of force undermines unity and may represent tacit acceptance of the forcible action,⁶ while states abstaining for instance from the resolutions on a New International Economic Order were indicating reluctance to accept their premise.⁷

Non-recognition of an unconstitutional regime change is another form of silence. But non-recognition, a political gesture that carries with it *de jure* consequences,⁸ may be offset by a pragmatic willingness to work with the unrecognised entity. This is illustrated by the succession of dealings with the Taliban, an unrecognised de facto authority in Afghanistan in the late 1990s until its overthrow by the US-led 'coalition of the willing' in 2001 and again following the withdrawal of opposing armed forces in August 2021. In 2020, for instance, the US concluded an agreement with the Taliban that was centred on US security and without reference to the Taliban's gender-based violence against women and girls, boys and non-binary persons.⁹ The 'Agreement for Bringing Peace to Afghanistan' – a misnomer if ever there was one – paved the way for the 2021 US withdrawal, the Taliban's ensuing takeover and its further systematic denial of women's rights. Despite non-recognition and non-acceptance of the Taliban's credentials by the UNGA, by January 2022 the UN Secretary-General could observe that 'the engagement of the international community with the Taliban has gradually increased'.¹⁰ While states may be urging the Taliban to accept inclusive government and advocating for human rights, dialogue with the Taliban implies pragmatic acceptance of the status quo¹¹ – a political regime founded on unbridled misogyny and sexism – and provides a stark illustration of how international law's silences are selective, gendered and inimical to peace.

---

⁴ *Fisheries case (United Kingdom v Norway)* 18 December 1951, 1951 ICJ Reports 116.

⁵ International Law Commission, Draft Conclusions on Identification of Customary International Law, adopted UNGAR 73/203, 20 December 2018, Conclusion 10.3: 'Failure to react over time to a practice may serve as evidence of acceptance as law (opinio juris), provided that States were in a position to react and the circumstances called for some reaction.'

⁶ eg UNGAR ES-11/1, 18 March 2022: Aggression against Ukraine was adopted by 141 states in favout, 5 against and 35 abstentions. Other states retained the silence of failing to vote, meaning that 52 states – over 25 per cent of UN membership – did not vote in favour of condemning Russian aggression against Ukraine.

⁷ See essay 5 'Peace in the UN Decade for Women'.

⁸ James Crawford, *Brownlie's International Law*, 9th edn (Oxford University Press, 2019) 134 ff for discussion of recognition/non-recognition.

⁹ Agreement for Bringing Peace to Afghanistan between the Islamic Emirate of Afghanistan which is not recognised by the United States as a state and is known as the Taliban and the United States of America, February 29, 2020 which corresponds to Rajab 5, 1441 on the Hijri Lunar calendar and Hoot 10, 1398 on the Hijri Solar calendar.

¹⁰ UN Secretary-General, The situation in Afghanistan and its implications for international peace and security, A/76/667–S/2022/64, 28 January 2022, para 12.

¹¹ 'Since the forcible takeover by the Taliban in August 2021, culminating in the fall of Kabul on August 15, the United States has shifted to a position of pragmatic engagement in Afghanistan': US Department of State, 'US Relations with Afghanistan', 15 August 2022.

The Taliban's erasure of women from public life is an extreme and visible instance of the gendered silence that women have long[12] been expected to maintain in public discourse and spaces,[13] even where there is apparent de jure equality. Patriarchy's gendered silence is imposed through legal means, governmental action and non-action, violence, ridicule, disinformation and gendered cultural norms. For example, those who do not fall within patriarchy's heteronormative order are often compelled 'to hide their identities and suppress their desires and personhood',[14] that is to remain silent for fear of violence and persecution. The power and violence of patriarchal silence is acutely experienced by those who disrupt official narratives with opposing or dissenting views, for instance with respect to preparedness for and pursuit of war. The gendered state does not tolerate any challenge to its right to use violence in self-defence, the conditions for which are typically unarticulated.[15] Law's silence paves the way for absolute violence.

Collective silences – social and through law – about structural and institutional racist[16] and misogynist violence,[17] about human rights abuses, and the continuing violence of imperialism, normalise those forms of violence and are themselves violent. Silence undermines possibilities for reparation, commemoration and thus for peace.[18] In the face of systematic injustice none of us should be at peace with ourselves, none of us silent.

Silence does not have a single meaning but is complex, layered[19] and interpreted variably according to culture, the standing of the people involved, their location and other contextual factors.[20] Silence can prevent a holistic understanding of how violence and its aftermath are experienced and thus inhibits both external peace and the peace of internal wellbeing.[21] For individuals,

> being unable to tell your story is a living death, and sometimes a literal one. If no one listens when you say your ex-husband is trying to kill you, if no one believes you when you say you are in pain, if no one hears you when you say help, if you don't dare say help, if you have been trained not to bother people by saying help.[22]

---

[12] It is evidenced from the 'very outset of the "tradition of Western literature"': Mary Beard, 'The Public Voice of Women' (2014) 36 *London Review of Books* (discussing *The Odyssey*); it is emphasised in the modern retelling of Greek classics, eg Pat Barker, *The Silence of the Girls* (2018) and *The Women of Troy* (2021).
[13] The 'history of silence is central to women's history': Rebecca Solnit, 'Silence and Powerlessness Go Hand in Hand', *The Guardian*, 8 March 2017.
[14] Independent Expert on protection against violence and discrimination based on sexual orientation and gender identity (IESOGI), Victor Madrigal-Borloz, Peace and Security, A/77/235, 27 July 2022, para 38.
[15] States tend to emphasise the right of self-defence without mentioning its conditions of necessity and proportionality, or even the requirement to report to the SC.
[16] eg 'White Silence is Violence: Black Lives Matter' *Global Integrity blog*, 5 June 2020.
[17] The MeToo social movement challenges the silence about misogynist behaviour of powerful men.
[18] IESOGI (n 14) para 31: 'Gender and sexual violence are one of the main obstacles hindering lasting peace and stability, as many women, and gender-diverse activists and human rights defenders are targeted on the basis of both their gender and/or sexual identity and their role as social leaders.'
[19] Ayşe Gül Altinay and Andrea Pető (eds), *Gendered Wars, Gendered Memories: Feminist Conversations on War, Genocide and Political Violence* (Routledge, 2016) 8.
[20] Martha Houston and Cheris Kramarae, 'Speaking from Silence: Methods of Silencing and of Resistance' (1991) 2 *Discourse and Society* 387.
[21] It can also impact health: Maytal Eyal, 'Self-silencing is Making Women Sick' *Time*, 3 October 2023.
[22] Rebecca Solnit (n 13).

International law's silence signposts what is permissible.[23] State sovereignty determines the need for state consent; accordingly, what is not prohibited or regulated by international law is permitted, making its silence the site of gendered and raced violence. Thus, private harm in war goes unregistered, devaluing its significance through silence. Despite normative advances, law's history of silence remains an obstacle that intensifies around conflict-affected sexual violence[24] that is predominantly committed against women and girls but also against men and boys and those who reject the gender binary.

In the second essay we turn our attention to sexism and misogyny as socially constructed obstacles that lie at the root of gender-based discrimination, violence, exclusion, and silencing of women. We have traversed this ground many times before. After all, feminism is 'the movement to end sexism, sexual exploitation, and sexual oppression'.[25] Sexism and misogyny are patriarchal markers of power. As mutually reinforcing socially entrenched dogmatologies, they sustain patriarchy's gender binaries that subjugate and normalise inequalities and violence directed principally but not exclusively at women and girls. Sexism and misogyny saturate popular culture: in the digital age they are fuelled in online spaces, shared, normalised, universalised. Yet, international law remains largely silent: the prevailing view among states is that neither sexism nor misogyny online or offline are harms meriting international prohibition. The normative silence permits sexist and misogynistic hate speech to be commodified: hate generates profit.[26] Sexism and misogyny are imbricated in racial extractivist capitalism.[27] Sexist hate speech thrives unabated online, silencing women and girls through self-censorship, normalising violence against women and spreading offline, creating further obstacles to gender equality and peace.

Sexism and misogyny permeate all walks of life, private and public. International law's doctrines, norms, architecture, and its institutions are shaped by an androcentricity calcifying a sexist heteronormative orientation. The fact that the protection and advancement of women's rights is primarily in soft law form signals law's sexist leanings.[28] Law's androcentricity is perpetuated by a dystopian logic in which neither states nor the fraternity of mainstream international lawyers consider sex/gender-based discrimination as a peremptory norm, namely one 'accepted and recognized

---

[23] *The Case of the SS Lotus (France v Turkey)* PCIJ ser A, no 10, 7 September 1927; see essay 15 'Strategic Practices: "Doing Our Own Thing"'.

[24] Narrating sexual violence has many meanings depending on context: Ayşe Gül Altinay and Andrea Pető (n 19) part I, 'Sexual Violence, Narration, Resistance'.

[25] bell hooks, *Feminist Theory: from Margin to Centre* (Pluto Press, 2000) 33.

[26] The commodification of hate cannot be divorced from the political economy of the gendered state. Nor should we lose of sight of the worrying global trend on the part of states to deploy hate as a mode of governance to divide and deflect, eg UK politicians' cynical turning peace protests into hate protests: Suriyah Bi, 'Suella Braverman's "Hate March" rhetoric is another desperate attempt to hold onto state power' *bylinetimes.com*, 7 November 2023.

[27] Cedric Robinson, *On Racial Capitalism, Black Internationalism and Cultures of Resistance* (Pluto Press, 2019) and *Black Marxism: The Making of the Black Radical Tradition* (University of North Carolina Press, 2000) ch 1.

[28] See essay 5 'Peace in the UN Decade for Women' and essay 6 'Revisiting the Past: Peace at Beijing and Beyond'.

by the international community ... as a norm from which no derogation is permitted and which can be modified only by a subsequent norm of international law having the same character'.[29] The mainstream position cannot be explained other than through the prism of sexism, since this refusal is impossible to square with and stands in stark contrast to racial discrimination, which is rightly treated as a *jus cogens* prohibition. The consequence is that while international law is equipped to name the racist state and act on it, it is unable to address the misogynistic one.

Sexism and misogyny operate at the intersection of race, class, and all other socially constructed markers of bifurcated difference rationalising relationships of subjugation.[30] Universalised by European colonialism, a 'paternalism that infantilized and feminized political subjectivities',[31] sexualised and racialised hierarchies were not extinguished by decolonisation but rather 'renegotiated', paving the way for the emergence of 'new, nationalist patriarchies across the anticolonial and postcolonial world'.[32] This in part explains why states, even those once subjugated by European imperialism and oppression, have little to gain from advancing women's rights.[33]

On occasion, international law's androcentricity is acknowledged by the gendered state. Take, for example, international humanitarian law (IHL). The sexist assumptions that framed the mindset of the drafters of the treaties are widely conceded by states and there have been efforts to reinterpret the law to take account of the different and particular experiences of women and girls in armed conflict.[34] Yet neither the 'gendering' of IHL's protections nor the more ambitious task of applying a gender perspective to the conduct of hostilities rules has delivered much practical change, as demonstrated in 2023 by the conflicts in Ukraine and in Palestine. Following the Hamas attacks of 7 October 2023, women and children have constituted over half the civilian deaths and injuries recorded in Gaza. They are the expendable casualties of war, decided upon primarily by male decision-makers and fought primarily between male weapons bearers. This raises again the value of 'adding' women into existing law when its structures and those interpreting and applying it are steeped in a sexist culture.

---

[29] Vienna Convention on the Law of Treaties, 1969. art 53. See essay 2 'Gender'.

[30] eg The Combahee River Collective, 'A Black Feminist Statement' (1982); Angela Davis, *Women, Race and Class* (Vintage Books, 1983) and Audre Lorde, 'Learning from the 60s', address delivered at Harvard University (1982) ('there is no such thing as a single-issue struggle because we do not live single-issue lives'), https://www.blackpast.org/african-american-history/1982-audre-lorde-learning-60s/.

[31] Vrushali Patil, 'From Patriarchy to Intersectionality: A Transnational Feminist Assessment of How Far We've Really Come' (2013) 38 *Signs* 847, 860 (examining the UNGA debates around the passage of the 1960 Declaration on Granting of Independence to Colonial Countries and Peoples). 'Enlightenment and sociological texts negotiated new, hardened configurations and binaries, spatializing and temporalizing them in the process. Such a remapping aligned heterosexual public men and domestic women with progress, placing other possibilities in other spaces and in other times. In this way, the alignment of dichotomous sexed bodies with binary gender roles and a certain kind of racialized, classed (hetero)sexuality was very much located within civilizational space and time': Vrushali Patil, 'The Heterosexual Matrix as Imperial Effect' (2018) 36 *Sociological Theory* 1, 15.

[32] Vrushali Patil, 'From Patriarchy to Intersectionality' (n 31) 861. We do not suggest that sexism and misogyny did not exist prior to colonialism.

[33] The 'coloniality of gender is still with us': Maria Lugones, 'Toward a Decolonial Feminism' (2010) 25 *Hypatia* 742, 746.

[34] See essay 13 'Strategic Practice: Peace and Equality through International Law'.

The final essay traces how international law's construction of crises and emergencies entrenches gender systems and militarism as structural obstacles to gender justice and peace. There is a great deal of critical feminist scholarship on the relationship between gender and militarism that reveals how gender sustains the logic of militarism – that force is the rational and optimum way to respond to any perceived threat. This in turn paves the way for the state to respond to public emergences, including health, with forcible measures. In crises such as war the logic of militarism becomes all-prevailing and all-consuming, rationalised through gender systems that make violence appear the natural and, at times, the only available option. International law fosters a militarised response as rational and expected, by bonding the occurrence of 'an armed attack' to a state's right to 'self-defence' through militarised force.[35] Article 51 of the UN Charter is silent on any other response. Instead, there is a chorus urging the use of militarised violence in response to violence, abstracting and sanitising through international law's lexicon the visceral brutality and destructiveness of war that will rip apart bodies, cause untold suffering, destroy lives.

The legal and institutional architecture created by the UN Charter is founded on the logic of militarism notwithstanding the prohibition on the use of force.[36] The fact that the Security Council is mandated with the legal power to authorise military force – even if as a last resort – rationalises, through law, military force to maintain or restore peace. The incoherence of this rationale requires the siloing of means from objectives. It is the law's siloing rather than its fragmentation that obstructs.

International law's obstruction to gendered peace manifests in ways additional to its construction of crisis. For instance, international law has been complicit in the outbreak of conflict. As Europe sought in 1919 to create sovereign states out of the collapse of the Ottoman and Austro-Hungarian empires, national, religious and ethnic identities were enshrined in international legal instruments as either the basis for territorial demarcation or to be protected as minorities. Neither proved stable, as was only too evident in the outbreak of World War II and again in the conflicts following the collapse of the former Yugoslavia and the Soviet Union. Yet nationalism has been upheld again through international law, for instance in the 1995 Dayton Accords[37] where, in the Agreement itself and subsequent state reconstruction, gender has been silenced[38] and peace is fragile.[39]

Gender is always enfolded into crisis narratives generated by states to justify responses, including military action. International law facilitates these narratives

---

[35] UN Charter, art 51: 'Nothing in the present Charter shall impair the inherent right of individual or collective self-defence if an armed attack occurs against a Member of the United Nations …'.
[36] ibid art 2(4).
[37] The General Framework Agreement for Peace for Bosnia and Herzegovina, Dayton, initialled 21 November 1995, signed Paris 14 December 1995, Annex 4, art III embedded the Republika Srpska as an Entity within Bosnia-Herzegovina with 'the right to establish special parallel relationships with neighboring states'.
[38] Nela Porobić Isaković and Gorana Mlinarević, 'Sustainable Transitions to Peace Need Women's Groups and Feminists' (2019) 72 *Journal of International Affairs* 173.
[39] Nela Porobić and Gorana Mlinarević, *The Peace That is Not: 25 Years of Experimenting with Peace in Bosnia and Herzegovina* (WILPF, 2021).

through legal ambiguity at the core of the UN Charter that leaves unresolved what constitutes a threat to international peace or security. What is a crisis and who decides? How do we, as feminist lawyers, overcome the obstacles created by our discipline's resistance to recognising that ideas about gender are central to the way international crises are identified and resolved, and how gender makes inevitable some decisions and others not?

All crises – not least war, the quintessential manmade crisis – have gendered effects that subsist long after states have moved on from the crisis that mandated urgent intervention. The end of a crisis is a patriarchal myth. The suspension of armed hostilities between the (mostly) male protagonists simply elides the ongoing gendered violence and oppression made possible through the re-entrenchment of gendered orders that continue to devastate women's lives.[40] Take for example Yemen, the site of multiple overlapping conflicts fuelled and perpetuated by foreign intervention. A decade after its outbreak, the main belligerents appear to have tired of war and its heavy financial burden.[41] Yemen's women and girls have paid a disproportionate cost.[42] War has set back by decades the progress being made to secure women's rights and enabled the reinstating of gendered norms particularly in Houthi-controlled areas.[43] The bodies of women and girls are controlled through the reinforcement of discriminatory misogynistic attitudes and regulations, including travel restrictions requiring them to be escorted by a male guardian (mahram); preventing access to reproductive health care; preventing women from engaging in paid work; gender segregation in public spaces; and control over dress.[44] Meanwhile, over 17 million Yemenis rely on foreign assistance; food insecurity remains acute, and malnourishment endemic, with women bearing much of the burden – as they always have.[45] Four million people have been internally displaced, 73 per cent of whom are women and girls, who face a heightened risk of gender-based violence, transactional sex for survival, and the sexual exploitation and trafficking that come with forced displacement. Poverty has worsened, affecting especially women-headed households. Yemen's healthcare, maternity services, water, sanitation and education systems have all but collapsed.[46]

Adding to their already dire situation, there is another crisis brewing for Yemen's women and girls and for feminist peace activism, paradoxically in the prospect

---

[40] The SC resolutions on women, peace and security (WPS) perpetuate the myth of the end of conflict, with their many provisions on post-conflict. In contrast see CEDAW Committee, General Recommendation No 30, on women in conflict prevention, conflict and post-conflict situations, CEDAW/C/GC/30, 18 October 2013, para 35: 'For most women in post-conflict environments, the violence does not stop with the official ceasefire or the signing of the peace agreement and often increases in the post-conflict setting. ... while the forms and sites of violence change, ... all forms of gender-based violence, in particular sexual violence, escalate in the post-conflict setting.'
[41] 'Saudi Officials Arrive in Iran to Discuss Reopening Diplomatic Missions' *The Guardian*, 8 April 2023.
[42] Human Rights Watch, 'Houthis Violating Women's and Girls' Rights in Yemen' 6 February 2023.
[43] In 2022, Yemen was ranked last globally in the UNDP's Gender Inequality Index.
[44] Letter to Yemen Minister for Foreign Affairs, Hisham Sharaf, from the Working Group on discrimination against women and girls; SR on cultural rights; SR on the right to education; SR on the right to health; SR on freedom of religion; and the SR VAWG, 2 December 2022.
[45] UN Yemen Sustainable Development Cooperation Framework 2022–2024, January 2022.
[46] See https://dppa.un.org/en/mission/special-envoy-yemen.

124 *Introduction to Part III*

of a peace that threatens to be deeply gendered. The warning signs are depicted in the image of a group of smiling men in a room with marble walls and floors lit by chandeliers delighting in a handshake between Madi al-Mashat, chair of the Houthis' political council, and Muhammad al-Jaber, the Saudi ambassador to Yemen, a gesture made possible by a tripartite agreement between Saudi Arabia, Iran and China.[47] Even the images released by the UN reaffirm the acceptability of sex and gender-based segregation and suggest that the need to 'consult' with women only arises once the male protagonists have reached agreement.[48] While the effects of the crises that have unfolded in Yemen are unique, that all crises have gendered effects that disproportionately disadvantage women and girls, is not. Nor are the gendered impacts of crises limited to war. All crises heighten existing inequalities and concurrently entrench inequalities,[49] creating mounting obstacles to peace, as is all too clear from the Covid-19 pandemic.

In the nineteenth and early twentieth centuries feminists campaigned for political rights, workplace rights, and peace – bringing together these different agendas in resistance to the structural inequalities of patriarchy. In the twenty-first century these objectives are less easily perceived as interwoven, a fragmentation that is reflected in specialist regimes of international law and institutions. The UNGA's Declaration on the Right to Peace originated within the Human Rights Council,[50] but the maintenance of international peace is the responsibility of the SC. Since adoption of the Beijing Declaration and PFA the UN has been committed to mainstreaming gender throughout the work of all UN bodies but in reality gender analysis with respect to women is centred within UN Women, CSW, the CEDAW Committee and the Working Group on Discrimination against Women and Girls. LGBTQI rights are now the domain of the UN IESOGI. There is, of course, overlap between the different bodies; since at least the Vienna World Conference on Human Rights 'all human rights are universal, indivisible and interdependent and interrelated'[51] and this is reflected in the work of many of the UN human rights treaty bodies and special procedures. Many of these bodies now introduce issues of gender into their work, as do many special agencies and regional bodies. Demarcation of mandates can nevertheless provoke dissension and claims that a body is acting outside its authority.[52] On the one hand, specialisation elicits marginalisation and exclusion, while on the other fragmentation across different bodies can inhibit joined up thinking, duplication and important issues falling between institutional mandates. Different approaches inhibit a coherent and sustained message about

---

[47] Patrick Wintour, 'Saudi Arabia Makes Peace Proposal for Yemen after Houthi Talks' *The Guardian*, 10 April 2023.

[48] UNSCR 1325, 31 October 2000, women and peace and security, urges member states to ensure increased representation of women at all stages of peace processes.

[49] CEDAW Committee, General Recommendation No 37 on the gender-related dimensions of disaster risk reduction in the context of climate change, CEDAW/C/GC/37, 13 March 2018, para 2: 'Situations of crisis exacerbate pre-existing gender inequalities and compound the intersecting forms of discrimination'.

[50] See essay 3 'Peace in International Law'.

[51] Vienna Declaration and Programme of Action, 25 June 1993, I, para 5.

[52] eg in SC open debates on WPS, Russia and China have argued that the Council is overstepping its mandate, eg S/PV.7533, 13 October 2015, 20–23.

inequalities rooted in patriarchy and aggressive capitalism that have become normalised. International law as a discipline founded on such inequalities of itself constitutes a significant obstacle to a holistic, gendered peace. This leaves feminist international lawyers with a choice between working within the system for such gains as might be possible and turning instead to other arenas for emancipatory change. This choice pervades the strategies discussed in Part IV of this book.

9

Silence as an Obstacle to Gendered Peace and Equality

I. INTRODUCTION

IN 2018 THE London-based Imperial War Museum hosted a Remembrance Day Debate entitled 'Why are we Silent when Conflict is Loud?'[1] We have since reflected on meanings and histories of silence, gender and peace. Communal silence is observed in public spaces to remember and honour certain deaths, notably of those who died in war. These are primarily men and a particular form of masculinity is constructed around their lives and their deaths, celebrating their courage, patriotism, and sacrifice in protecting those (women and children) dear to them. In many societies, respectful silence has become deeply embedded in the collective psyche. This has been formalised in the UK (and elsewhere) since 1919 when Edward George Honey,[2] a Melbourne journalist who had served in the Middlesex Regiment in World War I, wrote to the *London Evening Standard* proposing 'a silent tribute' – 'five minutes of national remembrance' – for 'these mighty dead'.[3] Through more political avenues the concept reached King George V who decreed a two-minute silence on the first anniversary of the Armistice: 'All locomotion should cease, so that, in perfect stillness, the thoughts of everyone may be concentrated on reverent remembrance of the glorious dead.' Silence denoted stillness. Accordingly, 'trams "glided into stillness," motors "ceased to cough and fume," and "mighty-limbed dray horses hunched back upon their loads"'.[4]

Nearly a century later, the culture of stillness and silence was repeatedly observed in Wootton Bassett (subsequently Royal Wootton Bassett) between 2007 and 2011 as the hearses of personnel killed in military service in Iraq and Afghanistan passed through the town. This was not the official silence of the annual Remembrance Day rituals; the government preferred silence to public reminders of the heavy toll of these unpopular wars. It was a spontaneous showing of respect by the town that

---

[1] In conjunction with the BBC: available at https://www.bbc.co.uk/sounds/play/m00011hq.
[2] Ironically, Honey preserved a form of silence even while setting in train public events by using a pseudonym, Warren Foster.
[3] Miyuki Jokiranta, 'The Little-known Origin of the Minute's Silence' *ABC News*, 8 November 2018.
[4] *Manchester Guardian*, 12 November 1919, cited in Caroline Davies, 'Armistice Day Silence Falls over Britain as Millions Honour the Dead' *The Guardian*, 11 November 2010.

stood 'proxy for the grief of the nation' as 'ordinary people ... standing still and quiet for a few moments in a mark of sorrow and gratitude'.[5] Their silence, observing 'the unwritten rules of conduct' reinforced the cultural norm; 'in contrast, the intentional breaking of silence was seen as taboo and deemed inappropriate'.[6]

Individuals can remember in silence who or whatever they wish, but collective silence writes an official narrative of national unity built on concepts of sacrifice and honour as the bases for citizenship. It creates a hierarchy of deaths by excluding those who are not designated the 'glorious dead', while essentialising those who died in wars. Many were not, however, willing heroes; they were conscripted,[7] were shamed into joining up, were executed for desertion[8] or 'cowardice' ('unmasculine' behaviour) or were simply invisible to the authorities – 'natives' from colonial territories, animals and, of course, women.[9]

Silence does not only determine who is to be honoured. It determines who can speak and is 'used to isolate people disempowered by their gender, race and class'.[10] The silence thus imposed makes it difficult for those who have been marginalised to speak out against official or mainstream policies. When they do so, they may be met with attempts to reimpose their silence by those holding power resorting to all the tools at their disposal – law,[11] public and private violence, custodial measures that are deliberately punitive[12] or allegedly protective,[13] ridicule and humiliation.[14]

Women's voices, when they dissent from prevailing views that favour war or arms escalation, are deemed hysterical or difficult.[15] Emphasis on (male) 'objectivity' as a guiding behavioural norm renders 'alternative perspectives from "unofficial

---

[5] Letter from the mayor of Wootton Bassett seeking restraint from the media that was converging on the town: 'The Myth of Heroes' Highway' *The Guardian*, 18 July 2009.

[6] Professor Mythen, cited in 'Royal Wootton Bassett Changed the Way Britain Marks "Consequences of War"' University of Liverpool, 28 May 2015.

[7] Conscription was introduced in World War I by the Military Service Act 1916.

[8] Local press was readier than national media to provide a space where 'otherwise voiceless individuals could speak': eg a Mrs Pitts wrote to her local newspaper in 1915 describing her husband, who had been shot at dawn, as a victim of war who should be remembered: Maggie Andrews, 'Commemorating the First World War in Britain: A Cultural Legacy of Media Remembrance' (2019) 12 *Journal of War and Culture Studies* 295.

[9] The Women's section of the Royal British Legion was not permitted to parade its standard at the annual Festival of Remembrance until 1953 despite women being responsible for the classic symbol of remembrance – the red poppy – and the major sellers of poppies for Remembrance Day: Maggie Andrews, ibid.

[10] Martha Houston and Cheris Kramarae, 'Speaking from Silence: Methods of Silencing and of Resistance' (1991) 2 *Discourse and Society* 387.

[11] Jennifer Robinson and Keina Yoshida, *How Many More Women? The Silencing of Women by the Law and How to Stop It* (Octopus Publishing Group, 2022).

[12] Arrests and detentions of Russian protestors against the 'military operations' in Ukraine that commenced 24 February 2022; Alexander Bidin, 'This is What it's Like Inside Russia's Anti-war Movement' *Open Democracy*, 28 February 2022; 'Russian Opposition Figure Ilya Yashin Jailed for Denouncing Ukraine War' *The Guardian*, 9 December 2022.

[13] 'Women in protective custody who have been ostracised by their families have almost no contact with the outside world' and are thus silenced: Jade Glenister, 'Good Intentions: Can the "Protective Custody" of Women Amount to Torture?' (2016) 16 *Equal Rights Review* 13.

[14] 'Women could be harshly punished and humiliated simply for talking too much or too publicly or in a tone of voice that seemed grating or nagging. ... The punishment for the crime – brutal and feared – was meant to draw a crowd and publicly humiliate the accused': Jane Brox, 'The Silence of Women' *Longreads*, 15 January 2019.

[15] Helen Lewis, *Difficult Women: A History of Feminism in 11 Fights* (Jonathan Cape, 2020).

sources" such as women peace activists ... as not credible or irrelevant, particularly if they question the dominant patriarchal view that military solutions and violence resolves conflict and ensures "security" and "peace"'.[16] This essay explores some of the tools engaged by those in positions of power to silence voices that dissent from war, violence and militarism and thus to preclude prospects of a gendered peace.

II. SILENCING THOSE PROTESTING WAR

In 1915 the government sought to silence the women from Britain who wanted to join the International Congress of Women (ICW)[17] in The Hague to speak out against the 'madness and the horror of war'.[18] First, the Home Secretary refused passports to the vast majority of the 180 women who applied to travel to the Netherlands. Second, the few who were issued with the required documents found the North Sea closed to shipping. Only three British women, who were already outside the country, were able to participate. Official silencing was augmented by media derision. Ignoring the women's courage in travelling in wartime (including American delegates who crossed the Atlantic) the *Evening Standard* dismissed the 'women peace fanatics' as 'a nuisance and a bore' and the *Daily Express* parodied them as 'peacettes'.[19] The US Women's Peace Party that sent delegates to the Congress was 'ridiculed as "silly" and "meddling with matters far beyond [their] capacity"'.[20] Undaunted, over 1,200 women went to The Hague from 12 countries. The ICW observed a minute's silence but not to laud masculine heroism. Rosika Schwimmer, a feminist and pacifist, recounted:

> we had one [woman attendee] who learned that her son had been killed – and women who had learned two days earlier that their husbands had been killed, and women who had come from belligerent countries full of the unspeakable horror, of the physical horror of war, these women sat there with their anguish and sorrows, quiet, superb, poised, and with only one thought, 'What can we do to save the others from similar sorrow?'[21]

They resolved to 'urge' governments to end the bloodshed, to establish a 'just and lasting peace' and, strategising to this end, delegated participants to convey their resolutions to the rulers of the belligerent states and the US President.[22]

Silencing those who protest war has continued unabated; in 2023 the Israeli Government has made it illegal to oppose the war in Gaza[23] and the UK Government

---

[16] Margaret E Thompson et al, 'Feminist Media Coverage of Women in War: "You are Our Eyes and Ears to the World"' (2007) 15 *Gender and Development* 438.
[17] See essay 7 'Women, Disarmament and Peace'.
[18] WILPF Resolutions, 1st Congress, The Hague, 1 May 1915, para 1. The Congress condemned all war, not just that then being fought.
[19] Peace Pledge Union (PPU), https://menwhosaidno.org/context/women/hague_1.html.
[20] John Craig, 'The Women's Peace Party and Questions of Gender Separatism' (1994) 19 *Peace and Change* 373, 389.
[21] PPU (n 19).
[22] ICW Resolutions (n 18).
[23] Orly Noy, 'The Silencing of the Anti-war Voices in Israel' *Jewish Voice for Labour*, 20 November 2023: Jewish protestors arrested/beaten for 'trying to hold a silent protest against the war'.

sought to discredit as 'disrespectful' a peace march on 11 November (Armistice Day) calling for a ceasefire in that war.[24]

III. SILENCE ABOUT THE EFFECTS OF WAR

Silence is maintained about what occurs in war, by governments that impose a shroud of secrecy[25] and by many who experienced war – both men[26] and women – after their return to 'normal' life. Gender roles and politics combine to create layers of silence, especially about the situation of women and those who reject the gender binary during the conflict. Women may be omitted from the war record as a way of maintaining the 'manly' enterprise of war,[27] or the post-war political environment may demand silence.[28] Silence intensifies around conflict-related sexual violence. Public silence may be demanded where allegations of sexual abuse would undermine the myth of the national 'honourable warrior' or where it implicates an organisation, as either perpetrators[29] or victims of sexual abuse.[30] Attempts to break that silence by drawing public attention to those killed and injured through rape and sexual violence have been strongly resisted by the state seeking to preserve its mythology intact. A striking example was the reaction of the Australian government to women when they sought in 1981 to lay a wreath at the national war memorial on Anzac Day[31] – 'the *One Day of the Year*'.[32] The 'masculine custodians of national memory' were outraged by the implications of sexual violence besmirching military honour. Fourteen of the 16 women were arrested and were accused of provocative, even 'terrorist', behaviour.[33]

---

[24] Ben Quinn and Vikram Dodd, 'Sunak Calls Armistice Day Pro-Palestinian Protests "disrespectful"' *The Guardian*, 3 November 2023.

[25] This may be attempted by denying access to independent media but is much harder to achieve in an age of social media.

[26] There is a vast literature: eg Ted Barris, *Breaking the Silence: Veterans' Untold Stories from the Great War to Afghanistan*, 2nd edn (Thomas Allen, 2012).

[27] Weronika Grzebalska, 'Militarizing the Nation: Gender Politics of the Warsaw Uprising' in Ayşe Gül Altinay and Andrea Pető (eds), *Gendered Wars, Gendered Memories: Feminist Conversations on War, Genocide and Political Violence* (Routledge, 2016) ch 5.

[28] Women who fought on the Republican side 'lost their voice', their 'existence in public space' and 'their right to express themselves as historical subjects': Sophie Milquet, 'Women's Memory of the Spanish Civil War: The Power of Words' in Ayşe Gül Altinay and Andrea Pető (eds), ibid, ch 9.

[29] The silence around sexual exploitation and abuse by UN peacekeepers is now being broken, although it remains a major concern: eg Jane Rasmussen, Personnel Conduct Officer, MONUC, End of Assignment Report, February 2006. The Secretary-General has committed to greater transparency and accountability for such abuse: Report of the Secretary-General on the Work of the Organization 2021, A/76/1, 2021, 134.

[30] Abby Stoddard, 'We Need to Talk: Overcoming the Culture of Silence around Sexual Violence in Humanitarian Operations' *Bond*, 17 August 2021.

[31] Anzac Day, 25 April, commemorates the landings of Australian and New Zealand forces at Gallipoli in 1915. It is marked with dawn vigils and services remembering all who have served and died in military and peacekeeping operations.

[32] This play by Alan Seymour exposes the different cultural aspects of Anzac Day; the dawn services and marches and alcohol-fuelled reunions later in the day. It reflects the view that the day is about 'old guys sitting around reminiscing about the glories of war': Meredith Burgmann, 'The Women against Rape in War Collective's Protests against ANZAC Day in Sydney, 1983 and 1984' (2014) 6 *Cosmopolitan Civil Societies Journal* 4222.

[33] Sean Scalmer, *Dissent Events: Protest, the Media and the Political Gimmick in Australia* (University of New South Wales Press, 2002).

Legislation authorised the arrest of anyone acting in a manner 'likely to disturb or disrupt' the Anzac Day Parade, or to 'give offence or cause insult' to those in the parade.[34] Similar actions followed in other Australian cities and elsewhere.[35] In Sydney in 1983 the Women against Rape collective marched before the main event on Anzac Day under a banner that read 'We mourn all women raped in all wars'.[36] The 'totally silent' march of around 300 women was met by 'a phalanx of police and eight paddy wagons'. Around 160 women were 'silently arrested';[37] participants were met with angry accusations of upsetting veterans and those mourning the dead, but all charges were subsequently dismissed.

Public discourse is not stable; governments may seek political traction from survivors' stories, moulded to suit their own agenda,[38] but they may be subsequently disavowed by change of government or policy and a return to official silence. Silence can be demanded through blocking media presence.[39] Silence can also denote cover up and unwillingness to acknowledge crimes committed by their own forces or allies. It can also be deliberately broken by misinformation, propaganda, used to dehumanise opponents, provoke and legitimise further violence in place of exploring paths to peace.[40]

Male[41] and female survivors of sexual violence in conflict, as well as of the violence that occurs in 'everyday peacetime life', may maintain private silence for reasons such as trauma, guilt, a culture of silence around sex and sexuality, patriarchal cultural norms, fear of stigma and exclusion from their families and communities, of reprisals[42] and – probably correctly – that no-one will be held to account and seeking justice will only cause further suffering.[43] A lapse of time before speaking out

---

[34] Australian Capital Territory Traffic (Amendment) Ordinance, 1981 (repealed by the Labour government in 1983).

[35] The UK War Widows Association began to hold a private ceremony at the Cenotaph the day before Remembrance Day, including laying a wreath of white chrysanthemums that was removed before the formal ceremonies: Maggie Andrews (n 8).

[36] Melbourne women's protest was against 'patriarchal war against women': Meredith Burgmann (n 32).

[37] Presumably it was the women who remained silent.

[38] Nayanika Mookherjee, *The Spectral Wound: Sexual Violence, Public Memories, and the Bangladesh War of 1971* (Duke University Press, 2015) (recounting how the Bangladesh government celebrated women raped by the Pakistani military as *birangonas* ('brave women') but that this imposed identity denied the diversity of their personal experiences).

[39] Israel has denied foreign reporters access to Gaza during the 2023 war; the Committee to Protect Journalists reports this as the deadliest conflict for media workers they have ever recorded, with a 'mass slaughter' of Palestinian journalists: Owen Jones, 'Who Will Shine a Light on the Atrocities in Gaza if All the Journalists are Wiped Out?' *The Guardian*, 29 November 2023.

[40] In winter 2023, we see all these in the context of the conflict between Israel and Palestine, with accusations that silence about the crimes committed by either side reveals bias and condones those crimes while claims on social media confuse facts and promote misinformation.

[41] Amalendu Misra, *The Landscape of Violence Sexual Violence Against Men in War* (Hurst, 2015); Charlotte Vercraeye, '"A Culture of Silence"; Sexual Violence against Men and Boys in Armed Conflict' Dr Denis Mukwege Foundation, guest blog.

[42] Witnesses in the former Yugoslavia feared revenge attacks against themselves or family members for testifying: *Prosecutor v Dusko Tadic, Decision on the Prosecutor's Motion requesting Protective Measures for Victims and Witnesses*, 10 August 1995, para 65. Additional factors include the 'possible social consequences of it becoming generally known … that a woman has been a rape victim and also the often acute trauma of facing one's attacker in court and being made to relive the experience of the rape': ibid, Judge Stephen, separate opinion.

[43] '[I]n the case of sexual violence, silence prevails, not only because of feelings of guilt, shame or fear of being stigmatized or ostracized by the community, but also because of the conviction that any complaint

may encourage disbelief. Silence may be a choice but is also forced upon many survivors as the safer option, as for instance where a raped person is accused of adultery, or for LGBTQI persons where homosexuality is criminalised or social exclusionary norms prevail. Those who are killed following sexual or other forms of gender-based violence are permanently silenced[44] and the record of these forms of violence as integral to the overall violence of conflict or genocide is lost.[45]

Gender and sexual violence form a major obstacle to lasting peace and stability 'as many women, and gender-diverse activists and human rights defenders are targeted on the basis of both their gender and/or sexual identity and their role as social leaders'.[46] This is exacerbated by the silence about these crimes (and indeed all the effects of war) when it is maintained by individuals, by communities and through lack of public acknowledgment. Silence – whether to maintain it or not – is strategic for individuals, communities and governments. For the former, maintaining silence can prevent inner peace; survivors of the Japanese system of military sexual slavery, the so-called 'comfort women', have said how 'the past [would] not let them rest and that they desire peace'.[47] Collective silence about sexual and gender violence in peace negotiations, in trials of accused persons or in public discourse entails an impoverished understanding of the nature and extent of the violence and perpetuates insecurity. Silence sustains impunity, which in turn sustains a culture of silence in a cycle that impedes peace.

IV. LEGAL SILENCING

Crimes of sexual and gender-based violence that are 'particularly targeted against women and girls'[48] constitute violations of international law under principles of state responsibility, international criminal law and human rights law. States are responsible for internationally wrongful acts attributable to them, including violations of international humanitarian law (IHL) and human rights law and are legally obliged to make reparation.[49] Perpetrators of international crimes, if convicted as individuals or under principles of command responsibility, face punishment. Until the 1990s there was, however, largely silence about crimes of sexual violence in international processes. Reparations for crimes of sexual violence formed no

---

would be futile owing to the lack of institutional protection, which highlights the extent of sexist cultural patterns': SR on the promotion of truth, justice, reparation and guarantees of non-recurrence, The gender perspective in transitional justice processes, A/75/174, 17 July 2020, para 21.

[44] 'Millions of women and girls are killed, brutalised and intimidated into silence every year': Rebecca Johnson, 'World Courts of Women: against War, for Peace' *Open Democracy*, 25 January 2016.

[45] The first reports of the genocide in Rwanda omitted accounts of the sexual violence committed especially against women and girls before they were killed: Human Rights Watch, *Shattered Lives: Sexual Violence during the Rwandan Genocide and its Aftermath* (1996).

[46] Report of the Independent Expert on protection against violence and discrimination based on sexual orientation and gender identity, Victor Madrigal-Borloz, A/77/235, 27 July 2022, para 31.

[47] Women's International War Crimes Tribunal for the Trial of Japan's Military Sexual Slavery, Case No PT-2000-1-T, Judgment, para 416.

[48] UNSCR 1820, 19 June 2008, preamble.

[49] International Law Commission, Responsibility of States for Internationally Wrongful Acts, UNGAR 56/83, 12 December 2001, Annex, arts 1–3, 31.

part of the peace treaties at the end of either World War I or II, nor were they appropriately prosecuted in international criminal tribunals. The obstacles were not because of unawareness of the commission of the crimes, nor because there was no applicable law.

The widespread allegations of rape and sexual violence in World War I were detailed in official reports and listed by the Commission on war crimes established by the Paris Peace Conference.[50] The entire list was disregarded and omitted from the 1919 Peace Treaty and momentum for an International War Crimes Court was lost.[51] Rape and sexual violence remained largely excluded from the post-World War II narrative and they were not explicitly included as crimes against humanity or violations of the laws and customs of war[52] within the jurisdiction of the Nuremburg Tribunal and the International Military Tribunal for the Far East (IMTFE). Evidence of sexual violence was admitted in the trials but was not prominent in the charges brought or judgments delivered. Judicial language and reasoning are gendered, matching that of male legislators and law enforcement agents.[53] The IMTFE prosecutors and judges were men who interpreted and applied the law in their own image,[54] thereby excluding its potential application to redress harms incurred by others. Over 50 years later, judges at the Tokyo Women's Tribunal, a Peoples' Tribunal[55] where survivors of the 'comfort women' system testified about the rapes and other abuse they had endured during World War II, based their opinion on the international treaties and customary international law binding on Japan in the 1930s and 40s. Evaluation of the women's accounts against the legal principles in force when the crimes were committed, interpreted through a feminist lens, highlighted that the law was not in fact silent about sexual slavery in conflict and that the Japanese state was responsible for its violation.

Rape was included as a crime against humanity in the Order giving jurisdiction over lesser alleged wartime criminals in Europe[56] and in trials held under the auspices of the UN War Crimes Commission.[57] Amidst the silence the voices of some women were heard in courts martial,[58] and as time passed in anonymous

---

[50] The Commission on the Responsibility of the Authors of the War and on Enforcement of Penalties, Report presented to the Preliminary Peace Conference listed rape and the abduction of women and girls: (1920) 14 *American Journal of International Law* 95, 114.

[51] The list of wartime offences produced by the UN War Crimes Commission (UNWCC) that could be charged through national jurisdictions included rape and forced prostitution: Dan Plesch et al, 'The Relevance of the United Nations War Crimes Commission to the Prosecution of Sexual and Gender-based Crimes Today' (2014) 25 *Criminal Law Forum* 349, 351.

[52] Charter of the International Military Tribunal, London, 8 August 1945, art 6(b) and (c); Charter of the IMTFE, Tokyo, 19 January 1946, art 5(b) and (c).

[53] Lucinda M Finley, 'Breaking Women's Silence in Law: The Dilemma of the Gendered Nature of Legal Reasoning' (1989) 64 *Notre Dame Law Review* 886.

[54] The image is that of white men; only three judges at the IMTFE (out of 11) were Asian. Indian Judge Pal placed Japanese actions in the context of allied behaviour including colonialism and racism; Western racial attitudes have indeed 'been a misfortune for mankind': IMTFE, Judge Pal, dissenting opinion, 316.

[55] See essay 15 'Strategic Practices: "Doing Our Own Thing"'.

[56] Control Council Law No 10, Punishment of Persons Guilty of War Crimes, Crimes Against Peace and Against Humanity, December 20, 1945, 3 Official Gazette Control Council for Germany 50–55 (1946), art II(c).

[57] eg trials held under the auspices of the UNWCC; Dan Plesch et al (n 51) 349.

[58] eg the courts martial held in Batavia received women's testimonies in addressing charges of forced prostitution: *Prosecutor v Washio Awochi*, XIII *Law Reports of Trials of War Criminals* 1 (1946); Temporary

accounts⁵⁹ and journalistic interviews.⁶⁰ Nevertheless, legal silence was largely maintained until the 1990s, when persistence by women activists secured the inclusion of crimes of sexual violence in the jurisdiction of the International Criminal Tribunals for the former Yugoslavia and Rwanda, the Special Court of Sierra Leone and the permanent International Criminal Court (ICC).⁶¹

Legal provision offers no guarantee that the silence that sustains impunity will be broken, and gendered obstacles to justice persist. The jurisdiction of the ad hoc international tribunals was limited by time and territorial space and that of the ICC depends on the territorial state or state of nationality of the accused being a party to the Rome Statute,⁶² unless there is SC referral. There is no retroactive jurisdiction.⁶³ The reality remains that international acknowledgment of the prevalence and severity of conflict-affected sexual violence, whether committed against women and girls, men and boys or those targeted for sexual or non-binary gender identity, has not greatly reduced legal silence in international criminal tribunals; conviction of perpetrators remains rare. Like the 'comfort women', Yazidi, Syrian, Rohingya and numerous other survivors of conflict-related sexual violence have found the major obstacle to be the lack of any international tribunal open to them to seek redress.⁶⁴

International crimes may also be prosecuted in national courts⁶⁵ but cases are infrequent.⁶⁶ This section briefly examines international law's complicity in silencing those seeking justice in national courts.⁶⁷ In an echo of patriarchal power over the household and family, states jealously protect exclusive territorial jurisdiction and control over their nationals. International law principles upholding the sovereign equality of states impose jurisdictional obstacles to prosecution of those accused of international crimes outside the territory where they were committed unless the accused is a national of the prosecuting state.⁶⁸ Jurisdiction based on the heinous

---

Court Martial in Batavia in the case of the Army Prosecution Officer, ex officio, against XX, 45 years old, born in Hiroshima-shi, Japan (1-10- 1902), Colonel in the Japanese army, https://www.law.cuhk.edu.hk/en/research/crj/document/Batavia-Judgment-No-72A-1947.pdf: Fred L Borch, *Military Trials of War Criminals in the Netherlands East Indies 1946–1949* (Oxford University Press, 2017).

⁵⁹ *A Woman in Berlin* is an anonymous diary account of the rapes committed by the Soviet military in Berlin in April/May 1945. Originally published in 1954, there was no reissue until 2003 after the author's death.

⁶⁰ eg Svetlana Alexievich, *The Unwomanly Face of War* (1985; Penguin 2018).

⁶¹ See essay 13 'Strategic Practice: Peace and Equality through International Law'.

⁶² Rome Statute of the ICC, 1998, art 12.

⁶³ ibid art 11.

⁶⁴ The state may be found in violation of international law in cases where sexual violence has been evidenced: eg *Application of the Convention on the Prevention and Punishment of the Crime of Genocide* (*Croatia v Serbia*), Judgment, 2015 ICJ Reports 3; *Application of the Convention on the Prevention and Punishment of the Crime of Genocide* (*The Gambia v Myanmar*) Preliminary Objections, 2022 ICJ Reports 1.

⁶⁵ The principle of complementarity bestows ICC jurisdiction only where the national courts are 'unwilling or unable' to exercise jurisdiction: Rome Statute of the ICC, 1998, art 17.

⁶⁶ The UN Secretary-General details trials that have taken place in the annual report to the SC of his Special Representative on conflict-affected sexual violence.

⁶⁷ See CEDAW Committee, General Recommendation No 33 on Women's Access to Justice, CEDAW/C/GC/33, 2015 for analysis of gendered obstacles to accessing justice.

⁶⁸ Additional contested bases of jurisdiction are the nationality of the victim (passive personality) or the adverse effects of the act on the interests of the prosecuting state (protective principle), principles that are favoured by powerful states to maintain their control.

nature of the crimes is an exception to the required territorial or nationality-based nexus between the crimes and the prosecuting state. Celebrated by human rights advocates and with some striking examples,[69] universal jurisdiction designates criminal accountability for the commission of atrocities above state sovereignty. It remains, however, controversial – not least because of the assertion of power by the state exercising jurisdiction and the assumption of judicial and moral superiority conveyed. States allowing for universal jurisdiction are predominantly in the Global North, allowing the construction of a narrative of contemporary violence elsewhere that disregards colonial and other complicity.[70]

Assertions of extraterritorial jurisdiction including legislation, with extraterritorial effect (prescriptive jurisdiction) and adjudicative jurisdiction in civil claims as under the US Alien Tort Claims Act[71] (and in earlier eras through the capitulation regimes in China, Japan and Ottoman Turkey), are further forms of legal imperialism that denigrate weaker states made subject to them. Despite its apparent legal neutrality, extraterritorial jurisdiction 'takes place amidst pre-existing social and political divides … a state can through the exercise of jurisdiction either strengthen or weaken prevailing social and political relations that can be captured using categories such as class, gender, race and caste'.[72] At the same time, powerful states resist the exercise of extraterritorial jurisdiction over their nationals, with the US even threatening the use of force to prevent its possibility.[73]

Universal jurisdiction – when provided for by national legislation and where generally[74] there is physical custody of an accused – is limited to the most egregious crimes. There is, however, no guarantee that these will include crimes such as the gender apartheid imposed by the Taliban since its takeover in Afghanistan in 2021.[75] There is a correlation between crimes for which universal jurisdiction is deemed appropriate and peremptory norms of international law (*jus cogens*): prohibition of crimes against humanity, for instance, is recognised as *jus cogens* and the ILC's Draft Articles on Crimes against Humanity specify states' obligation to establish jurisdiction over these crimes 'where the alleged offender is present in any territory' regardless of where the crimes were committed or the nationality of the offender – in

---

[69] 'First criminal trial worldwide on torture in Syria before a German court' European Center for Constitutional and Human Rights, 2022 (exercise of universal jurisdiction saw Syrian, Anwar R, convicted and sentenced to life in prison for state sponsored torture as crimes against humanity); the trial of Hissène Habré by the Extraordinary African Chambers in Dakar, Senegal for crimes committed in Chad is another celebrated example. See essay 14 'Strategic Practice: Giving Effect to Legal Change'.

[70] Belgian courts exercised universal jurisdiction with respect to the 1994 genocide in Rwanda: *Universal Jurisdiction Law and Practice in Belgium* (Open Society Justice Initiative, Briefing Paper, 2022).

[71] The Alien Tort Claims Act allows foreign nationals to bring civil claims in US courts for violations of public international law committed outside the US.

[72] BS Chimni, 'The International Law of Jurisdiction: A TWAIL Perspective' (2022) 35 *Leiden Journal of International Law* 29, 32.

[73] The American Service-Members Protection Act, 2002 (authorising military force to free an American citizen or citizen of an American ally brought to the ICC). The US is not a party to the Rome Statute of the ICC.

[74] The Rome Statute of the ICC, 1998, art 63(1) states that the accused shall be present at trial. There have been trials *in absentia* in international and national courts, notably the Special Tribunal for Lebanon that tried and convicted *in absentia* persons responsible for terrorist attacks in Beirut in February 2005.

[75] Karima Bennoune, 'The International Obligation to Counter Gender Apartheid in Afghanistan' (2022) 54 *Columbia Human Rights Law Review* 1.

essence, universal jurisdiction.[76] Acceptance of the Draft would clarify that when constituting crimes against humanity, rape and other forms of sexual violence are subject to universal jurisdiction. The same would be the case for gender-based persecution.[77] But the inherent gender bias in what are understood as *jus cogens*, and the contestations over the concept of gender[78] means that this cannot be assumed. Patricia Viseur Sellers has demonstrated that:

> neither normative nor positivist legal conceptualizations of jus cogens have grappled substantively with gender or other values that are prioritized by females or by gender minorities. By default, a masculine approach to peremptory norms persists, ... freedom from gender discrimination would disrupt and dislodge the gender hierarchies still embedded in jus cogens.[79]

Such mindsets might serve as a legal obstacle to the exercise of universal jurisdiction over embedded gender bias even if the practical and political hurdles could be overcome.

In a different understanding of jurisdiction, extraterritoriality extends to determining state responsibility under the human rights treaties for the commission by its agents of violations abroad. The treaties lack clarity with respect to their scope, freeing the UN human rights bodies and Human Rights Council special procedures to give an expansive interpretation to the extraterritorial obligation of states to respect, protect and fulfil human rights.[80] The CEDAW Committee, for instance, while acknowledging that states 'primarily exercise territorial jurisdiction', has clarified that 'States are responsible for all their actions affecting human rights regardless of whether the affected persons are in their territory'.[81] This explicitly applies to situations of armed conflict and emergency.[82] But faced with factual situations, the European Court of Human Rights (ECtHR) has been more circumspect. In interpreting article 1 of the European Convention,[83] the Court has clarified that

---

[76] The state may instead extradite the alleged offender to a state with jurisdiction under the principle of *aut dedere aut judicare*. In February 2024, the Ljublgana-Hague Convention that fills the jurisdiction gap in respect of jus cogens crimes opened for signature.

[77] The Rome Statute of the ICC, art 7(1)(h) includes persecution on the grounds of gender as a crime against humanity.

[78] See essay 2 'Gender'.

[79] Patricia Viseur Sellers, 'Feminist Approaches to International Law Jus Cogens: Redux' (2022) 116 *AJIL Unbound* 281.

[80] eg UN Human Rights Committee, General Comment No 31, 26 May 2004, the Nature of the General Legal Obligation Imposed on States Parties to the Covenant, para 10; Economic, Social and Cultural Rights Committee, General Comment No 24 on State obligations under the International Covenant on Economic, Social and Cultural Rights in the context of business activities, E/C.12/GC/24, 10 August 2017, para 25 ff; Joint General Comment No 3 (2017) of the Committee on the Protection of the Rights of All Migrant Workers and Members of Their Families and No 22 (2017) of the Committee on the Rights of the Child on the general principles regarding the human rights of children in the context of international migration; CMW/C/GC/3-CRC/C/GC/22, 16 November 2017.

[81] CEDAW Committee, General Recommendation No 28 on the Core Obligations of States Parties under Article 2 of the Convention on the Elimination of All Forms of Discrimination against Women, CEDAW/C/GC/28, 16 December 2010, para 12.

[82] ibid para 11; CEDAW Committee, General Recommendation No 30 on Women in Conflict Prevention, Conflict and Post-Conflict Situations, CEDAW/C/GC/30, 31 October 2013.

[83] Convention for the Protection of Human Rights and Fundamental Freedoms, Rome, 4 November 1950, art 1: 'The High Contracting Parties shall secure to everyone within their jurisdiction the rights and freedoms defined in Section I of this Convention.'

for the Convention to apply the person whose rights are allegedly violated must be physically within the spatial or personal control of the state party.[84] The former applies where the state has de facto effective control over an area abroad, while the latter arises where a state agent exercises authority and control over an individual. This reasoning has brought protection to some vulnerable persons and prevented states from avoiding their Convention obligations. For instance, in order to preserve territorial control, European states have sought ways to stop migration through border manipulation, creating – where possible – an impermeable border at sea or outsourcing the border to an enclave abroad such as Ceuta and Melilla in Morocco. States thus seek to keep violent or unruly behaviour outside their borders, maintain a 'civilised' stance and deny responsibility. The ECtHR has held that the Convention continues to apply to these extraterritorial situations.[85]

The Court has, however, excluded active hostilities from the Convention's scope where the objective of the fighting is 'to establish control over an area in a context of chaos'.[86] This has created a significant obstacle in Convention protection. It is hard to see why 'an armed conflict [is] a valid excuse for not accepting extraterritorial jurisdiction during the active stage of hostilities'. This apparent reinstatement of the legal distinction between IHL and human rights law makes little sense from 'the point of view of the victims and their rights, there is no difference between … State agents us[ing] physical force aimed at injuring or killing human beings, and [bombing and artillery shelling … to establish control]'.[87] This exclusion need not, however, apply to conflict-related rape and sexual violence. The Court's explanation that 'What is decisive in such [previous] cases is the exercise of physical power and control over the person in question'[88] precisely describes the act of rape. It is to be hoped that the Court would adjoin the movement for combating violence against women, including in conflict, with its earlier willingness to assert extraterritorial jurisdiction so as not to create a further obstacle to state responsibility for violation in situations of conflict, thereby additionally silencing survivors.

Extraterritorial application of human rights law requires states to ensure that their agents comply with the same legal standards of behaviour abroad as at home and may contribute to the realisation of human rights in other states. But it also provokes concerns about human rights imperialism: 'extraterritoriality sometimes allows powerful States to "put into effect laws that have an extraterritorial effect" in Global South States, through processes over which the latter States have little control and which are initiated without their consent in distant places'.[89] International law principles of jurisdiction support the masculine model of the hegemonic state by

---

[84] *Al Skeini v the United Kingdom*, ECtHR GC, Appl No 55721/07, 7 July 2011.

[85] *Hirsi Jamaa v Italy*, ECtHR GC, Appl No 27765/09, 23 February 2012 (Italy's exclusive *de jure* and de facto control over boat migrants in the Mediterranean brought them within the Convention's protection); *ND and NT v Spain*, ECtHR GC, Appl No 8675/15 and 8697/15, 13 February 2020 (Spain exercised jurisdiction over the individuals who arrived within the Spanish enclave of Melilla in North Africa).

[86] *Georgia v Russia (II)*, ECtHR GC, Appl No 38263/08, 21 January 2021.

[87] ibid Judge Lemmens, dissenting opinion.

[88] *Georgia v Russia (II)* (n 86) para 136.

[89] Independent Expert on human rights and international solidarity, Obiora Chinedu Okafor, International solidarity and the extraterritorial application of human rights: prospects and challenges, A/HRC/50/37, 19 April 2022, para 7.

upholding domestic autonomy and allowing intervention abroad in a new manifestation of the 'civilising mission'. It operationalises through law the structural power imbalance between states of the Global North and those of the Global South.

Establishing jurisdiction is not the end of the problem. The international law doctrine of state (sovereign) immunity protects states from having to answer for their activities before the national courts of another sovereign state, even where there is adequate applicable law and a jurisdictional basis.[90] Immunity blocks consideration of the legal merits of a claim, maintaining the power of the state to determine what is heard and adjudicated upon in the courts of another state. State interests in free-flowing trade and other economic dealings has lifted immunity for commercial activities but it is maintained for alleged human rights violations by the state and its high officials[91] even for violations of *jus cogens* norms.[92] This state-centric stance has been upheld by the ECtHR in cases involving alleged torture[93] and sexual abuse,[94] a conservative approach that perpetuates impunity and silences victims. Japan for instance, has been able to avoid answering legal claims for reparations brought by the former 'comfort women' as domestic courts around the world have upheld international law on sovereign immunity from jurisdiction.[95] Immunity also protects diplomatic staff[96] and the personnel of international organisations[97] from having to answer for their actions in domestic courts. It has been further extended through Status of Forces Agreements between states sending military forces to peacekeeping or security missions abroad and the receiving state, although the latter is unlikely to be in a position to protest.[98] Judges engage other techniques to block claims in national courts, for instance the 'political question' doctrine that renders them non-justiciable.[99] When used as another justification for declaring inadmissible the comfort women's claims, the irony becomes striking; women are not recognised as political actors, are excluded from political decision-making but then have that exclusion deemed political and as such beyond judicial determination.

The SC's WPS resolutions[100] reiterate states' responsibility to put an end to impunity and to prosecute those responsible for atrocities that include sexual violence[101]

---

[90] *Jurisdictional Immunities of the State (Germany v Italy: Greece intervening)*, 3 February 2012; 2012 ICJ Reports 99. In April 2022, Germany instituted new proceedings against Italy for failing to respect its jurisdictional immunity.

[91] ibid para 91: 'The Court concludes that, under customary international law … a State is not deprived of immunity by reason of the fact that it is accused of serious violations of international human rights law or the international law of armed conflict.'

[92] *Jurisdictional Immunities* (n 90) para 97.

[93] *Jones v United Kingdom* ECtHR, Appl No 34356/06 and 40528/06, 14 January 2014.

[94] *JC and Others v Belgium*, ECtHR, Appl No 11625/17, 12 October 2021.

[95] See essay 18 'Transformative Reparations and Gendered Peace'.

[96] Vienna Convention on Diplomatic Relations, 1961.

[97] eg Convention on the Privileges and Immunities of the United Nations, 1946. But see Christine Chinkin, 'United Nations Accountability for Violations of International Human Rights Law' 395 Collected courses of the Hague Academy (Brill, 2019).

[98] Aurel Sari, 'The Immunities of Visiting Forces' in Tom Ruys et al (eds), *The Cambridge Handbook of Immunities and International Law* (Cambridge University Press, 2019) ch 28.

[99] eg *You v Japan*, 150 F Supp 3d 1140, 1144–48 (ND Cal 2015); see essay 18 'Transformative Reparations and Gendered Peace'.

[100] See essay 6 'Revisiting the Past: Peace at Beijing and Beyond'.

[101] UNSCR 1325, 31 October 2000, OP 11.

and call upon states 'to strengthen legislation and enhance investigation and prosecution of sexual violence in conflict and post-conflict situations'.[102] But the resolutions are silent as to state immunity and as to states' responsibility for the extraterritorial acts of their own agents acting either individually or as members of an international or regional organisation, as donors acting through international financial institutions, or for the acts of non-state actors within their jurisdiction such as private militia, corporate bodies, or private military contractors.[103] Failure to address these obstacles to justice undermines the possibilities for peace.

Maintaining – or enforcing – silence about atrocities compromises external attempts at peace-making and internal peace and wellbeing: 'Ultimately, the wall of silence and the cloak of secrecy prevent these people [victims' families and close friends] from making any sense of what they have experienced and are the greatest obstacles to their recovery.'[104] A survivor of the Japanese 'comfort women' system lamented 'that she had not found peace' and would not do so 'until the Japanese government recognises the wrong it has done and compensates the people whom they have done wrong'.[105] Such desire for an end to historical silence, for acknowledgment of wrongs committed and of reparative measures owed is also felt collectively within communities, by indigenous peoples,[106] by the descendants of slaves, by those who endured colonial rule and by many others whose accounts have been suppressed by the narratives of the powerful and for whom public silence is less readily ordained.[107]

---

[102] UNSCR 2467, 23 April 2019, OP 14.
[103] CEDAW Committee, General Recommendation No 30 (n 82) paras 8–17; Committee on Economic, Social and Cultural Rights, General Comment No 24 (n 80).
[104] *El Masri v the former Yugoslav Republic of Macedonia*, ECtHR GC, Appl No 39630/09, Joint Concurring Opinion of Judges Tulkens, Spielmann, Sicilianos and Keller.
[105] Women's International War Crimes Tribunal (n 47) Judgment, para 416.
[106] Australian anthropologist WEH Stanner, in his 1968 Boyer lectures, *After the Dreaming*, broadcast by the Australian Broadcasting Company, described the European settler attitude toward the country's indigenous population as the 'Great Australian Silence'; the Canadian Truth and Reconciliation Commission regretted that 'For too long, Canadian governments chose denial over truth, and when confronted with the weight of truth, chose silence': Honouring the Truth, Reconciling for the Future, Summary of the Final Report of the Truth and Reconciliation Commission of Canada (2015) 372.
[107] See essay 18 'Transformative Reparations and Gendered Peace'.

10
Misogyny and Sexism in the Digital Age

I. INTRODUCTION

ONLINE VIOLENCE AGAINST women[1] – colloquially referred to as the 'shadow pandemic' – has soared to unprecedented levels across the globe. It is a pandemic that feeds on sexism and misogyny. Encapsulated by the acronym GTFO (one that is all too familiar to women who spend any time online) the violence should be understood as directed to the preservation of the patriarchal binary gendered order, online and offline.[2] Online hate speech, disinformation, and non-consensual intimate images are used to demean, silence, and/or drive from public spaces women and girls and anyone who is perceived to challenge the dominant order that privileges cis heterosexual men. It is a pandemic that has festered and spread through state inaction. It is stoked by a growing circle of men in high-profile public office who utilise digital technologies to disseminate their sexist and misogynistic ideas to an expanding global audience, normalising violence against women and girls (VAWG) online and offline, and entrenching the patriarchal order.[3] It is a pandemic fuelled by the commodification of misogyny and sexism through algorithms generated by 'Big Tech', compounding the structural obstacles to gender equality and peace. It is a pandemic that symbolises the surge in the global pushback, organised and coordinated, including by states, reversing decades of feminist activism and progress in advancing women's equality with men as a necessary condition to peace.[4]

Online VAWG is not the only means by which women are silenced in the digital age. The digital gender gap is a form of structural silencing effected through the denial of women's inclusion on an equal basis in an ever-growing digitised world. Structural silencing is global. It is maintained and normalised through unequal access to education,[5] the feminisation of poverty, discriminatory cultural norms, the

---

[1] Diverse terminology is used for the typologies of online violence and of umbrella terms, eg 'digital dimensions of violence against women' (VAW) has been used by international and regional human rights mechanisms to capture both online and technology facilitated VAWG. We use 'online VAW' to focus primarily on information and communication technologies.

[2] Emma A Jane, *Misogyny Online: A Short (and Brutish) History* (Sage Publications Ltd, 2017).

[3] eg Donald Trump had over 83 million followers on Twitter, with mainstream media reporting on, and thus repeating, his words. Narendra Modi boasts over 90 million.

[4] 'Türk urges Solidarity in Face of Gender Equality Backlash', OHCHR, 23 June 2023.

[5] CEDAW Committee, General Recommendation No 36 (2017) on the right of girls and women to education, CEDAW/C/GC/36, 27 November 2017, para 2.

construction of hostile spaces, the absence of law and non-enforcement of existing ones. Women are confronted by multiple layers of gendered obstacles that shape the political economy from the global to the local, preventing them from accessing, benefiting from, and shaping the digital world on an equal basis with men. Patriarchy's gender systems lie at the root of and sustain the structural silencing of women.

In the following section we offer some thoughts on misogyny and sexism as features and causes of gender-based discrimination and VAWG (online and offline) and on recent steps taken by the Council of Europe (CofE) in response. Notwithstanding these efforts, the gendered structural obstacles that silence and deprive women from enjoying their rights on an equal basis with men, online and offline, remain considerable and are multiplying. Feminists have devoted significant energy to developing strategies to address online VAWG and to overcome the barriers to digital inclusion.[6] These strategies are neither entirely problem-free nor without cost. This leads us to ask whether feminist activism needs to be reframed and to reflect on what remains outside the parameters of equality strategies. What do we miss? What do *we* fail to articulate and thereby help silence?

II. MISOGYNY AND SEXISM

For too many women and girls the digital space remains a hostile and toxic environment where they have witnessed and experienced first-hand sexist and misogynistic language and abuse. The attacks usually involve threats of violence, often of a sexual nature and specifically gendered. The distinct features of online attacks, their anonymity, relentlessness, and scale – facilitated by bots and automated agents – differentiate them from offline attacks and magnify the effects of the harm perpetrated.[7] Women are typically doubly attacked for their identity and for the opinions they express,[8] while those with intersecting identities are attacked along multiple vectors. For example, a UK study conducted since the outbreak of Covid-19 shows that Black women[9]

---

[6] For a summary, see Joann Lee and Hélène Molinier, 'Normative Frameworks on Gender Perspective in Technology and Innovation' *UN Women*, November 2022. On institutional efforts to overcome the digital divide, see eg CSW67, Innovation and technological change, and education in the digital age for achieving gender equality and the empowerment of all women and girls: Agreed conclusions, E/CN.6/2023/L.3, 20 March 2023.

[7] The 'acts can be committed at any time and from any place by primary perpetrators and amplified by secondary perpetrators, using digital space and tools that greatly enhance the rate, speed, replication, and permanence of the acts, with significant impacts on survivors': SR on the promotion and protection of freedom of opinion and expression, Gender justice and freedom of expression, A/76/258, 30 July 2021, para 64.

[8] SR on the situation of human rights defenders, Women human rights defenders, A/HRC/40/60, 10 January 2019, para 45. Women working to protect the rights of refugees, migrants, and minorities are especially targeted.

[9] Moya Bailey, *Misogynoir Transformed* (New York University Press, 2021): 'misogynoir' describes 'the anti-Black racist misogyny that Black women experience particularly in US visual and digital culture' and 'the uniquely co-constitutive racialized and sexist violence Black women experience as a result of their simultaneous and interlocking oppression at the intersection of racial and gender marginalization': *The Digital Misogynoir Report: Ending the Dehumanising of Black Women on Social Media* (Glitch UK, 2023) 10.

and non-binary people have experienced the highest rates of online abuse, often of a dehumanising nature, reproducing and amplifying the intersectional discrimination encountered offline and fuelling trends that were clearly discernible prior to 2020.[10]

Women are disproportionately targeted online and suffer disproportionately serious consequences.[11] The UN Secretary-General has reported on how '[d]isturbing trends of gender-based hate speech and incitement to violence fuelled conflict', and lead to further sexual violence. In another manifestation of silencing, 'Internet restrictions impeded the ability of survivors to access information, with frequent telecommunications shutdowns hindering access to helplines and other support services.'[12] The effects of online violence can be tangible and grave. Some victims suffer trauma, at times long-term, with socio-economic costs. Many have forcibly self-censored,[13] retreating from the digital space with the resultant loss of freedom of expression and public participation, consequences that are detrimental to society as well as to the individual concerned. Impunity for online VAWG is fostering a rise in sexist and misogynistic behaviour offline, demonstrated by studies showing how 'the disinhibited behaviour of men online has transferred to the street and other places'.[14] Rights activists view the digital realm as the 'new battleground' in the struggle for the rights of women and girls.[15] It is a global battle that is deeply political, organised, and coordinated and waged by states and non-state actors through gender disinformation campaigns and targeted gender-based violence.[16] It is a battle that many fear is being lost, which makes pressing the need for states to take urgent action to counter misogyny and sexism online and offline.[17]

The surge in retrogressive movements and the growing global backlash against feminism, gender equality, and women's empowerment has prompted feminist scholars to develop a more nuanced theoretical understanding of misogyny and sexism and their inter-relationship.[18] This work is needed to ensure the adoption

---

[10] 'Government Responses to COVID-19: Lessons on gender equality for a world in turmoil' (UN Women, 2022) 36. Intersectional discrimination is not registered and consequently unaddressed and silenced by law: Glitch UK, ibid.

[11] SR on violence against women, its causes and consequences, online violence against women and girls from a human rights perspective, A/HRC/38/47, 18 June 2018, para 28.

[12] UN Secretary-General, Conflict-related Sexual Violence, 14th Report, January–December 2022, S/2023/413, Fact Sheet.

[13] 'Measuring online violence and harassment against women journalists in Latin America' (UNESCO, 2021) on self-censoring by women journalists.

[14] Baroness Helena Kennedy, QC, *Misogyny – A Human Rights Issue* (Working Group on Misogyny and Criminal Justice, 2022) 9. Digital technologies have enabled the formation and radicalisation of Incel communities through 'echo-chamber dynamics' leading to mass killings: Stephane J Baele et al, 'From "Incel" to "Saint": Analyzing the Violent Worldview behind the 2018 Toronto Attack' (2021) 33 *Terrorism and Political Violence* 1667.

[15] SR on the freedom of expression (n 7) A/76/258 para 4.

[16] Foreign state-sponsored campaigns to target women politicians and feminist movements while autocratic political leaders have promoted gendered disinformation campaigns targeting especially women opposition leaders: Lucina Di Meco, 'Monetizing Misogyny' (#ShePersisted, 2023).

[17] eg studies show that violent extremist language in the incelosphere is steadily increasing: Stephane Baele et al, 'A Diachronic Cross-Platforms Analysis of Violent Extremist Language in the Incel Online Ecosystem' (2023) *Terrorism and Political Violence*.

[18] Kate Manne, *Down Girl – The Logic of Misogyny* (Oxford University Press, 2017); Irene Zempi and Jo Smith (eds), *Misogyny as Hate Crime* (Routledge, 2022). For earlier work see Andrea Dworkin, *Woman Hating* (Plume, 1974).

of laws and policies that can most effectively contribute to the eradication of both phenomena.

Misogyny is a term that has evolved over time. Its first popular usage is said to be a 1618 publication, *Swetnam, the Woman-hater*, and its protagonist, Mysogenos.[19] The anonymous work was one of several that appeared (including by Rachel Speght[20] and two other writers, both of whom are believed to be women) following the publication of Joseph Swetnam's virulent pamphlet, *The Arraignment of Lewd, Idle, Froward, and Unconstant Women*.[21] The *Oxford English Dictionary* defines 'misogyny' expansively, as the 'hatred or dislike of, or prejudice against women'. This definition tells us nothing about misogyny as a social or relational phenomenon, nor about its link to patriarchy.

Philosopher Kate Manne offers a more useful starting point, understanding misogyny as 'primarily a property of social environments in which women are liable to encounter hostility due to the enforcement and policing of patriarchal norms and expectations – often, though not exclusively, insofar as they violate patriarchal law and order'.[22] Misogyny operates to *enforce* women's subordination and to uphold male dominance and entitlement; women who are viewed as challenging the patriarchal gender binary order are especially 'punished', often through coercive means.[23] We see this played out online with women in public life – in politics, journalism, and human rights activism – being disproportionately targeted 'to intimidate, silence and drive them off the platforms and out of public life'[24] *because* they are women in a patriarchal world. Although women are the primary focus of misogyny, anyone whose identity or acts unsettles the patriarchal heterosexual binary order is at risk of attack, which is precisely why non-binary people are targeted.[25]

Male entitlement provides the assumption upon which misogyny operates.[26] In examining whether to list 'sex' as a hate crime, the Working Group on Misogyny

---

[19] See https://www.gutenberg.org/ebooks/58303.
[20] https://pages.uoregon.edu/dluebke/WesternCiv102/SpeghtMouzell1617.htm.
[21] See https://pages.uoregon.edu/dluebke/WesternCiv102/SwetnamArraignment1615.htm.
[22] Kate Manne (n 18) 19.
[23] Feminist scholars have shown how witch-burning was politically organised and orchestrated by ruling elites that disciplined women into accepting the patriarchal order. On the complex relationship between the misogynistic practices of witch-hunting, property ownership, and the expansion of capitalism through European colonialism, see Silvia Federici, 'Witch-Hunting, Globalization, and Feminist Solidarity in Africa Today' (2008) 10 *Journal of International Women's Studies* 21.
[24] Statement by Irene Khan, SR on freedom of expression, OHCHR, 18 October 2021: A letter to Facebook signed in 2019 by women legislators from 30 countries demanded that it 'stop the amplification of gendered disinformation' on its platform, stating, 'make no mistake, these tactics, which are used on your platform for malicious intent, are meant to silence women, and ultimately undermine our democracies': Lucina Di Meco (n 16) 27.
[25] This is captured, in part, by the term 'transmisogyny': Maria Marron, *Misogyny and the Media in the Age of Trump* (Lexington Books 2020) 2 ('leaders in this era of conservative populism have escalated misogynist remarks, demeaning women, minorities, and non-hegemonic males [and] although gender is the primary focus of misogyny, it also pertains to intersectionalities such as race, ethnicity, age, ability, and other variables not aligned with supremacist hegemonic masculinity and the patriarchal system').
[26] Male entitlement is intimately linked to white supremacy, manifesting in women of colour being doubly attacked: Kate Manne, *Entitled: How Male Privilege Hurts Women* (Crown Publishing, 2020).

and Criminal Justice in Scotland proposed defining misogyny as 'a way of thinking that upholds the primary status of men and a sense of *male entitlement*, while subordinating women and limiting their power and freedom' (emphasis added). It continues that 'conduct based on this thinking can include a range of abusive and controlling behaviours including rape, sexual offences, harassment and bullying, and domestic abuse'.[27] The Group of Experts on Action against Violence against Women and Domestic Violence (GREVIO), established to monitor implementation of the CofE's Istanbul Convention,[28] likewise notes that online VAW 'is rooted in the same context of women's inequality and *men's sense of entitlement* as the psychological, sexual and physical violence experienced by women and girls in the offline world' (emphasis added).[29] Male entitlement manifests in and founds the right to have *control over* women and girls which, by definition, is always coercive. It is enacted through personal, structural, and epistemic violence.

The term 'sexism' has also evolved over time, although its lineage is more recent. Coined in the 1960s by feminists, sexism names how patriarchy normalises the belief that women are inferior to men. The absence, until recently, of a definition of sexism in international law presented a normative obstacle since, however pernicious the consequences, *international* law provided little redress while the harm remained unnamed.[30] In March 2019 the CofE adopted a Recommendation on Preventing and Combating Sexism[31] which, with the accompanying Guidelines, defines sexism and details measures for eradicating online and offline sexism and hate speech.

The Recommendation defines sexism as:

[a]ny act, gesture, visual representation, spoken or written words, practice or behaviour based upon the idea that a person or a group of persons is inferior because of their sex, which occurs in the public or private sphere, whether online or offline, with the purpose or effect of:

 i. violating the inherent dignity or rights of a person or a group of persons; or
 ii. resulting in physical, sexual, psychological or socio-economic harm or suffering to a person or a group of persons; or
 iii. creating an intimidating, hostile, degrading, humiliating or offensive environment; or
 iv. constituting a barrier to the autonomy and full realisation of human rights by a person or a group of persons; or
 v. maintaining and reinforcing gender stereotypes.

---

[27] Helena Kennedy (n 14) 29.
[28] Council of Europe Convention on preventing and combating violence against women and domestic violence, Istanbul, 11 May 2011. It is the most comprehensive treaty on VAW, defining VAW as 'a human rights violation and form of discrimination against women'.
[29] GREVIO General Recommendation No 1 on the digital dimension of violence against women, 20 October 2021, para 24.
[30] The obligation to tackle both misogyny and sexism is implicit in international and regional human rights instruments that require states to guarantee human rights, gender equality and to prevent violence against women.
[31] Recommendation CM/Rec(2019)1 adopted by the Committee of Ministers of the Council of Europe, 27 March 2019.

The Recommendation recognises that sexism is reproduced through assumptions, beliefs, customs, traditions, theories, stereotypes, and social and cultural narratives to naturalise and consolidate biological difference as a basis for asserting that one sex is superior to the other resulting in discrimination against the supposedly inferior sex.[32] Although sexism affects both women and men, in that it has typically functioned to justify or rationalise patriarchal social orderings and relations across time and space, it is women who have been and continue to be disproportionately penalised and prejudiced. Sexism often goes unnoticed and unremarked, which is what makes it so harmful. Nor is sexism always coercive: it can manifest in unconscious and apparently benign bias, stereotyping, and discrimination. This does not prevent its consequences from being serious. Sexist beliefs and behaviour can result in domestic violence, hate speech, gender-based violence, and exclusion from public spaces deemed masculine, for instance peace processes.

The CofE Recommendation is welcome as a progressive commitment to gender equality. It fills a normative gap, serving as the 'prequel' to CEDAW and the Istanbul Convention, providing states with a well-developed blueprint for addressing the *causes* of gender-based discrimination and VAWG, online and offline.[33] Yet, as with many multilateral initiatives involving women's equality and combatting VAWG, the instrument is a non-binding recommendation. Moreover, its location within the European regional framework limits its geographical reach. The shortcomings of soft law instruments, the fragmentation of law pertaining to VAWG, and the institutional siloing that results, are obstacles that feminists have long identified.[34] And the very fact that women are still having these discussions demonstrates the embedded sexism that underpins law-making and law-enforcement by the gendered state.

III. OBSTACLES TO ADDRESSING ONLINE VAW

Over the last several years there has been a flurry of attempts to tackle online VAWG including at the regional level,[35] although such activities have not resolved the problems and have even thrown up further obstacles. An example of such activity was the conference hosted by Iceland (then holding the Presidency of the CofE) in December 2022 on online VAW that brought together the CofE divisions

---

[32] CEDAW, art 5 requires state parties to take appropriate measures to modify social and cultural patterns of individual conduct to eliminate 'prejudices and customary and all other practices which are based on the idea of the inferiority or the superiority of either of the sexes or on stereotyped roles for men and women': reiterated Istanbul Convention, art 12.1.

[33] Christine Chinkin, 'New European Recommendation Aims to Prevent and Combat Sexism' *LSE Blog*, 14 May 2019.

[34] Rashida Manjoo, 'Twenty Years of Normativity without Legality – United Nations Developments on Violence against Women, its Causes and Consequences' (2016) 3 *Queen Mary Human Rights Law Review* 1; SR on VAW, its causes and consequences, Adequacy of the international legal framework on violence against women, A/72/134, 19 July 2017; SR on VAW, Violence against women, its causes and consequences, A/HRC/41/42, 20 June 2019.

[35] eg EU Directive to Combat Violence against Women and Domestic Violence, COM (2022) 150 final, 8 March 2022; EU Digital Services Act, Regulation (EU) 2022/2065.

on Violence against Women and Cybercrime.[36] The aim was to explore how two separate CofE treaty regimes, the Istanbul Convention and the Budapest Convention on Cybercrime,[37] might align to investigate and prosecute online VAW more effectively. The initiative was welcomed by mainstream women's rights groups which have long demanded that states investigate and prosecute perpetrators of online VAW.[38] State inaction trivialised, effaced, and normalised the harms perpetrated online against women and girls, creating a vicious circle leading to ever more violence.

The Istanbul Convention, like the Budapest Convention, is open to *all* states, not just to member states of the CofE.[39] This enables it to fill a normative gap, in that there is no *international* treaty specifically on preventing and combating VAW.[40] However, and notwithstanding the prevalence of VAW across the world, only 37 states are parties[41] to the Istanbul Convention (and none from outside the CofE) in contrast to the Budapest Convention which boasts 68 states parties,[42] evidencing the gendered obstacles that feminist activists continue to confront when engaging with the state.[43]

Since its creation in 2015, GREVIO has repeatedly reminded states parties of their obligations to tackle online VAWG[44] pursuant to the Istanbul Convention.[45] Its first General Recommendation on the digital dimensions of VAW evidences its concern over state inaction and provides a comprehensive set of measures to prevent and combat online VAW in public and private life, based on the four pillars of the Convention: prevention; protection; prosecution; and coordinated policies.[46] It also notes that the Budapest Convention 'usefully complement[s]' the Istanbul Convention framework by providing a comprehensive set of legally binding standards to secure evidence and engage in cross-border co-operation.[47] Additional Protocol 2 to the

---

[36] See https://www.coe.int/en/web/cyberviolence/-/joining-forces-for-high-level-conference-on-digital-violence-against-women.

[37] Convention on Cybercrime, Budapest, 23 November 2001, in force July 2004.

[38] Critical feminists are more sceptical of carceral responses (criminalisation, increased policing, prosecution and imprisonment) that fail to address the root causes of heteropatriarchal violence whilst reconfiguring the state as women's protectors: Angela Davis et al, *Abolition. Feminism. Now.* (Penguin, 2022).

[39] Both instruments provide a template for enacting domestic legislation for states that choose not to become a party.

[40] The Istanbul Convention builds on and complements the work of the CEDAW Committee, which has further developed its framework for tackling VAWG: CEDAW Committee, General Recommendation No 35 (2017) on gender-based violence against women, updating general recommendation No 19, CEDAW/C/GC/35, 26 July 2017. The Committee clarified that the Convention applies in the digital sphere: ibid paras 20, 30.

[41] On 1 June 2023 the EU ratified the Convention, effective 1 October 2023.

[42] An additional 19 states have signed or been invited to accede.

[43] The UK took ten years to ratify the treaty, doing so (with reservation) in July 2022, in force November 2022; despite being in the midst of conflict, Ukraine ratified the treaty prior to the UK.

[44] Istanbul Convention, art 3(f): '"Women" includes girls under the age of 18'.

[45] The definition of VAW in Istanbul Convention, art 3(a) includes the digital dimension: GREVIO (n 29) para 33.

[46] ibid para 18.

[47] States parties to the ECHR must provide officials with the means for effective investigations and criminal proceedings of online crimes: *KU v Finland*, Appl No 2872/02, 2 March 2009. States must enable law enforcement agencies to obtain access to dynamic IP addresses and communication data to identify a private person who has violated another individual's right to private life; legislators must follow societal and technical developments and amend legislation to provide effective protection and to provide for electronic evidence for investigations of alleged violations.

Budapest Convention[48] aims to enhance inter-state cooperation and disclosure of electronic evidence by providing enforcement agencies with a legal basis for obtaining subscriber and traffic data information directly from service providers located in the jurisdictions of other states parties, surmounting the obstacles to effective investigations due to 'cloud computing, territoriality and jurisdiction'.[49] In short, the Protocol extends to law enforcement bodies significant additional powers unhindered by traditional conceptions of jurisdiction that bar states from enforcing sovereign rights on the territory of another state.[50]

Useful though these additional tools may be, impunity for online VAWG is primarily a structural issue that *cannot* be resolved by extending the investigatory powers of law enforcement agencies. In many states, existing legislation to prohibit and criminalise online VAWG remains deficient.[51] Even where laws exist, institutional sexism remains prevalent so that law enforcement agencies fail to investigate and courts trivialise VAWG, obstructing women's access to justice.[52] The compound effect is that women are typically denied gender justice for *online* VAWG, reproducing their experiences of the justice system in respect of *offline* VAW, including where there are no jurisdictional obstacles.

Sexism permeates law-making as it does law enforcement. For example, the Budapest Convention, despite its achievements, is gender-blind in that offences perpetrated against women and girls in the digital realm or by digital technologies are neither mentioned nor conceptualised within its framework, serving to silence online VAWG.[53] This silencing persists. The 2022 Explanatory Report to Additional Protocol 2 to the Budapest Convention, for instance, makes no references to online VAW when describing the different forms of cybercrime that have increased over the last two decades and which are considered by states to present 'a serious threat to human rights' warranting additional tools.[54] States' reluctance to prohibit and criminalise sexist hate speech – online or offline – is another example.[55] Although the International Covenant on Civil and Political Rights prohibits hate speech on the basis of national, racial or religious grounds that constitutes incitement to discrimination, hostility or violence, there is no mention of gender or sex.[56]

---

[48] Second Additional Protocol to the Cybercrime Convention on Enhanced Co-operation and Disclosure of Electronic Evidence, Strasbourg, 12 May 2022. The Protocol has 22 signatories to date.
[49] Explanatory Report to the Second Additional Protocol to the Cybercrime Convention, para 10.
[50] See essay 9 'Silence as an Obstacle to Gendered Peace and Equality'.
[51] Chioma Nwaodike and Nerissa Naidoo, 'Fighting Violence against Women Online: A Comparative Analysis of Legal Frameworks in Ethiopia, Kenya, Senegal, South Africa, and Uganda' (Internews & Policy, 2020) section V.
[52] CEDAW Committee, General Recommendation No 33 on women's access to justice, CEDAW/C/GC/33, 3 August 2015, paras 26–29.
[53] This silence is all the more pronounced given that Budapest Convention, art 9 requires states parties to adopt domestic legislation prohibiting different online acts pertaining to child pornography. In cybercrime state resources are directed primarily at countering terrorism, money laundering, major fraud, arms and drug smuggling, identity theft for the purpose of financial gain.
[54] Explanatory Report to the Second Additional Protocol to the Convention on Cybercrime para 5.
[55] SR on freedom of expression (n 7), Section E uses the term 'gendered hate speech'.
[56] ICCPR, art 20(2). CERD Committee, General Recommendation 35 on Combating racist hate speech, CERD/C/GC/35, 26 September 2013, interprets ICERD art 4 as prohibiting racist hate speech. CEDAW contains no provision on sexist hate speech. The CEDAW Committee has addressed sexist hate

This normative gap trickles down to the regional and domestic levels with, for instance, only 14 CofE states explicitly recognising sex or gender as a ground for hate speech and even fewer including a reference to the applicability of the law to the digital sphere.[57] Pressure from feminists operating within and outside international and regional institutional structures of law-making and -shaping is beginning to pay dividends but patriarchal resistance to change remains intransigent.[58]

Lawmaker resistance[59] is rooted in an androcentric worldview shaped by sexism. Violence is defined by male experience that does not recognise online VAWG within a continuum of violence experienced by women. As the Platform of Independent Expert Mechanisms on Discrimination and Violence against Women (EDVAW Platform) observes:[60]

> Physical acts of violence are often considered more serious than, and separate from, online and technology-facilitated experiences of violence, with many laws, policies and practices only applying to the offline world. However, such approaches fail to understand that violence against women is experienced as a continuum of online and offline experiences.[61]

Consequently, state responses tend to be piecemeal rather than holistic, often crafted in reaction to specific campaigns or tragedies.[62] This creates further normative gaps and obscures the knock-on rights violations that women experience, thereby depriving them from enjoying those rights on an equal basis with men.[63] Feminists

---

speech under art 5: Alexandra Timmer and Rikki Holtmaat, 'Article 5' in Patricia Schultz et al (eds), *The UN Convention on Elimination of All Forms of Discrimination against Women: A Commentary*, 2nd edn (Oxford University Press, 2022) 247.

[57] Sara De Vido and Lorena Sosa, 'Criminalisation of Gender-based Violence against Women in European States Including ICT-facilitated Violence' (European Commission, 2021) section 9.2. In most jurisdictions, legislation criminalising hate speech does not recognise sexist hate speech so there is no data. States that have legislated for sexist hate speech generally treat it as an aggravating factor – except Belgium, which recognises it as an autonomous offence.

[58] SR on the freedom of expression (n 7) has urged for gendered hate speech to be addressed within the international framework of hate speech and, in egregious cases, to carry criminal penalties. CofE Recommendation on combating hate speech, CM/Rec (2022) 16[1], 20 May 2022 expressly includes sex, gender and sexual orientation, online and offline, and in serious cases for criminal sanctions to apply.

[59] The UK government has opposed the introduction of the hate crime of misogyny following the Law Commission, Hate Crime Laws: Final Report (2021). The report concluded that making misogyny a hate crime may be 'more harmful than helpful' to victims of VAWG and to 'efforts to tackle hate crime more broadly': 'hate crime recognition would not be an effective solution to the very real problem of violence, abuse and harassment of women and girls in England and Wales and may in fact be counterproductive in some respects'. It noted that it would be difficult to prove in court, make prosecuting crimes against women and girls more difficult and introduce a hierarchy of serious crimes. The Report was criticised by women's rights groups, eg https://www.fawcettsociety.org.uk/news/joint-response-to-law-commission-review-of-hate-crime.

[60] The EDVAW Platform was launched in March 2018 at the initiative of the UN SR VAW to bring together seven international and regional mechanisms to harmonise and improve the implementation of international legal and policy frameworks on VAWG.

[61] 'The digital dimension of violence against women as addressed by the seven mechanisms of the EDVAW Platform', Thematic paper adopted by the EDVAW Platform at its 14th meeting, November 2022, 9.

[62] 'While many countries have introduced new laws to criminalise some forms of online and technology-facilitated abuse, many provisions have limits on their scope, as well as on their practical implementation. This is often due to laws being introduced because of specific campaigns or high-profile tragedies, rather than constituting a comprehensive and holistic response to all forms of online and technology-facilitated violence against women': ibid 28.

[63] Domestic legislation was failing to recognise online VAWG as a continuum of offline VAW and the harmful impact it had on social, economic, psychological and participatory rights: GREVIO, GR 1 (n 29)

have repeatedly urged states to recognise that women experience violence through a complex continuum and that measures to counter online VAW cannot be adequately addressed without taking account of this reality.[64]

Feminist activists have emphasised the need for 'a holistic and multisectoral approach'[65] to accountability that requires a mix of legal measures, criminal and civil, together with social responses including – but not limited to – enhanced training of state agents, designing education programmes, running national campaigns, and providing specialist services such as those elaborated by GREVIO.[66] Some states are rolling out more holistic programmes at the domestic level, although they remain the exceptions. Moreover, national efforts to counter online VAW without international collaboration will always be deficient, given the cross-border nature of online communities.[67] Building on the work of the CEDAW Committee and HRC Special Procedures,[68] each of these human rights mechanisms have provided separately and collectively concrete guidance to states[69] on combating sexism and sexist hate speech, online and offline. Yet, such calls largely go unheeded.

Confronted by the silence of the patriarchal state, feminist activists have resorted to self-help measures that paradoxically risk relieving the state of its core human rights obligations. The partial abdication by the state is rooted in a neoliberal political ideology that operates on the rationale that social problems can be resolved by empowering individuals to overcome the structural barriers present in all societies, thereby diverting attention from states' failure to dismantle those barriers. This rationale validates a 'light touch' approach by states, most notably in the digital sphere. It has also provoked the now all-too-common rejoinder to those who find themselves in the digital firing line that 'developing resilience' is what is required of them, while distracting attention from the gendered state's part in first creating the social problem.

States have been equally slow to regulate the activities of Big Tech that dominate the digital ecosystem, providing the platforms through which online VAW has been propagated.[70] Negotiations on a human rights treaty to regulate their activities as well as those of other transnational corporations have lasted over eight years, leaving

---

para 16. GREVIO considers 'the hateful abuse to which women are subjected in online environments' to not only amount to gender-based violence against women but to undermine a number of other human rights of women as protected by international law, including women's participatory rights: ibid para 13.

[64] Joanne Neenan and Christine Chinkin, 'International Law and the Continuum of Gender-based Violence' *LSE Blog*, 6 April 2017.

[65] Adriane van der Wilk, 'The Relevance of the Istanbul Convention and the Budapest Convention on Cybercrime in Addressing Online and Technology-facilitated Violence against Women' (CofE, December 2021).

[66] GREVIO, GR 1 (n 29).

[67] Thematic paper adopted by EDVAW (n 61) 29.

[68] CEDAW Committee, General Recommendation No 35 (n 40); SR VAW (n 11) online violence report.

[69] The mechanisms responsible for overseeing state compliance with the Protocol to the African Charter on Human and Peoples' Rights on the Rights of Women in Africa (Maputo Protocol) and the Inter-American Convention on the Prevention, Punishment, and Eradication of Violence against Women (Belém do Pará Convention) have elaborated measures for countering online VAW: Thematic paper adopted by EDVAW (n 61) 12–16.

[70] Statement by Irene Khan, SR on freedom of opinion and expression, UN GA 76th session (3rd Committee) 18 October 2021 ('The patriarchal norms of the real world are replicated on platforms, targeting young women and gender non-conforming people, especially those with marginalized identities').

the digital gatekeepers free to reproduce directly and indirectly the interests of capital, and entrenching the obstacles to equality and peace. Since corporate strategies are dictated by commercial calculations, technologies and algorithms that make content sticky and viral and therefore profitable are not only allowed but often *encouraged* to proliferate,[71] even though they generate sexist and gendered misinformation and ideology.[72] Misogyny and sexism are commodified through the political economy of the digital platforms.

The adoption of voluntary guidelines by Big Tech has done little to change the reality that responses to complaints by women who have been the target of online violence remain woefully inadequate.[73] In rejecting self-regulation as a solution, feminists have drawn attention to the fact that platform providers are not neutral hosts, just as the state is not a value-free receptacle. Patriarchal interests that intersect with profit determine what is privileged or expunged, who is heard or silenced in this sphere. The misogynist-racist online violence is not only symptomatic of, but *integral* to, the reproduction of the techno-patriarchal capitalist logic that underpins the operation of Big Tech, replicating the patriarchal/capitalist logic of the (neo)colonial state.

International human rights mechanisms have repeatedly drawn attention to the unprecedented powers exercised by these non-state actors that at times exceeds that of the state itself.[74] But they remain largely unconstrained by international law notwithstanding the enormous impact that corporate decisions have over human rights.[75] Big Tech may have the *responsibility* to respect human rights as elaborated in the UN Guiding Principles on Business and Human Rights[76] but, save where human rights obligations are translated into domestic law, remedies for rights violations remain unenforceable.[77] Some progress is being made at the regional level. The EU's

---

[71] SR on freedom of expression, On-line hate speech, A/74/486, 9 October 2019, para 40.

[72] CofE Recommendation on Preventing and Combating Sexism (n 31) II.B.7: 'Design of data-driven instruments and algorithms should factor in gender-based dynamics. ... Transparency around these issues should be improved and awareness raised about the potential gender bias in big data; solutions to improve accountability should be offered.'

[73] 'Putting the onus on women is a PR stunt – the platforms are the problem', letter to Big Tech senior personnel including Facebook/Instagram, Twitter, TikTok and Google from a women's collective, 1 July 2021. While Facebook has created an oversight board with the power to overturn decisions to censor material, this does not necessarily mean that steps taken to address VAWG are adequate. The inadequacy of self-regulation was made apparent when, in December 2022, after taking control of Twitter, Elon Musk disbanded its Trust and Safety Council, a group of 100 independent activists, academics and civil leaders that advised the company on tackling hate speech, leading to a sharp increase in online hate speech.

[74] 'Governments are no longer the primary regulators of speech ... in a reversal of the historic roles, private corporations have even become the de facto regulators of government speech': Richard A Wilson and Molly Land, 'Hate Speech on Social Media: Content Moderation in Context' (2021) 52 *Connecticut Law Review* 1029, 1032.

[75] eg Facebook's failure to address the violence perpetrated against the Rohingya community in Myanmar through the platform prompted significant criticism, including by the SR on freedom of expression (n 71) A/74/486, para 41. See Independent International Fact-finding Mission on Myanmar, Report, 8 August 2019 A/HRC/42/50, paras 70–75.

[76] UN SRSG, Guiding Principles on Business and Human Rights: Implementing the United Nations 'Protect, Respect and Remedy' Framework, Principles 11–24, A/HRC/17/31, 21 March 2011; SR on freedom of expression (n 7) IV.

[77] eg in Germany the Network Enforcement Law requires companies to act quickly to remove unlawful content and provides for substantial penalties for failure to do so. The attendant risk is one of overregulating

Digital Services Act introduces mandatory due diligence obligations on platform providers,[78] while the Inter-American Commission on Human Rights has launched a multi-stakeholder initiative to establish content moderation standards.[79] These developments are welcome but constitute only a fragment of the broader tapestry of work that is needed to dismantle the structures that give rise to online VAWG.

IV. EXCLUSION AND INCLUSION AS OBSTACLES

As with online VAW, the digital gender gap is the product and cause of inequality rooted in sexism, gender stereotyping, gender social norms, and patriarchal control.[80] Digital exclusion has taken on far greater political salience with the unprecedented pace at which all sectors of society transferred online post-2020,[81] leading to new forms of discrimination and exacerbating pre-existing ones. Within technologically advanced states, it was those women who were, prior to the pandemic, already disproportionately excluded from benefiting from digital technologies who found themselves doubly excluded with the shift to online work, social interaction, and the transfer of core state services online.[82] Meanwhile, in states with the least developed digital infrastructure, it was women and girls living in poverty in rural areas, migrant women and those with disabilities who were 'left behind', as revealed by the International Telecommunication Union's figures that show that women now represent a larger share of the 2.7 billion people worldwide with no access to digital technologies compared with pre-pandemic figures.[83]

In that digital exclusion deprives women and girls of opportunities to acquire and exchange knowledge and to fully participate in society, it represents an individual and collective loss. But exclusion constitutes more than lost *opportunities*. In a digitised world in which access to healthcare, education, social services, and justice,

---

content. An alternative legal entry point not yet explored is whether social media providers might be held directly responsible for violations of IHRL in that they are deemed to have 'effective control'.

[78] Regulation (EU) 2022/1925 of the European Parliament and of the Council, 14 September 2022. The Digital Services Act entered into force on 1 November 2022. The designated 'gatekeepers' have until March 2024 to ensure that they follow its obligations.

[79] The Americas Dialogue established by the SR on freedom of expression in collaboration with the IACommHR: https://www.americasdialogue.org/en/americas-dialogue/.

[80] Report of the Secretary-General on Innovation and technological change, and education in the digital age for achieving gender equality and the empowerment of all women and girls, E/CN.6/2023/3, 30 December 2022, paras 6–9.

[81] Studies show how lockdown measures accelerated digitisation of the economic sector by three to four years. Prior to the pandemic, even among the most technologically advanced sectors, the transition to remote working was estimated to take over a year; in the pandemic it took an astonishing average of 11 days to implement workable solutions: McKinsey & Company, 'How Covid-19 has Pushed Companies over the Technology Tipping Point – and Transformed Business Forever' 5 October 2020.

[82] eg, in the UK, more than half of those offline are women. Age, disability, rurality, poverty and race all compound exclusion: Hannah Holmes, and Gemma Burgess, 'Digital Exclusion and Poverty in the UK: How Structural Inequality Shapes Experiences of Getting Online' (2022) 3 *Digital Geography and Society*.

[83] International Telecommunication Union, 'Measuring Digital Development: Facts and Figures 2022' (three years after the outbreak of Covid-19, the digital gender gap, measured in absolute numbers, has increased by 20 million. Globally, men continue to gain greater access to the internet and mobile phone ownership than women. Women also lag behind men in the effective use of technology due to other dimensions of discrimination such as education and skill gaps and restrictions on autonomy).

among other rights, are increasingly being provided online (sometimes exclusively so) women and girls are disproportionately deprived from enjoying such rights on an equal basis with men and boys, thus compounding the obstacles to equality and peace. States' insistence that the right to digital access is an emerging rather than existing right in customary international law,[84] does not absolve them from the obligation not to discriminate. The CSW, at its 2023 session, sought to address this divide, urging states to prioritise 'digital equity' and elaborating on specific measures to close the gender digital divide.[85] CSW's Agreed Conclusions build on the legacy of the Beijing Declaration and PFA centring the traditional equality paradigm that assumes the problem of exclusion can be remedied through inclusion. Yet, in calling for equality there is a need to remain mindful of the gendered costs that are at stake and what inclusion entails. What do we miss – and thereby silence – in the process of demanding equality of access and use within the existing parameters of the digital architecture that is, after all, rooted in the logic of patriarchy and global racial capitalism?[86] Does inclusion, in and of itself, represent a form of submission to digital coloniality, an obstacle to equality and peace?

V. FINAL THOUGHTS

In closing, we step back and reflect not only on *who* is silenced in the digital age and *how* this is manufactured, but also on *what* is silenced – typically effected through siloing, intended or not. For example, in pressing for equality of access to and use of digital technologies, what falls from view is the extractivist-commodifying logic of capitalism upon which the digitised world is constructed. Feminists have been fierce critics of the gendered effects of capitalist systems,[87] yet the insights they offer are often treated as separate to the digital equality discourse that seeks gender equality within the existing structures of the global digital economy. A similar siloing occurs in respect of the huge environmental toll that digitisation exacts. Feminist activists and women from indigenous communities are frequently at the forefront of critical work exposing how the production of digital devices depends on extractive practices that destroy ecosystems and generate toxic waste and pollution; of how the construction and operation of server farms that rely on vast amounts of water deprive local communities and habitats; of how the disposal of digital devices in landfills leads to contamination of land and water; and of how the brunt of the harm created by digital technologies is disproportionately shouldered by the most marginalised women and in whose name we champion digital

---

[84] HRC resolution, Promotion, protection and enjoyment of human rights on the Internet, 13 July 2021, A/HRC/47/L.22, para 5; contrast SR on the promotion and protection of the right to freedom of opinion and expression, Frank La Rue, A/HRC/17/27, 16 May 2011; Human Rights Committee, General Comment No 34, Article 19: Freedoms of opinion and expression, CCPR/C/GC/5, 12 September 2011, para 15.

[85] CSW67, Agreed Conclusions (n 6) para 86(a)–(x).

[86] Gargi Bhattacharyya, *Rethinking Racial Capitalism: Questions of Reproduction and Survival* (Rowman and Littlefield International, 2018).

[87] Maria Mies, *Patriarchy and Accumulation on a World Scale: Women in the International Division of Labour* (Zed Books, 1986).

rights.[88] Likewise, what we also risk missing is the military-industrial-technological complex of the digital world that stretches back at least 50 years and the cascading gendered implications thereof.[89] We risk missing how surveillance capitalism, which forms the backbone of a patriarchal digital world, is exploited for political and economic gain at a disproportionate cost to women. And we risk missing how digital inclusion can become the very conduit through which patriarchy reasserts control over women's bodies and minds, entrenching the obstacles to security and peace.[90]

In March 2023 we went to see 'Women Talking', a film based on Miriam Toew's novel by the same name. Although the work is inspired by events that unfolded at a particular moment in time and place, the tragedy is the banality of the situation in which the women find themselves. Confronted by the violence of patriarchy, the women of the community must choose between three options: do nothing; stay and fight; or leave. The final choice made becomes almost secondary to the process of unravelling and understanding the complexities of the intersecting structures of oppression that give rise to women's subordination and the violence directed at them. The CSW is a platform that facilitates women talking. It is an opportunity to critically rethink feminist strategies going forward and to acknowledge that feminist battles must be fought on multiple fronts. Yet, sometime between Nairobi and Beijing peace – one of the three thematic strands (the other two being equality and development) – fell off the agenda.[91] Peace invites us to think about the structures that give rise to oppression and violence and opens up the conversation. There are no easy answers. But the point is that we need to keep talking, listening, and hearing one another and do so without being confined by the intellectual silos that prevent us from imagining alternative peaces.

---

[88] CSW67, Agreed Conclusions (n 6) para 22: 'the importance of ensuring the integrity of all ecosystems, including oceans, and the protection of biodiversity' and embraces the neoliberal logic that 'technology and innovation can assist countries in improving climate change adaptation and mitigation' thereby sidestepping the harm created by technologies to ecosystems and the environment that disproportionately impacts women.
[89] Roberto J González, 'Militarising Big Tech: The Rise of Silicon Valley's Digital Defence Industry' *TNI*, 7 February 2023.
[90] eg Sandra Duffy, 'Your Life is Not Your Own – *R v Foster* and the Criminalisation of Abortion' *sandraduffy.blog*, 13 June 2023.
[91] See essay 6 'Revisiting the Past: Peace at Beijing and Beyond'.

11

Crisis and Emergency: Entrenching Gender Systems and Militarism

I. INTRODUCTION

IN ITS CONTEMPORARY usage, 'crisis' denotes a disruptive event or situation demanding action. It is also a narrative device that qualifies what counts as an event, its significance, and ramifications.[1] We reflect here on the conceptual and material obstacles to peace that result from the gendered construction of crises by political elites and mainstream international lawyers, narratives that engender misgivings for us as anti-militarist feminists. We elaborate on our anxieties against the backdrop of the use of military force which has entrenched patriarchal gendered orders with catastrophic consequences for those made vulnerable by such force. The ever-greater securitisation and militarisation of crisis narratives constituted at the intersection of policy and law is a deeply troubling development, with far-reaching gendered consequences antithetical to equality and peace.

Crises narratives were proliferating in mainstream discourse well before the outbreak of Covid-19, the most significant global health crisis in over a century.[2] At times it seemed that the twenty-first century was being defined by multiple, overlapping, mutually constitutive, and interlinked crises, geographically defined, as with Yemen, Ethiopia, Afghanistan, Ukraine, Palestine, or thematically as with the global financial crisis, the climate emergency, food scarcity, war, human displacement and migrations, public health crises, and the crises of racism, sexism, transphobia, to name a few.[3] The ubiquity of such narratives spawned a growing body of scholarship,[4] with attention being directed to theoretical and epistemological inquiries around what constitutes a crisis, who decides, and the implications thereof.

---

[1] Janet Roitman, 'Framing the Crisis: COVID-19' *Arena Online*, 12 November 2021.

[2] In 1918–1919, approximately 500 million people, or one-third of the world population, became infected with the H1N1 virus, commonly referred to as the Spanish flu, which was spread worldwide by the movement of troops. Over 50 million are estimated to have died of the virus.

[3] Elke Krasny, 'Staying with the Crisis: A Feminist Politics of Care for Living with an Infected Planet' (2020) 16 *Escritura e Imagen* 307.

[4] Some scholars have called for the creation of an interdisciplinary field of crisis studies: Thomas Gammeltoft-Hansen et al, 'Crisis: Critical and Interdisciplinary Perspectives' (2022) 12 *Global Discourse* 456.

II. INTERNATIONAL LAW'S CRISIS NARRATIVES

Crisis has always been a central concern of international law. International lawyers portray a crisis as an event or situation that presents a serious threat to the sovereign state, to international 'peace and security' or the stability of the international order. The paradigmatic crisis is war or the threat of war. International lawyers' fixation with the crisis of war is perhaps only to be expected given contemporary international law's genealogy in the UN Charter: 'to save succeeding generations from the scourge of war'. Yet, as Hilary Charlesworth compellingly argues, the discipline's self-referential preoccupation with crisis comes at the cost of impoverishing law's development, narrowing its agenda, and limiting its potential.[5] The consequence is that dominant approaches restrict us from imagining the pursuit of equality, freedom, and peace other than through international law's prism of crisis or through a negative peace.[6] This is further limited by the gendered assumptions and norms upon which law defines and constitutes crisis.

Critical feminists are generally sceptical of crisis narratives tendered by the state, since naming a set of events or a situation as 'a crisis' is more than simply semantics or an empirical observation; it is a 'conceptual claim'[7] that is deeply political and gendered.[8] For feminists, the state's claim can often prove disquieting, because what constitutes a crisis is defined by a narrow class of political elites predisposed to a particular outlook. The dominance of cis heterosexual men as both architects and protagonists of crises erases women and all who do not conform to the gender binary and leads to a disregard for the intersectional gendered impact of crises. Narrowing is further effected with framing what constitutes a crisis through the parameters of a national security paradigm, with a bias towards privileging facts deemed to fall within the public domain to the exclusion of the private, and an obliviousness to 'the patriarchal male-dominant sex-gender order' we inhabit.[9] These tendencies are replicated through mainstream international law crisis narratives that privilege the public over the private and the spectacular over the banal,[10] obscuring the extant patriarchal order of the state and its use of coercive power to maintain its place within the gendered international order.

Feminists have also noted how through crisis narratives political elites problematise certain issues in ways that function to exclude the broader landscape – contextual, structural, and temporal. In other words, the sex-gender order is not the

---

[5] Hilary Charlesworth, 'International Law: A Discipline of Crisis' (2002) 65 *Modern Law Review* 377.
[6] See essay 3 'Peace in International Law'.
[7] Janet Roitman (n 1).
[8] Special Issue: 'Feminists Interrogate State of Emergency' (2013) 25 *Feminist Formations*.
[9] Cynthia Cockburn, 'Feminist Antimilitarism: Patriarchy, Masculinities and Gender Awareness in Antiwar Organizing' in *Gender and Militarism: Analyzing the Links to Strategize for Peace* (Women Peacemakers Program, May 24 Action Pack 2014) 33.
[10] Christine Chinkin, 'From the Spectacular to the Everyday: International Law, Violence and the Agenda for Women Peace and Security' in *Experiencing Violence* (British Academy, 2021); Vasuki Nesiah, '"A Mad and Melancholy Record": The Crisis of International Law Histories' (2021) 11 *Notre Dame Journal of International and Comparative Law* 232, 242 (noting how international law's crises focus on 'short, intense periods of extraordinary violence [that] normalizes systemic abuses and ordinary or "slow violence"' that it has contributed to creating). Austerity policies following the 2008 financial crisis exemplifies this.

only dimension that is effaced. This narrowing diverts attention from the structures of oppression that the state has had a hand in creating and maintaining, which are often at the root of the crisis it ostensibly seeks to address. For example, rather than scrutinising the logic of global capitalism that relies on the propagation of crises to survive,[11] global financial crises are typically traced by hegemonic states and international organisations to the poor practices of specific states (usually 'developing'), individuals (usually non-white, poor, and women) and singular entities that are treated as anomalies (Lehman Brothers) rather than as archetypical players.[12] Likewise, the crisis of migration and influx of refugees into countries of the Global North are framed as problems caused by criminal gangs that exploit the illegal trans-border transfer of people or with the 'illegal' migrant and resource-draining asylum seeker rather than with hegemonic policies that create structural inequalities, closed borders, poverty and war.[13] The crisis of nuclear weapons is when a state unreasonably threatens their use (as Putin has done in Ukraine), when an outlier state seeks their possession (North Korea, Iran) or when there is a threat of their acquisition by terrorists rather than with the militarisation of peace and security that rationalises their possession and accumulation by the permanent member states of the UN Security Council (SC). The myopic identification of crisis pre-determines responses through the selection of facts deemed relevant to the constitution of the crisis. International lawyers tend not to excavate the structural or historical causes of crises, though for a different reason. For the doctrinal lawyer, remaining within law's conceptual parameters is often justified as necessary to preserve a hermetically sealed self-referential system within which legal judgment can take place.[14] The consequence is that international lawyers can become participants in eliding law's structure and history in constituting the very crises that the discipline subsequently claims to address.[15]

International law's crises narratives obscure and silence the everyday lived crises experienced by the oppressed, diminishing the perpetual condition of crisis to which many are consigned. The ensuing despair is poignantly captured by Dionne Brand when, reflecting on the official responses by the US to the outbreak of Covid-19, she

---

[11] Financial markets thrive on volatility to maximise profit for the benefit of the few; for political consequences see Naomi Klein, *The Shock Doctrine: The Rise of Disaster Capitalism* (Penguin Books, 2007).

[12] Paula Chakravartty and Denise Ferrerira da Silva, 'Accumulation, Dispossession, and Debt: The Racial Logic of Global Capitalism' (2012) 64 *American Quarterly* 361 (reading the US subprime crisis through the dual lens of race and empire reveals how 'the predatory targeting of economically disposed communities was recast as a problem caused by the racial other', reproducing the patterns of accumulation/dispossession at the inter-state level that characterised colonialism and still persist).

[13] These narratives occlude the fact that low-income countries host a disproportionately large share of the world's displaced people: eg in 2022, 76 per cent of refugees were hosted by low- and middle-income countries: UNHCR, *Global Trends Report* 2022.

[14] eg the reasoning on facts relevant to legal judgment in *Janowiec v Russia* ECtHR GC (2013) 58 EHRR 792, para 110.

[15] eg China Mieville, 'Multilateralism as Terror: International Law, Haiti and Imperialism' (2009) 19 *Finnish Yearbook of International Law* 63 (damning critique of international law's multilateralism in Haiti); Vasuki Nesiah (n 10) (international law's history in facilitating slavery and racial oppression). The legal analyses on the 2023 Israel/Palestine conflict generated by IHL lawyers exemplifies this trait: eg many IHL lawyers were more focused on the scope of the precautionary obligation in attack and to give effective advance warning pursuant to Geneva Conventions Additional Protocol I, art 57(2)(c) than in taking into account the historical context of the mass forced displacement of Palestinians in 1948 and subsequently.

wrote 'I've been living a pandemic all my life: it is structural rather than viral; it is the global state of emergency of antiblackness'.[16] International lawyers do not usually regard structural violence – or the death and disability that result from socio-economic inequalities – as constituting a crisis, notwithstanding the fact that such violence causes several times more excess death and disability than suicide, homicide and warfare combined.[17] Structural violence simply does not constitute a crisis threatening the national security of the state, nor does it merit urgent action.

A. Arbitrariness of Law's Time

The concept of crisis is founded on a temporal fiction that assumes a definable beginning and end. International lawyers adopt and reproduce this fiction,[18] distinguishing between emergency and normality or war and peace to identify what law applies to curtail absolute sovereign power through the scope of legal responsibility.[19] For example, the unprecedented number of states that formally declared Covid-19 to constitute a state of emergency as a preliminary step towards derogating from some of their human rights treaty obligations prompted the international human rights community to engage in discussions over the scope and content of human rights law in times of emergency.[20] While some questioned whether derogation was necessary – pointing to limitation clauses within treaty texts[21] – others posited that derogation was preferred to demarcate the exceptionality of the powers being claimed by states and their (supposedly) limited duration.[22] The differences were primarily strategic, in

---

[16] Dionne Brand, 'On Narrative, Reckoning and the Calculus of Living and Dying' *Toronto Star*, 4 July 2020.

[17] Bandy X Lee, 'Causes and Cures VII: Structural Violence' (2016) 28 *Aggression and Violent Behavior* 109, 110.

[18] It is reflected in the mandates establishing legal entities such as commissions of inquiry that are extended as the crisis endures or mandates that are terminated notwithstanding the continued existence of a crisis: eg the Independent International Commission of Inquiry on the Syrian Arab Republic was established by Human Rights Council resolution S-17/1, 22 August 2011 and extended endlessly, most recently to March 2024.

[19] A legal finding of an armed conflict introduces the law of armed conflict, a separate legal regime that not only permits lethal force in armed conflict that would otherwise be unlawful but allows for the curtailment of rights, compounding the obstacles to equality and peace and reversing any progress made: Louise Arimatsu, 'The Democratic Republic of the Congo 1993–2010' in Elizabeth Wilmshurst (ed), *International Law and the Classification of Conflicts* (Oxford University Press, 2012) 146.

[20] 'Derogations by States Parties from Article 21 ICCPR, Article 11 ECHR, and Article 15 IACHR, on the Basis of the COVID-19 Pandemic', 3 March 2021 (right to peaceful assembly and association), https://www.rightofassembly.info/assets/downloads/Derogations_by_States_Parties_from_the_right_to_assembly_on_the_Basis_of_the_COVID_19_Pandemic_(as_of_3_March_2021).pdf; UN Human Rights Committee, Statement on derogations from the Covenant in connection with the COVID-19 pandemic, 30 April 2020, CCPR/C/128/2 (detailing when states could lawfully derogate from the Covenant); Alain Zysset, 'To Derogate or to Restrict? The COVID-19 Pandemic, Proportionality and the Justificatory Gap in European Human Rights Law' (2022) 4 *Jus Cogens* 285. The ECtHR rejected the claim that lockdown measures constituted a deprivation of liberty pursuant to ECHR, art 5(1): *Terhes v Romania*, Appl No 49933/20, 13 April 2021. The claimant did not raise ECHR, Protocol No 4, art 2 (freedom of movement) so the Court did not examine the validity of the derogation notified by Romania to the CofE.

[21] eg exceptions relating to measures necessary to protect public health.

[22] Alan Greene, 'States Should Declare a State of Emergency Using Article 15 ECHR to Confront the Coronavirus Pandemic' *Strasbourg Observers Blog*, 1 April 2020 (failure to derogate risks normalising

that the common position was to urge for normalcy. For feminists, the challenge has been to bring into these discussions an understanding of sovereign power as patriarchal power, a perspective that causes us to agonise over the very idea of normalcy and law's part in maintaining the status quo. We shared the view expressed by feminists across the world that a return to a pre-crisis 'normal' was no answer, as it would simply lead back to a point where repetition becomes inevitable. The crisis we feared was that there would be no change other than a return to the patriarchal violence of the gendered order. Return to 'normal' would be the crisis.

In redefining security as 'the absence of violence whether it be military, economic, or sexual', feminists have drawn attention to the patriarchal myth that crises end.[23] International lawyers also have difficulties in defining the end of crises.[24] Lawyers tend to treat protracted crises as fact and, in so doing, sidestep the question of law's part in constituting the new normal, as exemplified by the 'war on terror' or protracted occupations that deprive those entangled in law's crises of peace in perpetuity.[25]

B. Arbitrariness of Law's Facts

How international lawyers engage with facts is equally problematic in at least two inter-related respects. First, as Charlesworth observes, law's construction of crisis is, by definition, limited because it rests on 'truncated and selective understandings of events' to fit within its own normative parameters.[26] Context and history are usually the casualties of this process. Second, law insists on its distinction from facts, although both are mutually constituted. For example, in determining whether an armed conflict exists for the purpose of identifying the applicable law, international lawyers search for the relevant facts to support the criteria established by law: the intensity of the hostilities and an organisational element.[27] What is forgotten is that these criteria were extrapolated from a landscape of facts from which the International Criminal Tribunal for the former Yugoslavia (ICTY) concluded that an armed conflict exists when there is 'protracted armed violence between governmental authorities and organized armed groups or between such groups within a state'.[28] International lawyers adopt the two criteria condensed from the Tribunal's description (as though the law has always existed divorced from the facts) and through legal

---

exceptional powers). For a different view, see Martin Scheinin, 'COVID-19 Symposium: to Derogate or Not to Derogate?' *Opinio Juris blog*, 6 April 2020. CEDAW contains no derogation clause.

[23] J Ann Tickner, *Gender in International Relations: Feminist Perspective on Achieving Global Security* (Columbia University Press, 1992) 66.

[24] Marko Milanovic, 'The End of Application of International Humanitarian Law' (2014) 96 *International Review of the Red Cross* 163.

[25] Christine Chinkin, 'Women's Human Rights in Timor-Leste and Western Sahara' in Katlyn Thomas et al (eds), *Justice on Trial: Law Politics and Western Sahara* (IPJET, 2022) 205; *Legal Consequences Arising from the Policies and Practices of Israel in the Occupied Palestinian Territory, Including East Jerusalem* (Request for Advisory Opinion) ICJ, 19 January 2023.

[26] Hilary Charlesworth (n 5) 382.

[27] These criteria for qualification were set out by the ICTY in *Prosecutor v Tadić*, Decision on the Defence Motion for Interlocutory Appeal, 2 October 1995, IT-94-1, para 70.

[28] ibid.

technique and objective criteria (gendered though they are) filter 'relevant' from 'superfluous' facts to determine whether a crisis meriting the application of IHL exists. As a result, international lawyers produce crisis narratives that often have little affinity with unfolding events, which are always more complex, messy, fluid, intersectional, and contingent. But in doing so they assume that the law is sufficient, neutral, objective and even self-evident, which is why feminist international lawyers urge a gender analysis – in respect of both facts and law – to introduce alternative facts and to expose law's normative gaps and biases.[29] What facts, we ask ourselves, are silenced by law's gendered assumptions and norms?[30]

Obliviousness to the crises experienced by others is a form of repression that undercuts all possibility for equality and peace. It is the product of dominant crises narratives that privilege a patriarchal and siloed worldview in which events and facts are treated as isolated and disconnected from context, both spatially and temporally. This enables the gendered state, assisted by international law which it has created (and which created it), to define and privilege 'authentic' crises such as war and pandemics, whilst suppressing the crises of gender and racial inequalities, poverty and of violence against women. These are not characterised by states as 'crises' meriting urgent action, save as additional justifications for external intervention.[31] Intervention is the response made by (powerful) outsiders to what they perceive as a crisis in another country; international law principles on non-intervention[32] supposedly contain a crisis within national boundaries, upholding the sovereignty of the state in crisis, but this objective has become diluted and disregarded. Gender norms – often interwoven with race – play a vital part in the construction of international law's crisis narratives that knit together the protection of women's rights with the imperative of military intervention, as in the 2001 military intervention in Afghanistan. This co-option of women's rights enfolded into gendered crisis narratives to justify urgent military interventions incenses and causes us fear in equal measure.

III. MILITARISM, GENDER AND CRISES

Over two decades on, the legal basis for the use of force in Afghanistan by the self-identified 'coalition of the willing' remains contested.[33] Following the 9/11 attacks, international lawyers scrambled to fill what was claimed to be a normative gap in

---

[29] See essay 15 'Strategic Practices: "Doing Our Own Thing"'.

[30] Chrisine Chinkin et al, '*Bozkurt* Case, aka *Lotus* Case (*France v Turkey*): Ships that Go Bump in the Night' in Loveday Hodson and Troy Lavers (eds), *Feminist Judgments in International Law* (Hart Publishing, 2019) 34, 36–39.

[31] Karen Engle, '"Calling in the Troops": The Uneasy Relationship among Women's Rights, Human Rights, and Humanitarian Intervention' (2007) 20 *Harvard Human Rights Journal* 189; Anne Orford, *Reading Humanitarian Intervention: Human Rights and the Use of Force in International Law* (Cambridge University Press, 2009).

[32] UNGAR 2625, 1970, Declaration on Friendly Relations.

[33] Louise Arimatsu and Michael Schmitt, 'The Plea of Necessity: An Oft Overlooked Response Option to Hostile Cyber Operations' (2021) 97 *International Law Studies* 1171; Adil Ahmad Haque, 'Clearly of Latin American Origin: Armed Attack by Non-State Actors and the UN Charter' *Just Security blog*, 5 November 2019.

the UN Charter. The Charter was intended as a blueprint for promoting inter-state peace and to prevent inter-state war so that crises not arising out of relations between sovereign states simply did not fall into its original scope. International lawyers nonetheless assisted states to reshape treaty law, specifically article 51 of the Charter on self-defence, and the law of state responsibility to claim the legality of military force against an armed attack by a non-state actor (Al Qaeda) located in Afghanistan. Race and gender were enfolded into law's crisis narrative: first to circumvent the Taliban, the de facto government – whose treatment of women facilitated their depiction as medieval, uncivilised, outside of modernity and of international law and therefore unable to benefit from it; and second, to further justify military intervention as a means by which to liberate Afghan women from the Taliban's oppressive rule: 'the military intervention was saturated with the rhetoric of gender liberation'.[34] International law's construction of the crisis of 9/11 has, since then, encouraged further rewriting of the law[35] enabling hegemonic powers to resort to military force legitimised through international law. The programme of extra-territorial military bases, targeted killings and detentions flow from the original legal claim, creating cascading crises and mounting obstacles for peace and equality. Meanwhile, Afghan women are now largely forgotten.[36] As lawyers, the very fact that our discipline played a pivotal part in constructing the multiple crises that have continued to be disproportionately shouldered by Afghan women is difficult to absorb let alone square with our faith in the law.

The reinterpretation of the Charter's text has presented even those lawyers who supported an expansive reading with legal problems that are now difficult to unravel. Some have attempted to craft new legal arguments including, for example, a customary international law principle around the idea of 'unwilling and unable' that allows states to resort to armed force outside the text of the UN Charter.[37] Other lawyers have, for the most part, resisted this claim, as we have, but for different reasons.[38] As anti-militarist feminist lawyers we hold onto the belief that international law *is* the obstacle to the political crises of war and not an instrument through which to legally justify war and violence. The absence of a legal right to resort to violence is not a normative gap to be filled but a silence that calls for reflection and an opportunity to redirect minds to alternative options short of military force.

The task of anti-militarist feminists has again[39] become especially onerous over the last two decades, with the increasing dominance of a limited, militarised conception of security taking root – not least within the UN SC, which has primary responsibility for the maintenance of international peace and security.[40] This is made particularly

---

[34] Ratna Kapur '"The First Feminist War in All of History": Epistemic Shifts and Relinquishing the Mission to Rescue the "Other Women"' (2022) 116 *AJIL Unbound* 270, 271.

[35] eg reinterpretation and revival of UNSCR 678, 29 November 1990; 687, 3 April 1991 and 1441, 8 November 2002 to justify the 2003 invasion of Iraq; HL Deb, *Hansard*, 17 March 2003, col WA2.

[36] See essay 8 'Introduction to Part III'.

[37] Ashley Deeks, 'Unwilling or Unable: Toward a Normative Framework for Extra-Territorial Self-Defense' (2012) 52 *Virginia Journal of International Law* 483.

[38] Monica Hakimi, 'Defensive Force against Non-State Actors: The State of Play' (2015) 91 *International Law Studies* 1.

[39] See essay 4 'Introduction: Rewriting International Law's Histories'.

[40] UN Charter, art 24.

concerning by the more expansive understanding of what constitutes a threat to, or endangerment of, 'international peace and security' in the post-Cold War period. This has left us in a double bind, exemplified by the SC's WPS agenda, which while promoting as core to international peace and security the protection of women in conflict, has framed such protection within a narrow, militarised paradigm built on a gender binary and essentialist narratives.[41] SC resolutions pertaining to Covid-19 as constituting an 'endangerment to international peace and security'[42] introduced the risk that the public health crisis would be securitised and militarised,[43] thereby predetermining appropriate responses and by whom they could be made, with adverse implications for gender equality and peace.

Feminists have long viewed militarism as a serious impediment to both peace and equality. The militarised language used by mostly male political elites in responding to the outbreak of Covid-19, prompted us, as a gesture of feminist solidarity and resistance, to expose and critique the strategy.[44] The outpouring of militarised rhetoric diverted attention from the legal responsibilities of states and non-state actors. Equally troubling was the language of war, which enables political elites to invoke the collective 'we' and occlude the fact that risk is *never* equally distributed; it was, we thought, inappropriate, disingenuous and deeply offensive. Moreover, in that such rhetoric is 'dependent on the elevation of a particular construction of masculinity which necessitates a binary notion of gender', we viewed it as 'dangerous'.[45] Our fear was that the rhetoric of militarism would nurture an emboldened bellicose agenda to define immediate and long-term responses, priorities, and operational strategies, thereby creating new obstacles to gender equality and to peace while calcifying pre-existing ones.

War rhetoric is a powerful tool. In crises it can help to justify far-reaching restrictions on civil liberties whilst mobilising social solidarity and public support for incumbents. But its effectiveness is contingent on the prior 'peacetime' acceptance and assimilation of the ideas and norms of militarism and the extent to which social orders and institutional structures of governance from the local to the global are already shaped by its logic.[46] Crises do not produce militarism but rather rekindle existing forms of militarism and cultivate new ones that feed on gendered assumptions and patriarchal relations of power.

---

[41] See essay 6 'Revisiting the Past: Peace at Beijing and Beyond'.

[42] UNSCR 2565, 26 February 2021 and 2535, 1 July 2020 on Covid-19. It previously adopted two on ebola, UNSCR 2439, 30 October 2018 and 2177, 18 September 2014; and two on HIV/AIDS, UNSCR 1983, 7 June 2011 and 1308, 17 July 2000.

[43] Over the last decade critical scholars have noted how the politics of global health has been securitised and infectious diseases framed as security issues. Securitisation creates the conceptual basis upon which direct involvement by the armed forces becomes natural.

[44] Louise Arimatsu and Rasha Obaid, 'In Times of Crisis' *LSE Blog*, 9 June 2020; Christine Chinkin and Madeleine Rees, 'Our Male Leaders Declared War on the Pandemic. Our Response Must Match That' *LSE Blog*, 11 May 2020.

[45] Chinkin and Rees, ibid.

[46] Militarism is broader than war, comprising an underlying system of institutions, practices, values, and cultures: Laura Sjoberg and Sandra Via, 'Introduction' in Laura Sjoberg and Sandra Via (eds), *Gender, War, and Militarism: Feminist Perspectives* (Praeger, 2010) 7.

Feminist scholars have elaborated on how militarism and gender knit together to make relationships of oppression and war appear natural and reasonable. Unpacking this further, Cynthia Enloe identifies seven beliefs core to militarism:

> that armed force is the ultimate resolver of tensions; that human nature is prone to conflict; that having enemies is a natural condition; that hierarchical relations produce effective action; that a state without an army is naïve, scarcely modern and barely legitimate; that in times of crisis those who are feminine need armed protection; and that in times of crisis any man who refuses to engage in armed violent action is jeopardizing his own status as a manly man.[47]

In other words, binary gender systems are deeply implicated in rationalising and weaving together the logic of militarism which in turn rationalises patriarchy's gender systems of subjugation.[48] Feminist scholarship has further demonstrated how through war narratives militarised masculinities founded on stereotypical characteristics such as strength, authority, individualism, aggression and protection are privileged in contradistinction to stereotypical feminine traits, weak, passive, dependent and in need of protection, that consign women to the role of supporter and victim. Feminists have catalogued the ways in which socially constructed identities and norms are deeply imbricated in cultures of militarism that normalise particular configurations of power, relationships, and beliefs through structures and systems of governance at all levels of human interaction. Gender and militarism thus feed on and stoke each other thereby producing effects that adversely impact the rights of women to live in a world free of oppression, subordination, and violence.[49]

Failure to see the workings of gender in the crisis of conflict renders deficient mainstream accounts of the causes of conflict. This restricts international law's effectiveness, as exemplified by the conflict in Ukraine.[50] Patriarchy's binary gender systems saturate the conflict, its causes, how the conflict is shaped, fuelled and perpetuated and its gendered effects.[51] Gender norms operate in and through the figure of Putin, a hostage to his own gender binary narratives and a toxic militarised masculinity that upholds violent exercise of power, and through the policies of political elites in Ukraine and further afield. Gender systems, reinforced through law, determine who stays and who leaves, who can leave and who cannot, who is armed, with what, and by whom. Gender defines who lives, who dies, where and how.[52] The conflict is producing

---

[47] Cynthia Enloe, 'Understanding Militarism, Militarization, and the Linkages with Globalization using a Feminist Curiosity' in *Gender and Militarism: Analyzing the Links to Strategize for Peace* (Women's Peacemakers Program, 2014). See also Cynthia Enloe, *Bananas, Beaches and Bases: Making Feminist Sense of International Politics*, 2nd rev edn (University of California Press, 2014) for the linkages between US military bases abroad and women's insecurity.

[48] Militarism is 'gendered to the ground': Ann Scales, 'Soft on Defense: The Failure to Confront Militarism' (2005) 20 *Berkeley Journal of Gender, Law and Justice* 369, 388.

[49] We are not suggesting that women do not contribute to militarism and the socio-political processes of militarisation. Clearly, they do: bell hooks, 'Feminism and Militarism: A Comment' (1995) 23 *Women's Studies Quarterly* 58.

[50] On 24 February 2022, the Russian Federation launched a full-scale armed attack on Ukraine diverting global attention from the public health crisis to that of war, as well as from earlier Russian military activity in Eastern Ukraine and the annexation of Crimea in 2014.

[51] Louise Arimatsu and Christine Chinkin, 'War, Law and Patriarchy' *LSE Blog*, 5 April 2022.

[52] *Rapid Gender Analysis of Ukraine* (UN Women and Care International, May 2022).

and reproducing gender identities, reinventing and repackaging gender norms that are consumed globally through mainstream and social media, including videos that go viral. International law also saturates this conflict. International lawyers in the West have flocked to provide legal analyses, primarily supporting Ukraine,[53] and in response to Ukraine's strategic juridification of the conflict.[54] These interventions have not changed the course of the war and for the most part have become an exercise in providing a legal container for documenting violations and arguments for future accountability. International law is peripheral and mainstream legal interventions fail to recognise that at every level gender systems impact the war.[55] Neither conflict prevention nor law compliance in war can be secured without addressing the gender systems that are sutured into the fabric of militarism that make war and violence a rational pursuit.

Feminist concerns – that state framing of the global pandemic as constituting a threat to national security, and as analogous to war, coupled with the patriarchal rhetoric of militarism would prove detrimental for advancing equality and peace – were warranted in at least three ways. First, mainstream narratives by and large reproduced executive-generated pandemic narratives, thereby endorsing the qualities of a 'patriarchal protective masculinity' that have reinforced 'crisis leadership as a male domain'.[56] Second, by casting the virus as the 'foreign enemy' and a threat to national security, ideas around nationalism have been fostered, including through policies of 'vaccine nationalism' that have further entrenched the patriarchal state as protector.[57] Third, war rhetoric enabled executive branches to resort to operational tactics more common in wartime to enforce Covid-19 related regulations, upheld by the state enforcement agencies, thereby blurring the line between civil and military. The use of military labour, including by the UN, through militarised peacekeeping, to perform civil, humanitarian, policing, development and crisis management activities has become the new normal, with calls to reject militarised solutions largely ignored.[58] For many feminists, militarised framings are especially problematic in

---

[53] eg John B Bellinger III, 'How Russia's Invasion of Ukraine Violates International Law' (Council on Foreign Relations, 2022); 'Agora Essays: The War in Ukraine and the Future of the International Legal Order' (2022) 116 *American Journal of International Law* 687.

[54] Ukraine has commenced multiple cases: *Allegations of Genocide under the Convention on the Prevention and Punishment of the Crime of Genocide* (Ukraine v Russian Federation: 32 States intervening), order on provisional measures, 16 March 2022; *Application of the International Convention for the Suppression of the Financing of Terrorism and of the International Convention on the Elimination of All Forms of Racial Discrimination* (Ukraine v Russian Federation), order on provisional measures, 19 April 2017; *Ukraine v Russia (re Crimea)* ECtHR GC Appl Nos 20958/14 and 38334/18), admissibility decision 16 December 2020; *Ukraine and The Netherlands v Russia* ECtHR GC, Appl. Nos 8019/16, 43800/14 and 28525/20, admissibility decision 30 November 2022; and arbitral proceedings under annex VII of the UN Convention on the Law of the Sea.

[55] The critique we offer here applies equally to the 2023 Israel/Palestine conflict.

[56] Blair Williams and Brent Greer, 'All's Fair in Pandemic and War? A Gendered Analysis of Australian Coverage of Covid-19' (2023) 11 *Media and Communication* 91. While 'key workers' were depicted as 'heroic fighters on the frontline', the flipside of this militarised logic was the need for sacrifice of the lowest paid for the 'common good'.

[57] Thomas J Bollyky and Chad P Bown, 'The Tragedy of Vaccine Nationalism' (2020) 99 *Foreign Affairs* 96.

[58] Recommendations to prioritise demilitarisation and develop effective strategies for conflict prevention and nonviolent civilian protection in the SC-instigated Global Study have been ignored by the SC: Radhika

that the means by which to respond to perceived threats are narrowly construed and typically violent. An example is the Armed Forces of Liberia erecting in 2014 a razor wire cordon around the oldest slum in West Point, Liberia to contain the spread of Ebola.[59] As with war management, seeking to obliterate the threat through containment was prioritised over longer term prevention strategies. Similar tactics were deployed by states in response to Covid-19, while punitive methods used by the armed forces and law enforcement officials resulted in higher incidents of violence, disproportionately affecting women and those belonging to minority communities.[60]

This was unsurprising, as the government agencies charged with enforcement in times of crisis often come with a history of institutional sexism and misogyny, obstacles that women confront daily across the world. In the UK, for example, the decision by the police to prevent Reclaim These Streets – an organisation dedicated to countering violence against women – from organising a vigil following the kidnap and murder of a young woman, Sarah Everard, by a serving police officer displayed, at best, an insensitively to the concerns of women.[61] For feminists, this obliviousness is founded on an institutional culture of sexism and misogyny that manifested in the disproportionate force used to end the vigil. The decision to commence criminal prosecutions against the women contrasts with a pattern of resistance to investigating incidents of violence against women that continues to translate into record low conviction rates.[62] The exceptional powers extended to the police under the Covid-19 regulations are still felt today through aggressive policing that silences peaceful public protest and through draconian criminal penalties prohibiting public protest that now represent the new normal, a legacy that is replicated around the world.[63]

IV. CRISIS: ENTRENCHMENT AND REVERSAL

In spring 2020, as lockdowns kicked in around the world, feminist scholars across all disciplines turned their attention to the gendered dimensions of crisis in the shared knowledge that all crises produce gendered effects, typically reversing feminist gains made.[64] That crises such as war, natural disasters, and disease exacerbate pre-existing

---

Coomaraswamy et al, *Preventing Conflict, Transforming Justice, Securing the Peace: A Global Study on the Implementation of United Nations Security Council Resolution 1325* (UN, 2015) 15, 135.

[59] Daniel Hoffman 'Geometry after the Circle: Security Interventions in the Urban Grey Zone' (2019) 60 *Current Anthropology* 98.

[60] Amnesty International, *The State of the World's Human Rights for 2020/21*; and see report for 2021/22. In China the People's Liberation Army was responsible for implementing China's zero-tolerance policy, while the military was integral to shaping and/or implementing Covid-19 strategies in Uganda, South Africa, Nigeria, Italy, Spain, the UK, eastern Europe and across Latin America and Asia.

[61] The police were found to have violated the rights to the freedom of expression and assembly of the women: *Leigh & Others v The Commissioner of Police of the Metropolis* [2022] EWHC 527 (Admin) (11 March 2022).

[62] Independent Office for Police Conduct, *Operation Hotton* (2022) (report into the Metropolitan Police, concluding that sexism, misogyny and toxic masculinity were not isolated incidents).

[63] SR on the rights to freedom of peaceful assembly and of association, A/77/171, 15 July 2022, para 40 (expressing concern about the misuse of emergency measures to stifle peaceful protests and about the use of unlawful force during crisis situations).

[64] Naila Kabeer et al, 'Feminist Economic Perspectives on the COVID-19 Pandemic' (2021) 27 *Feminist Economics* 1.

gender inequalities is widely recognised, as is the fact that crises compound intersecting forms of inequalities against differently situated women, amplifying harms and the risks they confront.[65] As the CEDAW Committee elaborates, the very fact that pre-existing gender inequalities limit the control that women have over decisions governing their lives, makes them more likely to be exposed to gendered risks in crisis situations, natural and manmade.[66] For example, in 'natural' disasters men's survival rate is higher, due largely to pre-existing gendered social norms such as the division of care, survival skills, segregation, and even dress codes.[67] Crises fuel and produce new forms of violence against women.[68] In times of crisis, gender matters. States' failures to translate that knowledge into meaningful and adequate measures prior to, during, and post-crisis are obstacles to equality, freedom, and peace.

The shared anxiety among international rights bodies and feminists was that the pandemic would disproportionately exact a heavy toll on differently situated women, in particular those who confronted intersecting axes of discrimination, and that measures to contain the virus would exacerbate and create new obstacles to equality. It was against this backdrop that international human rights bodies rapidly released detailed Covid-specific Guidance Notes, reminding states to take extra care of those who were most likely to be at risk due to their socioeconomic situation and social roles, including women as caregivers.[69] States were likewise reminded of their international obligations to ensure that women, among other identified groups, were not directly or indirectly discriminated against in the design and implementation of measures taken in response to the pandemic.[70] And, as underscored by the CEDAW Committee, states parties to the treaty were required to take specific steps to address discrimination through the adoption of targeted laws, policies, mitigation and adaptation strategies, budgets and other measures.[71]

Feminist fears were justified. Although mostly anecdotal, there were early signs that lockdown measures were disproportionately and adversely impacting women across the globe.[72] Home confinement brought about a shocking, although not unanticipated, rise in domestic violence and femicide, making more visible the pre-existing crisis of violence against women and the failure to counter it. The 'domestic' as the

---

[65] CEDAW Committee, General Recommendation No 37 (2018) on the gender-related dimensions of disaster risk reduction in the context of climate change, CEDAW/C/GC/37, 13 March 2018, para 2.
[66] ibid para 3.
[67] ibid para 4.
[68] See essay 10 'Misogyny and Sexism in the Digital Age'.
[69] 'UN Human Rights Treaty Bodies Call for Human Rights Approach in Fighting COVID-19' (OHCHR, 24 March 2020).
[70] OHCHR Guidance Note on COVID-19 and Women's Human Rights, 15 April 2020; Guidance Note on CEDAW and COVID-19, 27 April 2020.
[71] CEDAW Committee General Recommendation No 37 (n 65) para 8; Independent Expert on the effects of foreign debt and other related international financial obligation of States on the full enjoyment of all human rights, particularly economic, social and cultural rights, Report, A/75/164, 31 July 2020, para 36: 'to redress the structural or system discrimination against women, it would be essential not only to provide them with access to health care and special financial support, but also to reinform social protection systems so as to prevent them from bearing the brunt of the economic crisis and the pandemic-response measures'.
[72] For millions in less affluent societies where there was no public safety net, the 'stay at home and shield' policy was not a feasible option: Reem Gaafar et al, 'Covid-19 Response in Sudan: The Pandemic vs. the Politics' *African Arguments Blog*, 28 January 2022.

space of safety is a patriarchal fiction. Some states did take mitigating steps to address the expected rise in such violence. However, this was largely driven by the rapid mobilisation of women's rights organisations and feminists holding key positions in the public sector who collectively urged additional protection measures.[73] The absence of women in decision-making spaces, including Covid-19 task forces, translated into gender-blind policies and widening inequalities.[74] Even when included, women were generally confined to policy areas coded female, such as public health, rather than economic policy, coded male, with far reaching social and economic consequences detrimental to women.

Lockdown policies exposed states' failure to address deeply engrained gender stereotypes, exemplified by the reinstatement of traditional gender roles within the home; women shouldered a greater proportion of additional care and home-schooling responsibilities, intensifying their time poverty.[75] Within academia, research outputs by women dropped dramatically, while men's outputs increased, widening the pre-existing gap.[76] Since professional progress is linked to research outputs, this setback is likely to have long-term consequences for women's equal representation within the higher echelons of the academy's hierarchical structure, reducing women's opportunities to contribute on an equal basis to the intellectual development of their respective disciplines. The loss is both individual and collective. This pattern was reproduced on a global scale and across all social fields, deepening existing economic, social, and political inequalities.

We subsequently learned that during the pandemic's first year women lost 46.6 million jobs globally, representing a 3.5 per cent loss compared to 2.9 per cent for men.[77] In contrast to previous economic downturns, this loss of livelihoods exacted a heavy and disproportionate toll on women due to their overrepresentation in sectors worst affected by lockdown measures, such as retail, hospitality and supply chains.[78] Further, the fact that most of the world's women in the paid economy were consigned to informal and precarious jobs with few, if any, rights and protections meant that they disproportionately experienced extreme poverty. The closure and/or online migration of social support and healthcare systems, including sexual and reproductive care, left women who were reliant on such services particularly vulnerable and exposed to different and compounded risks.[79] Pre-existing gendered structural

---

[73] 'Government Responses to COVID 19: Lessons on Gender Equality for a World in Turmoil' (UN Women and UNDP, March 2022) 46–48.
[74] Report of the Secretary-General, Women and Peace and Security, S/2020/946, 25 September 2020, para 3 (globally women formed 24 per cent of members of Covid task forces and lower in conflict-affected areas at 18 per cent).
[75] Home schooling was deeply racialised/classed re-entrenching disadvantage for children without access to learning technologies. See essay 10 'Misogyny and Sexism in the Digital Age'.
[76] Eunrang Kwon et al, 'The Effect of the COVID-19 Pandemic on Gendered Research Productivity and its Correlates' (2023) 17 *Journal of Informetrics* 109200.
[77] UN Women and UNDP (n 73) 15.
[78] The world's 10 richest individuals have seen their combined wealth increase by half a trillion dollars since the outbreak: Esmé Berkhout et al, *The Inequality Virus* (Oxfam International, 2021) 12.
[79] 'The Impact of COVID-19 on Women and Girls with Disabilities' (UNFPA and Women Enabled International, 2021); women with disabilities made particularly vulnerable, isolated and at higher risk of domestic violence due to their gender and disability.

obstacles to accessing social and healthcare services were made more onerous, as was access to gender justice, often deferred as non-urgent by decision-makers with androcentric worldviews.[80]

Global inequalities have widened since the pandemic.[81] Targeted interventions to reverse its gendered impacts, as recommended by international human rights bodies, remain largely unfulfilled.[82] For example, out of a total 3,099 social protection and labour market measures adopted between March 2020 and August 2021, only 380 measures – a meagre 12 per cent – prioritised women.[83] This is unsurprising: until there is parity in political representation and a redistribution of power coupled with a commitment to transforming gender norms and relations, policies and law will continue to privilege the interests of patriarchal elites.[84] The obstacles to gender equality and the potential for a meaningful peace for women and girls have ballooned: achieving the target of 'gender equality and empower[ing] all women and girls' by 2030 – SDG 5 – is, in the view of many, now not possible.[85]

If the pandemic revealed anything, it is how patriarchal privilege operates across the world, entangled with capitalism and militarism, enabling powerholders to consolidate and normalise binary difference and hierarchies through gender norms and identities that become deeply embedded within social structures. Crises bring into sharp relief the economic and political interests and values of ruling elites and in that process reveal who is expendable and who is not, typically defined by race, gender, and class.[86] The state of exception reveals the necropolitics of patriarchy that undergirds the state of normalcy.[87] For example, the lack of Personal Protective Equipment

---

[80] CEDAW Committee General Recommendation No 37 (n 65) para 3: 'the failure to address the structural barriers faced by women in gaining access to their rights will increase gender-based inequalities and intersecting forms of discrimination'; Brandi Moran, '"If She Was White, She Would Still Be Here": Canada's Murdered Women and Girls' *Al Jazeera*, 5 January 2022; Cristina Corujo, 'Months into State of Emergency, Puerto Rico Finally Approves $7 Million to Combat Gender-based Violence' *abc News*, 7 May 2021.

[81] eg the COVID-19 Global Gender Response Tracker launched in September 2020 by UNDP and UN Women to track government response measures across key sectors and assess them from a gender perspective.

[82] 'We must prioritize a gender-responsive recovery from COVID-19', OHCHR, 27 July 2021 (noting 18 months after the pandemic outbreak that 'the majority of socio-economic COVID-19 responses adopted by States are surprisingly gender-blind, often failing to address the specific needs of women'). Some states scaled up social protection for women in informal employment but such measures were rare and often short-term. Exceptions include Argentina, Brazil, Colombia, Kenya and Togo: Maja Gavrilovic et al, 'Gender-responsive Social Protection Post-COVID-19' (2021) 375 *Science*, issue 6585, 1111.

[83] UN Women and UNDP (n 73) 60.

[84] Supriya Garikipati and Uma Kambhampati, 'Leading the Fight against the Pandemic: Does Gender Really Matter?' (2021) 27 *Feminist Economics* 401.

[85] 'Progress on the Sustainable Development Goals: The Gender Snapshot 2022' (UN Women, 2022).

[86] As a condition of entry to the UK, migrant women are precluded from accessing public funds under the 'no recourse to public funds' policy, which, prior to the pandemic, was found to amount to indirect discrimination in breach of ECHR art 4 as disproportionately impacting women and people with disabilities. Although migrant women were entitled to benefit from the government's temporary Covid schemes, those operating in the informal economy were not eligible and the 'no recourse to public funds' policy excluded them from other benefits, leaving them destitute: 'Covid-19 and Economic Challenges for Migrant Women' (Women's Budget Group, Winter 2020/21).

[87] Achille Mbembe, 'Necropolitics' (2003) 15 *Public Culture* 11 (elaborating on the sovereign's power not only to 'let die' but to expose some people to conditions so precarious and detrimental that they will experience an untimely death).

(PPE) for health and social care workers – a feminised and racialised sector[88] – was the consequence of political priorities, decisions made and not made, not dismissible as an administrative oversight or explained away as a shortfall in supply. That the vast amount of available PPE was designed for men – and consequently placed working women at higher risk of exposure to the virus due to ill-fitting protective clothing – revealed the depth of gendered norms embedded within all societies across all walks of life.[89] It was not that lessons were not learned from the outbreak of Ebola in 2014, but that in a patriarchal capitalist system, some lives are worth less.[90] Likewise, in failing to take adequate account of the gendered dimensions of the labour market and caring inequalities faced by women, job retention schemes, pitched as benefiting all, disproportionately disadvantaged women, especially poor women from minority communities.[91] Such schemes, and other commercial initiatives to kick-start the economy, representing the largest public expenditure outside of wartime, have primarily benefited corporate elites whilst facilitating fraud and corruption on an unprecedented scale, the costs of which will ultimately fall to the taxpayer.[92] Feminists were concerned that governments worldwide would re-embrace austerity programmes that disproportionately penalise women, as they did following the 2008–2009 bailout of the financial sector.[93]

Our anxieties that the pandemic would embolden autocratic elites to manipulate the crisis to breach their human rights obligations by introducing retrogressive agendas, strengthening patriarchal norms, reinstating heteronormative gender roles, and silencing opponents and critics were not misplaced.[94] There are numerous examples: the introduction of laws to restrict and/or deny access to abortion, together with closing clinics deemed 'non-essential';[95] the use of disproportionate force against women protesting such measures;[96] the violent enforcement of women's dress codes by Iran's 'morality police' and by the Houthis in Yemen. These all represent a resurgence of patriarchy seeking to police and control women's bodies in the midst of the pandemic.

---

[88] Health and care services are some of the most feminised sectors of the global labour market, with women forming 70 per cent of the workforce. Nursing is one of the most low-paid sectors relative to skills.

[89] Jennifer Cohen and Yana van der Meulen Rodgers, 'Contributing Factors to Personal Protective Equipment Shortages during the COVID-19 Pandemic' (2020) 141 *Preventive Medicine*.

[90] The same is true of knowledge.

[91] eg UK HC, Women and Equalities Committee, *Unequal Impact? Coronavirus and the Gendered Economic Impact*, Fifth Report of Session 2019–2021, 26 January 2021; Abi Adams-Prass et al, 'Furloughing' (2020) 41 *Fiscal Studies* 591.

[92] eg UK HC, Committee of Public Accounts, *COVID Employment Support Schemes*, 40th Report of Session 2022–23, 23 February 2023.

[93] Total fiscal outlay for 2020–2021 is estimated to be at least four times higher than in 2008. Austerity policies had weakened public infrastructure and public health systems, compounding the effects of the pandemic.

[94] Human Rights Watch, 'COVID-19 Triggers Wave of Free Speech Abuse' (2021); Lana Baydas et al, 'Pushing Back against the Normalization of COVID-19 Related State of Emergency Restrictive Measures' *Open Global Rights*, 8 February 2022.

[95] Jessica Glenza, 'States Use Coronavirus to Ban Abortions, Leaving Women Desperate' *The Guardian*, 30 April 2020.

[96] Emma Beswick, 'Police Using "Excessive Violence" against Peaceful Protesters in Poland amid Abortion Row' *euronews*, 24 November 2020.

None of these developments occurred within a normative void. The backlash against human rights and women's rights – most notably sexual and reproductive rights – was already emerging over a decade earlier.[97] This pushback is a crisis that is gaining momentum, dividing and polarising opinion, as it is intended to do.[98] It is a crisis that has enabled states to reverse legal precedent protecting a woman's right to her bodily autonomy, revealing the fragility of feminist gains;[99] to control women's bodies by redefining them as a threat; to re-criminalise homosexuality;[100] to strip women of their parental rights if they will not conform to patriarchy's binaries;[101] and attempt to reimpose a biological binary.[102]

Crises make more visible the interlocking pathological patterns and structures of patriarchal gender systems, militarism, and capitalism that form the backbone of contemporary states and the international order, producing inequalities and fostering a predisposition to violence, inter-personal and inter-state. Feminists have long maintained that because all three systems of power are socially constituted, our ambitions for equality and peace are far from utopian. Repudiating dominant counternarratives founded on nature remains a site of struggle and feminist labour, as is overcoming our discipline's resistance to seeing gender in all crises or in seeing the crises of the everyday.

---

[97] See essay 2 'Gender'.
[98] 'Türk Urges Solidarity in Face of Gender Equality Backlash' (OHCHR, 23 June 2023).
[99] 'Access to Safe and Legal Abortion: Urgent Call for United States to Adhere to Women's Rights Convention, UN Committee' (OHCHR, 1 July 2022) (CEDAW Committee responding to the US Supreme Court's striking down of *Roe v Wade*).
[100] eg 'Uganda: UN Experts Condemn Egregious Anti-LGBT Legislation' (OHCHR, 29 March 2023).
[101] Barbie Latza Nadeau and Jack Guy, 'Italy Starts Removing Lesbian Mothers' Names from Children's Birth Certificates' CNN, 21 July 2023.
[102] *Semenya v Switzerland*, ECtHR, Appl Nos 10934/21; Decision, 11 July 2023.

Part IV

Strategic Practice: Gendering Law

12
Introduction to Strategic Practices

WOMEN ACROSS THE centuries[1] have devised strategies to overcome the obstacles to their pursuit of peace and equality, demonstrating how conflict and violence are gendered and a cause and consequence of patriarchy. Peace cannot be achieved or sustained unless this is recognised and acted upon. This requires a change in social hierarchies of power and in mindset to one that rejects misogyny, racism, colonialism, militarism, and pursuit of profit over personal and societal wellbeing. To this end, women have individually and collectively engaged in multiple tactics, typically non-violent, in pursuing strategies for peace and resistance[2] – occupying public spaces in rallies, marches, pilgrimages, establishing camps, situation rooms,[3] erecting statues,[4] producing literature, art and craftwork[5] and breaking down transnational[6] boundaries. Women have been creative, practical, outrageous[7] and disruptive[8] in challenging the gendered stereotypes that have been constructed and maintained through patriarchal power. They have also been solemn and respectful depending upon the circumstances. Tactics may be designedly performative, evoking ritual and symbolism.[9]

---

[1] *Lysistrata* by Aristophanes, portraying women seeking to end the Peloponnesian wars by denying sex to their partners was first performed in Athens in 411 BC.

[2] Cynthia Cockburn, *From Where We Stand: War, Women's Activism and Feminist Analysis* (Zed Books, 2007) details strategies engaged in by women's NGOs.

[3] West African women's NGOs have established Women's Situation Rooms to monitor election violence, mobilise against violence and mediate local conflicts. This has 'harnessed gender as a productive force for conflict prevention' by capitalising on women's national and international networks, on women's neutral position outside formal politics and on African discourses of motherhood: Paula Drummond et al, 'Mobilizing Gender for Conflict Prevention: Women's Situation Rooms' (2022) 16 *Journal of Intervention and Statebuilding* 249.

[4] 'Statues of peace', depictions of the 'comfort women', have been placed in public locations in cities worldwide as an enduring form of silent rebuke and memorialisation. See essay 18 'Transformative Reparations and Gendered Peace'.

[5] eg 'Material Power Palestinian Embroidery' exhibition, Kettle's Yard, Cambridge, 2023.

[6] eg the WILPF Peace Train that travelled from Helsinki to Beijing for the Fourth World Conference on Women in 1995.

[7] eg Code Pink, a US NGO, uses 'satire, street theatre, creative visuals, civil resistance, and … of course, wearing pink': https://www.codepink.org/about.

[8] Greenham women disrupted court hearings, making personal statements and reading aloud self-penned poems. 'And they sang. At one hearing they presented their case by way of a Gilbert and Sullivan opera, one singing her position and the others joining in as a chorus': Elizabeth Woodcraft, 'Greenham Women Plan "to Crowd the Prisons"', *Law Society Gazette*, 24 June 2019.

[9] Greenham provides numerous examples, including holding hands to encircle the base; dancing on the silos; cutting the fence; blockading the military transports: Kate Kerrow and Rebecca Mordan, *Out of the Darkness Greenham Voices 1981–2000* (The History Press, 2021).

They may be a spontaneous response to a particular situation or carefully planned and constructed. The endurance of many strategists and tacticians has been remarkable, exhibiting long-term staying power in the face of humiliation, ridicule and violence.[10] Indeed, as feminist thinker, writer and activist Cynthia Cockburn once noted: 'the feminist struggle against a male-dominant sex-gender order *is of itself* work for peace' (emphasis added).[11]

Strategising has involved determining the most effective way to achieve the objective, for instance to stop, reverse or modify a government policy or decision (such as that to go to or continue war); to carry out or support an independent inquiry process into some event or series of events and thus to repudiate misinformation and propaganda;[12] to educate, raise awareness and influence public opinion and perhaps to shame governments; to make women visible and to challenge the exclusion of women from commemorations.

Many strategies involve breaking the silences that have been imposed on women, especially with respect to their experiences of violence. 'Unsilencing' raises political, personal and ethical questions about who speaks for whom, when and with what consequences. Identifying silences and filling them or deciding upon their continuation[13] is thus an expression of feminist scholarship, politics and strategy but one that must be undertaken with caution and respect.[14] Women also use silence, for instance gathering silently in public spaces to message peace through the contrast with the noises of everyday life, or – more pointedly – with the cacophony of violence. A non-violent, usually silent, vigil is a preferred technique of Women in Black, a loose network of women peace activists worldwide.[15] Their silence is powerful and vocal:[16] 'Silence is the language that we speak, Silence, a language that voices our anguish.'[17] Black clothing signifies mourning for all who die in conflict; it 'does not represent surrender to mourning to sorrow; it is resistance against the killing of towns and of people, against the violence in everyday life'.[18] Women – mothers, grandmothers – demonstrate in silence, demanding an end to the silence

---

[10] See essay 9 'Silence as an Obstacle to Gendered Peace and Equality'.

[11] Cynthia Cockburn, 'Feminist Antimilitarism: Patriarchy, Masculinities and Gender Awareness in Antiwar Organizing' in 'Gender and Militarism', Women Peacemakers Program, 24 May 2014.

[12] Women's NGOs have long engaged in factfinding, eg WILPF, 8th Yearly Report, January–December 1923, 6–7 (recounting its Commission to the Ruhr 'to watch events, and to do whatever was possible to help the situation and to bring about conciliation between the French, British and German peoples'); a factfinding team from Women's International Democratic Federation (WIDF) toured North Korean cities to inspect war damage: Elisabeth Armstrong, *Bury the Corpse of Colonialism: The Revolutionary Feminist Conference of 1949* (University of California Press, 2023) 129.

[13] Ayşe Gül Altinay and Andrea Petö, 'Uncomfortable Connections: Gender, Memory, War' in Ayşe Gül Altinay and Andrea Petö (eds), *Gendered Wars, Gendered Memories: Feminist Conversations on War, Genocide and Political Violence* (Routledge, 2016): 'Feminist scholarship has historically been, among other things, a struggle for unsilencing – as well as a struggle for theorizing the intimate connections between silencing (from history and memory) and ongoing marginalization.'

[14] ibid.

[15] Cynthia Cockburn, *From Where We Stand* (n 2).

[16] Michael Drake, 'Commemorating the Fatalities of War' in Cassandra Ogden and Stephen Wakeman (eds), *Corporeality: the Body and Society* (University of Chester Press, 2013).

[17] Women in Black, Bangalore, India at https://womeninblack.org/vigils-arround-the-world/asia/india/.

[18] Stasa Zajovic, 'Being a Woman' in Tanya Renne (ed), *Ana's Land: Sisterhood in Eastern Europe* (Routledge, 2018).

shrouding the disappearances of their children. They have been met with insults,[19] stigmatisation,[20] violence,[21] denied information[22] and truth.[23] In human rights law, refusal to accept government denials or silence has contributed to the emergence of a 'right to truth'[24] – the antithesis of official, repressive silence.[25]

Strategies do not always achieve the hoped-for results; there has been seeming progress but also setbacks, unintended consequences, and new and unanticipated obstacles. There have been periods of great activity and some of apparent passivity, although work by feminist historians is excavating previously forgotten accounts. There have been some constants: WILPF has held triennial conferences and adopted resolutions that frequently propose new campaigns and strategies since its inception in the 1915 International Women's Congress.[26] Only world war has prevented its meetings. WILPF's longevity suggests success, but perhaps it should be seen as a failure as it has not achieved its vision: 'A world of permanent peace built on feminist foundations of freedom, justice, nonviolence, human rights, and equality for all, where people, the planet, and all its other inhabitants coexist and flourish in harmony.'[27] Indeed in 2024, with extreme violence in many parts of the globe, this seems as far away as ever and provokes the question: 'what would success look like?'

This question is especially apposite as war in Syria, Yemen, Tigray, Ukraine, Sudan, Israel/Palestine and elsewhere continue without apparent end in sight. Ukrainian feminists have voiced their dilemma, which resonates with that confronting their predecessors in the 1930s: how can they strategise for peace and an end to military

---

[19] CEDAW Committee, Report under article 8 of the Optional Protocol to the Convention, and reply from the Government of Mexico, CEDAW/C/2005/OP.8/MEXICO, 27 January 2005, para 111 (registering disbelief that the mothers' associations 'far from being supported and comforted, are mistreated and even threatened and harassed').

[20] 'Frequently, the mothers of persons who are disappeared are socially stigmatized by being blamed for not taking proper care of their disappeared children': UN Human Rights Council Working Group on Enforced or Involuntary Disappearances, General Comment on women affected by enforced disappearances, A/HRC/WGEID/98/2, 14 February 2013, para 11.

[21] Women members of Save Our Sons lost their jobs, were 'condemned as hysterical and naïve mothers, community dupes, rabble rousers, and bimbos', abused, assaulted, arrested, and jailed; 1965–72: SOS [Save our Sons] Australian Mothers Resist Vietnam War Conscription.

[22] Soviet mothers were bullied into silence about their sons' deaths in Afghanistan, eg a military commander shouted at a mother seeking information: 'That [information] cannot be divulged': Julie Elkner, '*Dedovshchina* and the Committee of Soldiers' Mothers under Gorbachev' (2004) 1 *Journal of Power Institutions in Post-Soviet Societies*.

[23] War crimes denial, including of the Srebrenica genocide, has intensified in the Republika Srpska; 61st Report of the High Representative for Implementation of the Peace Agreement on Bosnia and Herzegovina to the Secretary-General of the United Nations, 11 May 2022, paras 41–43.

[24] eg International Convention for the Protection of All Persons from Enforced Disappearance, 2006; UNGAR 65/196. Proclamation of 24 March as the International Day for the Right to the Truth concerning Gross Human Rights Violations and for the Dignity of Victims, 21 December 2010; UNGAR 68/165. Right to the Truth, 18 December 2013. See essay 18 'Transformative Reparations and Gendered Peace'.

[25] '[V]ictims of human rights violations and their next of kin have the right to know the truth. This right to the truth has been developed by international human rights law and its recognition is an important measure of reparation': *Plan de Sánchez Massacre v Guatemala*, IACtHR, Judgment of 19 November 2004 (Reparations), para 97.

[26] See essay 7 'Women, Disarmament and Peace' and essay 4 'Introduction: Rewriting International Law's Histories'.

[27] WILPF, Vision at https://www.wilpf.org/who-we-are/vision-values-and-approach/.

activity when their country is facing an existential crisis?[28] Ukrainian women have responded to the unprovoked violence with resourcefulness and strength. In Poland, for instance, they work through existing networks, dividing between themselves tasks generated by the conflict and the mass displacement of their sisters and assuming collective responsibilities for previously unthought of undertakings. They see their activities as essential for the war effort and for keeping alive the values of democracy and freedom to sustain a peaceful Ukraine when the fighting stops. They are those of women in war zones throughout history – strategies imposed by, and that evolve with, the circumstances. And elsewhere in 2024, women with extraordinary courage continue to protest vicious, life-threatening misogyny. Feminism requires strategies to end oppression, coloniality, racism and violence, which may include resorting to military strategies.[29] When, under what circumstances, by whom and to what ultimate end, are use of force and violence justified? These remain questions that feminists for peace and equalities struggle to answer. As in the 1930s in Europe, or in movements for national liberation from colonisation, those against war and violence under any circumstances find themselves marginalised from their sisters who consider that entering into dialogue with oppressors, or seeking a negotiated peace, would be to accept violent domination.[30]

Part IV looks at feminist strategising, mobilising, campaigning, lobbying, researching, seeking allies and persisting through any available forum (including those they have created for themselves) for a more inclusive international legal order, while recognising that legal strategies represent only a fraction of feminist activity across time and space. Women have seen international law as having a wider scope than inter-state regulation and as a potential site for domestic legal reform, a stance at odds with the traditional view of state sovereignty upheld by state (male) diplomats. From the founding of the League of Nations in 1919, women have evolved strategies for developing international legal standards for equality and social justice for inclusion into national legal systems.

Seeking change through law involves many steps: securing a foothold into law (national and international) by identifying lacunae and adverse language; seeking opportunities for reshaping the law; drafting reformed text and lobbying for its acceptance; forming alliances; making legal change work for women on the ground; monitoring implementation; and seeking accountability for non-compliance and violation. Language and format depend on immediate objectives and intended audience. Addressing a court, drafting a proposed treaty or seeking to hold a government to account entail formal legal argumentation. Policy language may be more suitable in an institutional setting (such as in addressing the SC) and an informal style preferable for public educational or campaigning purposes. We have both been involved in all these steps as we have sought to turn our academic expertise to practical ends. We have been struck by the randomness and messiness of much activity that has been undertaken hurriedly in response to opportunities that have arisen. On other

---

[28] See essay 4 'Introduction: Rewriting International Law's Histories'.
[29] Darya Tsymbalyuk, 'Why We as Feminists Must Lobby for Defence for Ukraine' *Open Democracy*, 16 March 2022.
[30] See essay 4 'Introduction: Rewriting International Law's Histories'.

occasions strategising has been long term and highly organised. The essays accordingly do not provide an orderly narrative but a personal account of how we have joined with scholars and activists worldwide in attempting to bring our feminism to bear on international legal discourse for the advancement of equality and peace. They centre on three different scenarios. First is seeking change or redressing omissions in legal texts; we have chosen human rights law and international criminal law as illustrative. Second is providing legal argument on points that arise either in judicial proceedings or government policy, looking for ways to influence decision-makers while navigating the dissonance between our feminist objectives and the constraints of legal formalism. In the third situation we have gone our own way, abandoning formal processes to offer a feminist vision of gender justice and of peace. The essays provide some instances where the language, concepts and mechanisms of international law have changed in response to feminist demands but the discipline overall remains impervious to the concept of a gendered peace. We finally ask whether women's attempts to enter the international legal domain have achieved success and whether they are even appropriate strategies to advance a feminist or gendered peace.

Figure 2 Celebrating the Life of Cynthia Cockburn, Women in Black, London, UK, 2019
Source: Personal collection, Louise Arimatsu.

13

Strategic Practice: Peace and Equality Through International Law

I. INTRODUCTION

For well over a century, feminist activists have seen international law as a site for the promotion of intra- and inter-state peace. We share that belief, notwithstanding law's imperfections including its gendered and colonial foundations and history. Although excluded by law from engaging in the political sphere, women active in the many nineteenth century peace movements that flourished in Europe and the US[1] made clear their support for the 1899 Hague Peace Conference[2] and attended side events.[3] They espoused the peaceful methods for avoiding recourse to war and violence that were institutionalised through the Hague Conventions[4] – conciliation/mediation, good offices, commissions of inquiry and arbitration.[5] Some women were especially active; for instance, Emily Hobhouse engaged in a solo fact-finding mission on the concentration camps set up by the British Government during the Boer war. Following her scathing denunciation of the camps, the Government appointed a 'Committee of Ladies' to visit and report on the camps.[6] Integral to its commitment to 'peace politics' the International Council of Women declared in 1899 that it would engage 'in every country to further and advance by every means in its

---

[1] The understanding of peace, for instance in the International Council of Women, was to prevent war between the 'civilised' nations, implicitly endorsing the use of violence to maintain the colonial status quo: Susan Zimmermann, 'The Politics of Exclusionary Inclusion: Peace Activism and the Struggle on International and Domestic Political Order in the International Council of Women, 1899–1914' in Thomas Hippler and Miloš Vec (eds), *Paradoxes of Peace in Nineteenth Century Europe* (Oxford University Press, 2015) 189, 194.

[2] Bertha von Suttner, author of *Lay Down Your Arms* (1889), was active at the 1899 Hague Peace Conference, organising her salon and arranging public meetings. She opposed the Conference's move away from disarmament to humanitarian provision in war. See essay 7 'Women, Disarmament and Peace'.

[3] The Hague Peace Conferences were 'the first time that women's associations lobbied so specifically and widely at a diplomatic multilateral meeting': Glenda Sluga, 'Women, Feminisms and Twentieth-Century Internationalisms' in Glenda Sluga and Patricia Clavin (eds), *Internationalisms: A Twentieth Century History* (Cambridge University Press, 2017) ch 4.

[4] Convention for the Pacific Settlement of International Disputes, The Hague, 1899; Convention for the Pacific Settlement of International Disputes, The Hague, 1907.

[5] Hague Convention, 1899, art 15: 'International arbitration has for its object the settlement of differences between States by judges of their own choice, and on the basis of respect for law.'

[6] HC Deb, *Hansard*, 4 March 1902, vol 104, col 369 ff. The Government's response recognised that women could occupy public roles as members of a commission of inquiry but the focus on women and children in the camps furthered an essentialised and problematic depiction of women as appropriately deployed only with respect to women's condition.

power the movement towards international arbitration'[7] and established a standing committee on Peace and Arbitration.[8] The International Congress of Women in 1915 similarly urged all governments 'to come to an agreement to refer future international disputes to arbitration and conciliation' and for a permanent court of international justice to settle 'differences of a justiciable character'.[9] Following the creation of the Permanent Court of International Justice (PCIJ) the Women's International League for Peace and Freedom (WILPF)[10] advocated for the Court's compulsory jurisdiction.[11] WILPF's ongoing commitment to 'law not war' is repeated in its 1929 resolution[12] urging governments to realise the renunciation of war as an instrument of national policy as stipulated in the then newly adopted Kellogg-Briand Pact.[13]

Figure 3 WILPF Banner for 1932 Disarmament Conference
Source: LSE Library archives.

---

[7] Susan Zimmermann (n 1) 190.
[8] Lady Aberdeen was President and Baroness von Suttner Secretary of the committee: ibid 192. Their positions typify the privileged, upper-class status of many women peace activists. This contrasts with the wider representation of working-class women in public marches and strikes, for instance the 1888 matchgirls strike. See essay 7 'Women, Disarmament and Peace'.
[9] WILPF Resolutions, 1st Congress, The Hague, 1915.
[10] See essay 4 'Introduction: Rewriting International Law's Histories'.
[11] eg WILPF Resolutions, 4th Congress, Washington DC, 1924: 'This Congress recommends National Sections to work in their own countries to induce their respective Governments to sign the optional protocol of the [PCIJ], thereby undertaking to submit to judicial decision legal disputes with other nations signing the protocol.'
[12] WILPF Resolutions, 6th Congress, Prague, 1929.
[13] General Treaty for Renunciation of War as an Instrument of National Policy, Paris, 27 August 1928.

In addition to advocating for peace through the instrumentalities of international law, women have perceived the international legal regime as a strategic entry point for securing equality, without which there could be no peace. Women sought to overcome domestic resistance to their political enfranchisement, make visible the realities of their lives and to break the silence about their experiences, especially of violence. This strategy of equality through international law and inclusion *in* international institutions has produced significant outcomes, founded upon the persistence of a relatively small number of women within the League of Nations and subsequently the United Nations,[14] backed by the much larger numbers of the global women's movement.[15]

II. FOOTHOLD INTO INTERNATIONAL LAW

Following the pioneering campaigns of the first generation of feminist activists and disappointment that the outbreak of World War II had prevented progress toward an equality treaty at the League of Nations, affirmation of women's equality within the institutional framework for the post-1945 international legal order was imperative. At first the outlook was unpromising. The proposals accepted at Dumbarton Oaks made little reference to human rights and none to discrimination.[16] Women's presence at the UN Conference on International Organization in San Francisco in 1945 was limited,[17] with around 21 representatives with political or technical functions and a handful of women's organisations among the plethora of other – mainly American – civil society associations. Their persistence, supported by some male delegates and smaller states, resulted in preambular affirmation of the 'equal rights of men and women'[18] and other relevant provisions in the UN Charter.[19] This small contingent of feminists had achieved a significant milestone in international law: the assertion of equality on the basis of sex as a matter of international concern

---

[14] Hilkka Pietilä, *The Unfinished Story of Women and the United Nations* (United Nations, 2007); Rebecca Adami and Dan Plesch, *Women and the UN: A New History of Women's Human Rights* (Routledge, 2022).

[15] See essay 4 'Introduction: Rewriting International Law's Histories' and essay 5 'Peace in the UN Decade for Women'.

[16] Washington Conversations on International Peace and Security Organization, Dumbarton Oaks, 1944, Proposals for the Establishment of a General International Organization, Chapter IX, section A, 1: 'With a view to the creation of conditions of stability and well-being which are necessary for peaceful and friendly relations among nations, the Organization should facilitate solutions of international economic, social and other humanitarian problems and promote respect for human rights and fundamental freedoms.'

[17] Six women were full delegates: Bertha Lutz (Brazil); Minerva Bernardino (Dominican Republic); Isabel Pinto de Vidal (Uruguay); Virginia Gildersleeve (US); Wu Yi-Fang (China) and Cora Casselman (Canada). They did not necessarily speak with one voice: the Latin Americans lobbied hard for explicit inclusion of women while Virginia Gildersleeve actively opposed such language: Katherine M Marino, *Feminism for the Americas: The Making of an International Human Rights Movement* (University of North Carolina Press, 2019).

[18] See essay 2 'Gender'.

[19] UN Charter, art 8 (women eligible for UN positions); arts 1(3); 55; 56 (human rights and fundamental freedoms for all without distinction with respect to race, sex, language, or religion); 68 (ECOSOC mandated to set up functional commissions); and 71 (NGO consultative status).

and peace and equality as mutually reinforcing objectives rather than as discrete and separate. One commentator has suggested that:

> [t]his most probably would not have happened without the involvement and active lobbying of women's organisations. They were clear about their aims and knowledgeable about international collaboration. They had access to the intergovernmental meetings and were experienced in dealing with official representatives… putting pressure on governments to include women in the delegations and lobbying to obtain support for women's requests.[20]

The immediate post-Charter generation of feminists pursued two complementary objectives: to ensure women's equal participation with men within the mainstream institutions that were engaged in shaping a post-war world; and the establishment of a dedicated architecture – institutional and normative – for the advancement of women's rights. Jessie Street, the only woman in the Australian delegation to San Francisco, told of a strongly supported recommendation for a commission on women[21] that would report directly to the Economic and Social Council (ECOSOC).[22] The Charter does not include any such provision[23] but the first session of the UN General Assembly (UNGA) in London in 1946 established the Commission on the Status of Women (CSW) as a sub-commission of the Commission on Human Rights (CHR). Determined efforts by its early members saw it upgraded to a full Commission of ECOSOC in 1947, mandated to promote women's rights in the 'political, economic, social and educational fields'.[24]

The next immediate objective was to ensure the incorporation of women's rights into the Universal Declaration of Human Rights then being drafted by the CHR. CSW members asserted their right to engage in the process and, with support from other feminists, secured sex inclusive language[25] ('all human beings', 'everyone'/ 'no-one', 'all members of the human family'[26]), provisions on equal pay, equal rights to marry, during marriage and at its dissolution and to security in widowhood. Jessie Street (then CSW vice-chair) unsuccessfully argued for a provision recognising women's right to be free from violence;[27] it would be another 45 years before the UNGA took such a step.[28] Other early measures for the under-resourced CSW were

---

[20] Torild Skard, 'Getting our History Right: How Were the Equal Rights of Women and Men Included in the Charter of the United Nations?' (2008) 1 *Forum for Development Studies* 37.

[21] The Inter-American Commission on Women, established at the 6th international conference of American States in Havana in 1928 to further peace and women's rights, provided a model.

[22] Jessie Street, 'UN Commission on the Status of Women: Without Distinction as to Sex', speech to the International Assembly of Women, Copenhagen, 21–24 April 1960.

[23] There was no formal vote on the Brazilian declaration proposing such a commission: Torild Skard (n 20).

[24] UN ECOSOC Resolution 11(II), 21 June 1946, Commission on the Status of Women. This placed CSW outside the 'mainstream' of human rights institutions: Hilary Charlesworth and Christine Chinkin, 'Between the Margins and the Mainstream: The Case of Women's Rights' in Bardo Fassbender and Knut Traisbach (eds), *The Limits of Human Rights* (Oxford University Press, 2019) 205.

[25] Elizabeth Evatt, 'Jessie Street & Human Rights', New South Wales Parliament House, 17 April 2008.

[26] Nevertheless the male pronoun ('his', 'him') is used throughout.

[27] Jessie Street (n 22).

[28] UNGAR, 48/104, 20 December 1993, Declaration on the Elimination of Violence against Women.

180 *Strategic Practice: Peace and Equality Through International Law*

to correct glaring injustices through the drafting of international treaties, followed by a more comprehensive condemnation of sex-based discrimination and assertion of women's right to equality with men through the Convention on Elimination of All Forms of Discrimination against Women (CEDAW) in 1979.[29]

III. MAKING LAW WORK FOR WOMEN: HUMAN RIGHTS

Once CEDAW – a legally binding treaty – came into force in 1981 and its monitoring Committee (CEDAW Committee) commenced work, further strategising was required to hold states parties to account and to make the Convention work for women on the ground.[30] Especially since the 1985 Nairobi conference,[31] feminist activists, lawyers and scholars have collaborated to this end, devising creative means to surmount the formal institutional boundaries and limitations established by states. Illustrative is the work of the International Women's Rights Action Watch (IWRAW) which since its founding in 1985[32] has worked together with national women's organisations in preparing shadow reports to provide the CEDAW Committee with an alternative picture to that proffered by states about their implementation of the Convention. Shadow reporting as a strategy was devised because CEDAW does not accommodate NGOs within the state reporting process, effectively silencing those for whom the treaty was drafted. IWRAW provided updates on the Committee's sessions, which served an important dissemination function in the pre-internet era when such information was not easily accessed. IWRAW has been followed by IWRAW Asia Pacific, created in 1993 'as a Global South-centric feminist organisation' to create links with women's groups on the ground and thus to facilitate the flow of information from such groups to the CEDAW Committee and in turn from the international back to the local level.[33]

In the early 1990s women's politicking through international institutions intensified and was pursued through multiple fora, notably the world conferences held throughout that decade.[34] Feminist international lawyers within the academy questioned why international law remained impervious to feminist

---

[29] Ellen Chester, 'Who Wrote CEDAW?' in Rebecca Adami and Dan Plesch (n 14) ch 7; see essay 5 'Peace in the UN Decade for Women'.
[30] Elizabeth Evatt, 'Finding a Voice for Women's Rights: The Early Days of CEDAW' (1987) 20 *George Washington International Law Review* 515.
[31] See essay 5 'Peace in the UN Decade for Women'.
[32] IWRAW was created by Arvonne Fraser from the US. Its early network included international law academics and women's rights practitioners: Rebecca Cook (Canada), Steve Isaacs (US), Alda Facio (Costa Rica), Jane Connors (Australia/UK), Andrew Byrnes (Australia), Shireen Huq (Bangladesh), Unity Dow (Botswana), Athaliah Molokomme (Botswana), Maggie Reibangira (Tanzania), Lyn Friedman (US), Isabel Plata (Colombia), Silvia Pimentel (Brazil), Chaloka Beyani (Zambia), Thandabantu Nhlapo (South Africa), Ramya Subrahmanian (India), and Shanthi Dairiam (Malaysia): Shanthi Dairiam, *Promoting the Equality of Women: IWRAW Asia Pacific's Journey* (IWRAW Asia Pacific, 2023) 24.
[33] Shanthi Dairiam (n 32) 26.
[34] See essay 6 'Revisiting the Past: Peace at Beijing and Beyond'. The 1990s global conferences took place in the context of economic globalisation and Western triumphalism at the collapse of the USSR, and largely promoted a liberal, albeit neocapitalist, agenda.

ambitions. Drawing on feminist theoretical insights from domestic law and other disciplines, scholars began to lay the conceptual foundations for a feminist analysis of international law, revealing how its androcentric colonial origins continued to exclude, normatively and institutionally, women from its ambit.[35] Analysis that law's normative gaps were rooted in the binary structure of law – public/private – coupled with gender binaries was welcomed by feminist activists as providing the theoretical foundations upon which strategies to advance women's rights and women's equality could be developed. One strategy was to enhance state responsibility for violations of women's rights.[36] This required recognition of gender-specific rights as human rights[37] and enhancing CEDAW's effectiveness through processes for holding states parties to account. Progress was achieved at the 1993 Vienna World Conference on Human Rights,[38] which expanded the international human rights agenda to include gender-specific violations, notably violence against women[39] and endorsed an optional protocol to CEDAW to introduce procedures to strengthen implementation of the Convention.[40] Further headway was made at the 1994 Cairo Conference on Population and Development and the Fourth World Conference on Women in Beijing in 1995, both of which reaffirmed 'the human rights of women and the girl child' as 'an inalienable, integral and indivisible part of universal human rights'.[41] At Cairo, the basic right of all couples and individuals 'to decide freely and responsibly the number and spacing of their children and to have the information, education and means to do so' was asserted.[42] These advancements were not entirely unproblematic. The 'universal' that we had criticised in our work applied equally to the assumption of 'woman' in Western liberal feminism, oblivious to difference. Moreover, political co-option was ever-present: Cairo conformed with US policy under the Clinton administration. The subjection of women's reproductive rights to the expansion

---

[35] eg Hilary Charlesworth et al, 'Feminist Approaches to International Law' (1991) 85 *American Journal of International Law* 613; Dorinda Dallmeyer (ed), *Reconceiving Reality; Women and International Law* (American Society of International Law, 1993).

[36] Especially influential was Charlotte Bunch, 'Women's Rights as Human Rights: Toward a Re-Vision of Human Rights' (1990) 12 *Human Rights Quarterly* 486 and the founding of the Center for Women's Global Leadership at Rutgers University.

[37] Articles on state responsibility in Rebecca Cook (ed), *Human Rights of Women: National and International Perspectives* (University of Pennsylvania Press, 1994) helped shape the debate on states' obligation to exercise due diligence in combating violence against women.

[38] The 1993 Vienna Conference 'witnessed the extraordinary success of efforts by women's rights activists worldwide to end the historic disregard of human rights violations against women. Indeed, women's human rights was perhaps the only area in which the World Conference can be said to have met the challenge of defining a forward-looking agenda': Donna J Sullivan, 'Women's Human Rights and the 1993 World Conference on Human Rights' (1994) 88 *American Journal of International Law* 152.

[39] This built upon CEDAW Committee, General Recommendation 19, Violence against women, 11th session, 1992.

[40] Vienna Declaration and Programme of Action, II, para 40: 'New procedures should also be adopted to strengthen implementation of the commitment to women's equality and the human rights of women.'

[41] International Conference on Population and Development (ICPD), Cairo, 5–13 September 1994, Principle 4; Beijing Declaration and Platform for Action, Report on the Fourth World Conference on Women, Beijing, 1995 (Beijing PFA), para 213.

[42] ICPD, Principle 8.

and rescinding of the global gag rule[43] by successive US Presidents illustrates the fragility of women's rights, their instrumentalisation and susceptibility to shifts in, especially, US policy.

The Beijing Platform for Action (PFA) expressed support for the CEDAW optional protocol.[44] NGOs, academics, the CEDAW Committee and CSW ensured that these political statements were acted upon; especially influential was a 1994 expert seminar organised in Maastricht by the International Human Rights Law Group to prepare a preliminary draft that could be fleshed out by CSW and the CEDAW Committee.[45] The Optional Protocol, adopted by the UNGA in 1999,[46] was innovative in providing an individual complaint procedure for violation of Convention rights that included economic, social and cultural rights and an inquiry on receipt of reliable information of 'grave or systematic violations'.[47] In addition to its concluding observations to states' reports and jurisprudence developed under the Optional Protocol, the CEDAW Committee has evolved the Convention through the adoption of general recommendations, interpreting CEDAW article 21 to allow this process to flourish,[48] often in conjunction with feminist champions of women's rights. It regularly holds consultation days with NGOs that in turn render assistance through undertaking research, preparing for and hosting seminars that allow members of the Committee working group to have informal discussions, air opinions and share potential texts and queries. These activities are mutually reinforcing: impetus for a general recommendation may lie in a shadow report;[49] general recommendations can galvanise NGO interactions with states; an individual communication might originate in the Committee's concluding observations.

Academic centres can provide a convening space, resources and a willingness to work behind the scenes[50] to assist the severely under-resourced Committee to secure the continued vitality of CEDAW. A significant proportion of our own work over the last few years has been in this vein, supporting the Committee's work, including through publicising its jurisprudence to practitioners working on

---

[43] 'What is the Global Gag Rule?' *Open Society Foundation*, April 2019.

[44] Beijing PFA (n 41) para 230(k).

[45] Andrew Byrnes, 'Slow and Steady Wins the Race?: The Development of an Optional Protocol to the Women's Convention' (1997) 91 *Proceedings of the Annual Meeting of the American Society of International Law* 383.

[46] Optional Protocol to the Convention on the Elimination of All Forms of Discrimination against Women, 1999.

[47] ibid art 8.

[48] CEDAW, art 21: 'The Committee ... may make suggestions and general recommendations based on the examination of reports and information received from the States Parties.' There were early divisions in the Committee (primarily along Cold War divides) about the use of article 21 to interpret the Convention: Elizabeth Evatt (n 30).

[49] CEDAW Committee General Recommendation No 39, Indigenous women and girls, CEDAW/C/GC/39, 26 October 2022 originated in a 2009 shadow report by the Indigenous Women's Movement from Guatemala; *Brief History of the Movement for a CEDAW General Recommendation on Indigenous Women* (January 2019).

[50] Max Lesch and Nina Reiners, 'Informal Human Rights Law-making: How Treaty Bodies Use "General Comments" to Develop International Law' (2023) *Global Constitutionalism*.

the protection of women's rights; facilitating knowledge exchange between it and regional courts;[51] identifying normative gaps; contributing to the production of general recommendations[52] and their dissemination through academic publications and social media. Our academic/activist feminist work has extended to more generally advancing thinking around combating sexism[53] and violence against women and accessing justice through work with, for instance, the HRC special procedures,[54] the UK government's Prevention of Sexual Violence Initiative and the Council of Europe. Through this work we seek to challenge the silos that impede gender justice and peace. We consciously question our own prejudices, biases, and preconceptions that come with privilege, both personal and institutional.

IV. MAKING LAW WORK FOR WOMEN: INTERNATIONAL CRIMINAL LAW

Feminists strategising to make international law inclusive have sought to make international humanitarian law (IHL)[55] responsive to women's experiences of armed conflict and to further its enforcement through international criminal law (ICL).[56] ICL is not grounded solely in proscriptions set forth in IHL; the criminalisation of aggression, for example, is founded in the *jus ad bellum*,[57] while crimes against humanity share the same ethical foundations as human rights law. Relevant applicable law had long existed but, following World War II, international decision-makers largely failed to interpret it through a feminist lens to secure gender justice for survivors of conflict-related sexual violence.[58] The pervasive silence about these crimes became the focus of much feminist strategising in the last decades of the twentieth century.

A strategy that evolved during the UN Decade for Women was the creation of safe spaces for women to speak out about the violence committed against them.[59]

---

[51] Sheri Labenski and Keina Yoshida, 'Where Would Women be Without CEDAW?' *LSE Blog*, 4 September 2019.

[52] eg assistance in the preparation of CEDAW Committee, General Recommendation No 35 on Gender-based Violence against Women updating General Recommendation No 19, CEDAW/C/GC/35, 2017 and General Recommendation No 38, 2020 on trafficking in women and girls in the context of global migration, CEDAW/C/GC/38, 20 November 2020.

[53] See essay 10 'Misogyny and Sexism in the Digital Age'.

[54] The then SR VAW, Dubravka Šimonović, was a Visiting Professor in Practice at the LSE Centre for Women Peace and Security. Members assisted her work on shelters, online violence and rape. We also worked with the SR on trafficking in persons, especially women and children, Maria Grazia Giammarinaro, for her report on linkages between the WPS agenda and trafficking, A/73/171, 17 July 2018. See also Christine Chinkin and Gema Fernández Rodríguez de Liévana, 'Human Traffic, Human Rights and Women, Peace and Security' in Soumita Basu et al (eds), *New Directions in Women, Peace and Security* (Bristol University Press, 2020) 189.

[55] IHL is especially gendered and, tellingly, a highly codified body of international law. Although there has been some progress in ensuring that the rules pertaining to protection are applied to take account of gender ('Addressing the Needs of Women Affected by Armed Conflict' ICRC 2004), whether the rules on the conduct of hostilities will be likewise revised remains to be seen.

[56] Christine Chinkin and Patricia Viseur Sellers, 'A Century and More of Feminist Architects' in Nienke Grossman et al (eds) *Oxford Handbook on Women and International Law* (Oxford University Press, forthcoming).

[57] See essay 3 'Peace in International Law'.

[58] See essay 9 'Silence as an Obstacle to Gendered Peace and Equality'.

[59] See essay 5 'Peace in the UN Decade for Women'.

Testimonies such as those given to the International Tribunal on Crimes against Women held in Brussels in 1976 underlined the role of violence in the oppression of women through the global incidence of wartime rape and the multiple other forms of 'everyday' violence that deny peace for women. Simone de Beauvoir expressed how women attendees 'denounce[d] the crimes perpetrated against us by the male-dominated nations in which we all live, and to develop strategies to combat them'.[60] Women activists identified violence against women as a site for action before the adoption of CEDAW, which nevertheless had no express provision condemning it. Contemporaneous academic research further bolstered the understanding of the prevalence and structural basis of violence against women.[61]

The opportunity for international legal reform came in the early 1990s with the relaxation of Cold War tensions but also the prevalence of 'new wars' with widespread attacks on civilian populations. Feminist objectives turned to seeking identification of sexual and gender-based violence as contrary to international law, ensuring the availability of fora with jurisdiction for their adjudication, their inclusion in indictments and reparation. In 1992 the CEDAW Committee boldly declared gender-based violence against women to constitute a violation of CEDAW, article 1 and that wars and related situations often lead to violence that requires 'specific protective and punitive measures'.[62] In the context of the conflicts in the former Yugoslavia, the UN Security Council (SC) emphasised that bringing to justice persons responsible for these crimes would 'contribute to the restoration and maintenance of peace'.[63] An all-male UN SC fact-finding mission made no finding of widespread conflict-related sexual violence[64] but the CHR Special Rapporteur deployed a team of medical experts who reported that 'rape has been used since the beginning of the conflict on a large scale as a means of implementing the strategy of ethnic cleansing'.[65] This, and similar reporting by NGOs and the media, spurred feminist activists to ensure the inclusion of crimes of sexual violence into the jurisdiction of any criminal court that might be established. These events coincided with feminist strategic activity around the Vienna Conference on Human Rights in June 1993. The Conference collapsed the boundary between IHL and human rights in its assertion that '[v]iolations of the human rights of women in situations of armed conflict are violations of the fundamental principles of international human rights and humanitarian law'.[66] The Statutes of the ad hoc International Criminal Tribunals for the former Yugoslavia (ICTY) and

---

[60] Dianne Russell, 'Report of the International Tribunal on Crimes against Women' (1977) 2 *Frontiers: A Journal of Women Studies* 1.
[61] eg Susan Brownmiller, *Against Our Will: Men, Women and Rape* (Simon and Schuster, 1975); Catherine McKinnon, *Sexual Harassment of Working Women* (Yale University Press, 1979).
[62] CEDAW Committee General Recommendation No 19 (n 39) para 16.
[63] UNSCR 808, 22 February 1993; UNSCR 827, 25 May 1993.
[64] Report of the SC Mission established pursuant to resolution 819 (1993), S/25700, 30 April 1993. Its all-male members were from France, Venezuela, Pakistan, Hungary, New Zealand and the Russian Federation.
[65] Report on the situation of human rights in the territory of the former Yugoslavia, submitted by Mr Tadeusz Mazowiecki, SR of the Commission on Human Rights pursuant to Commission resolution 1992/S-1/1 of 14 August 1992, E/CN.4/1993/50, 10 February 1993, Annex 2; the four medical experts were Dr Perran Moroy, Dr Elizabeth Murphy, Dr Shana Swiss and Dr Greta Forster.
[66] Vienna Declaration and Programme of Action, II, 38.

Rwanda (ICTR) excavated rape as a crime against humanity[67] from the 1945 Order that provided for jurisdiction over lesser alleged wartime criminals in Europe.[68] Early prosecutions before these bodies demonstrated the importance of explicit legal provision and of the appointment of personnel committed to giving effect to that law,[69] although it still took the intervention of a female judge in the ICTR, Navanethem Pillay, to allow a female witness to speak[70] about the sexual crimes committed against her and for the indictment to be amended for their inclusion.[71]

Recognition that the commission of 'unimaginable atrocities that deeply shock the conscience of humanity ... threaten the peace, security and well-being of the world'[72] contributed to the momentum that built in the 1990s for the establishment of a permanent international criminal court. Feminist activists further mobilised. In 1997, realising that 'without an organized caucus, women's concerns would not be appropriately defended and promoted', the Women's Caucus for Gender Justice was formed, a global network comprising over 300 NGOs. Its mission was to ensure a strong court, 'responsive to the principles of gender justice', with an 'overarching direction to eliminate discrimination and gender-based stereotypes in the discernment and application of the general principles'.[73] This vision contrasted with the court proposed by the International Law Commission (ILC) that listed only rape as a crime against humanity, made no requirement for gender expertise among the judges or for gender balance in its composition.[74] The 'extraordinary campaign' undertaken by the Caucus achieved a broad list of crimes of sexual and gender violence within the ICC's jurisdiction, persecution on the grounds of gender as a crime against humanity, provision for the participation and protection of victims and witnesses and for women staff and experts on sexual and gender violence on the Court. The successful strategy was celebrated as a key moment for the international women's movement. By 2000 the judges at the Tokyo Women's Tribunal noted that:

> largely as a result of the mobilisation and work of the international and grass roots non-governmental women's human rights movement, the contributions of feminists and jurists

---

[67] Statute of the ICTY, art 5(g); Statute of the ICTR, art 3(g). ICTR art 4(e) includes 'Outrages upon personal dignity, in particular humiliating and degrading treatment, rape, enforced prostitution and any form of indecent assault' as violations of art 3 common to the Geneva Conventions and Additional Protocol II; see also Statute of the Special Court for Sierra Leone, 2000, arts 2(g) and 3(e).

[68] Control Council Law No 10, Punishment of Persons Guilty of War Crimes, Crimes Against Peace and Against Humanity, December 20, 1945, 3 Official Gazette Control Council for Germany 50–55 (1946), art II(c).

[69] The appointment by Richard Goldstone, ICTY prosecutor, of Patricia Viseur Sellers as prosecutor and Legal Advisor for Gender to the ICTY was instrumental in prosecutorial gender strategies in the ICTY and ICTR; for Sellers' account of how civil society, experts and international criminal lawyers worked towards an ICL gender strategy see Patricia Viseur Sellers, 'Gender Strategy is Not Luxury for International Courts Symposium: Prosecuting Sexual and Gender-Based Crimes Before International/ized Criminal Courts' (2009) 17 *Journal of Gender, Social Policy and the Law* 3.

[70] See essay 9 'Silence as an Obstacle to Gendered Peace and Equality'.

[71] Akshan De Alwis, Interview with Navi Pillay: former UN HCHR, 6 October 2016.

[72] Rome Statute of the International Criminal Court, 1998, preamble.

[73] Women's Caucus for Gender Justice in the International Criminal Court, 'Recommendations and Commentary for December 1997 PrepCom on the Establishment of an International Criminal Court' (1997).

[74] ILC, Draft Statute for an International Criminal Court with commentaries adopted at its 47th session, 1994; 1994 2 YBILC, part two.

who are committed to examining gender issues, and the commitment of gender-inclusive prosecutors and judges, rape and other forms of sexual violence are becoming explicitly criminalised and increasingly prosecuted.[75]

V. REFLECTIONS

Prosecutions for conflict-related rape and sexual violence remain inadequate; nevertheless, that such acts can constitute war crimes, crimes against humanity and genocide and can be successfully prosecuted as such is now firmly established in ICL. This road is one that has required considerable labour on the part of feminists, including those of us working within academic institutions.[76] The resistance to – and cynical dismissal of – our work, that we experienced during those early years stays with us. The successes – albeit limited – in bringing feminist ideas and knowledge into human rights law and international criminal law have met with criticism, including from other feminist scholars.[77] Admittedly, the changes secured are largely cosmetic additions to the primary principles of these specialist regimes (recognising new manifestations of gender-based violence as international crimes and as human rights violations). We have had less success in our endeavours to disturb the secondary principles of public international law, such as those appertaining to state responsibility, sources or jurisdiction. Moreover, our successes have been bittersweet. State focus on sexual and gender-based violence (primarily in conflict and understood as what happens to women and girls) has reinforced the gender-binary, essentialising women as victims and men as perpetrators, promoting state intervention and implicitly upholding patriarchal, neoliberal and socially conservative policies.[78] We share the view of critics who argue that the 'crisis' of sexual violence against women has deflected attention from structural economic inequalities, peace and disarmament, lessening state responsibility for these aspects of governance.[79] And we look on with horror and despair when 'women's rights' are used to justify foreign intervention.[80]

---

[75] Tokyo Women's Tribunal, Case No PT-2000-1-T, Judgment, para 580. See essay 15 'Strategic Practices: "Doing Our Own Thing"'.
[76] Christine Chinkin, 'Rape and Sexual Abuse of Women in International Law' (1994) 5 *European Journal of International Law* 326.
[77] Hilary Charlesworth and Christine Chinkin, 'Feminist Approaches to International Law and International Law Approaches to Feminism: An Overview' in *Oxford Handbook on Women and International Law* (Oxford University Press, forthcoming).
[78] Karen Engle, *The Grip of Sexual Violence in Conflict: Feminist Interventions in International Law* (Stanford University Press, 2020).
[79] Karen Engle et al, 'Feminist Approaches to International Law' in Jeffrey Dunoff and Mark Pollack (eds), *International Legal Theory Foundations and Frontiers* (Cambridge University Press, 2022) ch 8; Karen Engle, 'Looking Back to Think Forward: What We Might Learn from Feminist Cold War Movements' (2022) 116 *AJIL Unbound*.
[80] See essay 11 'Crisis and Emergency: Entrenching Gender Systems and Militarism'; Ratna Kapur, 'The Tragedy of Victimization Rhetoric: Resurrecting the "Native" Subject in International/Post-colonial Feminist Legal Politics' (2002) 15 *Harvard Human Rights Law Journal* 1 (critiquing the 'victimisation' rhetoric engaged about women in the Global South, challenging the emphasis on sex as the locus of the oppression of women and arguing for a more complex understanding of women's lives to include race, wealth, class and religion etc).

Ratna Kapur has examined the discourse of women's human rights as a justification for US military operations in Afghanistan that commenced in 2001. She points to its reinforcement of binary distinctions – liberal/illiberal, civilised/uncivilised, saviour/victim – and the ensuing harms it has brought about. She decries the 'complete silence over the role of Western powers in creating the appalling conditions in which Afghan women live coupled with the pervasive racist and imperialist representation of Islam more generally as a monolithic, dogmatic, and deeply conservative force that invariably subordinates women' and urges alternative, non-liberal, understandings of 'gender, subjectivity, and peace'.[81]

Many of the above critiques appertain to the SC's Women Peace and Security (WPS) agenda.[82] The adoption of SC Resolution 1325 in 2000, bringing women's experiences of conflict and progress in IHL, human rights law and ICL within the SC's mandate for the maintenance of international peace and security, was welcomed as a further feminist success story. Twenty-three years later, the value of this strategy for enhancing the lives of women in conflict-affected areas has to be re-evaluated. The political will to resource WPS appropriately and to bring WPS principles into the SC's country-specific mandates has been lacking; the rhetoric has not been matched by practice.[83] From its outset, WPS did not challenge the structural factors that undermine gender equality[84] and peace: the price for SC endorsement of women's participation and protection against conflict-affected sexual violence was to forgo demands for disarmament.[85] 'Peace' is given no content except for the importance of women's participation in processes for conflict prevention as well as resolution.

In 2015 the 'emphatic conclusions of women ... from all over the world were that there must be an end to the present cycle of militarization, with its unprecedented levels of military spending, and that armed intervention by the international community and Member States must only be the last resort'.[86] Instead of heeding this call, the Council further securitised WPS by co-opting it and women into its counter-terrorist agenda.[87] There have been no further WPS resolutions since 2019,[88]

---

[81] Ratna Kapur, '"The First Feminist War in all of History": Epistemic Shifts and Relinquishing the Mission to Rescue the Other Woman' (2022) 116 *AJIL Unbound*.

[82] See essay 6 'Revisiting the Past: Peace at Beijing and Beyond'.

[83] 'Though there is a great deal of rhetoric supporting women, peace and security, funding for programmes and processes remains abysmally low across all areas of the agenda': Radhika Coomaraswamy et al, *Preventing Conflict, Transforming Justice, Securing the Peace: A Global Study on the Implementation of Security Council Resolution 1325* (UN, 2015) 14.

[84] The Council makes no gender analysis but equates gender with women; see essay 2 'Gender'.

[85] See essay 6 'Revisiting the Past: Peace at Beijing and Beyond' and essay 7 'Women, Disarmament and Peace'.

[86] Radhika Coomaraswamy (n 83) 394.

[87] UNSCR 2242, 13 October 2015. The 'international [Western] strategy of promoting women's roles in countering violent extremism ... reinforces gendered binaries of women's pacifism and men's warmongering that dominate globalized WPS discourses': Rita Manchanda, 'Difficult Encounters with the WPS Agenda in South Asia: Rescripting Globalized Norms and Policy Frameworks for a Feminist Peace' in Soumita Basu et al (n 54) 61, 63. See essay 11 'Crisis and Emergency: Entrenching Gender Systems and Militarism'.

[88] UNSCR 2467, 23 April 2019; UNSCR 2493, 29 October 2019.

and feminist activists are reconsidering their strategy: to persist with seeking further WPS resolutions from the SC, recognising the weakened state of that institution following its inability to prevent the gender-based persecution of Afghan women and girls; its inability to say anything meaningful both in respect of the 2022 invasion of Ukraine by Russia and the conflict between Israel and Palestine that have led to civilian deaths and injuries on a shocking scale; or to turn away from the SC and look elsewhere (the UNGA or HRC?) or abandon international law and its institutions altogether?

In this bleak assessment it must also be remembered that WPS (and international law more generally) does not operate only – or even mostly – within international institutions. Feminist strategies that focus on working through local NGOs for local implementation should be furthered. It is, for instance, remarkable that Ukraine – in the midst of existential conflict – has adopted a National Action Plan on WPS.[89] Encouragement of National Action Plans[90] must nevertheless be tempered with caution: those from the Global North portray WPS as an instrument of foreign policy, legitimising interventions into countries where women are deemed to need rescuing. But strategies that support and give effect to local women's priorities and initiatives through international law must be a preferred way forward.

Our work owes much to the scholarship of feminists, past and present, who provide us with the tools to critique and rethink our discipline, enabling us to better recognise the structural obstacles of power in the particular and in the difference. Their insights guide and enrich our work as academics and shape our politics. We have come to embrace activist-based scholarship, bridging theory and practice, along with many colleagues worldwide. Working with feminist activists we are often struck by their belief in the power of legal reform to achieve transformative change. We are more sceptical. There may be new treaty texts, resolutions, definitions in specialised legal regimes and gender relevant language in mainstream treaties but these do not change the fundamental principles of international law based upon state sovereignty. Treaty texts are hard fought but can be wilfully ignored or misinterpreted. We may have campaigned with feminist activists to insert a reference to gender in the Arms Trade Treaty,[91] but we were equally aware that by stipulating what was unlawful, the Treaty would protect the lawful arms trade, as defined by states. How – given what we know about militarism and the impact of weapons on the incidence of violence against women, ethnic, racial, religious and sexual minorities – could there ever be *legal* arms exports? At the intersection of patriarchy, militarism and capitalism, facilitated by international law, arms exports to Ukraine

---

[89] Christine Chinkin and Oksana Potapova, 'Women, Peace and Security: National Action Plans in the UK and Ukraine' (Peacerep, 2023).

[90] Mirsad Miki Jacevic, 'WPS, States and the National Action Plans' in Sara Davies and Jacqui True (eds), *The Oxford Handbook of Women, Peace and Security* (Oxford University Press, 2019) 273.

[91] Article 7(4): 'The exporting State Party, in making this assessment, shall take into account the risk of the conventional arms covered under Article 2 (1) or of the items covered under Article 3 or Article 4 being used to commit or facilitate serious acts of gender-based violence or serious acts of violence against women and children'.

and Israel have risen to unprecedented levels.[92] We nevertheless remain committed to international law in that its language and concepts open doors into the institutional structures of states and its organisations; without law we have no entry point. But we also fully recognise that, to the extent that feminist strategies rely on the androcentric tools of racial colonialism, they 'may never enable us to bring about genuine change'.[93]

---

[92] The surge in arms sales from Germany for example – whether to Ukraine or Israel – must be understood through multiple, intersecting prisms, economic, political/historical and military membership within NATO in which gender and race are imbricated: Sam Jones, 'German Arms Exports to Israel Surge as Berlin Backs Campaign against Hamas' *Financial Times*, 8 November 2023.

[93] Audre Lorde, 'The Master's Tools Will Never Dismantle the Master's House' in Audre Lorde, *Sister Outsider: Essays and Speeches* (Crossing Press, 1984) 110.

14

Strategic Practice: Giving Effect to Legal Change

I. INTRODUCTION

THE PREVIOUS ESSAY describes how feminist strategising and actions achieved changes in international human rights law (IHRL) and international criminal law (ICL) to make those specialist regimes more responsive to the lives and experiences of women and girls. Achieving relevant change in formal legal provision is only a first step. To advance feminist objectives, legal language and tools that have been obtained must be applied through a gender lens along with the political will to give practical effect to legal obligations. This pertains not only to gender-specific provisions but throughout the entire legal text. Lack of awareness, understanding of or hostility to feminist goals may prevent those responsible for applying the law from recognising possibilities for change.[1] Further strategies must be devised to ensure that earlier attainments are not undone by being ignored or discounted. One such strategy is that of the Women's Initiatives for Gender Justice[2] in monitoring the work of the ICC – the Judges, the Office of the Prosecutor and the Registry – against the gender norms in the Rome Statute. It makes recommendations for holistic integration of gender inclusive justice throughout all the Court's organs.[3] Gender inclusive justice is understood as:

> Justice that recognizes the gender dimensions of violence. It means justice that is neither blind nor deaf to the ways in which violence is perpetrated specifically against women [and LGBTQI+ people]. ... Of course, there are limitations to law and legal process. It isn't possible to end gender discrimination ... through prosecutions alone. Nonetheless, women survivors of conflict consistently call for the prosecution of gender-based crimes as an essential component of a comprehensive approach to sustainable peace and justice in their communities. The end of impunity is the beginning of peace.[4]

---

[1] Louise Chappell, *The Politics of Gender Justice at the International Criminal Court* (Oxford University Press, 2016) (analysing how implementation of the Rome Statute continues to be opposed and contested by what she terms adverse 'gender legacies').

[2] The successor body to the Women's Caucus for Gender Justice; see essay 13 'Strategic Practice: Peace and Equality through International Law'.

[3] States parties are reminded of their obligation to nominate women for election to the Court.

[4] Brigid Inder, Executive Director of Women's Initiatives for Gender Justice, *The International Gender Justice Dialogue* (opening plenary, 20 April 2010).

While the Rome Statute encapsulates the gender binary between women and men,[5] gender justice requires all involved in criminal processes to take account of power dynamics and of the 'lived experiences of LGBT and gender-diverse persons and communities in relation to and beyond sexual violence'.[6] Failure to do this entails these experiences being 'deliberately rejected and systematically ignored by law enforcement agencies, judicial systems, politicians, and conservative religious factions'.[7]

II. INTERVENTIONS INTO INTERNATIONAL LITIGATION

Feminist lawyers have not been satisfied with simply monitoring the work of international tribunals. They have sought to integrate gender into jurisprudence through commencing test case litigation and submitting *amicus* briefs into ongoing cases.[8] The former requires identification of appropriate cases and fora, a willing plaintiff, and an assessment of the risk of losing the case, both for the plaintiff and for the development of the law.[9] Submission of *amicus* briefs, which both authors have engaged in, is a form of protection against male dominated legal processes. It involves intervening in appropriate cases to present innovative interpretations of existing legal provisions (for instance that states have obligations to investigate rape and sexual violence under human rights treaties[10]), ensure that gender sensitive arguments are put to the court and to argue for transformative reparation.[11]

In the 1990s the excavation of ICL from the post World War II trials entailed numerous previously unasked questions coming before the newly constituted international tribunals. The long silence about crimes of sexual and gender-based violence meant that the discriminatory impact of the gender power imbalance had barely surfaced in ICL. The commencement of prosecutions provided women's human rights NGOs, legal scholars and practitioners with the opening to provide the tribunals with gendered perspectives on the questions before them.

Amicus briefs have been submitted at the invitation of a court or on the initiative of the *amici*; in the case of the former the court specifies the issues on which it is seeking assistance, although *amici* may go beyond the court's remit. *Amicus* briefs in

---

[5] See essay 2 'Gender'.
[6] Independent Expert on Protection against violence and discrimination based on sexual orientation and gender identity, A/77/235, 27 July 2022, para 35.
[7] ibid.
[8] For a useful report on this see Women's Initiatives for Gender Justice, *Judicial Approaches to Sexual and Gender Based Crimes at the International Criminal Court Structural Shortcomings, Critical Improvements and Future Possibilities of Intersectional Justice*, 2023.
[9] eg *Rosanna Flamer-Caldera v Sri Lanka*, CEDAW/C/81D/134/2018, 24 March 2022 (a lesbian, human rights activist, claiming for the first time before the CEDAW Committee that the criminalisation of lesbian sexual conduct violated CEDAW); Christine Chinkin and Keina Yoshida, 'CEDAW and the Decriminalisation of Same-sex Relationships' (2022) *European Human Rights Law Review* 288.
[10] eg in *MC v Bulgaria* ECtHR, Appl No 39272/98, 4 December 2003 Christine worked with Interights (a human rights NGO) on a third-party intervention to bring before the Court modern definitions of rape in European domestic legal systems and international law; Ivana Radačić, 'Rape Cases in the Jurisprudence of the European Court of Human Rights: Defining Rape and Determining the Scope of the State's Obligations' (2008) *European Human Rights Law Review* 357.
[11] See essay 18 'Transformative Reparations and Gendered Peace'.

which we have participated have covered a variety of issues: protective measures for victims and survivors;[12] seeking an amended indictment to include charges of rape and sexual violence; recognition of these crimes as of comparable gravity to other international crimes;[13] to expose stereotypes and myths that prejudice a fair trial.[14] As activist legal academics we have found participation, as individuals or as part of a feminist collective, in the drafting and submission of *amicus* briefs to be a way of contributing to a feminist jurisprudence. We discuss below a few examples of the many *amicus* briefs feminists have submitted to legal processes to demonstrate their overriding purpose – that failure to deliver gender justice is discriminatory and undermines sustainable peace by leaving in situ the gender systems and structures of power that founded the violence.

A. Jean Paul Akayesu

At the first trial before the International Criminal Tribunal for Rwanda (ICTR) female witnesses spontaneously told of rapes committed by militia under Akayesu's command in Taba commune. Rape was not included in the indictment brought by the prosecutor. The only female Judge, Navanethem Pillay, stopped the hearing to allow the prosecutors to investigate further and amend the indictment. An *amicus* brief was submitted to the Tribunal on behalf of over 40 signatories – women's human rights scholars, global NGOs, bodies from different parts of Africa, Asia and Latin America – who had worked 'to ensure recognition of and accountability for violence against women in the UN system, and, in particular, to guarantee gender justice in the operation of the International Criminal Tribunals'.[15] The fully legally referenced brief argued for an amended indictment that charged rape and other forms of sexual violence against Akayesu; failure to include such charges – despite evidence of sexual violence as integral to the genocide – suggested a lack of commitment to addressing these crimes, that they were less serious than other crimes committed in the course of genocide constituted a denial of equal justice and deprived survivors of 'recognition and vindication of their suffering', without which rebuilding their lives and self-esteem would be harder. The brief does not reflect that this would also deny the survivors internal and external peace. The Trial Chamber noted the amended indictment but made no reference to the *amicus* brief.[16]

---

[12] Christine submitted an *amicus* brief at the request of the prosecutor in the *Tadic* case before the ICTY. Another brief was submitted by Rhonda Copelon, Felice Gaer, Jennifer M Green and Sara Hossain: *Dusko Tadic v Prosecutor, Decision on the Prosecutor's Motion requesting Protective Measures for Victims and Witnesses*, 10 August 1995, para 10.

[13] eg *amicus* briefs in the *Akayesu* and *Hissène Habré* briefs, discussed below.

[14] eg *Velásquez Paiz v Guatemala*, IACtHR, Judgment of 19 November 2015 (preliminary objections, merits, reparations and costs): brief refuting gender stereotypes relating, inter alia, to a female murder victim's clothing and lifestyle.

[15] *Amicus* brief respecting amendment of the indictment and supplementation of the evidence to ensure the prosecution of rape and other sexual violence within the competence of the Tribunal, http://www.iccwomen.org/publications/briefs/docs/Prosecutor_v_Akayesu_ICTR.pdf.

[16] *Prosecutor v Jean Paul Akayesu*, ICTR-96-04, Judgment, 2 September 1998, para 23.

B. Hissène Habré

A 'select group of international experts, … leading academics, jurists, and practitioners specializing in the treatment of sexual violence under international criminal law'[17] submitted an *amicus* brief to the Extraordinary African Chambers in Dakar, Senegal[18] that tried Hissène Habré for crimes committed during his long authoritarian rule in Chad. The exercise of universal jurisdiction in an extraterritorial court owed much to civil society that had worked over decades with survivors of Habre's regime.[19] The brief was submitted mid-trial as testimony mounted of the 'multiple incidents of rape, sexual slavery, genital injury, forced nudity, and violations of reproductive health' committed by Habré or his high-level officials but which had not been charged.[20] An open letter to the Court from 'seventeen groups from across Senegal, eastern Democratic Republic of the Congo, the Netherlands and the United States'[21] called for an amended indictment, building on the similar action in *Akayesu*. The brief that followed was prepared rapidly since the trial was underway. Its aim was to aid the Court in discharging its responsibility 'to adjudicate acts of rape, sexual slavery, and other forms of sexual violence committed under the Habré regime and to properly characterize them as crimes against humanity, war crimes, and acts of torture under customary international law at the time of the alleged commission'. With no formal mechanism for filing an *amicus* brief, it could not be admitted into the trial record, although 'the Chamber could avail itself of any and all pertinent background documents'. A newspaper article brought the brief into the public domain. It seems likely that it was influential, as charges were amended to include sexual violence and Habré was convicted of rape and sexual slavery as crimes against humanity.[22]

C. Dominic Ongwen

In February 2021 an ICC Trial Chamber found Dominic Ongwen, a former commander in the Lord's Resistance Army, guilty of 61 war crimes and crimes against humanity committed in Northern Uganda between 1 July 2002 and 31 December

---

[17] Christine joined with many other feminists to add her signature to the brief but was not among its active drafters.

[18] Agreement between the Government of the Republic of Senegal and the African Union on the Establishment of Extraordinary African Chambers within the Senegalese Judicial System, Dakar, Senegal, 22 August 2012 (2015) 1 *African Journal of International Criminal Justice* 107.

[19] See essay 9 'Silence as an Obstacle to Gendered Peace and Equality'.

[20] *Amicus Curiae* brief of the Human Rights Center, University of California, Berkeley, School of Law, and International Experts on Sexual Violence under International Criminal Law, 'Rape and Other Forms of Sexual Violence as Crimes against Humanity, War Crimes, and Torture under Customary International Law' 8 September 2015.

[21] Kim Thuy Seelinger et al, 'Can We Be Friends? Offering an *Amicus Curiae* Brief on Sexual Violence to the EAC' in Sharon Weill et al (eds), *The President on Trial: Prosecuting Hissène Habré* (Oxford University Press, 2020) ch 17.

[22] On appeal Habré was acquitted of charges of rape allegedly committed by himself, although his conviction stood for such offences committed by persons under his authority and control.

2005.²³ Nineteen counts were for sexual and gender-based crimes, including forced marriage and forced pregnancy. Ongwen's lawyers filed an appeal against his conviction on multiple grounds.

The Appeals Chamber sought observations from 'qualified scholars and/or practitioners' on 'the legal interpretation of forced marriage, sexual slavery and forced pregnancy and the standards applicable to assessing evidence of sexual violence'.²⁴ This invitation presented an 'extraordinary' opportunity to contribute to the progressive development of international criminal law; if the Appeals Chamber accepted feminist legal arguments, they would be binding on the Court's future judgments, with the potential to filter down through domestic courts and tribunals. Within days, together with 42 feminist academics and international lawyers from around the world, we responded to a 'call to action', indicating our interest in collaborating.²⁵ We organised into four groups to tackle different areas of law: forced marriage; forced pregnancy; sexual slavery; and duress and evidentiary standards. All four groups were granted leave to intervene by the Court. Two colleagues have subsequently reflected on the process, describing the strategies and methods adopted; the practical, structural and intellectual barriers confronted; and the individual and collective anxieties experienced throughout the collaborative work.²⁶ They observed that the team was guided by the imperative that 'a gender strategy is not a luxury, [but rather] its absence is an absurdity'.²⁷

Adopting a gender perspective is core to how we, as feminist international lawyers, engage with the law to secure gender justice. This can involve presenting innovative legal arguments that go beyond the substance of the law and to the way in which courts engage with that law. For example, in citing article 21(3) of the Rome Statute, which requires that the Court's application and interpretation of the law 'be consistent with internationally recognized human rights, and be without any adverse distinction founded on grounds such as gender', we argued that the practical implication of this provision is 'the need to undertake a gender analysis when applying procedural and substantive law concerning both offences and defences in the Statute'.²⁸

Feminists typically encounter ethical dilemmas when intervening as experts, as did colleagues who prepared the sexual slavery brief.²⁹ The strategy of presenting a

---

²³ *Prosecutor v Dominic Ongwen*, ICC-02/04-01/15, convicted 4 February 2021; conviction upheld by the Appeals Chamber, 15 December 2022.
²⁴ Order inviting expressions of interest as amici curiae in judicial proceedings (pursuant to rule 103 of the Rules of Procedure and Evidence) ICC-02/04-01/15 A, 25 October 2021.
²⁵ We were both involved in this feminist collective effort.
²⁶ Alexandra Lily Kather and Angela Mudukuti, 'Symposium in Pursuit of Intersectional Justice at the International Criminal Court: Ongwen *Amici Curiae* Submissions from a Feminist Collective of Lawyers and Scholars' *Opinio Juris*, 2 May 2022.
²⁷ Patricia Viseur Sellers, 'Gender Strategy is Not Luxury for International Courts Symposium: Prosecuting Sexual and Gender-Based Crimes before International/ized Criminal Courts' (2009) 17 *Journal of Gender, Social Policy and the Law* 3, 23.
²⁸ Amici Curiae Observations on Duress and the Standards Applicable to Assessing Evidence of Sexual Violence, ICC-02/04-01/15 A A2, 22 December 2021, para 6.
²⁹ Amici Curiae Observations on Sexual- and Gender-Based Crimes, Particularly Sexual Slavery, and on Cumulative Convictions Pursuant to Rule 103 of the Rules of Procedure and Evidence, ICC-02/04-01/15 A A2, 23 December 2021.

compelling legal argument to ensure the progressive (and principled) advancement of international law but which concurrently casts doubt on the appropriateness of a charge for which the defendant has been found guilty, has the potential to backfire. As academics, we bear the brunt of our own argument, but as practitioners the risks and consequences are shouldered by others. While the Trial Chamber had posited that sexual slavery encompasses enslavement, our colleagues urged for the logic to be reversed: it is the crime of enslavement that encompasses all exercises of ownership, including any sexualised indicia of enslavement. They argued that 'all acts of a sexual nature, including control over sexuality, sexual integrity, and sexual and reproductive autonomy are *indicia* of the exercise of powers of ownership of [the crime] of enslavement in all its forms'.[30] This was not an exercise in legal semantics but a point of principle to facilitate gender justice.[31] The team considered that to develop the law on enslavement to address sexualised ownership over enslaved persons was a preferred strategy that would: capture other manifestations of enslavement as a crime against humanity; disrupt dominant misconceptions that enslavement does not include sexualised violence; enable the recognition of sexualised violence against enslaved men; and help to prevent the feminisation of sexual slavery.

Feminist strategies may focus on consolidating hard-won normative gains, as our colleagues did who worked on the forced marriage brief.[32] Forced marriage is not listed as a stand-alone crime in the Rome Statute and Ongwen was charged with the crime against humanity of 'other inhumane acts of a similar character [to those expressly enumerated in Article 7] intentionally causing great suffering, or serious injury to body or to mental or physical health'. Given that most victims are young women and girls, the very fact that forced marriage is *not* a listed offence demonstrates ICL's androcentric history.[33] Our colleagues argued that forced marriage has been recognised by the Special Court of Sierra Leone and the Extraordinary Chambers in the Courts of Cambodia as the crime against humanity of 'other inhumane acts'.[34] They maintained that it was a distinctive inhumane act in that, first, it constitutes a violation of relational autonomy and, second, it exposes the victim to a constellation of rights violations that extend in time. Developed under human rights law, relational autonomy is grounded in gender equality and the right to freely choose a spouse and enter into marriage with free and full consent.[35] Forced marriage is a deeply gendered act that strips one party – typically women – of their autonomy and free choice. It is a patriarchal practice that seeks to impose and

---

[30] Amici Curiae Observations on Sexual- and Gender-Based Crimes (n 29) para 2.

[31] Patricia Viseur Sellers and Jocelyn Getgen Kestenbaum, 'The International Crimes of Slavery and the Slave Trade: A Feminist Critique' in Indira Rosenthal et al (eds), *Gender and International Criminal Law* (Oxford University Press, 2022) 25.

[32] Amici Curiae Brief on Forced Marriage, ICC-02/04-01/15 A A2, 22 December 2021.

[33] *cf* Council of Europe Convention on preventing and combating violence against women and domestic violence, 11 May 2011 (Istanbul Convention) art 37.

[34] See https://api.research-repository.uwa.edu.au/ws/portalfiles/portal/163083971/FM_Amicus_Brief_22_Dec_2021.pdf.

[35] CEDAW, art 16; Protocol to the African Charter on Human and Peoples' Rights on the Rights of Women in Africa (Maputo Protocol), art 6(a).

maintain a relationship of exclusive male dominance over women and girls. The act is not necessarily sexual but is a form of gendered violence that is nearly always the basis for further violence, including sexual.[36] The *amicus* brief stands as a reminder of what is at stake.

Consolidating feminist gains was also the strategic aim of colleagues who worked on the forced pregnancy brief.[37] Unlike forced marriage, forced pregnancy is expressly listed in the Rome Statute as constituting a crime against humanity and war crime in international and non-international armed conflict.[38] Its inclusion in the Statute owed much to the concerted interventions throughout the Statute's negotiations by feminist activists, who were driven by their shared outrage over the atrocities, including forced pregnancy, perpetrated against women during the conflicts in the former Yugoslavia and elsewhere. Forced pregnancy is narrowly defined as the 'unlawful confinement of a woman forcibly made pregnant with the intent of affecting the ethnic composition of any population or carrying out other grave violations of international law' with the caveat that the definition 'shall not in any way be interpreted as affecting national laws relating to pregnancy'.[39] States thus retained the right to control the impregnated bodies of women in domestic law, as international criminalisation could not be allowed to interfere with patriarchal domestic abortion policies. The brief stressed that forced pregnancy constitutes a gender-specific crime and an attack on the 'reproductive integrity' of individuals assigned female at birth including trans and gender diverse people; moreover, the need to ground the crime in human rights law and as a violation of the 'personal and reproductive autonomy' of the victim was emphasised, as described by the Trial Chamber. The crime goes beyond forced impregnation in that it also involves preventing, by unlawful (forced) confinement, the victim from taking action to terminate the pregnancy should they wish to do so. It thus doubly violates the victim. Above all, the crime strips the victim of their personhood by treating them as nothing more than a vessel of reproduction.

Sometimes feminist interventions are directed to reaffirming the social imperative of criminalising and prosecuting gender-based violence, as was the case with the duress brief.[40] Feminist international criminal lawyers tend to concentrate on elaborating offences – recognising the need to think about gender in all crimes – and modes of liability, thereby neglecting legal defences, which nevertheless raise fundamental questions going to social priorities and ethics – deeply gendered – in the absence of law. Defences thus represent fertile ground for feminist reflection and analysis.

---

[36] The Special Court for Sierra Leone first considered forced marriage as a crime against humanity under ICL: see *Prosecutor v Brima, Kamara and Kanu*, Appeal Court, 22 February 2008.

[37] Amici Curiae Observations on the Rome Statute's definition of 'forced pregnancy' by Dr Rosemary Grey, Global Justice Center, Women's Initiatives for Gender Justice and Amnesty International, ICC-02/04-01/15-1938, 23 December 2021.

[38] Rome Statute of the ICC, arts 7(1)(g); 8(2)(b)(xxii); 8(e)(vi).

[39] ibid art 7(2)(f). There is no evidence that the use of 'woman' in the text was intended to exclude other pregnant persons from the scope of the crime including girls, transgender or intersex persons who are biologically capable of becoming pregnant.

[40] Amici Curiae Observations on Duress and the Standards Applicable to Assessing Evidence of Sexual Violence, ICC-02/04-01/15 A A2, 22 December 2021.

The brief on duress adopted two parallel strategies: the first was purely doctrinal, while the second aimed through a gender prism to highlight the operation of a patriarchal world grounded in violence.[41] Our political priority lay with the latter. Engaging the doctrine of prior fault, we argued that the defendant played 'an active role in creating, contributing to, and maintaining an environment [patriarchal] in which serious international crimes were sustained and/or normalized'. We urged the Court to:

> inquire into the broader gendered context in which the sexual and gender-based crimes took place, including an accused's role in creating and sustaining a discriminatory environment founded on coercion and violence ... and the ways an accused, through force, used their position of authority and power to promote a social order committed to maintaining inequalities including between women, men, girls, boys, lesbian, gay, bisexual, non-binary, and gender non-conforming persons.

A gender analysis 'would be attentive to the ways in which relationships of domination, oppression, and exploitation were normalised by an accused through ... the imposition of gender roles and stereotypes making sexual and gender-based violence inevitable'. Between the lines of our brief, we hoped our unarticulated plea would be heard: that by rejecting the applicability of the defence of duress, the Couer would not only affirm the imperative of gender justice but the imperative of gender equality in all societies in both war and peace.

On 15 December 2022, the Appeals Chamber unanimously confirmed the Trial Chamber's decision on Ongwen's guilt in respect of all 61 charges.

III. INTERVENTIONS INTO GENERAL INTERNATIONAL LAW

The *amicus* briefs discussed above directed the relevant court's attention towards manifestations of sexual and gender-based violence in patriarchal societies and the imperative of a gendered analysis. The discussion about examining criminal defences through a gender prism shows how looking beyond issues of violence and seeking entry points for gender analysis of broader issues of international law can expose the discipline's foundational gender and racial biases and suggest ways to counter them. Openings may be found in civil proceedings or in other sites for public engagement which offer opportunities for bringing feminist arguments into the mainstream. This next section describes two instances where we responded to opportunities to introduce some feminist thinking into issues of general international law and the quandaries we face as feminist lawyers addressing subjects that do not self-evidently raise questions of gender. Should we bring gender analysis into our opinion at the risk of losing the intended audience? Or should we remain within the parameters of classic legal argumentation, hoping thereby to win the legal point?

---

[41] The Defence also raised mental incapacity, but limited resources necessitated a collective strategic decision not to address this defence in the brief.

A. State Immunity

Decisions of national courts constitute subsidiary sources of international law[42] and domestic litigation sometimes offers opportunities for innovative legal argument through *amicus* intervention. One such example was the cases brought before the Seoul Central District Court in 2021 by former 'comfort women', for reparation for the serious violations of IHL and human rights by the Japanese military during World War II. Japan claimed sovereign (state) immunity from jurisdiction. It was 'the last throw of the dice' for the women, as Japan had successfully claimed immunity in lawsuits brought elsewhere around the world. The South Korean legal team sought the backing of international lawyers and invited the submission of *amicus* briefs: we responded. The brief drew on areas of international law where there had been feminist inroads to argue that gender analysis can be brought to overturn established principles of sovereign immunity under customary international law.[43] It argued that:[44]

> according state immunity to Japan for gender crimes committed against the so-called 'comfort women' is contrary to this [women, peace and security] Security Council agenda, reiterated through ten resolutions over a twenty-year period. The Council has recognised the importance of criminal trials in national courts of individuals accused of conflict-affected sexual violence and the responsibility of states to ensure access to justice. It is further inconsistent with calls to states to refuse amnesty for such crimes in peace processes to accord immunity from jurisdiction in national courts to answer for such crimes. Further Resolution 2467 emphasises the importance of a 'survivor-centred' approach to preventing and responding to sexual violence in conflict and post-conflict situations; protecting the state from answering for its actions does not accord with according priority to the needs and rights of survivors.

Hence:

> The assertion of state immunity from jurisdiction for consideration of such crimes is contrary to this repeated legal position, continues impunity and reinforces gender inequality. This cannot be the valid legal position today.

The legal reasoning was admittedly contrary to the International Court of Justice (ICJ) decision in the *Jurisdictional Immunities* case,[45] which denied any exceptions to state immunity based on the gravity of the offences, *jus cogens* or lack of any alternative forum. That case, however, involved no issues relating to gender-based and sexual violence and made no reference to gender. We argued that this limited its relevance to the present case, maintaining that:

> the law relating to state immunity must be reassessed through a gender lens, that is taking into account the evolution of gender equality and gender crimes in international law

---

[42] Statute of the ICJ, 1945, art 38(1)(d).
[43] See essay 9 'Silence as an Obstacle to Gendered Peace and Equality'.
[44] Extracts from *amicus* brief submitted by Christine Chinkin and Keina Yoshida to the Seoul District Court in *Kwak Ye-Nam et al v Japan*, October 2020.
[45] *Jurisdictional Immunities of the State (Germany v Italy: Greece intervening)*, 3 February 2012, 2012 ICJ Reports 99.

in the same way as it has been reassessed to take account of contemporary commercial practices ... state immunity is exposed as protecting the concerns of the sovereign (male) state, providing a shield to the masculinised activities of war. The restrictive immunity model is recognised when the interests of other men need to be protected (commercial activities) but not where those activities involve violations of human rights of women outside the legal frameworks of employment and commercial transactions. It is therefore imperative that the Court adopts a gender and human rights lens when considering the application of state immunity to this case.

In January 2021 the Seoul Central District Court boldly asserted that immunity is not a static value but that it evolves according to the international climate.[46] This approach, endorsing principles of human dignity, access to justice and human rights, was not repeated in a similar case a few months later when Japan's immunity was upheld by another chamber of the Seoul Central District Court.[47] In November 2023 the Seoul High Court reverted to the earlier decision and recognised the exception to immunity under customary international law and awarded the comfort women compensation. This decision, which Japan is apparently not appealing, is an outlier in that it does not correspond to mainstream opinion with respect to the law of state immunity. But it is a beacon, pointing to a world view that takes seriously violations of IHL and human rights and showing that state sovereignty need not prevail over individuals' interests. Existing exceptions to state immunity demonstrate that there is nothing inherently wrong or disruptive about the restrictive approach – it does not destroy diplomacy and inter-state relations. States can live and deal with each other without relying on immunity and could continue to do so with an exception based on serious violations of IHL and human rights. Placing a gender lens over state immunity exposes it as protecting the concerns of the sovereign (male) state and offers a way to link the evolution of international law on combating sexual and gender-based violence with mainstream doctrines of international law. It can be understood as a landmark in securing gender justice, not just for the 'comfort women' but, if followed by other courts, for other victims of conflict-affected sexual and gender-based violence.

B. Nuclear Weapons

In 2021 the UK branch of the Campaign for Nuclear Disarmament (CND) invited us to provide an opinion under international law on the legality of the UK Government's nuclear policy as set out in its 2021 *Integrated Review on Security, Defence, Development and Foreign Policy*. In our joint opinion[48] we engaged standard principles of treaty interpretation and legal analysis to argue that the policy breached the 1968 Treaty on the Non-Proliferation of Nuclear Weapons (NPT), the

---

[46] Seoul Central District Court, 34th Chamber, Case no 2016 Ga-Hap 505092 Compensation for Damage, *Kim, Kang-won v State of Japan*.
[47] Seoul Central District Court, 15th Civil Division, Case no 2016 Ga-Hap 580239 Judgment Summary, 21 April 2021.
[48] Available at https://cnduk.org/wp-content/uploads/2021/05/CND-legal-opinion-1.pdf.

200 *Strategic Practice: Giving Effect to Legal Change*

UN Charter's prohibition of the use of force and IHL. We also took the strategic decision to address the prohibition on discrimination on the grounds of sex and gender, maintaining that:[49]

> The use of nuclear weapons would also violate the prohibition of discrimination on the grounds of sex and gender and the requirement of equality between women and men as spelled out in many treaties to which the UK is a party.
>
> Research has revealed that the effects of nuclear weapons have different and disproportionate effects on women and girls and any threat or use of such weapons would violate the requirements of equality. As expressly recognised in the Treaty on the Prohibition of Nuclear Weapons, '*the catastrophic consequences of nuclear weapons cannot be adequately addressed, … and have a disproportionate impact on women and girls, including as a result of ionizing radiation*'.
>
> The CEDAW Committee has noted the heightened risks of violations to their rights faced by women and girls in situations of disaster. The Committee includes nuclear hazards and risks in its understanding of such disaster. It provides guidelines of the steps states should take in order to comply with their obligations under CEDAW with respect to such risk.
>
> Other human rights would also be violated by any use of nuclear weapons, including but not limited to: the right to be free from cruel, inhumane or degrading treatment; the right to health; freedom of movement indeed recognition of the 'dignity and worth of the human person' and to live in a '*social and international order in which the rights and freedoms*' can be realised.
>
> The UK's human rights obligations extend beyond its national borders with respect to all those within its jurisdiction. The CEDAW Committee has asserted that '*States parties are responsible for all their actions affecting human rights, regardless of whether the affected persons are in their territory*.'
>
> In a number of decisions, the European Court of Human Rights has considered the application of extraterritorial jurisdiction. It has held that 'in exceptional circumstances the acts of Contracting States which are performed outside their territory or which produce effects there ("extraterritorial act") may amount to the exercise by them of jurisdiction within the meaning of Article 1. The acts of state agents acting – legally or illegally – make the state accountable for violations of the Convention with respect to persons in the territory of another state, whether or not that other state is within the legal space of the Convention'. …. Rights violations caused by the UK's use of its nuclear weaponry, whether in wartime or peacetime, would thus engage the UK's responsibility wherever they occurred in the world.

Writing the opinion raised several dilemmas for us, going to substance and methodology and their interrelationship. We felt constrained and policed by international law's androcentric norms, doctrines and framing. Could we justify speaking to sex and gender discrimination in an opinion on nuclear policy? We considered ourselves bound by the language, style and reasoning of orthodox legal practice and opinion writing so we followed the formula. Moreover, if our opinion was to be taken 'seriously' (by the mainstream) the *lex ferenda* (aspirational law) and even emerging law not yet 'crystallised' as customary law could not form part of our opinion. Within

---

[49] In the extracts below from our joint opinion we have omitted all legal references.

international law's epistemic community, dominated by legal positivism, remaining faithful to the *lex lata* (existing law) was all important.[50] In search of binding law, we scrutinised the relevant texts while aware that negotiated language is always the site of contestation: the meaning of words is not fixed but is contingent on context, time, intention. Seeking to resolve uncertainty and ambiguity, we turned to the Vienna Convention on the Law of Treaties to guide our interpretation,[51] thereby putting our faith in yet another 'authoritative' text. We looked for guidance to the ICJ[52] but found its level of abstraction and at times opaque language[53] unhelpful. We have become adept at the strategy of using the master's tools to build rigorously constructed arguments, citing legal sources as delimited by yet another text, the ICJ Statute.[54] Every text functions to provide law with its normative force, protecting it from collapsing into violence. It is a double bind upon another, which cannot be untangled, although we attempted to do so by resorting to principles such as 'good faith'.[55] The fundamental principle of good faith is core to the 'trust and confidence that are inherent in international co-operation, in particular in an age when this co-operation in many fields is becoming increasingly essential'.[56] More explicitly, the Vienna Convention, article 26 requires states to perform in good faith treaties to which they are parties and in article 31 to interpret those treaties in good faith. We, however, question the 'good faith' of powerful states, here the nuclear weapon states that have deployed international law to serve their own interests as exhibited by their failure for over five decades to negotiate in good faith disarmament in accordance with article VI of the NPT,[57] or even to argue their position before the ICJ.[58] Nevertheless we embed ourselves in international law's dominant ontological and epistemological traditions as a means by which to secure progressive reform and, at times, simply to hold the line, even if temporarily.

Despite our care in following the precepts of our discipline, our opinion was dismissed by the Government. In response to a parliamentary question on whether, as 'academics at the London School of Economics have concluded' an increase

---

[50] On the distinction between codifying existing law and progressive development see ILC, Fifth report on peremptory norms of general international law (jus cogens) by Dire Tladi, Special Rapporteur, A/CN.4/747, 2022, para 26.

[51] Vienna Convention on the Law of Treaties, 1969, Section Three, Interpretation of Treaties.

[52] *Legality of Nuclear Weapons*, AO, 8 July 1996, 1996 ICJ Reports 226.

[53] The ICJ described the principle of distinction and the prohibition of unnecessary suffering as 'cardinal' and 'intransgressible' principles of customary IHL, terminology that is not part of the usual vocabulary of customary international law: ibid para 79.

[54] Statute of the ICJ, 1945, art 38(1); UN Charter, 1945, arts 92–96.

[55] Robert Kolb, *La bonne foi en droit international public: contribution à l'étude des principes généraux du droit* (Geneva Graduate Institute, 2001) 112–13.

[56] *Nuclear Weapons (Australia v France; New Zealand v France)* 1974 ICJ Reports, 253, para 46; 457, para 49.

[57] NPT, art VI: 'Each of the parties to the Treaty undertakes to pursue negotiations in good faith on effective measures relating to cessation of the nuclear arms race at an early date and to nuclear disarmament and on a treaty on general and complete disarmament under strict and effective control.'

[58] *Obligations concerning Negotiations relating to Cessation of the Nuclear Arms Race and to Nuclear Disarmament (Marshall Islands v United Kingdom)* 2016 ICJ Rep 833. The UK raised preliminary objections on jurisdiction and admissibility; the Court determined there to be no active dispute between the parties and deemed the case inadmissible.

in nuclear warheads constitutes a breach of the NPT, the Secretary of State for Defence replied, 'No, I think I would just say that I have it on better authority than those academics that we have not.'[59] It is unlikely that we will ever discover what (or who) comprises that 'better' authority, since the convention of attorney-client privilege effectively precludes any deliberative politics.[60] For the state to invoke this convention is to camouflage the violence of patriarchal sovereign authority. It is a mythical placeholder for a strategy to silence[61] and to skirt critical scrutiny and public accountability.

But did we expect a dialogue? After all, the history of nuclear weapons is a history clouded in patriarchal conventions.[62] Information pertaining to nuclear weapons is buried deep within the state's archives, hidden in perpetuity and an exception to the 20-year disclosure rule.[63] Nor has the ICJ been prepared to face head on the legality of nuclear weapons[64] or even to address the collective militarism of the nuclear weapons states.[65]

This is why feminist international lawyers refuse to remain silent in spite of our modest and (often) temporary successes. For many of us, it is the anger that comes with injustice that keeps us on track. The release of the UK's *Integrated Review* had angered us but we have embraced anger as necessary to our work, recognising it to be a 'powerful source of energy serving progress and change'.[66] Our anger extended to the timing of its release amid the pandemic, when health services were struggling for lack of human and material resources. The strategy outlined in the *Review* was the antithesis of the ambitions that had brought us together as feminist academics to rethink international law through the prisms of gender and peace, prompted by deeply held anxieties over the trajectory of contemporary global politics. Our misgivings over international law aside, the *Review* was a direct assault on international law, or more accurately, the *latest* of onslaughts by a government that viewed international law as an obstacle to its political agenda.

---

[59] HC Deb, *Hansard*, vol 701, 20 September 2021.

[60] Denisa Kostovicova and Tom Pashalis, 'Gender, Justice and Deliberation: Why Women Don't Influence Peacemaking' (2021) 65 *International Studies Quarterly* 263.

[61] See essay 9 'Silence as an Obstacle to Gendered Peace and Equality'.

[62] Note by the PM on Nuclear Testing, 31 July 1974: 'There is a long-standing convention that sensitive questions in the field of foreign affairs, defence matters and on security/intelligence are not necessarily brought before the Cabinet for decisions. A small group of Ministers sometimes have to assume responsibility, although clearly policies … could not be persued if it turned out that the Cabinet as a whole did not support them. The 1965 [nuclear weapon] test was not discussed in Cabinet. The decision to hold the recent test was not a policy decision. A decision not to hold it would however have been a policy decision because it would have prejudiced the effective fulfilment, in terms of time and money, of one of the options which we may wish to take.' CAB 3031/650, PRO, Kew, UK.

[63] In 2013 the UK public records disclosure rule was reduced from 30 to 20 years. Disclosed files on nuclear weapons are full of redactions and tabs documenting material that has been made doubly secret.

[64] The ICJ has been ambivalent about the legality of nuclear weapons, asserting that it 'cannot conclude definitively whether the threat or use of nuclear weapons would be lawful or unlawful in an extreme circumstance of self-defence, in which the very survival of a State would be at stake': *Legality of Nuclear Weapons* (n 52) para 105(2)(E). It has failed to rule on nuclear testing (*Australia v France; New Zealand v France* (n 56)) or on nuclear weapons states' obligations under the NPT (*Marshall Islands v UK* (n 58)).

[65] Nico Krisch, 'Capitulation in The Hague: The Marshall Islands Cases' *EJIL: Talk!*, 10 October 2016.

[66] Audre Lorde, 'The Uses of Anger: Women Responding to Racism' (keynote presentation at the National Women's Studies Association Conference, Storrs Connecticut, June 1981).

The invitation from CND posed a further quandary. Were we (and CND) even asking the right question? To assess whether the government's announcement of an increase in nuclear warheads constitutes a breach of the NPT is to accept a framing that pre-determines what is relevant to the discussion at hand.[67]

We wondered whether the more pertinent question was *why are we still discussing nuclear weapons over five decades after the adoption of the NPT*?[68] Feminists encounter this same problem time and again, exemplified by Virginia Woolf's account of an exchange she had just prior to the outbreak of World War II, when she was asked *how can war be prevented*?[69] And just as Woolf recognised that her answer – *Why fight?* – was of no value to those engaged in the political mainstream, we too concede that our question is not a response that fits within legal orthodoxy.

---

[67] 'Framings' are 'always an exercise of epistemic closure or limitation in the sense that frames tend to draw attention to selected aspects of a perceived "something" at the expense of a host of other candidates for attention producing in the process a set of muted or even invisible "others" – a whole range of unfocused-upon factors, features or subjectivities': Anna Grear, '"Framing the Project" of International Human Rights Law: Reflections on the Dysfunctional "Family" of the Universal Declaration' in Conor Gearty and Costas Douzinas (eds), *Human Rights Law* (Cambridge University Press, 2012) 17. See essay 11 'Crisis and Emergency: Entrenching Gender Systems and Militarism'.

[68] *cf* 'In sum, nuclear weapons are an unprecedented event which calls for rethinking the self-understanding of traditional international law. Such rethinking would reveal that the question is not whether one interpretation of existing laws of war prohibits the threat or use of nuclear weapons and another permits it. Rather, the issue is whether the debate can take place at all in the world of law. The question is in fact one which cannot be legitimately addressed by law at all since it cannot tolerate an interpretation which negates its very essence. The end of law is a rational order of things, with survival as its core, whereas nuclear weapons eliminate all hopes of realising it. In this sense, nuclear weapons are unlawful by definition': *Legality of Nuclear Weapons* (n 52) Judge Weeramantry, dissenting opinion, 522.

[69] Virginia Woolf, *Three Guineas* (1938).

15
Strategic Practices: 'Doing Our Own Thing'

I. INTRODUCTION

THE PREVIOUS ESSAYS discuss feminist strategies for reform of international law and its implementation, seeking a changed mindset that takes account of gender as integral to all legal decision-making. But inclusion has not been the only strategy pursued. Women have also resorted to their own methods when formal mechanisms fail to provide any space for their voices to be heard or when legal formalism sets gendered parameters. In this essay we discuss instances of women 'doing their own thing', including establishing parallel 'Track Two' peace processes, women's tribunals and rethinking the strictures of legal opinion writing.

II. PEACE PROCESSES

The first operative paragraph of UN Security Council (SC) Resolution 1325 on women and peace and security (WPS) urges 'increased representation of women at all decision-making levels in national, regional and international institutions and mechanisms for the prevention, management, and resolution of conflict'. The demand for women's participation in formal peace processes was constantly repeated throughout the twentieth century,[1] is a regular component of the WPS resolutions and a common theme for women addressing the SC today.[2] States parties to CEDAW have an obligation to ensure women's participation[3] but resistance to their

---

[1] See essay 5 'Peace in the UN Decade for Women' and essay 6 'Revisiting the Past: Peace at Beijing and Beyond'.
[2] 'Nearly all of the more than 200 women from civil society who have briefed the Security Council … demand direct and formal participation in all stages of peace processes': Report of the Secretary-General, Women and peace and security, S/2022/740, 5 October 2022, para 20.
[3] CEDAW Committee, General Recommendation No 30 on women in conflict prevention, conflict and post-conflict situations, CEDAW/C/GC/30, 18 October 2013, para 46(c) elaborating on CEDAW, arts 7 and 8.

presence in peace negotiations[4] remains high.[5] Excluded from formal peace processes women have been active in instigating and participating in track two, informal processes[6] that co-exist alongside formal peace processes. A good example (although not termed as such) was the 1915 International Women's Congress at The Hague. Attendees worked out their proposals and delegated members to deliver them to political leaders before the 1919 Peace Conference.[7] A more recent example is Yemen's Peace Track Initiative, a collective of women peace activists who developed an alternative roadmap to peace founded on feminist principles and a commitment to gender justice.[8]

Track two processes typically commence early in the conflict. A primary objective is to forge a peace, putting pressure on fighting parties to negotiate while in the meantime engaging in informal processes through many different means: dialogue, workshops, consultations with community leaders, religious leaders, differently situated women – internally displaced persons, combatants, prisoners of war, academics, health and education workers, diaspora, LGBTQI persons, rural and urban – conferences and rallies to bring diverse perspectives, generate options, prepare roadmaps for peace and strategies for their advancement. Women's involvement in track two processes does not assume an essentialist construction of women as inherently peaceful or as good at peace.[9] Their reasons for engaging in peace initiatives vary along with their experiences of conflict but are likely to be 'based on a pragmatic response to desperate situations rather than on an inherently pacifist orientation'.[10] There is no single model for track two processes, which are fluid, responsive to the situation and may fluctuate throughout the conflict. Women from the conflict zone may work in conjunction with international institutions (for example UN Women, representatives of the Secretary-General) or NGOs[11] that can offer resources, meeting places, research, contacts, but the emphasis is on local knowledge and local priorities. Track two processes may also generate local agreements, for instance for delivery of food and other essentials or for local ceasefires. There may be no clear dividing line between such activities and the many tasks undertaken by women

---

[4] Women may directly participate as delegates in party negotiation teams or in facilitating roles such as mediators. Women Mediators Networks have been formed in attempts to increase the incidence of active mediation by women.

[5] In 2021, women participated as party negotiators or delegates in all UN-led or co-led peace processes but women's representation was at 19%, down from 23% in 2020. Women were also absent from processes not led by the UN: eg in April 2022, no women were among the nearly 30 delegates from armed groups from the DRC at the Nairobi consultations; and the 2022 Chad peace talks had one woman among over 50 participants: Report of the Secretary-General (n 2) para 23.

[6] Agathe Christien, 'Advancing Women's Participation in Track Two Peace Processes' (Georgetown Institute WPS, Policy Brief, 2020).

[7] See essay 7 'Women, Disarmament and Peace'.

[8] Peace Track Initiative, 'Feminist Peace Roadmap in Yemen: A Guiding Framework for Mediators and Negotiators' March 2023.

[9] Hilary Charlesworth, 'Are Women Peaceful? Reflections on the Role of Women in Peace-Building' (2008) 16 *Feminist Legal Studies* 347.

[10] Judy El-Bushra, 'Feminism, Gender, and Women's Peace Activism' (2007) 38 *Development and Change* 131.

[11] eg WILPF brings together women from different conflict zones in 'solidarity dialogue' so they can learn from each other about potential pitfalls, prioritise, and assemble materials, data and arguments in preparing alternative scenarios for peace.

throughout conflict. Women support welfare needs (food, shelter rudimentary health care), negotiate local ceasefires or zones of safety, educate children, take on leadership roles, and in numerous other ways strive to hold the community together. Women's peace organisations have formed around such activities. They may operate at the grass roots community level, or at a national, regional or international level, and in turn provide training and support to other local groups.[12] The range of activities can break down political or other social divides,[13] thereby preparing the groundwork for peace at a local level.

Track two processes have transformative potential, but much depends on their inclusivity (not just involving elite or diaspora participants, for instance). Additional strategising may be needed to find ways to feed their insights and recommendations into formal negotiations between the warring parties; a receptive individual or institutional mediator,[14] or liaisons with those at the negotiation table, are likely to be instrumental in achieving this. Research suggests that the success of track two processes may lie in legitimating formal peace processes rather than in influencing outcomes. Peace agreements reflect compromises between warring parties, but it may be women who have effectively prepared the way for negotiation, an 'inequitable division [that] marginalizes the often-transformative vision of the peace that women in informal peace processes can advocate'.[15] Where women can input into peace settlements, evidence suggests that they seek inclusion of provisions for gender equality, security (including from domestic violence and other forms of violence), and socio-economic and humanitarian needs that are often overlooked by male fighters and leaders.[16]

III. WOMEN'S COURTS AND TRIBUNALS

Peoples' Tribunals[17] have been part of the civil society landscape since the Russell Tribunal was established during the Vietnam War to hear testimony and deliver an independent critical analysis of the war's legality.[18] Feminist strategies of protest and critique have generated a proliferation of women's courts and tribunals that 'aim to provide a different sort of justice and the acknowledgment, support and

---

[12] Judy El-Bushra (n 10).
[13] Cynthia Cockburn, *The Space Between Us: Negotiating Gender and National Identities in Conflict* (Zed Books, 1998).
[14] Nelson Mandela, as facilitator in the Burundi peace process in 2000, engaged with the Track Two All-Party Burundi Women's Peace Conference and is credited with ensuring that many of their demands were included in the peace accord: 'Remembering Nelson Mandela's work to bring women to the table during peace talks in Burundi' (UN Women, 6 December 2013).
[15] Anjali Kaushlesh Dayal and Agathe Christien, 'Women's Participation in Informal Peace Processes' (2020) 26 *Global Governance* 69.
[16] Marie O'Reilly, 'Why Women? Inclusive Security and Peaceful Societies' (Inclusive Security, 2015).
[17] Andrew Byrnes and Gabrielle Simm (eds), *Peoples' Tribunals in International Law* (Hart Publishing, 2018).
[18] The Universal Declaration on the Rights of Peoples, Algiers, 1976 was a foundational document for the Permanent Peoples' Tribunals.

memorialisation of gendered harms that victims and survivors feel is lacking in official courts'.[19] Each has its own history, constitution and methodology but has given space and voice to dissenting views and to those who are silenced by mainstream law and politics.[20] Grounded in legal analysis and accountability,[21] they offer a transformative vision beyond the law to 'challenge the master narratives of our times'.[22]

Women have sought to realise gender justice[23] in the more than 30 sessions of the radically feminist World Courts of Women,[24] that originated in Asia and have been convened around the world to confront multiple forms of women's oppression. Women's Courts underline that women are not to be silenced and that their personal experience of violence, discrimination and oppression is a political issue. The intersection between political and personal is given aesthetic expression (women sing, weep, laugh and yell during the trials), representing both survival and resistance. Women's testimonies, the space they occupy and the affectivity they express, help to create different kinds of judicial system and juridical practices. Women's Courts aim at evolving new concepts of justice through an:

> unfolding of space, an imaginary: a horizon that invites us to think, to feel, to challenge, to connect, to dance, to dream. It is an attempt to define a new space for women, and to infuse this space with a new vision, a new politics.[25]

They have examined many issues: violence, violence against identified women (Dalit, indigenous women), the effect on women of HIV/AIDS, of uranium mining, of Covid, war and peace.

Women have also held one-off tribunals, focusing on the commission of war crimes and crimes against humanity in a specific conflict setting. The following section discusses as illustrative one such tribunal, the Women's International War Crimes Tribunal for the Trial of Japan's Military Sexual Slavery, a Peoples' Tribunal that was held over a week in Tokyo in December 2000.[26]

The court martial proceedings[27] that addressed the forced prostitution of Dutch women detained following the Japanese invasion and occupation of Batavia in the

---

[19] Gabrielle Simm, 'Peoples' Tribunals, Women's Courts and International Crimes of Sexual Violence' in Andrew Byrnes and Gabrielle Simm (n 17). Examples include hearings on sexual violence in Phnom Penh in 2012 and the Judicial Council for the Women's Court, Sarajevo, 2015.
[20] Dianne Otto, 'Beyond Legal Justice: Some Personal Reflections on Peoples' Tribunals, Listening and Responsibility' (2017) 5 *London Review of International Law* 225.
[21] By providing for some form of 'judgment', women's courts and tribunals differ from proceedings that hear only personal testimonies.
[22] Dianne Otto, 'Beyond Legal Justice' (n 20).
[23] See essay 14 'Strategic Practice: Giving Effect to Legal Change'.
[24] Corinne Kumar, *Singing in the Dark Times* (Bangalore, Karnataka: El Taller and Asian Women's Human Rights Council, 2001).
[25] https://vimochana.co.in/courts-of-women/#:~:text=The%20Courts%20of%20Women%20are, new%20vision%2C%20a%20new%20politics.
[26] Christine Chinkin (UK and Australia) was one of four judges, with Judge Gabrielle Kirk McDonald (US); Judge Carmen Argibay (Argentina) and Judge Willy Mutunga (Kenya).
[27] Fred L Borch, *Military Trials of War Criminals in the Netherlands East Indies 1946–1949* (Oxford University Press, 2017). See essay 9 'Silence as an Obstacle to Gendered Peace and Equality'.

Dutch East Indies (present day Indonesia) in 1942 had afforded a rare insight into what has otherwise been the 'long and torturous silence'[28] surrounding the so-called 'comfort women'. In the late 1980s and 1990s the now elderly women began to recount their experiences to NGO investigators[29] and UN mandate-holders,[30] through writings[31] and commencing lawsuits[32] for reparation. Their accounts were backed by historical research.[33] Now that they were ready to speak out, the women found that there was no forum through which they could receive justice.

The Tokyo Women's Tribunal – like the Women's Courts and other women's Tribunals[34] – was a response by women's civil society[35] to fill this lacuna. It was 'established to redress the historic tendency to trivialise, excuse, marginalise, and obfuscate crimes against women, ... even more so when they are committed against women of subordinated ethnicities'.[36] Its authority derived 'not from a state or intergovernmental organisation but from the peoples of the Asia-Pacific region, and indeed, the peoples of the world to whom Japan owes a duty under international law to render account'.[37] The Women's Tribunal did not purport to replace formal legal mechanisms but had as its key strategy to create a public forum for the development of the historical record based on the survivors' oral testimony and to apply principles of international law to those facts.[38]

Breaking silence is not just about speaking out, becoming empowered to speak, but is also about controlling the form and substance of what is said.[39] Accordingly, unlike in a formal court where testimony is constrained by the legal rules of evidence and procedure, the women told their stories in their own words, supported by legal

---

[28] Charter of the Women's International War Crimes Tribunal 2000 for the Trial of Japanese Military Sexual Slavery (Tokyo Women's Tribunal), preamble, https://archives.wam-peace.org/wt/wp-content/uploads/2020/02/Appendices.pdf.
[29] Ustinia Dolgopol and Snehal Paranjape, *Comfort Women: An Unfinished Ordeal* (International Commission of Jurists, 1994).
[30] SR VAW, its causes and consequences, Ms Radhika Coomaraswamy, Report on the mission to the Democratic People's Republic of Korea, the Republic of Korea and Japan on the issue of military sexual slavery in wartime, E/CN.4/1996/53/Add.1 4 January 1996; Commission on Human Rights, Final report submitted by Ms Gay J McDougall, SR, Contemporary Forms of Slavery, Systematic rape, sexual slavery and slavery-like practices during armed conflict, E/CN.4/Sub.2/1998/13, 22 June 1998.
[31] eg Jan Ruff-O'Herne, *50 Years of Silence* (Penguin Australia, 2008).
[32] Tokyo Women's Tribunal, Case No PT-2000-1-T, Judgment, note 12 and paras 990–93 for lawsuits completed or in progress in 2000 at https://archives.wam-peace.org/wt/wp-content/uploads/2020/03/Judgement.pdf.
[33] Professor Yoshiaki Yoshimi publicised his research on the 'comfort women' in 1992. His book *Comfort Women: Sexual Slavery during the Japanese Military in World War II* was published in Japanese in 1995 and in English in 2000.
[34] eg Women in Black was instrumental in designing the Sarajevo Women's Tribunal, working with nine other women's groups from across the former Yugoslavia.
[35] An International Organizing Committee comprised civil society organisations from Japan and from areas where women were victims of the 'comfort women' system (South and North Korea, China, Taiwan, the Philippines, Indonesia, Malaysia and others). It was supported by an International Advisory Committee of scholars and human rights activists: Tokyo Women's Tribunal, Charter (n 28).
[36] Tokyo Women's Tribunal, Judgment (n 32) para 5.
[37] ibid para 8.
[38] ibid.
[39] Martha Houston and Cheris Kramarae, 'Speaking from Silence: Methods of Silencing and of Resistance' (1991) 2 *Discourse and Society* 387.

counsel. Survivor testimony (in their own language[40]) was supported by documentary evidence, assembled through painstaking archival research by volunteers in all the territories from where the women were 'recruited' through abduction, coercion or misrepresentation. Additional oral testimony was provided by legal experts, historians and psychologists. The Japanese government was invited to present its case; in its absence an *amicus curiae* brought before the Tribunal its anticipated arguments. Controversially, the Tribunal heard evidence from two former Japanese soldiers who had used the 'comfort stations'. Closing statements were given by the two chief prosecutors and a preliminary judgment was delivered after a day's deliberation. A detailed judgment was then prepared and delivered in The Hague in December 2001.

As an informal Peoples' Tribunal, the Tokyo Tribunal was not constrained by the tenets of international law such as the legal divide between state responsibility for international wrongful acts and individual criminal liability; it was bestowed with jurisdiction over Japan for the commission of international wrongs and over named individuals for the commission of crimes against humanity.[41] The central strategy was the fiction that the Tribunal was a continuation of the International Military Tribunal for the Far East (IMTFE); the accused were those who had been tried by the IMTFE in 1945 and were now facing charges of sexual slavery 'as if' they had faced such charges at that time.[42] This obviated the necessity of determining the accused's presence and activities in the theatre of war; such details were determined from the IMTFE records. It also avoided the constraints of extraterritoriality and claims of immunity from jurisdiction.[43] The exception to this fiction of continuity was the Emperor Hirohito, who had faced no trial for Japan's wartime atrocities but was now accused before a Women's Tribunal.

As with many Peoples' Tribunals,[44] the strategy was to engage legal symbolism and ritual (the judges wore legal attire; witnesses testified under oath; cross examination followed). The judgment analysed the law binding upon Japan in the 1930s and 40s when the crimes were committed and took account of contemporary law to show how the then current developments in international criminal law were grounded in the past. The Tokyo Tribunal was above all a Women's Tribunal, dominated by women survivors, activists and organisers.[45] Hearing women's voices, not just as victims but as survivors empowered through telling what had happened to

---

[40] CEDAW Committee, General Recommendation No 33, on women's access to justice, CEDAW/C/GC/33, 23 July 2015, para 17(b) emphasises the importance of interpreters to assist survivors in giving evidence.

[41] Charter (n 28) art 2: 'The Tribunal shall have jurisdiction over crimes committed against women as war crimes, crimes against humanity and other crimes under international law …. The Tribunal shall also have jurisdiction over claims involving State responsibility under international law'.

[42] Karen Knop, 'The Tokyo Women's Tribunal and the Turn to Fction' in Fleur Johns et al (eds), *Events: The Force of International Law* (Routledge, 2010) ch 11.

[43] Charter (n 28) art 6 denied immunity for state actors, regardless of their position as head of state or otherwise.

[44] 'If one purpose of such a process is to empower those whose rights have been violated, then creating materials that improve their knowledge and understanding of the law and its limits should be an integral part of the holding of people's tribunals': Ustinia Dolgopol, 'The Tokyo Women's Tribunal Transboundary Activists and the Use of Law's Power' in Andrew Byrnes and Gabrielle Simm (n 17).

[45] This is not to imply there were no men involved. There were male lawyers and researchers. Willy Mutunga from Kenya was a Judge.

them, having it believed and understood as a crime against humanity, was strategically central to the process. Recognition by a Peoples' Tribunal (and the thousand or more attendees) does not substitute for formal acknowledgment and legal reparation from the state[46] but informal commemoration carries its own weight. In sum 'women non-governmental organisations did what governmental organisations failed to do'.[47] In the words of one participant, reflecting on the Tribunal 20 years later, 'we redefined interpretations of humanitarian law and international law and human rights law. We gendered the whole framework'.[48]

The past and current situation of the 'comfort women' provides substantive and methodological insights and illuminates the linkages between feminist strategies, peace and transformative justice. The Tribunal judgment recognised this nexus between peace and justice, that the post-World War II Peace Treaties were inherently gender biased in that women did not, either as individuals or as a group, participate in their negotiation, that military sexual slavery and rape formed no part of the negotiation, and that such gender blindness continues the culture of impunity for crimes perpetrated against women in armed conflict. This deprived the women 'of the possibility of living in peace with themselves and with their families and communities'.[49] Twenty years after the Tokyo Tribunal, and over 80 years since the commission of the offences, Japan still does not speak directly to the women, electing to address them only through diplomatic sources and public, limited attempts at apology without acknowledgment of the state's responsibility under international law.[50] Such steps make for an uneasy and unstable peace between the countries and deprives the women of justice and peace.

IV. SUBVERTING LEGAL FORMALISM

In the previous essay we discussed the limitations imposed by legal formalism in writing our joint opinion on the legality of the UK's policy to increase its nuclear warheads. But what would we have written had we given rein to our feminist inclinations and not felt constrained by international law's traditions?

The 'freedom' to discard the constraints of legal formalism was an idea we had explored as academics involved in The Feminist International Judgments project.[51] The project allowed us to show how international law can be re-visioned and what some of the key judgments of international and regional tribunals might have looked

---

[46] See essay 18 'Transformative Reparations and Gendered Peace'.
[47] Judge Gabrielle Kirk McDonald, Documentary, 'The International Women's Tribunal: Gender Just Peace' at https://www.lse.ac.uk/women-peace-security/research/Gendered-Peace.
[48] Indai Sajor, ibid.
[49] Tokyo Women's Tribunal, Judgment (n 32) para 1068.
[50] The Government of the Republic of Korea and the Government of Japan announced a 'state to state' Agreement at a Joint Press Occasion on 28 December 2015. Japan acknowledged its responsibility, without specifying legal responsibility and, with 'sincere apologies and remorse', agreed to contribute to a previously established Foundation to assist the former 'comfort women'. Not all surviving 'comfort women' have been willing to receive money from the Foundation.
[51] Loveday Hodson and Troy Lavers (eds), *Feminist Judgments in International Law* (Hart Publishing, 2019).

like if feminist judges willing to disrupt the foundations of the discipline had sat on the Bench. The rewritten judgment in the *SS Lotus* case[52] (which we renamed the *Bozkurt* case) rejects the iconic starting point of international law, state sovereignty whereby states have freedom to act as they please unless they have consented to an explicit prohibition. The new principle of the *Bozkurt* case drew upon traditional sources – the League of Nations Covenant – and non-traditional sources – the Resolutions adopted by the 1915 International Women's Congress in The Hague.[53] It reconfigures state sovereignty as resting on interdependence and cooperation: 'Turkey's exercise of jurisdiction in support of her own nationals should not be feared by France but embraced … as an assurance of sovereign equality and that justice can be achieved through cooperation.' This reimagining shows how feminist strategies can be turned to an international order that prioritises peace: a transformative reconfiguration of sovereignty which, 'if it had been adopted by the PCIJ in 1927 may well have laid the foundation for a more cooperative, less divided, more equitable, less state-centric, more peaceful and less militaristic international community'.[54]

The Feminist Judgments project allowed us simultaneously to situate ourselves outside the law (and to write unencumbered by patriarchal and disciplinary traditions) but remain within it, occupying an uneasy space but with emancipatory potential. The project was inspired by long-standing feminist discussions around who has authority to speak, who is heard and whose knowledge counts, not least within our discipline, which is founded on a legacy of epistemic violence, gendered and racialised.[55] These questions are not purely academic but are core to the practice of law that materialises in the shape of separate and dissenting opinions of judges, including those who have sat on the International Court of Justice (ICJ). The struggle to do justice within the confines of law and to articulate a different politics in law's language can involve finding alternative accounts of law in history and philosophy,[56] in change over time,[57] and in giving preference to the 'overriding importance of the fundamental principles of humanity, and of equality and non-discrimination' to overcome the 'inter-State paradigm in contemporary international law'.[58]

To return to the question: what might we have written? Perhaps we would have contextualised the *Integrated Review* within the UK's gendered, militarised, white supremacist colonial history that made it a given that it would acquire nuclear weapons in the early 1950s. We might have argued that the UK's intended increase of nuclear warheads continued a pattern of disregard for its international treaty obligations, including article 2(4) of the UN Charter, exemplified by its nuclear testing

---

[52] *SS Lotus (France v Turkey)* 1927 PCIJ, Series A, No 10.
[53] See essay 4 'Introduction: Rewriting International Law's Histories'.
[54] Dianne Otto, 'Feminist Judging in Action: Reflecting on the Feminist Judgments in International Law Project' (2020) 28 *Feminist Legal Studies* 205.
[55] See essay 11 'Crisis and Emergency: Entrenching Gender Systems and Militarism'.
[56] *Legality of Nuclear Weapons*, Advisory Opinion, 8 July 1996, 1996 ICJ Reports 226, 443 Judge Weeramantry, dissenting opinion.
[57] *Reservations to the Convention on the Prevention and Punishment of the Crime of Genocide* AO, 28 May 1951, 1951 ICJ Rep 15, 50 Judge Alvarez, dissenting opinion.
[58] *Accordance with international law of the unilateral declaration of independence in respect of Kosovo*, AO, 22 July 2010, 2010 ICJ Rep. 403, 525, Judge Cançado Trindade, separate opinion.

programme which constituted an unlawful use of force on the territories and on the bodies of those who occupied distant lands in wanton disregard for the health, wellbeing and environmental consequences.[59]

Perhaps we would have critiqued the entire *Review* for perpetuating militarised responses to 'threats', normalising those responses and making the acquisition and possession of nuclear weapons and their use thinkable. Consequently, the UK's intention to increase its number of nuclear warheads not only constituted a breach of the Treaty on the Non-Proliferation of Nuclear Weapons, but the logic underpinning its reasoning evidenced its continued commitment to gendered and other socially constructed systems of discrimination and power (eg racism, classism, heteronormativity and ableism) and failure to dismantle them in accordance with its UN Charter and human rights obligations, including CEDAW.

Perhaps we would have situated the *Review* within the UK's other commitments under the Charter, such as to: 'save succeeding generations from the scourge of war' (preamble); 'establish conditions under which justice and respect for the obligations arising from treaties and other sources of international law can be maintained' (preamble); 'live together in peace with one another as good neighbours' (preamble and Declaration on Friendly Relations); and 'take other appropriate measures to strengthen universal peace' (article 1). We might have pointed out that its unilateral insistence on advancing its nuclear arsenal – the very antithesis of peace – constituted a failure to discharge its responsibility as a permanent member of the SC for maintaining peace and security (article 24) and to formulate plans 'for the establishment of a system for the regulation of armaments' (article 26). Indeed, we might have questioned whether such failure should deprive it of its permanent status on the SC, alongside of course the other four permanent members.

Perhaps we would have posited that evidence is mounting of a rule of customary international law prohibiting nuclear weapons, including the coming into force of the 2017 Treaty on the Prohibition of Nuclear Weapons less than four years after its adoption and the succession of UNGA resolutions that may not of themselves be legally binding but 'when repeated in a stream of resolutions, as often and as definitely as they have been, [they] provide important reinforcement to the view of the impermissibility of the threat or use of such weapons under customary international law'.[60] We could have argued that the 'persistent objector'[61] rule was inapplicable to the prohibition on nuclear weapons, an erga omnes obligation and in any case 'from the standpoint of the creation of international custom, the practice and policies of

---

[59] In the words of Tony Debrum, co-agent for the Marshall Islands: 'During the "testing" [no fewer than 67 atomic and thermonuclear weapons were deliberately exploded as "tests" in the Marshall Islands] …, several islands in my country were vaporized. Many, many Marshallese died and … many suffered birth defects never before seen and cancers': *Obligations concerning Negotiations relating to Cessation of the Nuclear Arms Race and to Nuclear Disarmament (Marshall Islands v United Kingdom)* Verbatim Record, 11 March 2016, 11.

[60] Judge Weeramantry (n 56) 532.

[61] James Crawford, *Brownlie's Principles of Public International Law*, 9th edn (Oxford University Press, 2019) 26: 'with the increasing emergence of communitarian norms, reflecting the interests of the international community as a whole, the *incidence* of the persistent objector rule may be limited'.

Subverting Legal Formalism 213

five [nuclear weapon states] States out of 185 seem to be an insufficient basis on which to assert the creation of custom, whatever be the global influence of those five'.[62]

Perhaps we would have maintained that the UK has the obligation to provide victim assistance and environmental remediation for its nuclear weapons testing programme and under customary international law to provide full and adequate reparation for all resulting harm and in particular the gendered effects of its testing programme. And we could have argued for imagining an updated Martens clause better suited to the twenty-first century and the cause of peace.[63]

But we did none of this; we were effectively silenced by the need to stay within international law's structures and traditions.

---

[62] Judge Weeramantry (n 56) 533. There are now 193 member states of the UN and 9 states with nuclear weapons.

[63] Convention (II) with respect to the Laws and Customs of War on Land, The Hague, 29 July 1899, preamble: 'Until a more complete code of the laws of war is issued, the High Contracting Parties think it right to declare that in cases not included in the Regulations adopted by them, populations and belligerents remain under the protection and empire of the principles of international law, as they result from the usages established between civilized nations, from the laws of humanity, and the requirements of the public conscience': Christine Chinkin and Patricia Viseur Sellers, 'A Century and More of Feminist Architects' in Nienke Grossman et al (eds) *Oxford Handbook on Women and International Law* (Oxford University Press, forthcoming) for such an imagining.

16

Enriching Strategic Practice: Some Reflections

THE ESSAYS IN this part outline feminist strategies for achieving greater normative inclusivity within international law in the pursuit of gender equality and peace. But have these strategies been successful? And what does success mean?[1]

From one perspective the successes have been considerable. We can point to specialised treaties on combating violence against women, progressive language in general treaties and some gender-aware jurisprudence. These are supplemented by a growing body of soft law, a plethora of declarations, resolutions, guidelines, gender policies and reports where we can rightfully claim impact. On the other hand, these examples are scattered and ad hoc, belying any notion that feminist principles imbue the structural foundations of international law. Our misgiving about the law for achieving transformative change notwithstanding, we have proactively engaged with others in pursuing these strategies: advising on inclusive treaty language, drafting briefs, writing opinions and working with the UN human rights bodies and with feminist activists. All of these interventions have required us to speak through and with international law's gendered lexicon and reasoning to secure material change. At times we eschew pragmatism and forge our own paths.

Yet with pragmatism there is always an element of loss and the risk of superficiality and betrayal. At every turn pragmatism calls for a reckoning that is deeply personal: what, we repeatedly ask ourselves, is the scope of our ethical responsibility? And to whom do we owe that responsibility?[2] The questions haunt us even as we continue to turn to the task at hand as we remain convinced that without legally affirmed standards there is no starting point: if crimes are not named, if there is no prohibition of gender-based violence, if reparations are not demanded then space for progress is closed down. And once they have been named and prohibited, fresh strategies are needed to pressure governments and others to give effect to those standards and to hold violators to account. There remains a

---

[1] Hilary Charlesworth observes that 'while the rest of the discipline ignores us [feminist scholars] feminists have created a veritable industry of internal critique': Hilary Charlesworth, 'Talking to Ourselves? Feminist Scholarship in International Law' in Sari Kouvo and Zoe Pearson, *Feminist Perspectives on Contemporary International Law Between Resistance and Compliance?* (Hart Publishing, 2014) ch 2.

[2] Resistance only from outside/within. The danger is that we will lose our ability to think critically: 'a paradoxical and unstable mixed position: critical and disenchanted engagement': Janet Halley, *Governance Feminism* (University of Minnesota Press, 2018) xvi.

utility to the 'rule of law' that accepts that some order is better than the exercise of power based on the will of individuals. Even while acknowledging that the structure of the law serves the interests of a particular system, the law's ability to constrain the worst abuses of autocratic power is better than having no available constraints.[3]

But too much weight cannot be put on law; legal reform must be only one among many strategies.

In the nineteenth and early twentieth centuries feminist activists campaigned for peace, combining it with demands for equal political rights, workplace rights and economic and social justice. International law and institutions were targeted as spaces where domestic resistance to women's advancement could be challenged and the dual agendas for peace and for human rights pursued. Today, agendas have shifted and peace has been lost as a stand-alone objective, except in disarmament, a somewhat specialised (marginalised) area of international law.

Can the strategy for enhancing women's visibility in international law be aligned with a strategy for peace? Or does the intensive campaigning for the former mean a decline in the latter through law? Are strategies for peace best pursued through protest, silent vigils and peace camps? Law does not deliver peace but regulates human activity and, in the case of international law, state activity. The cases brought by and against the Greenham women demonstrate how authorities resort to law to prevent what is seen as disruptive behaviour,[4] how protestors can use the law[5] and legal argument can be turned against the law-makers.[6] It is deeply ironical that those seeking peace face being arrested for violating that peace. International law may be looked to as a higher law, justifying breach of local law.[7] But international law is flawed. It may successfully offer an alternative to violence where recourse is had to peaceful dispute resolution methods but it does not challenge the bases of power that sustain inequalities and enable violence and war. The ICJ can determine that the US used violence illegally against Nicaragua, or that Serbia failed to prevent genocide in Srebrenica, but it must uphold state sovereignty and consent. It cannot change the foundations

---

[3] Ustinia Dolgopol, 'The Tokyo Women's Tribunal Transboundary Activists and the Use of Law's Power' in Andrew Byrnes and Gabrielle Simm (eds), *Peoples' Tribunals in International Law* (Hart Publishing, 2018).

[4] The Ministry of Defence introduced bye-laws restricting movement on Greenham Common, thereby criminalising the Greenham women's movements.

[5] 'The women pursued claims in the civil courts, still using these occasions to generate media interest ... actions against the police in the County Court for damages for injury suffered during evictions. ... appeals in the County Court against injunctions or eviction orders relating to their presence on Greenham Common. ... they pursued their demand for the right to vote since, for those who lived there, the camp was their main residence': Elizabeth Woodcraft, 'Greenham Common Women's Peace Camp 1981–2000' in Erika Rackley and Rosemary Auchmuty (eds), *Women's Legal Landmarks: Celebrating the History of Women and Law in the UK and Ireland* (Hart Publishing, 2019) 363, 366.

[6] The House of Lords upheld the protestors' challenge to the bye-laws: *Director of Public Prosecutions v Hutchinson; Director of Public Prosecutions v Smith* [1990] 2 AC 783. Lord Taylor, Lord Chief Justice, delivering the 1992 Richard Dimbleby lecture said 'it would be difficult to suggest a group whose cause and lifestyle were less likely to excite the sympathies and approval of five elderly judges. But it was five Law Lords who ... held that the Minister has exceeded his powers in framing the byelaws so as to prevent access to common land': at http://www.greenhamwpc.org.uk/.

[7] The Greenham women argued their actions to be justified by the Convention on the Prevention and Punishment of the Crime of Genocide, 9 December 1948. The case failed, but this and prosecutions involving the Greenham women caused media attention and raised awareness.

of international law in colonialism and racism. The ICC can find Dominic Ongwen guilty of forced marriage, torture, rape, sexual slavery, enslavement, forced pregnancy and outrages upon personal dignity,[8] but it cannot redress the oppression, gender stereotypes and inequalities that are the structural backdrop to their commission.

International law's foundations in colonialism, slavery, racism and patriarchy make it an improbable tool with which to address these inbuilt forms of oppression. As argued by Hilary Charlesworth, international law is a discipline of crisis that sustains a band aid approach that looks for short-term measures that provide the appearance of action but leave untouched its underlying biases.[9] Seeking 'headline responses' to extreme conflict-related violence deflects attention from the 'slow violence' of the everyday and contributes to the neglect of gender dynamics in international relations. Vesuki Nesiah has demonstrated how apparently progressive institutional reform can legitimise and empower the world order that enabled the crisis to erupt in the first place. Close examination 'may reveal that these histories frame and reframe the crisis-space of these moments in ways that deny and distract from the legacies of racial and gendered capitalism'.[10]

Does this mean that women's attempts to make international law more gender inclusive have no relevance to the goal of a gendered peace? We do not believe this to be the case and believe two issues should be separated. First is to ask whether the law addresses women or their interests and then to extend the question to ask whether the law recognises the fluidity of gender and other axes of oppression. We need continued strategies to this end, as feminists have devised for well over a century. Second is that experience shows us that unless civil society activists and lawyers ask these questions, they are unlikely even to enter an international agenda. The recent situation with the International Law Commission's definition of gender in the Draft articles on Prevention of Crimes against Humanity illustrates the imperative of inclusive participation to make audible the voices of those who are otherwise not heard, and as a form of resistance. Simply calling for increased participation by women, as in the Women, Peace and Security (WPS) resolutions, is inadequate; those participating must be committed to change and to have the tools to make it happen. We believe that peace discourse – a culture of peace – is impossible without taking account of gender[11] and in turn gender discourse must be directed toward ending violence and promoting peace. Unless women, and others committed to ending militarism, power politics and violence, come forward and ask where peace is to be found in the WPS agenda, and more broadly in international law, the silence will continue. Seeking progress through demanding participation in the instrumentalities of international

---

[8] *Prosecutor v Dominic Ongwen*, ICC-02/04-01/15, convicted 4 February 2021; conviction upheld by the Appeals Chamber, 15 December 2022.

[9] See essay 11 'Crisis and Emergency: Entrenching Gender Systems and Militarism'.

[10] Vasuki Nesiah uses the Nuremberg Tribunal and the Mixed Commissions that were established to adjudicate allegations of continued slave trading after its abolition to develop her argument: Vasuki Nesiah, '"A Mad and Melancholy Record": The Crisis of International Law Histories' (2021) 11 *Notre Dame Journal of International and Comparative Law* 232.

[11] Equality between women and men through an integrated gender perspective is one of eight action areas in UNGAR 53/243, 1999, UN Declaration and Programme of Action on a Culture of Peace, but the wording replicates the binary women/men.

law is playing within the existing order. This is limited but 'sometimes we need to play feminism "straight"'.¹² But we must also explore 'ways of overturning convention and tradition, of disrupting expectations and confounding categories' through protests, through disruptive peace camps, through occupying public spaces: we should seize opportunities to play it 'queer'; moments 'when we should veer off the path of respectability, integration and adaptation; ... should side-step the homorelational world and instead carve new spaces for ourselves'¹³ for a different international order and a gendered peace.

Figure 4
Source: LSE Library archives.

The first strategy has been to make women visible and, subsequently, to give effect to gender diversity and gender equality in international legal doctrine. The second was to break the silence about sexual violence as a war crime, crime against humanity and as integral to genocide and to end impunity. Neither is directly relevant to securing peace.¹⁴ Attention in the early 1990s was directed primarily toward process, ensuring that the newly established international criminal tribunals had jurisdiction over crimes of sexual violence and seeking gender balance in their composition. The Beijing Platform for Action in 1995 called for women's increased participation in decision-making about conflict, accountability for conflict-related sexual violence, disarmament and weapons control.¹⁵ At the outset of the twenty-first century, civil society turned its attention to the UN Security Council (SC), and Resolution 1325 was lobbied for as a women's human rights and peace agenda. The resolution incorporates both strategic demands: it calls for women's increased participation and

---

¹² Sasha Roseneil, *Common Women, Uncommon Practices* (Cassell, 2000).
¹³ ibid.
¹⁴ The preamble to the Rome Statute of the ICC recognises that 'such grave crimes threaten the peace, security and well-being of the world'.
¹⁵ See essay 6 'Revisiting the Past: Peace at Beijing and Beyond'.

representation, implementation of the specialist regimes of international law protecting women in armed conflict and accountability for conflict-related sexual violence against women. But disarmament and weapons control are absent from the WPS agenda. They are advocated for, as well as for language that reflects the gendered harms of weapons, in a separate strand of activism outside and beyond the SC.[16] In this sense the rubric 'women, peace and security' is misleading: peace is not overtly addressed throughout the WPS resolutions and there is little reference to conflict prevention. The SC's ambition appears limited to making war safer for women, a position that was rejected by Bertha Suttner in the nineteenth century and by the Women's Congress at The Hague in the twentieth. Integration of WPS with the agendas for countering terrorism and violent extremism[17] plays into the militarised and territorially expansive agenda of the US, minimises personal agency by assuming all wartime sexual conduct is rape, and continues assumption of victimhood for women – all contrary to peace.[18] In another sense, the WPS rubric is only too accurate: the agenda has no place for those who do not conform to the gender binary around which it is constructed. 'Gender' throughout is synonymous with women.

---

[16] There is some such language in the Convention on Cluster Munitions, 2008, preamble; the Arms Trade Treaty, 2013, preamble and art 7; Treaty on the Prohibition of Nuclear Weapons, 2017, preamble.
[17] UNSCR 2242, 2015.
[18] Karen Engle et al, 'Feminist Approaches to International Law' in Jeffrey Dunoff and Mark Pollack (eds), *International Legal Theory: Foundations and Frontiers* (Cambridge University Press, 2022) ch 8.

Part V

Transforming International Law

17

Introduction to Part V

IN THIS FINAL section we consider possibilities for a transformed international law – a law that no longer reproduces the structures of oppression and exploitation upon which it was founded and no longer serves to justify violence, hegemonic, inter-state, inter-communal, inter-personal. In its current orientation international law is too often the means through which structural injustices and violence are legitimised and perpetuated.[1] Can it be reimagined to *prevent* structural injustices and violence? To date, feminist strategies have had some positive results, although often we feel that they manifest only at the edges of international law and struggle to dismantle the structures of violence and inequalities. This begs the question: is international law trapped by its genealogy so that its past already determines its present and future? We would like to think not.

International lawyers on the margins have long been attentive to law's shortcomings. There is no shortage of critical analyses exposing the imperial violence upon which law is constituted; its heteropatriarchal and racist underpinnings; its silences that perpetuate subjugation and injustices; its ordering that preserves militarised hierarchies;[2] and its anthropocentrism that facilitates capitalist extractivism.[3] But rather than step away, most have sought to reclaim the project from its patriarchal homogenising imperialist anchor in the belief that international law holds the potential not only to 'limit and resist power'[4] but to redefine relationships, values, and facilitate structural transformation.[5] The paradox of working with law's tools within law's framing is not lost on us.[6] That said, there is now an expectation that

---

[1] Mohsen al Attar 'At World's End: Palestine, the ICJ, and a New Dawn in International Law' *Opinio Juris blog*, 9 January 2024.
[2] The status of the permanent five members of the Security Council creates a hierarchy established in the UN Charter that is replicated in the Treaty on the Non-Proliferation of Nuclear Weapons.
[3] For a glimpse into the annihilation and destruction of nature in North America and on Indigenous struggles to fight back see Winona LaDuke, *All Our Relations: Native Struggles for Land and Life* (Haymarket Books, 2015).
[4] Antony Anghie, *Imperialism, Sovereignty and the Making of International Law* (Cambridge University Press, 2005) 318. In contradistinction, states tend to invoke international law to justify violence.
[5] But see Makau Mutua, 'What is TWAIL?' (2000) 94 *Proceedings of the American Society of International Law Annual Meeting*: 'the regime of international law is illegitimate … it is a predatory system that legitimizes, reproduces and sustains the plunder and subordination of the Third World by the West'.
[6] Mohsen al Attar, 'TWAIL: a Paradox within a Paradox' (2020) 22 *International Community Law Review* 163. See essay 15 'Strategic Practices: "Doing Our Own Thing"'.

disputes between states are articulated in law's language and the legitimacy of force used must be in conformity with international law. It is not the violence, per se, but the non-compliance with international law (evidenced by the effects of the violence) that generates widespread censure and admonishment. Thus, law is the instrument that enables critique of the author(s) of violence and grounds demands for state and individual accountability. Law's language may abstract and sanitise but it can still be drawn upon to assert the right to resist, the right to return and the right to justice and to peace.

International law has been a tool of resistance; its incommensurability, incoherence and fragmentation – that worry some – can simultaneously provide the instrumentality to challenge oppressive power.[7] Law's institutional structures (notwithstanding their imperial genealogy) are the sites through which international law is being reshaped, reimagined and new law founded. International law is no longer in the exclusive hands of states, nor for that matter a language confined to the privileged few within the legal 'fraternity' in or outside governments. The 'invisible' college of international lawyers has become visible and vocal. It comprises, inter alia, civil society, human rights special procedures, academics, and – as we portrayed throughout this book – women acting individually and collectively.[8]

Children and young people too are creatively invoking international law to bypass states to secure climate justice, the right to a future. The attempt to hold states responsible for 'failing to take necessary preventive and precautionary measures to respect, protect and fulfil their right to life, health and culture' pursuant to the Convention on the Rights of the Child (CRC)[9] may have been dismissed on admissibility grounds[10] but what it achieved was to draw attention to the abject failure by states to take adequate steps to meet their legal obligations owed to children under multiple legal regimes. Moreover, the claim coupled with global environmental activism, prompted the CRC to issue General Comment No 26 (2023) on children's rights and the environment, with a special focus on climate change.[11]

Likewise, persistent efforts by a group of law students from the University of the South Pacific in Vanuatu to secure an Advisory Opinion from the ICJ on the obligations of states in respect of climate change have achieved initial success with the decision in March 2023 by the UN General Assembly to request the Court for an opinion.[12] The ICJ has been asked to identify state obligations 'to ensure the protection of the

---

[7] These facets of law do not deprive law of its binding nature or from being applied in a particular context. Far more problematic is the tendency to compartmentalise and silo, attributes traced to the Enlightenment's obsession with categorisation.

[8] Oscar Schachter, 'The Invisible College of International Lawyers' (1977–1978) 72 *Northwestern University Law Review* 217.

[9] Communication to the Committee on the Rights of the Child, *Sacchi et al v Argentina, Brazil, France, Germany and Turkey*, 23 September 2019.

[10] *Sacchi et al v Argentina et al*, Decision adopted by the Committee under the Optional Protocol to the Convention on the Rights of the Child, No 104/2019, 11 November 2021, CRC/C/88/D/104/2019.

[11] General Comment No 26 (2023) on children's rights and the environment, with a special focus on climate change, CRC/C/GC/26, 22 August 2023. The General Comment involved an extensive consultation process with children in 121 countries.

[12] UNGAR 77/276, 29 March 2023; Pacific Islands Students Fighting Climate Change, https://www.pisfcc.org/.

climate system and other parts of the environment from anthropogenic emissions of greenhouse gasses for states and for present and future generations' and to specify the legal consequences of significant harm caused to the climate system with respect to states and in particular small island developing states and peoples and individuals of the present and future generations.[13] When delivered,[14] it will be the first authoritative statement on climate change issued by the ICJ. The Court has been given the opportunity to expound on the concept of intergenerational responsibility,[15] the rights of climate refugees, including the intersectional effects of climate change on differently situated people, most notably Indigenous Peoples, and in that regard to delve into evolving law on climate reparation. The burden on the Court is enormous. For what is at stake is whether it can deliver an opinion that does not undermine the faith (neither utopian nor purely strategic) placed by young people in international law and its institutions to effect change.[16]

Indigenous Peoples are also engaging with international law in creative ways, stretching its content to more effectively claim their rights and to advance their cosmovisions, their legal systems[17] and cultural norms, long suppressed by colonial and post-colonial states. For example, claims articulated by Indigenous Peoples have furthered the expansion of the contours of international human rights law from one that privileges individual rights – founded on a European tradition – to extend to group or collective rights.[18] This was cemented with the adoption of the 2007 UN Declaration on the Rights of Indigenous Peoples (UNDRIP)[19] which recognises Indigenous Peoples as 'distinct peoples who possess collective rights', especially in relation to self-determination. Described as a watershed instrument, UNDRIP is the outcome of decades of collective labour by Indigenous Peoples[20] to build on ILO

---

[13] ICJ, Request for Advisory Opinion, Obligations of States in Respect of Climate Change, 2023.
[14] Statute of the ICJ, 1945, art 65: 'The Court may give an advisory opinion on any legal question' requested by a body authorised by the Charter to do so.
[15] Maastricht Principles on the Human Rights of Future Generations, 3 February 2023; UN Secretary-General, 'Our Common Agenda Policy Brief 1: To Think and Act for Future Generations' March 2023; Margaretha Wewerinke-Singh et al, 'In Defence of Future Generations: A Reply to Stephen Humphreys' (2023) 34 *European Journal of International Law* 651.
[16] What has still garnered inadequate attention is the impact of militarisation (rather than war itself) on the environment, ecosystems, and climate change and the potential of international law to address this. On the protection of the environment *in* conflict, see Karen Hulme, 'Using International Environmental Law to Enhance Biodiversity and Nature Conservation during Armed Conflict' (2022) 20 *Journal of International Criminal Justice* 1.
[17] The right of Indigenous Peoples to 'maintain their own judicial structures and systems is a fundamental component of their rights to autonomy and self-determination' albeit subject to international human rights standards, including those elaborated under CEDAW: CEDAW Committee, GR 39 on the rights of Indigenous women and girls, 31 October 2022, CEDAW/C/GC/39, para 25.
[18] Article 1 of both the ICCPR and ICESCR asserts the collective right to self-determination; the African Charter on Human and Peoples' Rights, Banjul, 27 June 1981, arts 19–24 set out collective rights including the right to peace; see essay 3 'Peace in International Law'.
[19] UNGAR 61/295 13 September 2007. Report of the SR on Indigenous People, 11 August 2008, A/HRC/9/9; Megan Davis, 'Indigenous Struggles in Standard-Setting: The United Nations Declaration on the Right of Indigenous Peoples' (2008) 9 *Melbourne Journal of International Law* 439.
[20] Since the late 1980s, Indigenous Peoples have brought cases to the UN human rights treaty bodies that have actively developed a body of jurisprudence to advance their rights, individual and collective, to take account of their specific historical, cultural, social and economic circumstances.

Convention 169[21] and the jurisprudence of human rights bodies[22] which recognised the special connection of Indigenous Peoples with their lands, territories and resources. Rather than defining the content and form of the relationship, UNDRIP requires states to provide special protection and to recognise that Indigenous Peoples' lands should be protected in accordance with their own systems and traditions,[23] which effectively allows for a wholly different paradigm to exist in parallel to the state. In other words Indigenous Peoples' strategising is challenging international law's traditional state-centricity 'expanding mainstream sources of legal authority'[24] and reshaping fundamental norms of international law.[25] A notable example of this has been the struggle by Indigenous Peoples in Canada to have the Indian Residential School System and the treatment of Indigenous women, girls and 2SLGBTQI+[26] people recognised as genocide within the meaning of the 1948 Genocide Convention. Informed by decolonial and Native feminist theorising, two national inquiries concluded that Canada's policies constituted cultural/colonial genocide.[27] The obstacle to justice was the absence in the Convention of any reference to 'cultural' genocide, an outcome of political pressure exerted primarily by settler states that was at odds with Raphael Lemkin's original elaboration of genocide, core to which was cultural genocide.[28] A legal impediment (silence) had been created in 1948 by a political decision (European colonialist). In October 2022, following intensive campaigning,

---

[21] International Labour Organization, Convention (No 169) Concerning Indigenous and Tribal Peoples in Independent Countries, adopted 27 June 1989 by the General Conference of the International Labour Organization at its 76th session, entered into force 5 September 1991.

[22] eg the IACtHR established that indigenous territorial rights encompass a broader concept than property which is related to the collective right to survival as an organised people with the control of their habitat as a necessary condition for the reproduction of their cultural life, their own development and to carry out their life plans: *Yakye Axa Indigenous Community v Paraguay* (Merits, Reparations and Costs) Judgment, 17 June 2005, Series C No 125.

[23] UNDRIP, art 26. The Declaration does not admit a veto over extractivist development projects (although it requires that any state interference with those rights be subject to consultation and free, prior and informed consent) evidencing how far we have yet to go to decolonise international law: Carsten Stahn 'Reckoning with Colonial Injustice: International Law as Culprit and as Remedy?' (2020) 33 *Leiden Journal of International Law* 823, 825.

[24] S James Anaya and Antony Anghie, 'Introduction to the Symposium on the Impact of Indigenous Peoples on International Law' (2021) 115 *AJIL Unbound* 116.

[25] Clare Charters, 'The Sweet Spot Between Formalism and Fairness' (2021) 115 *AJIL Unbound* 127, showing how Indigenous Peoples' thinking on and around self-determination has altered the very understanding of self-determination under international law.

[26] This is the Canadian Government's acronym for the Canadian community: '2S: at the front, recognizes Two-Spirit people as the first 2SLGBTQI+ communities; L: Lesbian; G: Gay; B: Bisexual; T: Transgender; Q: Queer; I: Intersex, considers sex characteristics beyond sexual orientation, gender identity and gender expression; +: is inclusive of people who identify as part of sexual and gender diverse communities, who use additional terminologies': https://women-gender-equality.canada.ca/en/free-to-be-me/2slgbtqi-plus-glossary.html.

[27] Honouring the Truth, Reconciling for the Future: Summary of the Final Report of the Truth and Reconciliation Commission of Canada 2015. National Inquiry into Missing and Murdered Indigenous Women and Girls, A Legal Analysis of Genocide 2019. The majority of commissioners were from indigenous communities.

[28] Raphael Lemkin, *Axis Rule in Occupied Europe* (1943) 79: genocide is 'the disintegration of the political and social institutions, of culture, language, national feelings, religion, and the economic existence of national groups, and the destruction of the personal security, liberty, health, dignity, and even the lives of the individuals belonging to such groups': Loeora Bilsky and Rachel Klagsbrun, 'The Return of Cultural Genocide?' (2018) 29 *European Journal of International Law* 373.

Canada's parliament unanimously recognised the residential school system as genocide, opening up the debate on how genocide should be understood in both treaty and customary international law.²⁹

Indigenous Peoples have also been at the forefront of rethinking on the protection of ecosystems, the environment and climate justice. They are playing a pivotal role in shaping and guiding the content and trajectory of international law to forge a radically different vision of being in the world that recognises 'human beings' embeddedness in and coexistence with nature'.³⁰ The incorporation into domestic law of Indigenous Peoples' cosmologies recognising the universe as agentive and sentient and all matter and phenomena – persons, plants, animals, rivers, winds, mountains, seas – as expressions of life force or spirit, interconnected and intersubjective,³¹ is challenging the dominant androcentricity of European philosophy³² underpinning international law that treats nature as an object, to be altered, possessed, and owned, facilitating capitalist consumerism and extractivism.³³ States have adopted different approaches to encapsulate the 'rights' of Nature. Ecuador, for example, amended its constitution in 2008 to recognise Nature's right to *exist*.³⁴ Colombia and Aotearoa New Zealand, on the other hand, have conferred natural entities (specific rivers/ park) with *legal personality*,³⁵ coupled with the appointment of guardians. Although both approaches remain inherently anthropocentric and the fit between Indigenous and settler legal and philosophical concepts imperfect,³⁶ ecological jurisprudence

---

²⁹ See also *Bringing Them Home: Report of the National Inquiry into the Separation of Aboriginal and Torres Strait Islander Children from Their Families* (Commonwealth of Australia, 1997), finding that forcible removal of Aboriginal children from their parents involved both systematic racial discrimination and genocide as defined by international law.

³⁰ Maria Akchurin, 'Constructing the Rights of Nature: Constitutional Reform, Mobilization, and Environmental Protection in Ecuador' (2015) 40 *Law & Social Inquiry* 937, 960. Many, if not most, Indigenous Peoples have never distinguished between nature and culture: Erin O'Donnell et al, 'Stop Burying the Lede: The Essential Role of Indigenous Law(s) in Creating Rights of Nature' (2020) 9 *Transnational Environmental Law* 403, 405; Alessandro Pelizzon, 'Earth Laws, Rights of Nature and Legal Pluralism' in Michelle Maloney and Peter Burdon (eds), *Wild Law – In Practice* (Routledge, 2014) 176.

³¹ Natalie Avalos, 'Indigenous Stewardship: Religious Praxis and Unsettling Settler Ecologies' (2023) *Political Theology* 13.

³² The articulation of nature into the fragmented language of land, territories, and resources is problematic in that it introduces categories that are divorced from one another, thereby framing the discourse within a European tradition.

³³ International law facilitates this process through the operation of international trade and investment law, enabling states and transnational corporations to acquire land and extract resources in the Global South and in spaces occupied by the most marginalised for the benefit of the Global North and the privileged. Extraction and consumption on an unprecedented scale has destroyed ecosystems, polluted air, land and water, making vast areas of the earth uninhabitable.

³⁴ Constitution of the Republic of Ecuador, 2008, Title II, ch 7, art 71 on the Rights for Nature states: 'Nature or Pachamama, where life is reproduced and exists, has the right to exist, persist, maintain and regenerate its vital cycles, structure, functions and its processes in evolution'.

³⁵ In Aotearoa New Zealand, Te Urewera (a national park) and the Whanganui River were recognised as having legal personality following negotiations with Maori iwi. Legislation adopted in 2017 expressly acknowledges the Whanganui River as a living being, corresponding with Maori tradition and protected by a guardianship scheme involving the Maori people, that sets aside the colonial paradigm that treated the river as an object of ownership and management rather than as a subject to be respected and protected. In Colombia, the Rio Atrato is likewise recognised as having legal personality.

³⁶ Wapshkaa Ma'IIngan, 'Aki, Anishinaabek, kaye Tahsh Crown' (2010) 9 *Indigenous Law Journal* 107. UNDRIP, art 28, addressing reparation, cites restitution but in doing so uses multiple verbs to capture the

represents a step towards disrupting the western dualist tradition, including the separation of human history from natural history,[37] universalised through colonialism. Reflecting on the process through which the rights of Nature to exist was integrated into Ecuador's constitution, Maria Akchurin notes how:

> this story was not only an instance of an alternative philosophy becoming incorporated into a legal framework, but also an important case of how indigenous politics influenced nonindigenous systems of authority and created the space for a different understanding of nature/society relations to be conceptualized, described, and incorporated into the constitution, pushing the boundaries of existing ideas about rights, authority, and the state.[38]

While the idea of the rights of Nature is still in its nascent stage, it is garnering greater traction across the world, prompted by the emerging field of 'earth law' and 'ecology jurisprudence'[39] on the back of domestic legislation.[40] At the international level it is acknowledged within the UN's *Harmony with Nature* rubric, an inter-governmental initiative that seeks to strengthen the protection of the environment through a more holistic, Earth-centric approach drawing together multilateral initiatives on sustainable development, environmental protection, international law and alternative knowledge traditions.[41] As a *legal* concept, the rights of Nature has yet to formally migrate to the international sphere, although it is making inroads within regional systems, most notably, the Inter-American and, more belatedly, the African[42] human rights systems. For example, the Inter-American Court of Human Rights has read the rights of Nature into the right to a healthy environment which:

> protects the components of the environment, such as forests, rivers and seas, as legal interests in themselves, even in the absence of the certainty or evidence of a risk to individuals. This means that it protects nature and the environment, not only because of the benefits they provide to humanity or the effects that their degradation may have on other human rights, such as health, life or personal integrity, but because of their importance to the other living organisms with which we share the planet that also merit protection in their own right. In this regard, the Court notes a tendency, not only in court judgments, but also in Constitutions, to recognize legal personality and, consequently, rights to nature.[43]

---

relationship between Indigenous Peoples and land, including 'traditionally owned, or otherwise occupied or used' and which has been 'confiscated, taken, occupied, used or damaged'. Not all the provisions of UNDRIP are universally supported by all Indigenous communities; different communities have their own distinctive histories, cultures and priorities.

[37] Dipesh Chakrabarty, *The Climate of History* (University of Chicago Press, 2021) 201.
[38] Maria Akchurin, 'Constructing the Rights of Nature: Constitutional Reform, Mobilization, and Environmental Protection in Ecuador' (2015) 40 *Law & Social Inquiry* 937, 961.
[39] Sometimes referred to as 'wild law' or 'earth jurisprudence' or 'ecological jurisprudence'.
[40] For domestic legislation and jurisprudence from across the world see https://www.harmonywithnatureun.org/rightsOfNature/.
[41] UNGAR 77/169, Harmony with Nature, 28 December 2022.
[42] African Commission on Human and Peoples' Rights, ACHPR/Res 372 (LX) 2017, Resolution on the Protection of Sacred Natural Sites and Territories.
[43] *The Environment and Human Rights*, IACtHR Advisory Opinion OC-23/17 of 15 November 2017, para 62. The right to a healthy environment or quality of life are anthropocentric and must be understood separately from the rights of Nature. Climate Emergency: Scope of Inter-American Human Rights Obligations, Resolution No 3/2021, IACHR and REDESCA.

The abstraction and denaturalisation of time and space by modernity made possible their separation and regulation through international law.[44] International law's time and space are grounded in a European philosophical tradition, a dualist ontology, staunchly committed to binary oppositions, universalised through (and shaped by) the forces of imperialism and colonialism that continue to exclude and silence alternative conceptions of being in the world.[45] International law's time and space order the world, quantifying and qualifying, cutting and dividing. It is able to construct the present as if it has no history, to separate land from sea, humans from ecosystems. The law's temporal and spatial signposts provide the socio-legal constructed state (founded on law's time and space) with rights and permissions enabling it to extract, to use, to cause suffering and harm, to annihilate with profound implications for gender justice and peace. International law's proclivity for privileging the future over the past, and the immediate over the distant past, has enabled the erasure of historical injustices and their gendered, racialised legacies that structure the present and determine the future.[46] Those calling for gender and racial justice are fighting back, developing new tools including through the idea of transformative reparations. The topic has gained far more prominence over the last two decades as a promising site through which law can facilitate the dismantling of the structures of patriarchy and European imperialism by engaging with the past.[47] For those seeking gender, racial and, more recently, climate justice, the key to transformative reparation 'often lies in active acknowledgment of past and continuing injustice and taking appropriate corrective responsibility for it'.[48]

Transformative reparations, the topic of the first essay, are disruptive of extant orders of power. They offer a conduit through which prevailing structures and relationships of power (extractivist, violent, gendered, raced), each of which gave rise to the harm in the first place (slavery, genocide, dispossession, forced displacement), can be overturned in law's lexicon. Legal interventions alone cannot deliver on transformative change: social and economic inequalities have deep roots.[49] Nonetheless, transformative reparations have the potential to redistribute 'authority and meaning-making'[50] across history, culture, the political economy and law itself.

---

[44] Russell West-Pavlov, *Temporalities* (Routledge, 2013) 25. Modernity introduced a culture of abstraction – of the abstract individual with abstract rights engaging in monetary exchanges determined by the abstract value of goods.
[45] Mark Rifkin, *Beyond Settler Time: Temporal Sovereignty and Indigenous Self-Determination* (Duke University Press, 2017).
[46] eg in South Africa, the focus on the proximate past of apartheid meant freedom was equated with civil rights rather than the restoration of sovereignty to the dispossessed peoples of South Africa.
[47] Imperialism is the ideology upon which colonial practices – including the transatlantic slave trade – were normalised through the creation of racial and gendered hierarchies that persist to this day. Both sex and race were used to naturalise inequalities on biological grounds. Imperialism has multiple facets and must be understood as a political, economic and cultural system: Edward W Said, *Culture and Imperialism* (Vintage Books, 1994).
[48] Albie Sachs, 'Foreword' in Jacqueline Bhabha et al (eds), *Time for Reparations: A Global Perspective* (University of Pennsylvania Press, 2021) viii. Reparation claims are not solely – or primarily –concerned with monetary compensation, despite what some states infer.
[49] Mari Matsuda, 'Looking to the Bottom: Critical Legal Studies and Reparations' (1987) 22 *Harvard Civil Rights and Civil Liberties Law Review* 323.
[50] Sarah Riley Case, 'Looking to the Horizon: The Meanings of Reparations for Unbearable Crises' (2023) 117 *AJIL Unbound* 49.

These initiatives – whether by children, Indigenous Peoples, environmentalists, feminists, and those calling for racialised and gender justice – point in the direction of a pluriversal law: law that is no longer limited to being inter-*national* or confined to being *uni*-versal but law that values alternative knowledge traditions and strives for multiplicities.[51] The opening of law to alternative cosmologies and temporal and spatial imaginaries is helping to provide more fruitful foundations for advancing just orders conducive to intra- and inter-communal peace by disrupting dominant binaries that give rise to hierarchies which form the bedrock of international law. What would happen if law confronted its past to do justice today? What would law look like if it were to centre peace?

In the second essay we address these questions through the teaching of peace in international law. The teaching of peace is a topic saturated in gendered assumptions. Typically, peace studies is treated as a separate topic among a collection of subject matters/disciplines rather than integral to all areas of study, whilst in the teaching of international law, it is rarely mentioned. This absence strips international law of its potential to advance peace. The marginalisation and absence of peace in education is hard to reconcile with the right to education as protected by international law. For example, article 13 of the ICESCR (which reproduces article 26 of the UDHR) stipulates that:

> education shall enable all persons to participate effectively in a free society, promote understanding, tolerance and friendship among all nations and all racial, ethnic or religious groups, and further the activities of the United Nations for the maintenance of peace.

The first action area in UNESCO's strategy for fostering a culture of peace is education, as a tool to change values and gendered stereotypical attitudes, and to encourage behaviours that reject violence.[52] The potential of education for empowering women and girls and promoting gender equality[53] is demonstrated by the determination of misogynist regimes to prevent girls from attending and receiving schooling and to close educational institutions that disseminate values different from their own.[54] We reflect on the absence of peace in the teaching of international law and suggest how this might be reversed. The neoliberal agenda that promotes profits over wellbeing leaves little or no space for education about peace.[55]

---

[51] Arturo Escobar, *Pluriversal Politics: The Real and the Possible* (Duke University Press, 2020).

[52] UNESCO – *Mainstreaming the Culture of Peace* (Paris, Culture of Peace Co-ordination, 2002).

[53] CEDAW Committee, General Recommendation No 36, on the right of girls and women to education, CEDAW/C/GC/36, 27 November 2017, para 1: 'Education plays a pivotal, transformative and empowering role in promoting human rights values and is recognized as the pathway to gender equality and the empowerment of women.'

[54] Report of the Special Rapporteur on the situation of human rights in Afghanistan, A/78/338, 1 September 2023, especially paras 41–43.

[55] As part of the Gendered Peace project, Sheri Labenski developed a syllabus and materials for a course on 'Gender and Peace' to be available through the Brilliant Club (a UK NGO) to schools in London.

18
Transformative Reparations and Gendered Peace

I. INTRODUCTION

IT IS A firmly established principle of international law that states have the obligation to make reparation for internationally wrongful acts or omissions attributable to them.[1] The International Law Commission lists restitution, compensation, and satisfaction as forms of reparation for the commission of an internationally wrongful act.[2] Restitution seeks to place the wronged state in the situation it was in prior to the violation or to restore the status quo to the point in time *immediately* before the wrongful act.[3] Restitution treats the *violation* of the rule as disruptive to the extant order, inter-state stability and peace; it is mostly agnostic to the normative order it seeks to reinstate. Pecuniary compensation puts a monetary value upon the harm (material and moral injury[4]) and its consequences. International law has not generally been concerned with the nature and content of the compensatory demands, although such demands following armed conflict can be felt (and are intended) as punitive in effect,[5] detrimental to sustainable peace[6] and contributing to further conflict.[7] If an injury cannot be made good by restitution or compensation, states must 'give satisfaction', which may comprise an acknowledgment of the breach, an

---

[1] *The Factory at Chorzów (Germany v Poland)* Jurisdiction, PCIJ Series A, No 9, 26 July 1927, 21: 'It is a principle of international law that the breach of an engagement involves an obligation to make reparation in an adequate form'.
[2] Articles on the Responsibility of States for Internationally Wrongful Acts, UNGAR 56/83 of 12 December 2001, annex, art 34.
[3] Restitution is 'to re-establish the situation which existed before the wrongful act was committed': ibid art 35.
[4] ibid art 31.
[5] Treaty of Versailles, 1919, art 231 affirmed Germany's legal liability for damage caused by the war. Art 232 recognised that Germany's liability had to be limited by its resources. Reparations for specified damages were determined by a Reparations Commission in 1921. These articles were particularly loathed by Germany and the source of 'uneasy consciences' among the allies: Margaret MacMillan, *Peacemakers: The Paris Conference of 1919 and Its Attempt to End War* (John Murray, 2001) 204.
[6] WILPF expressed its deep regret at the 'financial and economic proposals' of the proposed Peace Treaty, condemning a hundred million people to 'poverty, disease and despair which must result in the spread of hatred and anarchy within each nation': WILPF Resolutions, 2nd Congress, Zurich, Switzerland, 1919.
[7] UNGAR ES-11/5, 14 November 2022, Furtherance of remedy and reparation for aggression against Ukraine.

expression of regret, a formal apology, a guarantee of non-repetition or other appropriate acts.[8]

Reparation in international law is not confined to inter-state wrongdoings. Under international human rights law (IHRL), states are required to provide reparation for human rights violations committed against individual(s) within the state's jurisdiction. The multi-layered obligation to respect, ensure respect and fulfil human rights requires states to take appropriate measures to prevent violations, to undertake investigations of alleged violations, to provide victims with access to justice, and to provide effective remedies, including reparations.[9]

Transformative reparation is a relatively recent concept that has emerged from transitional justice[10] and IHRL. The following section charts transformative reparation as advanced by international and regional human rights mechanisms and, most notably, as a tool to interrupt the cycles of gendered violence. We then turn to how these mechanisms – often in tandem with feminist activism – are developing transformative reparation in the context of historical wrongs, to surmount and dismantle patriarchy's structural obstacles in the quest for gender and racial justice as necessary to peace. In the final section we reflect on how the developments in IHRL are shaping the trajectory and content of inter-state law, unsettling some of its core doctrines and disrupting prevailing inter-state relationships of power founded on gendered and racial injustices. Reparations for historical injustices are contested through international law's temporal doctrines and principles, asking whose time matters and accordingly whose life matters – concerns that have always been core to feminist struggles.

II. TRANSFORMATIVE REPARATION TO BREAK THE CYCLE OF GENDERED VIOLENCE

The right to reparation is founded on the right to an effective remedy as recognised in international and regional human rights treaties. The forms of reparation recognised in IHRL parallel those applicable to states, namely restitution, compensation, and satisfaction but additionally include rehabilitation and guarantees of non-repetition.[11] Although the UN General Assembly's adoption of the 2005 Basic Principles and Guidelines[12] was welcomed by feminist activists as helping to clarify the scope and

---

[8] Articles on the Responsibility of States (n 2) art 37.

[9] UNGAR 60/147, 16 December 2005, Basic Principles and Guidelines on the Right to a Remedy and Reparations for Victims of Gross Violations of International Human Rights Law and Serious Violations of International Humanitarian Law (Basic Principles and Guidelines).

[10] Report of the Secretary-General, The rule of law and transitional justice in conflict and post-conflict societies, S/2004/616, 23 August 2004. Administrative reparation schemes have been introduced by states to respond to large scale human rights violations perpetrated in armed conflict or in situations of widespread political violence.

[11] Articles on the Responsibility of States (n 2) art 30 is a weak provision on non-repetition under the heading 'General principles' not 'Reparation for Injury'. It notes that a state responsible for the commission of an internationally wrongful act has the obligation to 'to offer appropriate assurances and guarantees of non-repetition, if circumstances so require'.

[12] See n 9.

content of reparations,[13] the failure to apply a gender perspective prompted women's civil society activists to draft the 2007 Nairobi Declaration,[14] which calls on states to take account of gender in tailoring reparations, since all harms have gendered dimensions. States had also failed to register that, for many victims of gender-based violence, restitution – ie a return to the situation immediately prior to the violation – was precisely *not* what was sought.[15] Restitution left untouched the conditions that had given rise to the harm experienced. The Nairobi Declaration thus asserts that 'reparation must go above and beyond the immediate reasons and consequences of the crimes and violations; they must address structural inequalities that negatively shape women's and girls' lives'.

SR VAW, Rashida Manjoo enlarged on the Nairobi Declaration and for the need to link individual reparation and structural transformation since 'violence perpetrated against individual women generally feeds into patterns of pre-existing and often cross-cutting structural subordination and systemic marginalization'.[16] Further, the guarantee of non-repetition requires states to recognise that 'adequate reparations for women cannot simply be about returning them to where they were before the individual instance of violence, but instead should strive to have transformative potential'.[17] Reparations provide an opportunity to address the structural causes of violence, including sexual and gender-based violence founded on patriarchal assumptions about masculinity. It follows that in the context of post-conflict reparation schemes, states 'should aspire, to the extent possible, to subvert, instead of reinforce, pre-existing structural inequality that may be at the root causes of the violence the women experience before, during and after conflict'.[18] Guarantees of non-repetition 'trigger a discussion about the underlying structural causes of the violence and their gendered manifestations and a discussion about the broader institutional or legal reforms that might be called for to ensure non-repetition'.[19] If non-repetition is to have any meaningful effect, dismantling the 'patriarchal and sexual hierarchies and customs'[20] that produce the situation in which violations occur in the first place is critical.

The two-pronged approach – integrating gender and aiming for transformation – as elaborated in the Nairobi Declaration is endorsed by the CEDAW Committee, which emphasises that 'an assessment of the gender dimension of the harm suffered is essential' so that reparations are gender-sensitive, promote women's rights and

---

[13] The Basic Principles were criticised for omitting reparations for historical violations; SR on contemporary forms of racism, racial discrimination, xenophobia and related intolerance, Reparations for racial discrimination rooted in slavery and colonialism, A/74/321, 21 August 2019, para 38.
[14] Nairobi Declaration on Women's and Girls' Right to a Remedy and Reparation, 2007.
[15] Nairobi Declaration: 'reintegration and restitution by themselves are not sufficient goals of reparation, since the origins of violations of women's and girls' human rights predate the conflict situation'. Restitution is not irrelevant, but without taking account of gender and the need for transformation, restitution is likely to be inadequate and, in certain contexts, counterproductive to gendered peace.
[16] SR VAW, Reparations for women subjected to violence, A/HRC/14/22, 23 April 2010, para 24.
[17] ibid para 31.
[18] ibid.
[19] Report of the SR VAW (n 16) para 62.
[20] Guidance Note of the UN Secretary-General, Reparations for conflict-related sexual violence, June 2014.

prevent the reoccurrence of violations.[21] Other international human rights mechanisms have underscored the need for a gender analysis to understand the 'complexity of the harm suffered and its consequences', since only then can measures be crafted to effectively address the particular needs of victim/survivors and avoid directly or indirectly reproducing patterns of gender/intersectional discrimination that create the harm in the first place.[22] Transformative reparations represent a means by which to interrupt the cycles of violence and to nurture inter-personal and inter-societal peace. Accordingly, states should devise reparative programmes that are gender sensitive and promote women's rights and which seek not simply to repair the direct harms but to transform social structures and relationships, including gender relationships and stereotypes.[23]

Reparations have particular importance for women, as 'they can provide acknowledgement of their rights as equal citizens, a measure of justice, crucial resources of recovery and contribute to transforming underlying gender inequalities'.[24] By calling for enhanced access to justice[25] to 'strengthen institutional safeguards against impunity' and recalling the applicable provisions of international law on the right to an effective remedy for violations of human rights, SC Resolution 2467 (2019) brings these obligations directly into the Women, Peace and Security (WPS) agenda[26] as a step toward transformative gender justice. Such programmes should include institutional and legislative reforms, as well as reparative measures devised in close cooperation with local women's organisations and civil society.[27] This links to another human rights principle[28] and a pillar of the WPS agenda, inclusive participation that is not confined to the 'prevention, management, and resolution of conflict',[29] but also encompasses the design, implementation and monitoring of transnational justice mechanisms and reparations.[30] Without the participation of directly affected women

---

[21] CEDAW Committee, General Recommendation No 30 on women in conflict prevention, conflict and post-conflict situations, CEDAW/C/GC/30, 18 October 2013, para 79.
[22] SR on the promotion of truth, justice, reparation and guarantees of non-recurrence, The gender perspective in transitional justice processes, A/75/174, 17 July 2020, paras 27 and 62.
[23] CEDAW Committee, General Recommendation No 30 (n 21) para 79.
[24] Radhika Coomaraswamy et al, *Preventing Conflict, Transforming Justice, Securing the Peace: A Global Study on the Implementation of Security Council Resolution 1325* (UN, 2015) 115.
[25] Basic Principles and Guidelines (n 9) para 12: victims of human rights violations or of international humanitarian law 'shall have equal access to an effective judicial remedy as provided for under international law.'.
[26] UNSCR 2467, 23 April 2019. The resolution's survivor-centred orientation also signifies preference for restorative or reparative remedies.
[27] CEDAW Committee, General Recommendation No 33 on women's access to justice, CEDAW/C/GC/33, 3 August 2015, para 19. For examples of reparative measures recommended by the Committee to states see Sheri Labenski, *The Right to Reparations for Sexual and Gender-based Violence* (LSE Centre for WPS, 2020).
[28] Human rights special procedures have stressed the importance of victim participation in reparations processes; eg SR on the promotion of truth, A/HRC/34/62, 27 December 2016, para 53; SR on Contemporary Forms of Racism, Human rights obligations of Member States in relation to reparations for racial discrimination rooted in slavery and colonialism, A/74/321, 21 August 2019, para 40.
[29] UNSCR 1325, 31 October 2000, OP 1.
[30] Nairobi Declaration (n 14) Section 2: 'A. In order to achieve reparation measures sensitive to gender, age, cultural diversity and human rights, decision-making about reparation must include victims as full participants, while ensuring just representation of women and girls in all their diversity. .... B. Full participation of women and girls victims should be guaranteed in every stage of the reparation process, i.e. design,

and girls, initiatives are likely to reflect elite men's experience of violence and their concerns, priorities, and needs regarding redress; the same is true of participation for other unrepresented and marginalised groups. Failure to ensure such participation misses an opportunity for victims to instil historical context and to gain a sense of agency that may, in and of itself, be an important form of rehabilitation, especially when victims come to perceive themselves as actors of social change.[31]

At the regional level, human rights bodies have been innovative in conceiving of the concept of transformative reparations. For example, the African Commission on Human Rights notes:

> [t]he ultimate goal of redress is transformation. Redress must occasion changes in social, economic and political structures and relationships in a manner that deals effectively with the factors which allow for [commission of harm]. This transformation envisages processes with long-term and sustainable perspectives that are responsive to the multiple justice needs of victims and therefore restore human dignity.[32]

In its view, the aim of guarantees of non-repetition is 'to break the structural causes of societal violence' and 'offer an important potential for institutional and social transformation that may be required to address the underlying causes of violence'.[33] Within the Inter-American system, transformative reparation has evolved as an aspect of post-conflict reconstruction. It has been pioneered especially by the Inter-American human rights institutions[34] that have detailed for states the substance of reparative programmes, aiming to transform the lives of individual survivors and their families, as well as engineering structural change within communities and the state. The *Cotton Field* case concerning the deaths of women and girls in Ciudad Juárez, Mexico is illustrative.[35]

The Inter-American Court of Human Rights (IACtHR) made a slew of orders that addressed not only the deaths of the three women whose families had brought the case but also took account of the hundreds of other women who had been murdered or disappeared. Measures related first to the ongoing investigation into the deaths of the three women and into all other similar investigations to ensure that they are carried out promptly, integrate lines of inquiry into similar patterns in the area,

---

implementation, evaluation, and decision-making.' *cf* ACHPR, Resolution on the Right to a Remedy and Reparation for Women and Girls Victims of Sexual Violence, 42nd Ordinary Session, Brazzaville, Republic of Congo, 15–28 November 2007: 'Ensure participation of women in the elaboration, adoption and implementation of reparation programmes'.

[31] Reparative processes 'must engage those disproportionately affected ... as co-creators and owners of knowledge and solutions from the very start of response processes': Nkita Yasmin Shah and Florence Waller-Carr, 'The Radical Potential of Feminist Approaches to Relief and Recovery' (LSE Centre for WPS, June 2022).

[32] ACPHR, General Comment No 4 on the African Charter on Human and Peoples' Rights: The Right to Redress for Victims of Torture and Other Cruel, Inhuman or Degrading Punishment or Treatment (Article 5), ACPHR 21st Extra-Ordinary Session, 23 February to 4 March 2017, Banjul, The Gambia, para 8.

[33] ibid paras 45 and 48.

[34] The IACtHR has developed its approach in many cases including those involving violence against women: eg *Plan de Sánchez Massacre v Guatemala*, Judgment, 29 April 29, 2004 (merits); *Miguel Castro Castro Prison v Peru*, Judgment, 25 November 2006 (merits, reparations and costs); *Caso Lopez Soto v Venezuela*, Judgment, 26 September 2018 (merits, reparations and costs).

[35] *González, Monreal and Monarrez ('Cotton Field') v Mexico*, Judgment, 16 November 2009 (merits, reparations, and costs).

keep victims' families fully informed, are performed by officials highly trained in cases involving discrimination and gender-based violence, are appropriately resourced to ensure their independence and impartiality and incorporate guarantees for the safety of all involved in the processes. A second set of requirements related to publicity for the proceedings 'so that Mexican society is aware of the facts', encompassing publication and dissemination of the Court's judgment in newspapers, on the radio and television, public acknowledgment by Mexico of its international responsibility for the violations, and commemorative measures such as a monument to be determined through widespread consultation. A third set of measures required the sanctioning of officials who committed irregularities in the course of the earlier investigations, including investigating complaints filed by the victims' families about harassment and persecution; a fourth to the standardising of all protocols, manuals, prosecutorial investigation criteria, expert services, and services to ensure compliance with international standards in cases of disappearance; a fifth to the creation and update of webpages and databases of all material relevant to the disappearances; a sixth to ongoing education and training programmes and courses on human rights and gender and elimination of gender stereotypes; and a seventh on the immediate provision, free of charge, of appropriate and effective medical, psychological or psychiatric treatment through specialised state health institutions to be made available to all the next of kin. Finally, compensation for pecuniary and non-pecuniary damage to the families of the three named victims in the case was ordered.

The Court's judgment is extraordinarily thorough, seeking to cover all aspects of the traumatic events. It both looks back by redressing violative behaviours by state officials and forward to preventing future violations. In other cases, the Court has ordered a housing programme, free medical treatment for all victims, specialised programmes of psychological and psychiatric treatment for collective, family and individual treatment, legislative reform addressing sexual violence and processes to combat it, reform of administrative and investigatory processes, mandatory gender-sensitive and human rights training programmes for legislators, judges, law enforcement personnel, individually-tailored educational opportunities for survivors and their families, access to credit, land restitution, land redistribution, and means to transform that land into a source of livelihood. It has also required the setting up of local bodies to assess needs and, in conjunction with local civil society, to advise on appropriate ways forward with time limits for the state to report back on its implementation of the Court's orders.

Reparation under international criminal law (ICL) has lagged behind IHRL, although international humanitarian law has long recognised the right to reparation.[36] The International Criminal Court (ICC) is, however, expressly mandated to establish principles with respect to reparations for victims including restitution, compensation or rehabilitation,[37] and through the Trust Fund for Victims (TFV) has approved a

---

[36] Fritz Kalshoven, 'State Responsibility for Warlike Acts of the Armed Forces: from Article 3 of Hague Convention IV of 1907 to Article 91 of Additional Protocol I of 1977 and Beyond' (1991) 40 *International and Comparative Law Quarterly* 827; *Jurisdictional Immunities of the State (Germany v Italy)*, 3 February 2012, 2012 ICJ Rep. Judge Cançado Trindade, dissenting opinion, paras 66–68; Tokyo Women's Tribunal, Case No PT-2000-1-T, Judgment, para 1052. See essay 15 'Strategic Practices: "Doing Our Own Thing"'.

[37] Rome Statute of the ICC, 1998, art 75.

range of service-based collective reparations, including psychological support, medical care, schooling and university support, short and long-term training courses, and income generating activities.[38] But it cannot direct states to undertake the type of redistributive activities and structural changes that would disrupt the gender order to minimise the recurrence of conflict-related sexual and gender-based violence that is anticipated by transformative reparations. The Global Survivors Fund (GSF)[39] is filling an important gap by providing for the immediate reparative needs of survivors of conflict-related sexual violence and working with survivors for longer term development of comprehensive programmes but, as with the TFV, what it cannot deliver is structural transformation.

Neither ICL nor the GSF must be allowed to detract from the core principle of reparation: an obligation of the state under IHRL owed to those whose rights have been violated and that offers the possibility of transformed social and political structures. Reparations are additional to the state's obligations with respect to economic, social and cultural rights that are owed to all persons within its jurisdiction whether or not they are victims of violations. Reparations must be accorded in addition to any general social programmes. Conflating welfare assistance with reparations – as is often the case – poses the risk of weakening the international law doctrine of state responsibility that is at the core of the international legal order and rule of law.

III. TRANSFORMATIVE REPARATION TO BREAK THE CYCLE OF GENDER INJUSTICE

Those seeking reparation for the crimes of slavery and colonialism do so against two temporal registers: for the historical crimes perpetrated and for their contemporary discriminatory effects, structural and experienced, due to state failure to redress the original harms. Colonial and settler states tend to invoke the intertemporal rule to bar the former claim, and lack of causation to avoid the latter.[40] But even where these issues present no obstacle, siloed legal regimes, the lack of fora through which claims can be adjudicated, procedural requirements, and the doctrine of state immunity[41] create further legal barriers for victims seeking gender justice. In addition to these legal obstacles, women find themselves unable to access justice by the gendered state. Illustrative are the experiences of the women who were subjected to sexual slavery by the Japanese military during World War II in the Asia-Pacific region – the so-called 'comfort women'.[42] The very fact that states continue to prevent them from claiming their right to reparation forecloses the opportunity to address and dismantle the

---

[38] eg *Prosecutor v Thomas Lubanga Dyilo*, 9th Decision on the TFV's administrative decisions on applications for reparations and additional matters, ICC-01/04-01/06, 22 September 2022 (public redacted version) para 13.

[39] The GSF is the initiative of Nobel Laureates Dr Denis Mukwege and Nadia Murad; launched in 2019, it promotes a survivor-centred approach to reparative treatment.

[40] The intertemporal rule mandates that a state can only be held responsible for a breach on the basis of the laws in effect at the relevant time. Law also demands that cause of harm and its effect be proximate for there to be legal responsibility.

[41] See essay 9 'Silence as an Obstacle to Gendered Peace and Equality'.

[42] See essay 15 'Strategic Practices: "Doing Our Own Thing"'; see also https://wam-peace.org/en/.

structural inequalities – gender and race, among other axes of discrimination – that founded the programme of sexual slavery run by Japan's military and political elites, grounded in the logic of settler colonialism.[43]

The brutality and scale of Japan's wartime slavery system, rooted in sexism, misogyny, racial and imperial superiority, deeply enfolded within the patriarchal and militarised state structure is well documented. What is buried is the abject failure by the International Military Tribunal for the Far East to charge any individual for crimes perpetrated against the estimated 200,000 women from Burma, Indonesia, China, Japan, Korea, Taiwan, the Philippines, and Timor Leste[44] as indicative of the gendered and raced views prevalent among those who were purportedly acting to secure *international* justice. There were no legal impediments,[45] and masculine forms of slave labour were prosecuted.[46] The women were erased at the intersection of gender and race.

Over the years, the women have continued to struggle for reparation and against intersectional erasure by Japan and by their own states that, for different reasons, have sought to forget the past. For example, in 1998, Malaya Lolas,[47] a collective established by Filipina survivors of the Japanese 'comfort stations', requested the Philippines Government to assist in filing a claim for reparation against Japan but, after some delay, were notified that pursuant to the 1951 Treaty of Peace and 1956 Reparations Agreement with Japan – neither of which had taken account of the crimes perpetrated against the women – demands for further reparations had been waived by the state.[48] In 2004 Malaya Lolas petitioned the Supreme Court to find the waiver void as contrary to the *erga omnes* obligation not to provide immunity for crimes against humanity, including sexual slavery. In 2010, the Court rejected the petition on the grounds that such matters were the exclusive prerogative of the executive branch. In 2016 Malaya Lolas submitted individual complaints to a number of UN special procedures and in 2018, in response to requests for further information by three UN Special Rapporteurs, the Philippines Government reiterated that the Reparations Agreement with Japan foreclosed any discussions. In 2019, Malaya Lolas submitted a communication to the CEDAW Committee arguing that the Philippines had violated CEDAW, articles 1 and 2(b) and (c). In 2023, the Committee found the Philippines Government had breached its treaty obligations by failing to address the institutionalised system of wartime sexual slavery and its consequences for victim/survivors for nearly four decades.[49] The women had received inadequate social support, reparation, benefits and recognition commensurate with the harms they suffered as survivors while, in contrast, Filipino war veterans – predominantly male – had been accorded special treatment, including educational and healthcare benefits, old age, disability and death pensions.

---

[43] Critics of European settler colonialism are often blind to the politics of settler colonialism by non-Europeans: Lachlan McNamee, 'Settler Colonialism', https://aeon.co/essays, 5 October 2023.
[44] See essay 15 'Strategic Practices: "Doing Our Own Thing"'.
[45] As explained by the judges of the Tokyo Women's Tribunal (n 36) paras 511–34.
[46] Patricia Viseur Sellers, 'Wartime Female Slavery: Enslavement' (2011) 44 *Cornell International Law Journal* 115.
[47] Literal meaning 'free grandmothers'.
[48] The Reparations Agreement made no mention of the crimes perpetrated against the women.
[49] *Natalie Alfronzo et al v The Philippines* CEDAW/C/84/D/155/2020, 8 March 2023.

The Committee issued two sets of recommendations, the first addressing the women's needs – including 'an official apology ... for the continuous discrimination that they have suffered' – and the second directed to societal transformation. The latter include: to establish an effective nationwide reparation scheme to provide all forms of redress to victims of war crimes; to remove restrictive and discriminatory legal and policy provisions relating to redress for civilian victims of war; to establish a state-sanctioned fund to provide compensation and other forms of reparation; to create a memorial to commemorate the suffering inflicted and to honour the women's struggle for justice; and to:

> mainstream in the curricula of all academic institutions, including in secondary and university education, the history of Filipina victims/survivors of wartime sexual slavery, as remembrance is critical to a sensitive understanding of the history of human rights violations endured by these women, to emphasize the importance of advancing human rights, and to avoid recurrence.[50]

If implemented, CEDAW's recommendations have the potential not only to make a real difference to the women's lives in practical terms and in terms of their self-esteem[51] but also to occasion structural change with far-reaching societal effects across the Philippines. But it is also a decision that reaches beyond the Philippines' borders, with ramifications for all states parties to CEDAW that have hitherto done too little to provide effective and non-discriminatory reparations to survivors of sexual slavery dating back nearly a century. Separately, the CEDAW Committee has repeatedly pressed Japan to provide full and effective redress and reparation, including compensation, satisfaction, official apologies, and rehabilitative services to all those women brutalised under its wartime 'comfort station' programmes.[52] Importantly, the Committee considers that it is not precluded *ratione temporis* from addressing the matter in that the serious violations have an ongoing effect on the victim/survivors, compounded by the continued lack of effective remedy.

IV. ADVANCING GENDERED PEACE THROUGH REPARATIONS

The past is never past.[53] Death does not extinguish the cascading effects of some harms that are passed on inter-generationally. As powerfully put by Carol McBride of the Native Women's Association of Canada (NWAC) on the 'national day set aside for honouring the victims and survivors of the Indian residential schools':

> for Indigenous people – for us, as Indigenous women, girls, Two-spirit, transgender and gender diverse people – the residential schools are not just a thing of the past. They are very much a part of our present. Those are not just the bodies of children being discovered on the sites of the former schools. They could be the auntie or uncle who was taken as a

---

[50] ibid para 11.
[51] SR on promotion of truth (n 28) paras 37–40.
[52] CEDAW Committee, Concluding observations on the combined seventh and eighth periodic reports of Japan, CEDAW/C/JPN/CO/7-8, 10 March 2016, paras 28–29.
[53] Karen Barad, *Meeting the Universe Halfway: Quantum Physics and the Entanglement of Matter and Meaning* (Duke University Press, 2007) ix.

child and never returned home. They could be the response to the question that followed our grieving parents and grandparents to their graves. The people who were damaged by the abuses of those schools still walk among us. Their wounds have been passed on to their children and grandchildren. This is multi-generational harm.[54]

Contemporary structural injustices – gendered, raced, intersectional – cannot be adequately addressed until such time that states take responsibility for historical injustices as a step towards dismantling the odious, predatory and extractivist relationships of power to break the cycle of oppression, discrimination, and violence. As the CEDAW Committee emphasises in the context of Indigenous women and girls:

> [i]t is critical for States parties to address the consequences of historic injustices and to provide support and reparations to the affected communities as part of the process of ensuring justice, reconciliation and the building of societies free from discrimination and gender-based violence against Indigenous women and girls.[55]

The Committee's call for reparations comes amidst a growing global movement for reparation for historic injustices such as slavery, the slave trade and the violence of colonialism.[56]

States acknowledge that past injustices, when left unaddressed, can have continuing and cascading effects, both individual and societal. For example, the 2001 Durban Declaration and Programme of Action[57] recognises that Africans and people of African descent, people of Asian descent and Indigenous Peoples were victims of slavery and colonialism and that those histories are sources of the racism, racial discrimination, xenophobia and related intolerance that they experience today.[58] The link between the past and contemporary forms of discrimination is also acknowledged in the preamble to the 2007 UN Declaration on the Rights of Indigenous Peoples (UNDRIP).[59] While the Durban Declaration names slavery and the slave

---

[54] Statement by NWAC President Carol McBride on National Day for Truth and Reconciliation, 29 September 2023.

[55] CEDAW Committee, General Recommendation No 39 on the rights of Indigenous women and girls, CEDAW/C/GC/39, 31 October 2022, para 12.

[56] OHCHR, Promotion and protection of the human rights and fundamental freedoms of Africans and of people of African descent against excessive use of force and other human rights violations by law enforcement officers, A/HRC/47/53, para 3: recognising that '[t]he murder of George Floyd on 25 May 2020 … the mass protests that ensued … represent a seminal point in the fight against racism' and considering 'the long-overdue need to confront the legacies of enslavement, the transatlantic trade in enslaved Africans and colonialism and to seek reparatory justice': Jacqueline Bhabha et al, *Time for Reparations: A Global Perspective* (University of Philadelphia Press, 2021).

[57] Report of the World Conference against Racism, Racial Discrimination, Xenophobia and Related Intolerance, Durban, South Africa, 2001. The Declaration was adopted by 134 states in favour, two against (US, Israel) and two abstentions (Australia, Canada). Since its adoption, several states, including 'those most implicated by its analysis of the historical roots of racism' signalled their 'intent to abandon the Durban process' and boycotted the UN's twentieth anniversary commemoration. These states are 'among some of the greatest beneficiaries of colonialism, slavery and the transatlantic slave trade': SR on contemporary forms of racism, racial discrimination, xenophobia and related intolerance, Twentieth anniversary of the Durban Declaration, A/76/434, 22 October 2021, para 12.

[58] ibid paras 13–14. The link between historic enslavement and contemporary racism is recognised in CERD Committee, General Comment No 34, Racial discrimination against people of African descent, CERD/C/GC/34, 30 September 2011.

[59] UNGAR, 61/295, 2 October 2007, preamble: Indigenous Peoples have 'suffered from historic injustices as a result of, inter alia, their colonization and dispossession of their lands, territories and resources,

trade as crimes against humanity, it is silent on reparations, the outcome of a political compromise.⁶⁰ UNDRIP is also silent on reparations.⁶¹ Neither Declaration describes colonialism as a crime against humanity.

The UK, for one, has made its position unambiguous. In a 2022 statement elaborating on its vote against a HRC resolution seeking concrete action against racism, its spokesperson asserted that states are not required 'to make reparations for the slave trade and colonialism, which … were not, at that time, violations of international law'.⁶² Some states have acknowledged their colonial histories (albeit begrudgingly) but there is resistance to accepting *legal* responsibility, including for colonial crimes perpetrated within living memory, with the passage of time typically raised as a bar to avoid state responsibility, as with the UK.⁶³ Apologies, when tendered, have been guarded to avoid legal consequences,⁶⁴ as with Japan. And truth commissions, while serving an important function, are often limited to making recommendations that are all too rarely implemented, as with Canada.⁶⁵ That international law provides

---

thus preventing them from exercising, in particular, their right to development in accordance with their own needs and interests'. UNDRIP was adopted by 144 states in favour and 4 against (Australia, Canada, New Zealand, US) and 11 abstentions. Since then, states opposing it have reversed their position.

⁶⁰ Gay McDougall, 'The World Conference against Racism: Through a Wider Lens' (2002) 26 *The Fletcher Forum of World Affairs* 135, 138. The outcome document provided the foundation for the Caribbean Community (CARICOM) *Ten-Point Plan for Reparatory Justice* (2014).

⁶¹ Report of the Expert Mechanism on the Rights of Indigenous People, 2 September 2019, A/HRC/EMRIP/2019/3/Rev.1 para 71: UNDRIP should be 'the main framework for recognition, reparation and reconciliation' and that 'recognition of indigenous peoples, as well as reparation and reconciliation relating to past and current injustices, are essential elements for the effective implementation of the Declaration'.

⁶² Statement by UK Human Rights Ambassador to the UN Human Rights Council, 7 October 2022, delivered prior to voting against HRC Resolution 51/32, From rhetoric to reality: a global call for concrete action against racism, racial discrimination, xenophobia and related intolerance.

⁶³ In *Mutua and others v FCO* [2012] EWHC 2678 (QB), the UK government did not dispute the systematic abuse and torture inflicted during the Mau Mau Uprising (1952–1963) in Kenya by British colonial officials, but argued that the case was time barred, that too much time had elapsed since the events and a fair trial was no longer possible. The Court's rejection of these arguments led to a public apology by the Government, the construction of a permanent memorial commemorating the victims of colonialism, and compensation. Another case brought by Kenyans for large-scale abuse perpetrated during the Kenyan Emergency of that period was dismissed by another court on the grounds that it would not be 'equitable' to lift the limitation period given the passage of time: *Kimathi and others v FCO* [2018] EWHC 2066 (QB). In *Keyu and others v FCO* [2015] UKSC 69, the court dismissed an appeal to order a public inquiry into the 1948 Batang Kali massacre (then under British Colonial administration) because 'it had been brought too late'. In *Hacienda Brasil Verde Workers v Brazil*, IACtHR, (Preliminary objections, merits, reparations and costs) 20 October 2016, para 508 (11) the Court ordered Brazil to adopt measures precluding the applicability of limitation periods to the international crime of slavery. The Rome Statute of the ICC, art 29 provides that crimes within the Court's jurisdiction 'shall not be subject to any statute of limitations'.

⁶⁴ In Canada in July 2022, Pope Francis delivered a carefully worded 'apology' to the First Nations, Inuit, and Métis people in which he avoided any mention of the sexual abuse rampant in Canada's Catholic-run Indian Residential Schools and placed blame for wrongdoings on individuals. The institutional complicity of the Catholic church in Canada's policy of removing children from their families, communities and Nations was condemned as 'cultural genocide' by the Truth and Reconciliation Commission of Canada which identified 94 'Calls to Action', including a Papal Apology; 'Honouring the Truth, Reconciling for the Future' 2015: https://nctr.ca/about/history-of-the-trc/trc-website/.

⁶⁵ eg seven years after Canada's Truth and Reconciliation Commission identified 94 Calls to Action, only 13 Calls had been completed: 'Calls to Action Accountability: A 2022 Status Update on Reconciliation' (Yellowhead Institute, December, 2022). The same pattern of delay and non-implementation is seen in respect of the 231 Calls for Justice identified by Canada's National Inquiry into missing and murdered Indigenous women and girls. *Reclaiming Power and Place: The Final Report of the National Inquiry into Missing and Murdered Indigenous Women and Girls* (2019) was welcomed by women's groups as providing

the legal tools to deny justice for historical wrongs on the basis that the causal link between the past and present is too tenuous[66] or that the act in question was not prohibited at the material time[67] has led to calls for its decolonisation.[68] Third World Approaches to International Law (TWAIL) scholarship,[69] which locates international law's origins in the histories of the oppressed and in the colonial encounter, has long sought to 'unearth the perversions of Eurocentrism that pervade international law'[70] and impede justice.[71] For some, this entails excavating alternative histories outside Europe that have hitherto been suppressed, to uncover (an)other account(s) of international law, for example, to reveal that from its inception in around 1450, transatlantic chattel slavery was not only strongly resisted but widely condemned by those outside of Europe.[72] Thus, long before the adoption of the 1926 International Convention to Suppress the Slave Trade and Slavery and certainly by the early nineteenth century, slavery was condemned under customary international law.[73]

These interventions are necessary.[74] But in that they seek 'international law's redemption within itself', they leave undisturbed international law's structures and doctrines, founded on a European onto-epistemology that treats slavery and colonialism as events rather than as the structures of imperialism that shape the global order.

---

the blueprint for securing transformative change. NWAC observed that implementing the calls would 'right past wrongs' and help build 'a society within which First Nations, Inuit, and Metis families can raise their children with the same safety, security, and human rights that non-Indigenous families do, along with full respect for their rights': 'Reparations and Remembrance in Canada for Indigenous Women, Girls and Gender-Diverse Persons' 20 April 2020, 7. Three years on, the government has failed to make meaningful progress: NWAC report, 1 June 2023, https://nwac.ca/special-reports/score-card-documents.

[66] On identifying the indicia of causality, see Philippe Sands, 'Contemporary Institutionalized Racism as a Breach of International Human Rights Norms' in Justine N Stefanelli and Erin Lovall (eds), *Reparations under International Law for Enslavement of African Persons in the Americas and the Caribbean* (American Society of International Law, 2022) 146, 155. The victim/wrongdoer binary that structures law works against the idea of intergenerational harm.

[67] Statement by UK Human Rights Ambassador (n 62). European states repeatedly invoke the intertemporal rule in judicial processes: SR on the promotion of truth, 'Transitional justice measures and addressing the legacy of gross violations of human rights and international humanitarian law committed in colonial contexts', A/76/180, 19 July 2021, paras 26–28.

[68] SR on contemporary forms of racism, racial discrimination, xenophobia and related intolerance, 'Reparations for racial discrimination rooted in slavery and colonialism', A/74/321, 21 August 2019 para 58.

[69] For TWAIL scholarship see Deborah Z Cass, 'Navigating the New Stream: Recent Critical Scholarship in International Law' in Gerry Simpson (ed), *The Nature of International Law* (Routledge, 2001).

[70] Mohsen al Attar and Shaimaa Abdelkarim, 'Decolonising the Curriculum in International Law: Entrapments in Praxis and Critical Thought' (2023) 34 *Law and Critique* 41, 43.

[71] Vasuki Nesiah, 'Crimes against Humanity: Racialised Subjects and Deracialized Histories' in Immi Tallgren and Thomas Skouteris (eds), *The New Histories of International Criminal Law: Retrials* (Oxford University Press, 2019) 167.

[72] Patrick Robinson, 'The Ascertainment of a Rule of International Law Condemning Transatlantic Chattel Slavery' in Justine N Stefanelli and Erin Lovall (eds) (n 66) 171.

[73] The 1814 Treaty of Ghent (Great Britain and US) and the 1815 Vienna Declaration recognised the principle of humanity which called for the respect of the inherent dignity and personhood of all human beings: Patrick Robinson, Introduction to the Report on Reparations for Transatlantic Chattel Slavery in the Americas and Caribbean (American Society of International Law, 8 June 2023).

[74] E Tendayi Achiume and Gay McDougall, 'Anti-Racism at the United Nations' (2023) 117 *AJIL Unbound* 82, 87: 'for international lawyers and legal scholars invested in challenging racial domination in myriad forms, the work is and always has been to remain clear-eyed about how our very discipline is the vehicle though which such domination is codified, while making the most of any and all opportunities to short-circuit this domination'.

We also wonder whether decolonising international law paradoxically preserves the logic of imperialism, given a tendency among advocates to focus primarily on race (reproducing the silos of European colonialism) and pay inadequate attention to the gendered aspects and consequences of slavery and colonialism that perpetuate intersectional inequalities faced by women and girls and non-binary people.[75] Decolonising our thinking cannot be achieved without seeing the operation of patriarchy's gender systems.[76] Might provincialising international law offer a more fruitful avenue to advance gender and racial justice?

Underpinning disagreements over reparations for historical injustices is the broader question over whose time and life matter, and what harms merit reparation.[77] Human rights mechanisms are chipping away – where they can – through memorialisation and education as means of satisfaction, exemplified by CEDAW's decision in the *Malaya Lolas* case.[78] Memorialisation has garnered comparatively little attention from international lawyers, who typically treat it as external to law. Memorialisation can give voice/presence to victims of historical injustices, bonding the past with the present and future and thereby contributing to the prevention of the recurrence of rights violations and assisting in 'building a culture of peace'.[79] Official decisions involving what and who merits remembrance – and how – are never neutral: official memorialisation projects continue to privilege pasts that exclude the oppressed and marginalised, reinforcing gendered and racialised norms and hierarchies.[80] Public commemorations, memorials and monuments reproduce patriarchal histories that focus on the lives and deaths of men – often militarised – and on male experiences, while commemorations and memorials dedicated to women's struggles for justice are rare.[81] CEDAW's recommendation 'to create a memorial to commemorate the suffering inflicted and honour [the women's] struggle for justice'[82] surfaces patriarchy's oppression and violence, not in one particular place and not at one singular moment in time, but in all places, past and present. In the absence of state action, civil society has taken direct action both to take down and set up memorials in public spaces. Thus, the *Statue of Peace*, funded, created, and erected by Korean women activists, faces the Japanese embassy in Seoul and is the site of weekly gatherings.[83] It stands as a reminder of legal responsibilities avoided and memories of pasts suppressed by powerholders, who insist on putting the past behind, a position that is only accorded

---

[75] eg Durban Declaration and Programme of Action adopts the Rome Statute definition of gender; See essay 2 'Gender'.

[76] Patricia Viseur Sellers, 'Sexualized Practices and Institutions of the Slave Trade and Slavery' in Justine N Stefanelli and Erin Lovall (eds) (n 66) 63.

[77] eg states have introduced reparation programmes for victims of terrorism, but not necessarily for victims of sexual and gender-based crimes.

[78] Basic Principles and Guidelines (n 9) para 22 lists 'commemorations and tributes to the victims' and an accurate account of the violations that occurred in legal training and 'in educational materials at all levels'.

[79] SR promotion of truth, 'Memorialization processes in the context of serious violations of human rights and international humanitarian law: the fifth pillar of transitional justice', A/HRC/45/45, 9 July 2020, para 21.

[80] See essay 9 'Silence as an Obstacle to Gendered Peace and Equality'.

[81] The Monument to the Women of World War II in Whitehall, London was not erected until 2005; the Cenotaph was opened in 1920.

[82] *Natalie Alfronzo et al v The Philippines* (n 49) para 11(4).

[83] See essay 12 'Introduction to Strategic Practices'.

to the privileged. Japan has unsuccessfully demanded its removal.[84] Over time, replicas of the statue have appeared across the world, injecting it with a broader symbolic meaning for a new generation of women activists, inspiring them to continue in the fight for gender and racial justice and peace denied by states.

Figure 5 Peace Statue, Memorialising the 'Comfort Women' (YunHo Lee, 2015)

Source: https://www.flickr.com/photos/137346712@N07/22940589530/in/photolist-6Ad48H-7eQ8oy-ArMJem-6AhaQy-AXbw2G-ArUCbe-oJUKoJ-yWuowF-73xhSD-78SkSN/.

For the most part, states have failed to take seriously their duty to preserve memory and, not unexpectedly, of their own histories of oppression.[85] This responsibility is closely interlinked to the collective right to truth,[86] both of which are necessary to advancing inter-personal and inter-state peace. The inclusion of the histories of the struggles for gender and racial justice in mainstream education texts is foundational to instilling in all societies the importance of advancing human rights for all as a basis for peace. The decisions and reports of international human rights bodies such as CEDAW, the judgments of courts and tribunals, the reports of national and international truth commissions are among just some of the growing body of

---

[84] Japan has blocked South Korea's efforts to instigate documents appertaining to the 'comfort women' into UNESCO's Memory of the World Register.

[85] Updated set of principles for the protection and promotion of human rights through action to combat impunity, E/CN.4/2005/102/Add.1, 8 February 2005. Principle 3: The Duty to Preserve Memory: 'A people's knowledge of the history of its oppression is part of its heritage and, as such, must be ensured by appropriate measures in fulfilment of the State's duty to preserve archives and other evidence concerning violations of human rights and humanitarian law and to facilitate knowledge of those violations. Such measures shall be aimed at preserving the collective memory from extinction and, in particular, at guarding against the development of revisionist and negationist arguments.'

[86] Basic Principles and Guidelines (n 9) para 22(b). See essay 12 'Introduction to Strategic Practices'; *Bámaca-Velásquez v Guatemala* (Reparations) IACtHR 22 February 2002, Series C No 91, para 77: 'preventive measures ... begin by revealing and recognizing the atrocities of the past ... Society has the right to know the truth regarding such crimes, so as to be capable of preventing them in the future'. The IACtHR has also ordered that the results of investigations be publicly disclosed, so that society learns the truth: *Caracazo v Venezuela* (Reparations) IACtHR, 29 August 2002, Series C No 95, para 118.

knowledge that, if integrated into mainstream education texts, have the potential to transform societies.

The reality of the weakness of implementation of international legal norms – even non-compliance with court orders – remains, thereby undermining their effectiveness in achieving the changes sought. Victims and survivors may look outside the law for restorative justice. They may, for instance, draw strength from the inventiveness and creativity of those who use art forms – literature, music, tapestry and quilt making,[87] street art,[88] dance, puppetry, acting, museum exhibits[89] and many others – to recount and memorialise what has occurred, to depict the impact of events on populations and to offer ways forward. Art forms can provide graphic descriptions of atrocities, render visible the contributions of those whose contributions have been lost in the mists of time, or who have been deliberately marginalised out of existence,[90] and provide expressions of hope. Participating in artistic ventures can promote individual and community wellbeing, enrich understandings of peace and of different ways of being. They are threatened by the closing space for civil society in many jurisdictions that must be resisted. While recognising the importance of alternative forms of reparation, we nonetheless must not lose sight of the fact that, just as legal framing presents a particular account of events, so too do artistic portrayals that are crafted from a particular perspective and with a specific objective in mind. We must acknowledge the complexities inherent in attempts at constructing narratives in whatever form in pursuit of transformative justice.[91]

---

[87] As part of the United Kingdom Research and Innovation Global Challenges Research Fund-funded Hub on Gender Justice and Security, Christine visited the newly opened Museum in Mampuján, Colombia where, as part of the reparations programme, women have produced an array of tapestry and quilt work depicting what had occurred in their village during the conflict and their current lives. Women described the restorative impact of designing and sewing these pieces of artwork.
[88] Bill Rolston and Sofi Ospina, 'Picturing Peace: Murals and Memory in Colombia' (2017) 58 *Race and Class* 23 (street art in Colombia speaking to the protracted violent political conflict and the emerging peace process, articulating the memory of violence and representing victims' demands for acknowledgment, reparation and justice).
[89] Kazuyo Yamane and Ikuro Anzai, *Museums for Peace Worldwide* (International Network of Museums for Peace, 2020). We have both worked with the Women's Active Museum on War and Peace, Tokyo, which commemorates the 'Comfort Women'.
[90] Fareda Banda, *African Migration Human Rights and Literature* (Hart Publishing, 2020) 28–29.
[91] ibid.

19
Searching for Peace in Teaching International Law[1]

I. INTRODUCTION

PEACE WAS ONE of the three objectives of the four World Conferences on Women held between 1975 and 1995[2] and was understood as inextricably linked with the other two objectives of equality and development.[3] A reiterated strategy for the attainment of peace was education and training for peace, including education against violence in personal relationships and social interactions,[4] and for fostering a 'culture of peace'.[5] Peace education was deemed desirable 'for all members of society' as part of 'formal and informal education processes'.[6] This focus on education for and about peace[7] led us to question why 'peace' is not a subject generally found in university law school curricula.[8] In some countries, for instance Japan, peace is taught within the context of constitutional law. In many common law jurisdictions, including the UK, the concept of peace and how it relates to the law and justice is not taught in public law modules. Yet if law is about constraining and regulating violence, peace should be integral to all legal education.

Public international law (PIL) – the legal regime governing state behaviour – might be an appropriate place for peace education, given the state's monopoly on the use

---

[1] Keina Yoshida is a co-author of this essay, which was first presented at a workshop on Gendering Peace Education at the LSE Centre for WPS, October 2021 under the auspices of the ERC advanced grant on Gendered Peace.

[2] See essay 5 'Peace in the UN Decade for Women' and essay 6 'Revisiting the Past: Peace at Beijing and Beyond'.

[3] See essay 5 'Peace in the UN Decade for Women'.

[4] 'Include in educational programmes and methodologies a special emphasis on education against violence particularly violence in relationships between women and men': Programme of Action for the Second Half of the United Nations Decade for Women: Equality, Development and Peace, Copenhagen, 1980, para 168.

[5] 'Consider establishing educational programmes for girls and boys to foster a culture of peace, focusing on conflict resolution by nonviolent means and the promotion of tolerance': Platform for Action, Beijing, 1995 (Beijing PFA) para 146(d).

[6] Forward-Looking Strategies for the advancement of women for the years 1996–2000, Nairobi, 1985, paras 255–56.

[7] UNGAR 71/189, 19 December 2016, Declaration on the Right to Peace: 'International and national institutions of education for peace shall be promoted'.

[8] There are exceptions. The University of Oslo has run courses on the right to peace and international law and peace.

of violence[9] and its stated purpose 'to maintain international peace and security'.[10] University PIL courses typically follow the UN Charter's linkage between peace and security, addressing the prohibition of the use of force in international relations and the collective security system,[11] thereby denoting peace as negative peace – the absence of war.[12] The general course may be supplemented with elective offerings across a range of topics including the conduct of international and non-international armed conflict (international humanitarian law (IHL)), international criminal law, dispute resolution and human rights law. Taken together, these suggest various components of a wider understanding of peace than solely absence of conflict and national security – accountability for the commission of war crimes, crimes against humanity and genocide, economic and social justice, guarantees of economic, social, cultural, civil and political rights and the rule of law, but the study of peace as a stand-alone concept is largely absent from international law teaching.

This led us to consider a further question: given the long history of women's peace activism and the centrality of peace for women's advancement, as recognised by its inclusion as one of three objectives of the UN Decade for Women, its continuation (at least in the slogan[13]) for the 1995 Beijing Women's Conference and its reiteration in the Security Council's agenda on women, peace and security (WPS), should it be included in courses on women's human rights or gender and human rights?[14] But if peace were to be included in such courses, would this marginalise it as a 'women's' or 'gender' issue and contribute to gender stereotyping by portraying women as passive and 'peace-loving' and men as warlike, violent and as protectors against the violence of other men?[15] We decided to explore these questions through some informal discussions with colleagues engaged in teaching PIL, or some designation of women or gender and human rights.

We reflect here on these discussions on the place of peace pedagogy in PIL and associated subjects. We first consider the public role of teachers of international law and the place of peace within the discipline, more specifically in human rights law.[16] We outline the basis of our discussions with colleagues and expand on our findings through three themes: the lack of peace education within PIL and human rights teaching; the ambiguities which come from thinking about peace within the framework of international law; and the teaching of peace outside of the law school context in

---

[9] Anthony Giddens, *The Modern State and Violence* (Polity Press, 1985): the state as a 'bordered power container'.
[10] UN Charter, 1945, art 1.
[11] ibid art 2(4) and chapter VII.
[12] 'This coupling [international peace and security] signals an understanding of peace as reliant on (state) security': Dianne Otto, 'Queerly Troubling International Law's Vision of "Peace"' (2022) 116 *AJIL Unbound* 22.
[13] See essay 6 'Revisiting the Past: Peace at Beijing and Beyond' – subsuming of peace into women and armed conflict.
[14] Beijing PFA (n 5), para 69: 'Education is a human right and an essential tool for achieving the goals of equality, development and peace.'
[15] The SC WPS resolutions reinforce these stereotypes: Christine Chinkin, *Women, Peace and Security and International Law* (Cambridge University Press, 2022) 31.
[16] We did not have similar discussions with teachers of IHL, as we considered that regime to be primarily about minimising the harms of conflict rather than seeking peace.

what has been termed 'compensatory' legal education. We reflect on why teaching peace within legal education matters or should matter. This essay aims to contribute to ongoing reflective scholarship and practice in international legal pedagogy and to question the discipline's assumption of violence as 'normal'[17] and its marginalisation of peace.

II. THE ROLE OF TEACHERS OF PUBLIC INTERNATIONAL LAW

Gerry Simpson identified what he described as a 'malaise' among PIL teachers which results from their fear of being consigned to the periphery of a law department.[18] PIL is a compulsory undergraduate[19] subject in very few law schools and is not a prerequisite for professional qualification. It must therefore compete with other optional subjects that are seen by many students as providing a more solid grounding for globalised legal practice or with commercial/profitable take up, for instance company law, market transactions, tax, property or intellectual property law. In an era when universities are increasingly required to be entrepreneurial and compete globally, greater focus is directed toward private rather than public international law.[20] When a general PIL course is offered, its expanded scope (foundational issues – sources, sovereignty, jurisdiction etc – as well as specialist regimes – refugee law, law of the sea, dispute settlement, criminal law etc) curtails the space for human rights and this is even more the case for a concept such as 'peace'. Universities are essentially conservative institutions[21] and international law may be regarded as a radical deviation from conventional, national law.[22] When international human rights law is available as a distinct module, there are questions about its scope and how it is to be presented: is it about domestic law (constitutional law, civil liberties, in the UK the Human Rights Act 1998) or as a special regime of international law? If the latter, should it be primarily about the UN system or an applicable regional system? And is there any place

---

[17] *cf* Dianne Otto's description of the importance of 'queering' international law, that it involves a 'fundamental critique of its regimes of the normal that, together, regulate our relations with each other and the planet': Dianne Otto (n 12).

[18] Gerry Simpson, 'On the Magic Mountain: Teaching Public International Law' (1999) 10 *European Journal of International Law* 70.

[19] It is problematic to write generally about the level of legal education as this varies across jurisdictions: for instance, law is generally an undergraduate degree course (LLB) in the UK and other law schools following the UK model; it is a graduate course in the US (JD); and part of a joint honours degree in many Australian universities. Many law schools offer taught postgraduate degrees (LLM), and supervised doctorates (PhD; SJD) and various combinations of taught courses and thesis writing.

[20] Vasuki Nesiah, 'A Flat Earth for Lawyers without Borders? Rethinking Current Approaches to the Globalization of Legal Education' (2013) 5 *Drexel Law Review* 371, 381.

[21] 'As state and market subsidised sites of knowledge production and transfer, universities are conservative in character, beginning and ending with their law faculties': Mohsen Al Attar and Shaimaa Abdelkarim, 'Decolonising the Curriculum in International Law: Entrapments in Praxis and Critical Thought' (2021) 34 *Law and Critique* 41, 42.

[22] Research and publication on gender issues may be viewed as outside any branch of law, including international law: Joseph Weiler, 'The Strange Case of Dr Ivana Radačić', *EJIL Talk*, 5 April 2013. Dr Radačić had been denied advancement in the University of Zagreb Law Faculty despite a long publication record on, inter alia, women's human rights, sex discrimination and the rape jurisprudence of the European Court of Human Rights.

for what are now the many specialisms within human rights law – children's rights, minority rights, rights of indigenous persons, disability rights, rights of refugees and internally displaced persons, women's rights, LGBTQI rights etc? A general human rights module is unlikely to be able to accord more than a couple of lectures or seminars to any of these of these specific regimes. In the case of women's human rights there might be mention of CEDAW and perhaps the treaties and jurisprudence on violence against women and how it has come to be understood as a matter of human rights, but there is likely to be scope for little else.

There has been a trend among PIL teachers to reflexivity, to consider the 'how and why' of their work[23] as well as their public role.[24] Some international lawyers have taken a very visible stance in challenging, for instance, state torture and state failure to comply with international obligations.[25] Many of us shared the belief that we could not keep silent about the illegality under international law of the invasion and occupation of Iraq in 2003 by the self-designated coalition of the willing,[26] Russia's aggression against Ukraine in 2022 and Israel's war against Palestine in 2023.[27] Yet in condemning illegal acts of force, there has been ambivalence about identifying the pre-existing conditions as violating peace. There has, for instance, been a tendency to represent peace as ending in Ukraine on 24 February 2022 without exploring the implications of that position – that it reinforces the limited definition of peace as absence of overt conflict while discounting other events since the collapse of the USSR, including the annexation of Crimea, occupation of Eastern areas of the country and the Minsk Agreements (2014 and 2015).[28]

Anthea Roberts expounds that 'what counts as international law depends in part on how the actors concerned construct their understandings of the field and pass them on to the next generation'.[29] She argues that international lawyers' vision of their field implicates and weighs upon 'which areas are significant, which actors are important, which principles are fundamental, which sources are relevant'. She and other scholars such as Gerry Simpson have sought to interrogate 'international lawyers' romantic

---

[23] Christine Schwöbel-Patel perceives a shift in the literature on teaching in international law from 1990 that reflects changes in the discipline from being primarily of concern to foreign ministries to one that has expanded its reach to 'global universities, a global knowledge economy, and a much-debated juridification of international relations': 'Teaching International Law' in *Oxford Bibliographies*, 24 February 2021.

[24] eg ILA, Committee on Teaching of International Law, Final Report, in *Report of the 74th Conference, The Hague, 2010*; George Rodrigo Bandeira Galindo, 'Some (Short) Reflections on (My) International Law Teaching Experience in Brazil' *Afronomics Law*, 19 September 2020; Antony Anghie and JR Robert Real, 'Teaching and Researching International Law in Asia (TRILA) Project' (NUS Centre for International Law, 2020 Report); Sari Kouvo, 'Teaching International Law in Times of Change and Crisis' (2021) 4 *Nordic Journal on Law and Society* 1.

[25] eg Philippe Sands, *Torture Team: Rumsfeld's Memo and the Betrayal of American Values* (St Martin's Press, 2008); Philippe Sands, *The Last Colony A Tale of Exile, Justice and Britain's Colonial Legacy* (Weidenfeld & Nicolson, 2022).

[26] Letter in *The Guardian*, 7 March 2003; for reflections on the public role of teachers of international law brought to a head by the letter see Matthew Craven et al, 'We Are Teachers of International Law' (2004) 17 *Leiden Journal of International Law* 363.

[27] UNGAR ES-11/1, 2 March 2022. See 'Ukraine and the International Order' (2022) 116 *AJIL Unbound* and the many statements made by international lawyers: 'Public Statement: Scholars Warn of Potential Genocide in Gaza' *TWAIL Review*, 17 October 2023.

[28] These same observations apply for all situations of occupation and dispossession, *de jure* and *de facto*.

[29] Anthea Roberts, *Is International Law International?* (Oxford University Press, 2017).

understanding of themselves and their field as universal and cosmopolitan'.[30] In light of this sentimentalism within international legal scholarship, it remains baffling that the concept of peace – so central to international relations – is largely absent from the terrain of international law.

In 2021, the British Institute of International and Comparative Law held a webinar series seeking to redress the position that 'reflections and collaborations on the practice of teaching international law remain relatively rare'.[31] Perhaps one reason is that teaching PIL is not easy or straightforward for those who wish to depart from the 'subject mainstream'.[32] As Mohsen Al Attar and Shaimaa Abdelkarim have reflected:

> When lecturing about international law, deciding *where to begin* is as difficult as deciding *where to end* and which *path to take*. Yet, despite international law's distinctiveness, its important and popularity grow, provoking the need for deeper engagement with the associated pedagogy.[33]

Scholars across disciplines have explained how Euro-centric colonial practices are foundational to academic studies and to the development of legal regimes such as international law,[34] creating 'ontological and teleological challenges'[35] for those seeking to teach international law from a critical perspective. Engagement with PIL pedagogy mirrors debates on decolonising the curriculum taking place in other disciplines, including but not limited to international relations, conflict studies, politics, governance and gender studies.[36] Al Attar and Abdelkarim explain that the 'deeper engagement' they call for manifests via the 'Decolonising the Curriculum' movement in law faculties around the world, drawing attention to the epistemic violence of international law and its pedagogy. They argue that '[t]o teach international law is to augment Eurocentrism within its praxis, and the alternatives are limited and unsatisfactory'.[37] They conclude that 'international law must be decolonised, but it cannot; its entire framework, even its legitimacy is derived from colonial ambitions and forms of governance'.[38] They offer restructuring knowledge production through

---

[30] Gerry Simpson, *The Sentimental Life of International Law: Literature, Language, and Longing in World Politics* (Oxford University Press, 2021).

[31] British Institute of International and Comparative Law, Teaching International Law Webinar Series, 2021. Christine Schwöbel-Patel (n 23): 'it is notable that there are only relatively few contemporary scholarly contributions dedicated specifically to the teaching of international law'.

[32] Rohini Sen, 'Teaching International Law in Asia: The Predicated Pedagogue' *Afronomics Law*, September 2020.

[33] Mohsen Al Attar and Shaimaa Abdelkarim (n 21) 41.

[34] eg Antony Anghie, *Imperialism, Sovereignty and the Making of International Law* (Cambridge University Press, 2012); Balakrishnan Rajagopal, *International Law from Below: Development, Social Movements and Third World Resistance* (Cambridge University Press, 2003).

[35] Rohini Sen (n 32).

[36] Maria Lugones, 'Toward a Decolonial Feminism' (2010) 25 *Hypatia* 742: 'Decolonising gender … is racialized, colonial, and capitalist heterosexualist gender oppression as a lived transformation of the social'.

[37] Mohsen Al Attar and Shaimaa Abdelkarim (n 21) 3; Rohini Sen (n 32): 'Eurocentric international law is institutionalised imperialism and scholars such as myself are its diminished objects … And within the academe, we [teachers of international law in the Global South] have to make a conscious choice to accept or reject this inheritance.'

[38] Mohsen Al Attar and Shaimaa Abdelkarim (n 21) 7.

what they term a 'process of disenchantment',[39] the consequence of which is that to teach peace through and with international law is at best incoherent. Other scholars have championed a Marxist approach to international law as a method for overcoming mainstream deficiencies; nonetheless Marxism too has serious shortcomings, not least for its gender-blindness.[40]

Alongside critiques highlighting the coloniality and ongoing structural violence of international law, feminist international lawyers have pointed to its roots in patriarchy.[41] Ntina Tzouvala has argued for the need 'to examine the teaching of international law in higher education institutions as an essential step for safeguarding the future of women in international law'.[42] Some gendered and feminist perspectives have entered into law school curricula, including the teaching of international law, although they remain largely the equivalent of a footnote to a standard international law text.[43]

A few academics have sought to foreground 'peace' rather than war and conflict in their teaching of PIL. Cecilia Bailliet, writing back in 2014, explained that:

> Upon reflecting that many of my lectures addressed the use of drones, extraordinary rendition, torture, targeted killing, etc., I became concerned about the type of education we were providing the next generation of lawyers. It occurred to me that although we were emphasizing the prohibition of certain actions, we were failing to comprehensively present non-violent approaches, which seek to prevent or resolve conflict and strengthen peace.[44]

Bailliet accordingly designed a new course entitled 'The Right to Peace' that covers a range of legal topics including non-discrimination, gender equality, fair trade, sustainable development, transitional justice, governance, democracy and disarmament. She recognises this as an unconventional way of teaching international law. In similar vein, Dianne Otto reflects on how peace education could be reimagined.[45] She queries what peace can mean to us and to our students in this 'time of endless wars', expanding arms sales, heavily securitised borders, environmental degradation and other horrors. How can we international lawyers understand and explain how the project of universal peace has failed so profoundly? Otto speculates on teaching PIL as a vision of peace, challenging scholars and teachers of international law to reimagine peace in the classroom, moving beyond international law's negative conception of

---

[39] ibid: 'Unlike decolonisation, disenchantment opens up a speculative space to those objects that do not fit within the dominant epistemology. Disenchantment forces us to be attentive to the complexities in decolonisation (like decoloniality) that are not merely pedagogical questions as the decolonising the curriculum movement frames them.'

[40] BS Chimni, 'An Outline of a Marxist Course on Public International Law' (2004) 17 *Leiden Journal of International Law* 1.

[41] Rohini Sen, 'Critical Pedagogy Symposium: The Emotional Labour of Teaching – A Feminist Critique of Teaching Critical International Law', *Opinio Juris*, 3 September 2020.

[42] Ntina Tzouvala, 'The Future of Feminist International Legal Scholarship in a Neoliberal University: Doing Law Differently' in Susan Harris Rimmer and Kate Ogg (eds), *Research Handbook on Feminist Engagement with International Law* (Elgar Publishing. 2019) 269.

[43] Hilary Charlesworth, 'Talking to Ourselves: Feminist Scholarship in International Law' in Sari Kouvo and Zoe Pearson (eds), *Feminist Perspectives on Contemporary International Law* (Hart Publishing, 2011).

[44] Cecilia M Bailliet, 'Untraditional Approaches to Law: Teaching the International Law of Peace' (2014) 12 *Santa Clara Journal of International Law* 1.

[45] 'Rethinking Peace Education in a Time of Endless War', Lecture as part of the FILPS project delivered at the LSE Centre for WPS, October 2019.

peace as a binary with war and the use of force. Drawing on Agamben, Otto argues that the 'bare peace' of the UN Charter treats most life – human and non-human – as expendable,[46] an approach that along with our gendered way of thinking must be destabilised in seeking a transformative approach to peace.

These reflections from critical international legal scholars suggest some ways in which international law could be taught from multiple perspectives to challenge its foundational violence and its complicity in relegating peace to militarised security. These engagements are underpinned by an understanding that how we teach PIL matters, because it affects how students understand and will practise and teach the subject in the future. In a 2019 lecture Joseph Weiler emphasised the importance of international law teaching in training the lawyers of tomorrow in the context of the neoliberalisation of universities.[47] In an environment of globalised legal education that has oriented the curriculum towards market priorities,[48] he recognised there are subjects 'which it is our responsibility [as academics] to teach'. Yet reflections on whether teaching in international law should encompass peace and the importance of peace to the training of tomorrow's lawyers remain largely absent.[49]

III. PEACE IN HUMAN RIGHTS COURSES?

But perhaps we should not be looking in PIL courses for the teaching of peace; maybe a more plausible home would be in a course on international human rights law, since 'recognition of the inherent dignity and of the equal and inalienable rights of all members of the human family is the foundation of freedom, justice and peace in the world'.[50] The linkage between peace and human rights is furthered through the assertion by the UN General Assembly (UNGA) that 'peace is a vital requirement for the promotion and protection of all human rights for all' and in turn that 'peace is promoted through the full enjoyment of all inalienable rights derived from the inherent dignity of all human beings'.[51] Perhaps surprisingly, since it was adopted in 1979 during the UN Decade for Women with its objectives of equality, development and peace, CEDAW has no provision relating to a right to peace. In contrast, peace is a significant theme in the Protocol to the African Charter on Human and Peoples' Rights on the Rights of Women in Africa (Maputo Protocol). It is extolled as an African value along with equality, freedom, dignity, justice, solidarity, and democracy. Article 10(1) sets out women's right to a 'peaceful existence and … to participate in the promotion and maintenance of peace'. As components of women's rights to life,

---

[46] The lecture drew on: Dianne Otto, 'Rethinking "Peace" in International Law and Politics from a Queer Feminist Perspective' (2020)126 *Feminist Review* 19; Gina Heathcote and Dianna Otto (eds), *Rethinking Peacekeeping, Gender Equality and Collective Security* (Palgrave Macmillan, 2014) 23; Dianne Otto (ed), *Queering International Law: Possibilities, Alliances, Complicities, Risks* (Routledge, 2018).
[47] The Eli Lauterpacht Lecture 2019, 'Taking Teaching Seriously: How to Teach Treaty Interpretation'.
[48] Vasuki Nesiah (n 20) 375.
[49] Even proposals for a critical alternative international law course do not centre peace as such: eg BS Chimni (n 40).
[50] UDHR, 1948, preamble; ICCPR, 1966, preamble; CESCR, 1966, preamble.
[51] UNGAR 71/189, 19 December 2016, Declaration on the Right to Peace. See essay 3 'Peace in International Law'.

integrity, and security of the person, the Maputo Protocol requires states parties to take appropriate and effective measures to 'actively promote peace education through curricula and social communication in order to eradicate elements in traditional and cultural beliefs, practices and stereotypes which legitimise and exacerbate the persistence and tolerance of violence against women'.[52]

Article 10 – the only stand-alone right to peace and peace education in a legally binding human rights treaty[53] – strengthens the argument for inclusion of peace into a course on women's human rights. Despite this and the reference to peace in the international Bill of Rights, our instinctive feeling was that peace is not taught in international human rights law courses, nor indeed in courses on gender or women's human rights. But even if there is no explicit inclusion of peace in such a course, topics such as economic and social rights, reproductive and sexual rights,[54] harmful stereotypes and violence against women and LGBTQI persons[55] could be seen as an implicit form of peace education.

This led us to conversations about teaching women's human rights and, more broadly, feminist legal education in international law which we have been having over the years. The LSE Law Department course on Women's Human Rights[56] persuaded many women students looking for careers in human rights to pick the LSE for their postgraduate work.[57] The Law Department's[58] decision to cancel the course raised questions for us about the role and responsibilities of law schools in educating the next generation of lawyers, academics and policy makers, vis-à-vis the transformative potential that education plays in fostering gender and other equalities. It also made us want to hear about the experiences of those in the academy in different parts of the world who had taught – or who are continuing to teach – this or related subjects.

Our concern was that courses on women's human rights law are falling out of fashion. This led us to question whether this is so and, if it is, why this might be

---

[52] Maputo Protocol, art 4.

[53] The African Charter on Human and Peoples' Rights, art 23(1) provides: '1. All peoples shall have the right to national and international peace and security.' See essay 3 'Peace in International Law'.

[54] ACHPR, General Comment No 2 on Article 14.1(a), (b), (c) and (f) and Article 14.2(a) and (c) of the Protocol to the African Charter on Human and Peoples' Rights on the Rights of Women in Africa, 28 November 2014 is important for women's wellbeing, and thus peace.

[55] UNGAR 48/104, 20 December 1994, Declaration on the Elimination of Violence against Women expresses the concern that 'violence against women is an obstacle to the achievement of equality, development and peace'; Report of the Independent Expert on protection against violence and discrimination based on sexual orientation and gender identity, A/77/235, 27 July 2022, para 31: 'gender and sexual violence are one of the main obstacles hindering lasting peace and stability, as many women, LGBT and gender-diverse activists and human rights defenders are targeted on the basis of both their gender and/or sexual identity and their role as social leaders'.

[56] Despite efforts to secure the continuation of a course on Women's Human Rights as part of the LLM programme at the LSE, it was shelved following Professor Chinkin's retirement in 2015. The course was introduced by Jane Connors in 1993, then at the School of Oriental and African Studies, as part of the LLM of the University of London. It was co-taught by Professor Fareda Banda (SOAS) and Christine Chinkin (LSE) for many years until the LSE introduced its separate LLM. Professor Banda has continued teaching the course at SOAS.

[57] This included co-author Keina Yoshida, who is a leading practitioner in women's and LGBTQI human rights.

[58] The LSE Gender Department offers a course on Gender and Human Rights which does not have a legal focus.

the case. It seemed to us that proponents of including women's human rights in a law school curriculum must overcome scepticism by those in charge of law degree programmes because of the subject's association with three areas of law, none of which is perceived as mainstream in legal education: PIL, human rights and some variation on women or gender and law. Neither gender nor peace fit readily into the bureaucratic and managerialism of contemporary law schools, nor the 'neoliberalisation of universities' referred to by Professor Weiler above. In addition, there is the ever-present cynicism from some within law schools about international law as 'real' law and the usefulness of human rights law as a tool for combating the inequalities and violations that are only too evident throughout the globe. We wished to investigate these themes with colleagues, but first we briefly explain the methodology we adopted for our conversations.

IV. CONVERSATIONS ABOUT TEACHING PEACE

A. Methodology

We drew upon socio-legal methodologies to enrich our understandings of what is and is not taught in law schools. Seven conversations took place in September and October 2021 with law professors and teachers from four different continents, who brought with them experience of teaching in their current institutional settings and elsewhere. Others have reported on the 'global' conversations engaged in through teaching with feminist judgments,[59] now expanded into the Feminist Judgments in International Law project.[60] We looked for regional diversity in teaching experiences, including from Europe, Asia, Africa, Latin America and Australia. The conversations were held online and followed a semi-structured format. The views are presented anonymously. We reached out to those who had either written about or taught peace, gender and human rights or women's international human rights law. We were interested to know whether peace had been included in the syllabus of any such course, thus focusing on the individual academic's approach rather than the institutional affiliation.[61] Many of those we spoke to had founded courses on gender and conflict, women's human rights or similar courses and occupy positions of privilege or authority within university hierarchies (professorial positions) or within the UN gender architecture. This gave them a freedom to elect which modules they would teach, including introducing new electives and determining the course content. They also carry more authority with students when raising issues deemed by some to be controversial, such as feminism and gender. Early career staff are not always able to choose their subjects,[62] but

---

[59] Bridget J Crawford et al, 'Teaching with Feminist Judgments: A Global Conversation' (2020) 38 *Pace Law Faculty Publications* 2.
[60] Loveday Hodson and Troy Lavers (eds), *Feminist Judgments in International Law* (Hart Publishing, 2019).
[61] Contrast this with Anthea Robert's approach to studying international law academics in elite universities: Anthea Roberts (n 29).
[62] This may not always be the case, for instance when a person is appointed specifically to teach a course on women's human rights because the previous teacher has left the institution.

are expected to teach on undergraduate compulsory law modules; they may also be more hesitant to express views or to raise subjects which are outside the mainstream curriculum. We recognise the limited sample size and hope that our discussions will spark further research and dialogue on this topic and help 'change the conversation'[63] towards recognition of peace pedagogy in international law.

This is not a legal biography project, but a form of life writing that has infused this essay following conversations with colleagues. We did not intend to delve into their lives but – perhaps inevitably – the teaching of peace or subjects relating to women or gender was for many of them a deeply personal endeavour forming part of their feminist activism and praxis. These discussions build on the methodology of conversation which we, like others, have used throughout our broader projects on feminist and gendered peace.[64] Conversations or 'everyday talk' is a qualitative methodology which has been developed particularly by Black feminists in the USA who have highlighted how it can centre thinking which is considered to occur at the margins.[65] The conversations also provided important instances of connection during the global pandemic when the everyday talk that was previously taken for granted at the informal parts (coffee breaks, mealtimes) of international law events were no longer taking place. The conversations allowed people to talk about their experiences but also their emotions and opened up spaces not only for knowledge-sharing but also for connection and care.[66]

B. 'I Don't Teach Peace': Triage in Law School

Our conversations confirmed that the right to peace or concepts such as peace are rarely taught in women's human rights courses. As one professor explained:

> I only talk about peace once. I explain that universal human rights is part of the project that the UN sits upon, in terms of achieving world peace, and that human rights is a component to world peace. That's it. That's all I say in international human rights law or with women, war and peacebuilding. Now I reflect that I could have taught it quite differently.

Even in specific courses on women or gender and human rights there was 'no time for peace'. Some teachers reflected on the practical constraints of teaching a time limited module:

> I don't teach peace. Why don't I teach peace? It wasn't a discussion that I had with myself. I have 9 sessions [18 hours] and it weighs on me that I am perhaps the only time that my students will study this. I am triaging what can they not know before leaving. I feel like an emergency worker, and I have a very short amount of time to get things across. Sometimes I teach students who will never attend another women's rights class.

---

[63] Vasuki Nesiah (n 20) 378.
[64] Sarah Smith and Keina Yoshida (eds), *Feminist Conversations on Peace* (Bristol University Press, 2022).
[65] Barbara Smith, 'A Press of Our Own Kitchen Table: Women of Color Press' (1989) 10 *Frontiers* 11; Patricia J Williams, *The Alchemy of Race and Rights* (Harvard University Press, 1991); Ellen Kohl and Priscilla McCutcheon, 'Kitchen Table Reflexivity: Negotiating Positionality through Everyday Talk' (2015) 22 *Gender, Place and Culture: A Journal of Feminist Geography* 10.
[66] Patricia Williams (n 65); bell hooks, *Feminist Theory: From Margin to Center* (1984).

The concept of triaging was also overlaid by those who teach on women, or gender, or feminism being asked by colleagues to teach gender components in other courses. One teacher said she had become the 'gender person on call' within the department, with students increasingly expecting a gender perspective on courses such as IHL or international criminal law. This ate into the professor's time to research and to study other topics, including peace:

> I feel I would have to study and I would need to learn more about the peace framework. And I have no time. Saying I would like to incorporate a new concept, it would also have to be time that I would take away from something else.

Those we talked with generally found that while discussion in women's human rights courses ranged widely, including around issues of multiple and intersecting forms of discrimination and identity (as well as the law), 'there is very little time spent to discuss very fundamental issues such as peace'. One international law teacher reflected that this was a common experience both within the law faculty and within UN human rights treaty bodies or international institutions, where members are time-pressed during the limited official working hours. The mechanics of getting through the agenda items and complying with the mandate are demanding, leaving little time for additional topics. Since the right to peace is not spelled out in any UN human rights treaty, it is not likely to be elaborated upon through a General Comment or Recommendation.

As we had intuited, the conversations suggest that the right to peace, the UNGA and UNESCO's plea to foster a culture of peace, and the obligation to provide peace education in the Maputo Protocol have made little inroad into the realities of legal education.[67]

C. A Preference for Violence and Conflict Over Peace

In the press to get through large law school curricula there was little time to consider what peace means within or for international law. Instead, those we spoke to reflected that they teach on violence or conflict. Their experience suggests that students are more attracted to such courses, rather than to ones on peace. Gina Heathcote has described an experiment she has undertaken: in addition to the module she was teaching on Gender, Armed Conflict and International Law she set up another module on Gender, Peace and International Law.[68] The second course proved less popular than the first. She asks: 'Why is armed conflict so desirable as a field of study; but peace is overlooked or less desirable'? This conundrum raised for her the need to interrogate 'what we are talking about when we talk about peace'. She found that the topics students wanted to address – conflict resolution, conflict-related sexual violence, women's participation, transitional justice – all relate to peace. When peace

---

[67] The Maputo Protocol is only binding upon states parties but those teaching women's human rights could use the provision to consider what a right to peace might mean for women.
[68] Gina Heathcote et al, 'Teaching Feminist Peace through Encounters with Female Violence' in Sarah Smith and Keina Yoshida (n 64) 181, 182.

is addressed in a PIL course, participants said that it was often in the context of conflict and peace-making (peace processes), peacebuilding or peacekeeping. As one international law professor stated, 'peacebuilding seems more concrete' than an abstract concept of peace and was also a way of bringing the WPS agenda into the discussion. She continued: 'It's interesting isn't it? It's always peacebuilding or peace-making, but the concept of peace standing on its own, doesn't seem to figure anywhere, yet conflict or war is central'. This limited perception of peace led some to comment that while peace was 'relevant' or 'topical' it was hard to see how the concept could stand on its own outside of courses on the use of force or IHL. Some professors felt that this was further underpinned by a feeling amongst some students that concepts such as peace, or even gender or race discrimination, were not relevant to them, to their future careers or their country contexts. Law schools of course prefer to continue modules that are popular with students.

D. Conceptual Ambiguity: Reclaiming Peace and its Possibilities

There is not always silence about the right to peace or legal conceptions of peace in law schools around the world. In different jurisdictions, teaching on these subjects depends on constitutions and domestic legal frameworks. The domestic context creates ambiguities and differences in meaning. An international law professor from Japan explained that her country has a pacificist constitution and that peace, and jurisprudence relating to peace, is taught in law schools. She gave examples of litigation on Japanese involvement in Iraq, and the taxation of citizens to fund the self-defence army and explained how these relate to a constitutional right to peace. She described active teachers' unions on peace education in Japan that work on producing materials on peace for children. A critical question for her was 'For whose benefit do we use the law?' She explained a phenomenon which is apparently unique to Japan, that the best law students from prestigious universities do not aspire to be lawyers or judges but to be bureaucrats or to work for companies with higher salaries. This is a crucial issue for those who teach law in Japan, with discussion about how to teach and make visible topics such as peace and gender equality for the next generation of those who do enter the profession.

Another professor told us that 'you've been looking for peace in all the wrong places' and questioned our narrow assumptions about where human rights education is to be found. She pointed out that peace was found in the common law under concepts such as 'peace bonds', 'peace orders' or 'keeping the peace'. We were challenged to look outside of the context of international law or even of law faculties:

> If we talk about the right to peace or peace education, it shouldn't be limited to the law. It should involve international relations, politics, economics, overseas development assistance. And also beyond institutions of education to the home and community meetings: What of my granny's Thursday Methodist ladies club/ men's group?

Peace was seen by some as having been 'sapped' of its emancipatory and positive content, and instead co-opted as a securitised, militarised discourse. This was especially the case in the context of the WPS agenda, where militarised notions of national security predominate within the UN Security Council (SC) and peace as a concept is barely mentioned. Maybe international lawyers should join with NGOs and activists to 'reclaim peace' as an emancipatory idea.

Alongside the co-option of the term 'peace', one professor raised the risk of reinforcing gendered binaries by teaching peace only in courses or classes relating to women's human rights or gender and conflict:

> I use a lot of images and a lot of quotes for students to think about how gender works as a category to support militarism. I talk about women's movements and the history of women's peace movements, but then have to ask the question of why these movements haven't been more effective? Why have they been side-lined? Why haven't they had the kind of impact that I hope to have, and it comes back to a discussion about how peace is dismissed as a feminised, a kind of weak, position, or concept. So we get to peacemaking and peacebuilding. And obviously, yes, women's rights are part of that. But we still have a problem with gender. So the question I suppose that I try to explore with them is how to move away from the gender binary in our work on peace, in our thinking about peace. And in the peacebuilding context. How can we think about women's anti-war activism in a less binary gendered way, which it just seems to feed?

For some law professors, it was alternative sources such as women's activism and mobilisation or even alternative sites of justice such as peoples' tribunals that allowed for an introduction of the concept of peace or gendered peace into law school courses. The marginalisation of peace in the teaching of PIL – a subject committed to the maintenance of international peace and security – demonstrates how securitised international legal discourse is, and how the lawyers and law teachers of the future are overwhelmingly not being exposed to ideas, debates and work on peace during their law school education.

V. COMPENSATORY LEGAL EDUCATION

In university curricula PIL may be regarded as a radical deviation from conventional, national law. We were told how in some jurisdictions, courses such as women's human rights or gender and the law are viewed with hostility[69] and are rare. Indeed, one law professor told us that in her region there was no education within law schools on human rights and women's rights. An option that some participants mentioned is a dedicated law clinic on women's human rights within the university system, but these are often less well regarded by law school hierarchies, for instance in terms of promotion or standing. The lack of availability of relevant courses has meant that 'compensatory' courses have been developed to close the lacunae, such as intensive extra-curricular or summer school courses.[70] We have both taught on such courses,

---

[69] The 'gender backlash' in parts of Eastern Europe have made it difficult for teachers wishing to teach such courses there; see essay 2 'Gender'.

[70] We were told about the Women's Human Rights Training Institute, founded in Sofia, Bulgaria in 2002 to make up for the lack of teaching about women's rights in Eastern Europe and as part of the transition from socialism: Isabel Marcus, 'Compensatory Women's Rights Legal Education in Eastern Europe: the Women's Human Rights Training Institute' (2017) 39 *Human Rights Quarterly* 539.

which are provided for a broad range of audiences, including military personnel, peacekeepers, police officers, government officials, and NGOs.

Many of the participants spoke of short courses and compensatory legal education as places where women's rights, or peace might be taught. In some circumstances, these courses have emerged due to a 'women's rights or gender person' being at the university. As one colleague who was involved in setting up such a course explained, there was no place for her in the university to teach women's human rights or transitional justice. Since she 'couldn't teach what she wanted', she and a colleague instead had the idea of setting up a specialist course targeted at those in positions of power. She explained:

> we would take people in positions of power and we would train them on human rights. It was a very fundable project and we could see results very quickly. We had some judges changing their adjudication. Not only having these massive thinkers but also getting massive results.

The unwillingness to introduce a course on women's human rights or peace in this teacher's experience was in stark contrast to the attitude in another law school where, the participant told us that almost everyone in the faculty was supportive of feminism and nearly all core courses had a feminist component, creating an environment for the introduction of women or gender courses.

We heard of another form of compensatory education: training undertaken by consultants who often combine their own legal education (for instance reissuing the materials from the human rights courses they took) with their experience working in international or regional agencies and NGOs. Such consultancies are often awarded for the training of ministry and other public officials. The format does not lend itself to innovation or the introduction of new topics such as peace.

Some discussants were critical of compensatory courses. Short courses and diplomas on subjects such as transitional justice, women's human rights, gender and human rights or WPS are offered at expensive rates and attract those in privileged professional positions, with employers sometimes paying for their employees to attend. In turn, the hope within departments or by those running the course is that those in decision-making positions will now have some sort of gender awareness and that there will be a direct impact on public policy or legal adjudication. This is one form of compensatory education aimed mainly at the elite, with the benefit of potential impact, but it also brings a financial benefit for the institution. It is nevertheless a far cry from the aspiration of peace education for all, at all levels.

VI. WHY DOES TEACHING PEACE AND WOMEN'S RIGHTS MATTER?

Although limited in number, our conversations reinforced our intuition that peace holds little sway in law school curricula and that, even in courses where it could intellectually be accommodated and would add a critical dimension, there was little reference to peace. But does this matter? Would the inclusion of peace into an already crowded law school market-oriented curriculum have any added value to legal education? There are several responses to why we believe it would. First, law faculties occupy central roles in the reproduction of knowledge, in governing elites, and in hierarchies of expertise: 'curricular choices are teleological, shaping not just what students read but also privileging particular histories and constructions of knowledge'.[71] In 'global universities' there is a danger of a disconnect, especially at the local level between 'what society needs and law schools supply'.[72] It is imperative that this market-driven orientation does not entirely displace concepts of social justice, one component of which is peace. Law school education should not replicate the normalisation of violence but should encourage students (and teachers) to engage conceptually with thinking about whether it makes or could make a contribution to peace. Following from this, inclusion of peace into what is largely a conservative legal education would challenge the assumption of peace as feminised, passive or radical ('leftist') and might help shift mindsets away from militaristic solutions towards more constructive cooperative approaches to state-building at local, national, regional and international levels. Second, teaching peace would open a space for 'alternative sources to expand feminist methodologies on peace', including for instance art projects, 'craft activism', exploratory walks to find peace in the city. In these ways, Gina Heathcote considered that 'feminist peace education is as much about breaking down a hierarchy of actually who gets to speak and how we speak'.[73] And third, academics shape legal fields, and influence students – who in turn influence legal categories and thinking as scholars and legal practitioners, working in courts, government, international institutions, NGOs, private corporations and elsewhere. Law is also seen as a training for non-legal careers, with law graduates going into other sites of public life – politics, policy decision-makers. Thinking about the dichotomy between war/peace, negative/positive peace through a feminist lens opens the way to breaking down other binaries that sustain the privilege accorded to militarised masculinity – gender binaries; civilian/non-civilian; human/non-human; natural/material. Peace education plays an essential role in recognising the interconnection of inequalities and destruction of the environment and the planet.

As with all critical approaches to PIL, peace education furthers understanding of the limitations of the discipline by exposing its hypocrisies and refusal to engage with its own history:[74] what kind of international law is it if it cannot embrace the teaching of peace? And what kind of international lawyers are we if we do not challenge ourselves by thinking outside the mainstream and seeking transformation? Peace education could be a conduit for a different way of thinking about the world in place of the hegemonic, masculinist word of the SC and PIL. But what is apparent – from albeit a very small sample – is that this is not the case: concepts of gendered peace with the framework of international law are not evolving through legal education.

In this essay our focus has been on the absence of peace in the teaching of international law. We write against the backdrop of the silencing of critique and of all alternative methodologies that grew out of oppression and resistance to dominant pedagogies. The intellectual battles being fought are compartmentalised and siloed; debate is narrowed and divorced from context. To resituate these polarised angry exchanges through the prism of peace may help people to better understand what is at stake and offer better solutions for a gendered peace.

---

[71] Mohsen Al Attar and Shaimaa Abdelkarim (n 21).
[72] Vasuki Nesiah (n 20) 376.
[73] Gina Heathcote (n 68) 183.
[74] Rohini Sen, 'Teaching International Law in Asia' (n 32).

Index

Abdelkarim, Shaimaa   248
abortion   84, 87–8, 167, 196
access to justice   146, 198–9, 230, 232, 235–7, 239
accountability
  holistic approach   148
  individual criminal responsibility   8–9, 28, 38, 209, 222
  international humanitarian law (IHL)   245
  sexual and gender-based violence (SGBV)   217–18
  soft law   97–8
  state   42, 44, 202, 222, 245
  strategic practices   174, 192, 207, 217
  universal jurisdiction   134
  violence against women and girls (VAWG) in UN system   192
activism   49–57, 59 *see also* disarmament and women's activism; protests
  strategic practices   172, 176, 178–9, 188
  woman-only organising   16, 50–53, 71, 110–111, 172
  World War I, activism in   50–3
ad hoc international criminal tribunals   82, 95, 133, 217 *see also* International Criminal Tribunal for the former Yugoslavia (ICTY); International Criminal Tribunal for Rwanda (ICTR)
Addams, Jane   49, 50
Afghanistan, conflict in   9, 29, 56
  gender apartheid and   9, 29, 134
  legal basis for use of force in   158–9
  regime change, non-recognition of unconstitutional   118–19
  Security Council   188
  September 11, 2001   158–9
  Taliban   9, 28–9, 118–19, 134, 159
  United States, withdrawal from   118
  women's rights, denial and co-option of   158–9, 187
Africa *see also* African Charter on Human and Peoples' Rights (ACHPR) (Banjul Charter)
  African Commission on Human Rights   233
  African feminisms   69
  Bandung Conference 1955   42, 58, 61, 106
  Beijing Conference, African women at Nairobi Women's conference 1985   69–70

African Charter on Human and Peoples' Rights (ACHPR) (Banjul Charter)
  Maputo Protocol   43, 250–1, 254
  life, integrity, and security of the person, women's right to   250–1
  right to peace   39, 43, 250–1
  stereotypes   251
  violence against women and girls   251
Agamben, Giorgio   250
Agenda 21 (UNCED)   21
Agenda for Peace 1992 (UN Secretary-General)   15, 90–1, 93–4
aggression, international crime of   36–8, 183
Ahmed, Sara   3
Akayesu case (ICTR)   192, 193
Akchurin, Maria   226
Al Attar, Mohsen   248
Alston, Philip   40–1
amicus briefs   191–7, 198
Annan, Kofi   95
annual day of peace   77–8
anti-gender movements   31–3
apartheid   9, 65, 66, 72, 78, 80, 82
  gender   9, 29, 134
  international criminal law   9
  jus cogens   29
  silence   134
arbitration and conciliation   7, 50, 101, 103, 176–7
archival work   1–2
armed conflicts *see also* Afghanistan, conflict in; Gaza, war in; international humanitarian law (IHL); Ukraine, Russia's invasion of; World War I; World War II
Beijing Declaration and Platform for Action (PFA)   90–8
colonialism   35, 94
complicity of international law   122–3
conflict resolution, participation in   92–4, 96
Declaration on the Protection of Women and Children in Emergency and Armed Conflict 1974   90
existence, criteria for   157
Geneva Conventions   35, 93
human rights   93, 136

260   Index

humanitarian intervention   11, 37
international criminal law   38
intervention, co-option of women's rights to justify foreign   186
Iraq War 2003   10, 247
new wars   30, 82, 184
occupation   35, 69, 80, 157, 247
reparations   231, 235
sexual and gender-based violence conflict-affected/related   93, 136, 184, 218, 235
state responsibility   159
strategic practices   173–4
Vietnam War   206
war crimes   95, 132, 186, 193–7, 207
Women, Peace and Security agenda   95–7, 217–18
Yemen   10, 28, 123–4, 167, 205
Yugoslavia, conflicts in the former   56, 95, 122, 184
arms *see* **disarmament and women's activism; weapons**
Arms Trade Treaty 2014   22, 112, 188
ASEAN Human Rights Declaration 2012   42
Asia
    Asia Pacific region   85, 208, 235
    Asia Women's Conference 1949   61
    Bandung Conference 1955   42, 58, 61, 106
    Beijing Women's Conference, Asian women at   85
    colonialism   69
    International Women's Rights Action Watch (IWRAW)   180
    World Courts of Women   207
asylum-seekers and migrants   10, 136, 155
Australia, protests on Anzac Day in   129–30
authoritarianism   16, 57, 71, 85, 193

Bailliet, Cecilia   249
Ballantyne, Edith   71
Bandung Conference 1955   42, 58, 61, 106
Banjul Charter *see* **African Charter on Human and Peoples' Rights (ACHPR)**
Begtrup, Bodil   59
Beijing Women's Conference
    Africa   84, 89
    alliances and networks   88
    armed conflicts   90–8
    Asia-Pacific region   85
    attendance, level of   81
    Caribbean region   85, 88
    CEDAW Optional Protocol   182
    Central and Eastern Europe   83–4
    Central and South America/Latin America   85–6, 88
    Cold War   80, 82, 83, 90

Commission on the Status of Women (CSW) (UN)   79, 80–1, 90, 182
equality, development and peace objectives   79, 81, 91, 99, 244
lesbians   89–90, 91
Pacific women at   85
regional preparatory meetings (prepcoms)   81, 83
religion   84, 87
UN Decade for Women, as context of   79–81, 90, 92–4, 99
United States   83, 88
Beijing Declaration and Platform for Action (PFA) 1995   6, 27, 56, 79–99, 245
    critical areas of concern   80
    Declaration 2020   108–9
    development   79, 81, 91, 99, 244
    disarmament   93–4, 108–9
    education for peace   80, 94
    gender, definition of   21
    Global North   82, 84, 87
    Global South   86–8
    Holy See and   21, 87–88
    human rights   86, 90–1, 94, 96, 98, 181
    indigenous women, marginalisation of   88–9
    interpretative declarations   81
    national level, progress at   94–5
    NGO forum   83, 91
    NGOs/civil society   81, 86–7, 95
    participation of women   80, 82, 96, 217
    peace in the Declaration and PFA   90–4
    post-Beijing   94–7
    private sector, strategic objectives and actions to be taken by   81
    reservations   81
    review by UNGA   95
    roadmap for empowerment   81
    sidelining peace   79
    soft law   56, 97–8
    UN bodies, strategic objectives and actions to be taken by   81
    violence against women and girls (VAWG)   80, 82–3, 85, 92, 94–9, 217
Benjamin, Walter   1
Big Tech   139, 148–50
biological sex   21, 24
    essentialism   18, 32, 110
    immutability   32
Boer War, concentration camps in   176
borders
    Cold War   82
    migrants   136, 155
    securitisation of   249
    violence   43

Brand, Dionne   155–6
British Institute of International and Comparative Law (BIICL)   248
Budapest Convention on Cybercrime 2001   145–6

Cairo Conference on Population and Development 1994   21, 181
campaigning *see* activism
Canada, residential schools in   224–5, 237–8, 239
capitalism   9, 20, 57, 62, 68, 87, 120, 125, 151, 152, 155, 166, 168, 188, 216
carceral feminism   9
caregivers, women as   164
Caribbean region   85, 88
CEDAW; *see* Convention on the Elimination of All Forms of Discrimination against Women
CEDAW Committee   124, 236–7
 academic centres and   182–3
 Covid-19 statement on   164
 equality and non-discrimination   24, 26, 43, 72, 76, 77, 164, 180, 204, 236–7
 extraterritoriality   135
 General Recommendations   21, 23–4, 76, 182
 implementation of CEDAW   180
 intersectionality   23
 memorialisation   237, 241
 NGOs/civil society, consultation with   182
 shadow reporting   180, 182
 social constructionist concept of gender   23
 strategic practices   180
 violence against women and girls (VAWG)   184
Central and Eastern Europe (CEE)   83–4 *see also* Soviet Union and satellite states
Central and South America/Latin America   49–50, 59, 61, 65, 69, 71, 88
Charlesworth, Hilary   10, 154, 157, 216
Charter of Economic Rights and Duties of States   66
Churchill, Winston   105
civil and political rights   7, 38–9, 49, 51, 65, 69, 92, 146
civil society *see* non-governmental organizations (NGOs)/civil society
climate justice   222–3, 225
Clinton, Bill   181–2
Cockburn, Cynthia   172, 175
Cold War
 Beijing Women's Conference and   80, 82, 83, 90
 colonialism   65
 disarmament   101, 105–6
 end of   82
 Friendly Relations Declaration   7, 42, 65
 proxy conflicts   65, 82
 feminists from socialist countries   68, 83–84
 UN Decade for Women   56, 58, 65, 67–8, 78
collective right to peace   34, 39, 42
collective security   35, 37, 245
colonialism   5, 9, 11, 18, 20, 50, 52, 57, 63, 66, 68, 69, 72, 82, 94, 104, 121, 171, 189, 216, 226, 227, 235, 238–41 *see also* decolonisation
coloniality   43
crimes against humanity   239
Euro-centric colonial practices   240, 248
genocide   224
Global South   18
imperialism   46, 55, 58, 61, 66, 72, 90, 94, 102, 119, 121, 134, 136, 227, 240, 241
international law and   10
reparations for   235, 238–41
self-determination   30, 65
settler colonialism   236
strategic practices   181, 189
Third World feminisms   69
transformation of international law   223, 226, 227
UN Decade for Women   61–3, 65, 69
violence, use of   61
World War I   52
'comfort women'
 access to justice   235–7, 239, 241–2
 apologies to   210, 237
 courts martial proceedings   208
 human rights   199
 memorials   237, 241
 reparations   198–9, 208, 235–7, 239, 241–2
 sexual and gender-based violence   131, 132, 137–8
 silence   208
 South Korea   198–9
 Tokyo Women's Tribunal 2000   207–10
Commission on the Status of Women (CSW)   59–60
 armed conflicts   90
 Beijing Declaration and Platform for Action (PFA)   79, 80–1, 90–1, 182
 CEDAW   180
 Commission on Human Rights (CHR)   179
 Declaration on the Elimination of Discrimination against Women (DEDAW)   60, 72–3
 disarmament   105
 ECOSOC   59–60, 105, 179
 UN Decade for Women   62–3
Committee against Torture (CAT)   23
Committee on the Elimination of Racial Discrimination (CERD)   23
common heritage of mankind   40
communist ideology   49, 62

compensation 229, 234
compensatory legal education 246, 256–7
Conference on International Organization (UN), San Francisco, 1945 178
conferences *see also* Beijing Women's Conference; Copenhagen Women's Conference 1980; Mexico City Women's Conference 1975; Nairobi Women's Conference 1985
   final documents of global summit meetings 56, 59
   state practice, evidence of 98
   strategic practices 180–1
   UN Decade for Women 58–63
conservative/right-wing movements 16, 31
Convention on the Elimination of All Forms of Discrimination against Women (CEDAW) *see also* CEDAW Committee
   Commission on the Status of Women (CSW) 180
   Copenhagen Women's Conference 1980 63
   disarmament 108, 200, 212
   entry into force 76
   implementation 180–1
   Optional Protocol to 94, 181–2
   participation of women, ensuring the 204–5
   peace processes 204–5
   preamble 43, 73, 78
   ratification 77, 94
   reparations 241–2
cooperation between states 7, 42–5, 62, 65, 146
co-option of women's rights 64, 158–9, 186–7
Copenhagen Women's Conference 1980
   CEDAW for signature, opening of 63
   development 41, 244
   disarmament 108
   equality and non-discrimination 41, 244
   NGO forum 71
   objectives 63
   outcome documents 72, 76–7
   participation of women 75
   Plan of Action 66
   peace 63, 71, 75
   politicisation 66–7
   violence against women and girls (VAWG) 75
Cotton Field case 233–4
Council of Europe (CofE)
   Budapest Convention on Cyber Crime 145–6
   Istanbul Convention 25, 143–5
   Recommendation on Preventing and Combating Sexism 2019 143–4
courts martial 132
Covid-19 2–3, 6, 43, 124, 153, 253
   academia, effect on women in 165
   aggressive policing 163
   caregivers, women as 164
   derogations from human rights 156–7
   domestic violence and femicide, growth in 164–5
   emergency, states of 156
   equality and non-discrimination 164–7
   gender roles, reinstatement of traditional 165
   gendered effects 163–6
   human rights 156–7, 166–8
   militarisation 6, 160, 162–3, 166
   policing women's bodies 167
   social support and healthcare systems, closure of 165–6
   time poverty of women 165
   vaccines 45, 162
Crawford, James 56
crimes against humanity
   apartheid 9, 29, 65, 66, 72, 78, 80, 82
   colonialism 239
   Draft Articles on Crimes against Humanity 22, 134
   erga omnes obligations 236
   forced pregnancy 195
   gender, definition of 22
   gender persecution 8–9, 27–8, 135
   jus cogens 134
   sexual and gender-based violence 25, 132–3, 193–7, 217
   sexual slavery as 131–2, 193–5, 208–10, 216, 235–237
criminal law *see* international criminal law (ICL)
crises and emergencies 153–68 *see also* Covid-19
   backlash against human rights and women's rights 168
   crisis, definition of 153
   critical feminist theory 154
   derogations from human rights 156–7
   entrenchment of gender systems 122, 163–8
   equality and non-discrimination 153, 154, 158, 160, 163–4
   forcible measures 122
   gendered construction of crises 122, 153
   gendered effects 123
   global financial crises 155
   justification of responses 122–3
   militarism 122, 153, 155, 158–63, 166, 168
   natural disasters 164
   non-intervention principle 158
   patriarchy 123, 153–4, 157–8, 160–2, 165–8
   repression 158
   securitisation 153
   time 156–8, 227, 228, 230, 235, 239, 241
   violence against women and girls (VAWG) 156–7, 163–4
critical feminist theory 122, 154
critical race theory 32, 68
Cuban missile crisis 1962 107

culture of peace   94, 99, 216, 228, 241, 244, 254
customary international law
  Beijing Declaration and Platform for Action (PFA)   98
  erga omnes obligations   29, 212, 236
  genocide   225
  international litigation   193
  jus cogens   29, 120–1, 134–5, 137, 198
  nuclear disarmament   200–1, 212–13
  opinio juris   29, 98
  reparations   240
  silence   118, 132
  slavery   240
  soft law   20–1, 37, 43, 56, 77, 97–8, 118, 120, 144, 214
  state practice   29, 98

DAWN   87
Dayton Accords   95, 122
de Beauvoir, Simone   64, 184
Declaration on the Elimination of Discrimination against Women (DEDAW)   60, 72–3
Declaration on the Elimination of Violence against Women 1993   21
Declaration on the Granting of Independence to Colonial Countries and Peoples 1960   43
Declaration on the Protection of Women and Children in Emergency and Armed Conflict 1974   90
Declaration on the Right to Peace 2016   41–4, 113, 124
Declaration on the Rights of Indigenous Peoples (UNDRIP) 2007   223–4, 238–9
decolonisation
  curriculums   248–9
  Declaration on the Granting of Independence to Colonial Countries and Peoples 1960   43
  process   9, 61
  international law   240–241
  reparations   241
  resistance to   61–2
democracy   78, 80, 82, 84–7, 174
development
  Beijing Declaration and Platform for Action (PFA)   244
  Charter of Economic Rights and Duties of States   66
  Copenhagen Women's Conference 1980   41, 244
  disarmament   108
  discourse and practice   20
  General Assembly, resolutions on   41
  Nairobi Women's Conference 1985   41, 70, 244
  New International Economic Order (NIEO)   66–7
  UN Decade for Women   55, 66–7, 70, 71, 76

digital technology
  misogyny and sexism   120–1, 139–52
  social media   32, 130
disarmament *see also* nuclear disarmament
  armed groups and proliferation of small arms   114
  arms race   65, 71, 74, 82, 101–5, 109–10, 113
  Arms Trade Treaty   112, 188
  autonomous systems   112
  Beijing Declaration and Platform for Action (PFA)   93–4, 108–9
  Biological Weapons Convention 1972   108
  biotechnology   112
  Chemical Weapons Convention 1992   108
  Cluster Munitions Weapons Convention 2008   112
  Copenhagen Women's Conference 1980   108
  expenditure, rise in weapons   10, 101–2, 108, 112
  female/male, coded as   105, 110, 114
  gender prism, through a   109–12
  Hague Congress 1915   102–3
  humanitarian disarmament   111–12
  international humanitarian law   112
  League of Nations   103–5
  militarism   104, 113, 187–8
  motherhood   111
  Nairobi Women's Conference 1985   74, 108
  Non-Aligned Movement (NAM)   58, 65, 106
  patriarchy   104–5, 111, 113–14, 202
  Peace and Disarmament Committee   104
  Peace and Disarmament Conference 1899   7
  private sector, regulation of   103–4
  Prohibition of Nuclear Weapons Treaty 2017 (TPNW)   112
  Security Council   108–9, 111
  small arms   114
  technical and scientific knowledge, development of   103–4
  UN Decade for Women   108–9
  universal/total disarmament   7, 103–4, 106, 109, 112–13
  WILPF   102–3, 105–8
  women's international and transnational activism   100–14, 215
  Women's Disarmament Committee (WDC)   104
  World Disarmament Conference 1932   100–1, 104, 177
discrimination *see* equality and non-discrimination
drug trafficking   38
Dumbarton Oaks   178
Durban Declaration and Programme of Action 2001   238

Echeverría, Luis 66
economic, social and cultural rights 7–8, 39, 65–6, 228, 235
ECOSOC (UN Economic and Social Council)
  Commission on the Status of Women (CSW) 59–60, 105, 179
  NGOs/civil society 64
education *see also* teaching international law
  culture of peace 244
  feminist legal education 251
  institutions of peace 43
  reparations 241, 243
  right to education 228
  truth commissions 243
emergencies *see* crises and emergencies
Enloe, Cynthia 4, 161
entrenchment of gender systems 122, 163–8
environment 8, 11, 38, 41, 43, 78, 83–4, 151, 213, 222–3, 225–7, 258
equality and non-discrimination *see also* Convention on the Elimination of All Forms of Discrimination against Women (CEDAW);
  Beijing Declaration and Platform for Action 21–2, 79, 81, 91, 99, 244
  Copenhagen Women's Conference 1980 41, 244
  Covid-19 and 164–7
  crises and emergencies 153, 154, 158, 160, 163–4
  Declaration on the Elimination of Discrimination against Women 60, 72–3
  indigenous peoples 69, 85, 88–9, 138, 151, 223–4, 237–8, 247
  international litigation 191–2
  intersectionality 18, 70, 88, 121, 141, 232, 236, 238, 241
  LGBTQI+ 31–2, 96, 124, 131, 190–1, 205, 224, 247, 251
  misogyny 120–1, 140–3, 147–8, 163
  Nairobi Women's Conference 1985 41, 244
  patriarchy 28, 46, 50, 60, 70, 124–5, 140, 186, 230
  racial inequality 16, 44, 69, 72, 76, 88, 158, 171, 212, 238
  reparations 232–8
  sexism 6, 44, 120–1, 141, 143–4, 146–8, 150, 236
  strategic practices 174, 176–89, 214–15
  structural inequalities 46, 50, 70, 124, 140, 230–1, 236, 238
  UN Charter 59
  UN Decade for Women 40, 63, 79
erga omnes obligations 29, 212, 236
essentialism
  anti-essentialism 18, 110
  biological sex 32, 110

stereotyping 16, 53, 74–5, 96, 186, 245
  Women, Peace and Security (WPS) agenda 160
European Convention on Human Rights (ECHR) 135–7
Everard, Sarah 163
evidentiary standards 194, 208–9
Extraordinary African Chambers in Dakar, Senegal 193
Extraordinary Chambers in the Courts of Cambodia (ECCC) 195
extraterritorial jurisdiction
  typologies of 134
  human rights 135–8
  universal jurisdiction 134–5, 193

fair trial, right to a 192
family
  values 31, 87
  violence 75–6, 80
fascism 10, 31–2, 53–4, 104
femininity 18–19, 74
feminisms, definition of 5–6, 69–70
Feminist International Judgments project 210–11, 252
First World War *see* World War I
forced marriage 8, 75, 194, 195, 216
forced pregnancy 194, 196, 216
foreign intervention 71, 80, 123, 186
formalism, legal 175, 210–13
Forward-Looking Strategies for the Advancement of Women *see* Nairobi Women's Conference's Forward-Looking Strategies for the Advancement of Women (FLS)
Fourth World Conference on Women *see* Beijing Women's Conference and Beijing Declaration and Platform for Action (PFA) 1995
Friendly Relations Declaration 7, 42, 65, 212

Gaza, war in
  arms to Israel, supply of 188–9
  Hamas attack 121
  protests 128–9
gender-based violence *see* sexual and gender-based violence (SGBV); violence against women and girls (VAWG)
gender 15, 17–33
  analysis 16, 17–20, 28, 124, 158, 194, 197, 198, 232
  apartheid 9, 134
  backlash 11, 17, 31, 98, 141, 168
  human rights 17, 23–5, 28
  identity 5, 16, 23–5, 27, 89, 110, 113, 119, 131, 133, 140, 142, 161, 162, 166

ideology   16, 31, 98
justice   26, 29, 83, 85, 146, 166, 175, 185, 190–2, 194–5, 197, 205, 227–8, 232, 235–7
persecution   8–9, 27–8
relational, as   18, 24
sexual and gender-based violence (SGBV)   25, 29, 99, 131, 184, 186, 191, 197, 231, 235
social constructionist concept of   5, 12, 16–19, 22–5, 27, 31, 120–1
stereotypes   16, 24, 96, 102, 143, 165, 171, 197, 216, 232, 234, 251
theory of   17–20, 28, 31–3
women, as synonymous with   22, 218
General Assembly (UNGA)
annual day of peace, designation of   77–8
Charter of Economic Rights and Duties of States   66
culture of peace   254
Declaration on the Elimination of Violence against Women 1993   21
Declaration on the Right to Peace 2016   41–4, 113, 124
disarmament   106
International Women's Year, designation of 1975   62–4, 108
nuclear disarmament   212
Nuremberg Principles adoption of   37–8
participation of women   73
Sustainable Development Goals   97
Geneva Conventions 1949   35, 93
genocide   186, 217, 224–5
global financial crises   155
Global North
civilising mission   82, 84
feminisms   58, 66–70
migrants and asylum-seekers   10, 155
New International Economic Order (NIEO)   66–7
triumphalism   82
Women, Peace and Security (WPS) agenda   188
Global South
Beijing Declaration and Platform for Action (PFA)   86–8
feminisms   16, 69–72
grassroots forum meetings   86–7
neoliberalism   67
New International Economic Order (NIEO)   66–7
Non Aligned Movement (NAM) TWAIL   240
Global Survivors Fund (GSF)   235
globalisation   5, 43, 78, 82, 246, 250
good faith   82, 201

good neighbourliness   7, 8, 212
Grassroots Organisations Operating Together in Sisterhood (GROOTS)   86–7
Greenham Common   2, 71, 111, 215
Group of Experts on Action against Violence against Women and Domestic Violence (GREVIO)   143, 145, 148
Guiding Principles on Business and Human Rights   149–50

Habré case   193
Hague Appeal for Peace   96
Hague Women's Congress 1915   50–2, 102–3, 128, 205, 211, 218
Hague Conventions 1899 and 1907   7, 101, 104, 176
hate speech   120, 141, 142–3, 146–8
Heathcote, Gina   254, 258
Helsinki Accords 1975   65
heteronormativity   18–19, 32, 44, 119–20, 167, 212
Hirohito, Emperor of Japan   209
historical wrongs, reparations for   230, 235, 238–41
histories, rewriting international law's   49–61
HIV/AIDs   85
Hobhouse, Emily   176
Holy See   21, 31, 88
Honey, Edward George   126
human rights   7–8, 23–5, 26, 36, 39, 43, 59, 72, 82, 84, 112, 180–3, 184
access to justice   146, 198–9, 230
African human rights system   39, 43, 250–1, 254
backlash   11, 18, 31, 98, 141, 168
Beijing Declaration and Platform for Action (PFA)   86, 90–1, 94, 96, 98, 181
civil and political rights   7, 38–9, 49, 65, 146
Covid-19   156–7, 166–8
crimes against humanity   183
derogations   156–7
development right to   40
disarmament   112, 200
economic, social and cultural rights   7–8, 39, 65–6, 72, 228, 235
effective remedy, right to an   230, 232
European Convention on Human Rights (ECHR)   11, 135–7
extraterritoriality   135–7
fair trial, right to a   192
international litigation   194
investigations   230
law clinics   256
law courses   250–2
life, right to   39
peace, right to   37, 39, 40
reparations   230–5, 241–2
state immunity   199

state responsibility 30, 76, 131, 199
teaching international law 228, 245, 246–7, 250–7
Tehran World Conference on Human Rights 1968 39, 72, 74
torture 11, 23, 137, 193, 216, 247
treaty bodies 23
Universal Declaration of Human Rights 38, 179
Vienna Conference on Human Rights 1993 21, 124, 181, 184
violence against women and girls (VAWG) as violation of 75–7
Women, Peace and Security 187

immunity *see* state immunity
Imperial War Museum (IWM) 3, 126
impunity 131, 133, 137, 141, 146, 190, 198, 210, 217
Indigenous Peoples 69, 75, 88, 138, 151, 247
  Beijing Declaration and Platform for Action (PFA) 88–9
  Canada, residential schools in 224–5, 237–8, 239
  climate justice 223, 225
  colonialism 223, 226
  Declaration of Indigenous Women 89
  lands, territories and resources 94, 224
  marginalisation 88–9
  nature, rights of 225–6
  reparations 237–8, 237–9
  UN Declaration on the Rights of Indigenous Peoples (UNDRIP) 2007 223–4, 238–9
individual criminal responsibility 8–9, 36–8, 209
Integrated Review on Security, Defence, Development and Foreign Policy 199–202, 210–13
Inter-American Commission on Human Rights (IACommHR) 150
Inter-American Commission of Women 54, 86
Inter-American Court of Human Rights (IACtHR) 226, 233–4
intergenerational responsibility 223, 237
International Council of Women 1899 176–7
International Court of Justice (ICJ) 56, 198–9, 201–2, 211, 215, 222–3
International Covenant on Civil and Political Rights (ICCPR) 38–9, 65, 146
International Covenant on Economic, Social and Cultural Rights (ICESCR) 38–9, 65–6, 228
International Criminal Court (ICC), *see* Rome Statute of the
  amicus briefs 193–7
  Appeals Chamber 27, 194–7
  Office of Public Counsel for Victims 26

Ongwen case 193–7, 216
Prosecutor's Office (OTP) 26–8
Policy on the Crime of Gender Persecution 27–8
Policy Paper on Sexual and Gender-Based Crimes 26
Registry 190
Trial Chamber 193–7, 216
Trust Fund for Victims 26, 234–5
Women's Initiatives for Gender Justice 190
international criminal law (ICL) *see* crimes against humanity
  aggression 36–8, 183
  gender, concept of 17, 25–8
  genocide 186, 192, 217, 224–5
  international humanitarian law (IHL) 183
  reparations 234–5
  sexual and gender-based violence (SGBV) 25, 29, 183
  war crimes 95, 132, 186, 193–7, 207
International Criminal Tribunal for the former Yugoslavia (ICTY) 157, 184
  rape as a crime against humanity 185
  sexual and gender-based violence (SGBV) 133, 185
International Criminal Tribunal for Rwanda (ICTR) 185
  Akayesu case 192, 193
  amicus brief 192, 193
  rape as a crime against humanity 185
  sexual and gender-based violence (SGBV) 133, 185
international financial institutions (IFIs) 67, 81
international human rights law (IHRL) *see* human rights
international humanitarian law (IHL) 93, 131, 136, 183, 184, 199, 200, 245
  crises 158
  disarmament 112
  Geneva Conventions 1949 35, 93
  gendering of 121, 183, 254
  human rights law and 92, 136, 184
  reparations 131, 198, 234
  sexual and gender-based violence (SGBV) 93
  Women, Peace and Security 187
International Labour Organization (ILO) 2, 52, 59
International Law Commission (ILC)
  Articles on Responsibilities of States for Internationally Wrongful Acts (ARSIWA) 9, 229
  Draft Code of Offences against the Peace and Security for Mankind 1954 37–8
  Draft Convention on Crimes against Humanity 29, 134, 212, 216

Convention on the Freedom of the High
    Seas   107
drug trafficking   38
environment, wilful damage to the   38
gender, definition of   22, 29
permanent criminal court   38, 185
reparations   229
International Military Tribunal for the Far East
    (IMTFE)   132, 209, 236
International Tribunal on Crimes against Women,
    Brussels, 1976   64, 75–6, 184
International Women's Rights Action Watch
    (IWRAW)   180
International Women's Suffrage Alliance   102
International Women's Year (IWY) 1975   62–4,
    108, 236
International Year for the Culture of Peace
    2000   99
International Year of Peace 1986   40
intersectionality   70, 112, 121, 141, 232
    Beijing Declaration and Platform for Action
        (PFA)   88
    CEDAW Committee   23–4
    Covid-19   164
    crises and emergencies   154
    reparations   232, 238, 241
intervention
    civilising mission   137
    co-option of women's rights as
        justification   186–8
    humanitarian intervention   11, 37
    non-intervention principle   7, 30, 36, 42, 71,
        72, 158
    state responsibility   30
Iran   9, 29, 167
Iraq War 2003   10, 247
Istanbul Convention 2011   25, 143–6

Japan *see also* 'comfort women'; Tokyo Women's
    Tribunal 2000
    Asia, occupation of   69
    constitutional law courses   244
    Hiroshima and Nagasaki, bombing of   104
    International Military Tribunal for the Far East
        (IMTFE)   132, 209, 236
    peace, constitutional right to   255
    Women's Active Museum on War and Peace
        (WAM), Tokyo   3
jurisdiction *see also* extraterritorial
    jurisdiction
    prosecution, obstacles to   132, 133–4, 138
    temporal jurisdiction   230, 235, 237
    territorial jurisdiction   133–8
    universal jurisdiction   134–5, 193
jus cogens (peremptory norm)   29, 77, 120–1,
    134–5, 137, 198

Kapur, Ratna   187
Kellogg-Briand Pact 1928   7, 177
Kennedy, John F   107
King, Angela   95
Kosovo, NATO's action in   56
Kyoto Museum for World Peace   3

Labenski, Sheri   4
Landmines Treaty 1997   111–12
Latin America/Central and South America
    49–50, 59, 61, 65, 69, 71, 86, 88
League of Nations   50, 52–4, 59, 98, 103–5, 174,
    178, 211
Lemkin, Raphael   224
LGBTQI+
    anti-gender movements   31–3
    binaries, reinforcing gendered   256
    CEDAW Committee   23
    discrimination against   10, 16, 19, 27, 31
    gender identity   4–5, 16, 23–5, 27, 88–91, 115,
        133, 162
    gender justice   191
    Independent Expert on Sexual Orientation and
        Gender Identity (IESOGI)   124
    intersectionality   19
    lesbianism   89–90, 91
    online abuse   141–2
    reparations   241
    violence   96, 190
    Women, Peace and Security (WPS) agenda   96
live in peace, right to   7, 74
London School of Economics (LSE)
    film festival   3
    LSE Women's Library   1–2
    Women's Human Rights   251
Lorde, Audre   11
Lotus case (*Bozkurt* case)   8, 211

mainstreaming, gender   21–2, 84, 95, 124, 145
Malaya Lolas   236, 241
Manjoo, Rashida   231
Manne, Kate   142
Martens clause   213
Marxism   249
masculinity   6, 18–19, 74, 110, 114, 126, 160, 161,
    162, 231, 258
McBride, Carol   237–8
memorialisation   207, 241, 243
Mexico City Women's Conference 1975   40–1, 58,
    62–4, 70
    Coalition of Latin American women   69
    International Year of Peace   40
    NGOs/civil society   72
    NIEO   66
    outcome documents   63, 66, 72, 73, 75, 76–8
    politicisation   66–7, 70–1

UN Decade for Women   58, 66–8, 70–3, 76–9
  violence against women and girls   75
migrants and asylum-seekers   10, 43, 136, 150, 155
militarisation/militarism   20, 46, 52, 94, 171, 188, 202, 216, 256
  core beliefs   161
  Covid-19   6, 160, 162–3, 166
  disarmament   104, 113–4, 187–8, 202, 212
  crises and emergencies   122, 153, 155, 158–63, 166, 168
  pacifism and anti-militarism, limits of   16, 53
  patriarchy   236
  peacekeeping   162–3
  security, military solutions and   35, 101–3, 105, 108–9, 113, 128
misogyny   16, 44, 118, 139–52, 171, 172, 174, 236
  backlash against feminism   141
  colonialism   121
  commodification   149
  continuum of VAWG   147–8
  crises and emergencies   163
  definition of   142–3
  equality and non-discrimination   120, 147–8, 150–1
  gendered state   121
  impunity   141, 146
  intersectionality   121, 140, 152
  male entitlement   142–3
  patriarchy   139–40, 142–4, 148–52
  self-censorship   120
  social construction   120–1
  stereotyping   144
  violence against women and girls (VAWG)   46, 139–41, 144–50
  Working Group on Misogyny and Criminal Justice (Scotland)   142–3
Mosley, Oswald   54
mothers/motherhood   52, 53, 111, 172

Nairobi Women's Conference 1985 *see also* Nairobi Women's Conference's Forward-Looking Strategies for the Advancement of Women (FLS)
  Africa, attendees from   69–70
  Asia, attendees from   69–70
  NGO forum   71
  NIEO   67
  outcome documents   72, 77
Nairobi Women's Conference's Forward-Looking Strategies for the Advancement of Women (FLS)   20–1, 56, 63
  conceptualisation of peace   72
  disarmament   74
  participation of women   73
  violence against women and girls (VAWG)   75

national security   154, 156, 162, 256
nationalism   30, 84, 104, 121
NATO's action in Serbia and Kosovo   56
natural disasters   164
nature, rights of   8–9, 225–6
negative peace   6–7, 34–7, 38, 72, 94, 249–50
neoliberalism   43, 67, 78, 82, 148, 228, 250
Nesiah, Vesuki   216
New Agenda for Peace   45–6
New International Economic Order (NIEO)   40, 43, 66–7, 78, 118
new wars   30, 82, 184
New World Order   82
Non-Aligned Movement (NAM)   58, 65, 106
non-discrimination *see* equality and non-discrimination
non-governmental organizations (NGOs)
  Beijing Women's Conference   81, 86–7, 95
  campaigns   16, 77, 182
  disarmament   105
  ECOSOC consultative status   64
  grey literature   55
  Nairobi Declaration 2007   231
  NGO fora   55, 63–4, 66–7, 71–2, 83, 91
  Tokyo Women's Tribunal 2000   208, 210
  Women, Peace and Security (WPS) agenda   217, 256
  women's courts and tribunals   206–10
non-repetition, guarantees of   230, 231, 233
non-violent resistance   54
nuclear disarmament   8, 45, 74, 92–3
  arms race   101, 105
  CEDAW   200, 212
  CND   199–203
  Cold War   101, 106
  Cuban missile crisis 1962   107
  customary international law   200–1, 212–13
  Declaration on the Right to Peace 2016   43
  environmental remediation   213
  Greenham Common   111
  good faith   201
  Hiroshima and Nagasaki, bombing of   104
  human rights violated by nuclear weapons   200
  ICJ   201–2
  Integrated Review on Security, Defence, Development and Foreign Policy, legality of UK's policy in   199–202, 210–13
  Limited Test Ban Treaty 1963   107
  militarism   202, 212
  non-nuclear weapons states   112
  Non-Proliferation Treaty (NPT) 1968   82, 108, 199–202, 210–13
  nuclear free zones   36, 106
  nuclear weapons states   106, 107, 112, 202

Outer Space Treaty 1966   107
peace camps   65, 71, 111, 215, 217
persistent objector rule   212
preserving peace, nuclear weapons as   105
Prohibition of Nuclear Weapons Treaty 2017
    (TPNW)   112, 212
protests   65, 71, 107
reparations   213
Review Conference of Nuclear
    Non-Proliferation Treaty   82
SALT II   65
START   65
testing   36, 82, 85, 101, 106–8, 212–13
WHO   106–7
WILPF   106–8
Women Strike for Peace initiative (WSP)   107

occupation   35, 63
Office of the United Nations High Commissioner
    for Human Rights (OHCHR)   3, 25
Ongwen case (ICC)   193–7, 216
Oosterveld, Valerie   26
opinio juris   29, 98
Otto, Dianne   249–50
Outer Space Treaty 1967   107

pacifism   16, 53–4, 56, 61, 102, 128, 205, 255
Papacy   21, 31, 88
participation of women
    Beijing Declaration and Platform for Action
        (PFA)   80, 82, 96, 217
    conflict resolution   92–4, 96
    Copenhagen Women's Conference 1980   75
    decision-making about peace   72–3
    disarmament   100, 104
    Mexico City Women's Conference 1975   73
    Nairobi Women's Conference 1985   73
    peace processes in   204–5
    reparations   232–3
    UN Decade for Women   72–3, 74–5, 77
    Women, Peace and Security (WPS)
        agenda   216–18
    workloads, unequal distribution of   73
patriarchy   4–6, 16–20, 32, 55, 58, 87, 94, 104,
        152, 172, 216, 249
    binary differences, hierarchies of   19, 24, 142
    crises and emergencies   123, 153–4, 157–8,
        160–2, 165–8
    disarmament   104–5, 111, 113–14, 202
    equality and non-discrimination   28, 46, 50,
        60, 70, 124–5, 140, 186, 230
    masculinity   231
    militarism   113, 188, 236
    misogyny   139–40, 142–4, 148–52
    nationalism   121

normalisation   18, 125, 143
resistance to change   147
sexual and gender-based violence   197
silence   117, 119–20, 124–5, 128, 130, 133, 140,
    148, 202
structural inequalities   46, 50, 70, 124, 140, 230
transformative reparations   227, 241
violence against women and girls   148–50
Peace and Disarmament Conference 1899   7
peace camps   2, 65, 71, 111, 215, 217
peace caucuses   81, 91
peace, concept of   15, 34–46, 72–6
peace, culture of *see* culture of peace
peace processes   78, 80, 84, 96, 144, 198, 204–6
peace, right to *see* right to peace
peace societies, participation of women in   49
peaceful, stereotype of women as   53, 92–3, 96,
    205, 245
peacekeeping operations   6, 41, 82, 96, 137, 162
people's tribunals   206–7, 209, 256
Permanent Court of International Justice
    (PCIJ)   177, 211
persecution   8–9, 27–8, 135
Persinger, Mildred   63–4
Pillay, Navanethem   185, 192
Platform for Action *see* Beijing Declaration and
    Platform for Action (PFA) 1995
populism   16, 31
post-structuralism   18, 27
Prevention of Sexual Violence Initiative (UK)   183
private sector   81, 103–4
progressive development of international
    law   194–5
prostitution/sex work   67, 72, 75, 85, 93, 207
protests   45, 49, 128–31, 163, 167, 174, 206, 215
    see Greenham Common, Reclaim these
        Streets, Women in Black
    disarmament   104, 111
    nuclear disarmament   65, 71, 107, 111
    war, against   128–31
proxy conflicts   82
Putin, Vladimir   9, 155, 161

queer theory   5, 18, 27

race/racialism *see* colonialism   36, 52, 63, 66,
        70, 88, 120, 121, 146, 158–9, 166, 236,
        238, 241
    apartheid   29, 65, 82
    critical race theory   32, 68
    Jim Crow laws   49
    reparations   238, 241
    Terrell, Mary Church   49
    violence   120, 236
    WILPF   71

Reagan, Ronald   65, 67
Reclaim These Streets   163
Rees, Madeleine   6
regime change   118–19
rehabilitation   233–4, 237
religion/religious   24, 36, 41, 84, 87, 122, 146, 188, 191, 205, 228
　Holy See   21, 31, 88
　reproductive rights   87–8
Remembrance Day   126
reparations   131–132, 137, 214
　transformative reparations   227, 229–43
reproductive rights   31–2, 84, 87–8, 168, 181–2
responsibility to protect (R2P)   37, 45
restitution   229, 231, 234
restorative justice   243
right to peace   4, 37–44, 250–1
　collective   34, 39, 42, 74
　individual   34, 39, 42, 74
　live in peace, right to   7, 74
　New International Economic Order (NIEO)   40, 43
　resource distribution and consumption   40
　social justice   40
　women's right to peace   4, 15, 43, 250–1
　zones of peace   40
right-wing movements/regimes   16, 31, 65, 69, 71
Roberts, Anthea   247
Rome Statute of the International Criminal Court   21, 38, 133
　aggression, crime of
　crimes against humanity   26–8, 95, 193–7
　evidentiary standards   194
　forced marriage   194–5, 216
　forced pregnancy   194, 195, 196, 216
　gender, definition of   21, 22, 26
　Ongwen case   193–7, 216
　persecution   27–8
　sexual and gender-based violence (SGBV)   27, 95, 133, 185
　sexual slavery   194–5, 216
　war crimes   95, 193–7
Royal Wootton Bassett   124
Russia; see Ukraine, Russia's invasion of
Rwanda see International Criminal Tribunal for Rwanda (ICTR)

safe spaces   183
satisfaction   229–30
Schwimmer, Rosika   128
second wave feminism   68
Second World War see World War II
Secretary-General (UN)   22, 60, 118, 205
　Agenda for Peace 1992   15, 90–1, 93–4
　disarmament   113

hate speech   141
　New Agenda for Peace   45–6, 113
　Special Adviser on Gender Issues and Advancement of Women   95
　Summit of the Future 2024   113
securitisation   6, 153, 160, 187, 249, 255–6
Security Council   3, 11, 41, 122, 155 see also Women, Peace and Security (WPS) agenda
　collective security   37
　hegemonic masculinity   258
　maintenance of international peace and security   122, 124, 159–60, 187
　national security   256
　Permanent Members   106, 155
　sexual and gender-based violence (SGBV)   41, 184, 218
　Ukraine, Russia's invasion of   188
　Yugoslavia, conflicts in the former   184
self-defence, use of force in   36, 122, 159
Sellers, Patricia Viseur   2, 135
Senegal, Extraordinary African Chambers in Dakar   193
Serbia, NATO's action in   56
sexism
　definition of   143–4
　commodification of   149
　Recommendation on Preventing and Combating Sexism 2019 (CofE)   143–5
　stereotypes   144
sexual rights   84
sexual and gender-based violence (SGBV)
　armed conflicts   82, 93, 136, 184, 186, 217, 218, 235
　'comfort women'   131, 132, 137–8
　crimes against humanity as   25, 132–3, 193–7, 217
　genocide as   217
　human rights, as violation of   26, 184
　impunity   131, 133, 137
　international criminal law   25, 26, 27, 95, 133, 183, 185, 186
　international humanitarian law (IHL)   93
　International Military Tribunal for the Far East (IMTFE)   132
　non-repetition, guarantees of   231
　Nuremberg Military Tribunal (NMT)   132
　patriarchy   197
　Prevention of Sexual Violence Initiative (UK)   183
　prosecutions, lack of   132, 138, 186
　reparations   131–2, 230–1, 234–5
　sexual slavery   194–5, 216
　silence   120, 129–38, 217
　state immunity   198–9
　UN War Crimes Commission   132
　universal jurisdiction   135

war crimes, as   95, 132
Yugoslavia, conflicts in the former   184
sexual slavery *see also* **'comfort women'**   194–5, 207–10, 216
silence   126–38, 221, 227
   collective silences   119, 126–7, 131, 138
   'comfort women'   208
   cover-ups   130
   culture of   131
   customary international law   118, 132
   impunity   131, 133, 137
   legal silencing   131–8
   private silence   130–1
   protests   117–18, 128–31
   Remembrance Day   126
silos, creation of   6, 44, 122, 128, 144, 151–2
Simpson, Gerry   246, 247–8
Singh, Sophia Duleep   49
Sinichi, Ago   3
Sipila, Helvi   76
slavery   235, 238–41 *see also* 'comfort women', sexual slavery
social justice   10, 40, 49, 50, 54, 69, 72, 87, 174, 215, 245, 258
social media   32, 130, 162, 183
soft law   43, 76–77, 97–8, 118, 120, 144, 214
   final documents of global summit meetings   56
   international fora, gender in   20–1
   peace, right to   37
solidarity rights   39, 40–1, 45
South America *see* Central and South America/Latin America
South Korea, 'comfort women' in   198–9, 242
sovereign equality of states   35, 36, 67, 132, 211
Soviet Union and satellite states *see also* Cold War   39, 106, 107
   collapse of   41, 82, 90–1, 122
   communist ideology   49, 62
   Cuban missile crisis 1962   107
   feminists from   67–8, 83–84
   politicisation of peace   39, 70–1
   WIDF   61–2, 64, 69
Special Adviser on Gender Issues and Advancement of Women   95
Special Court for Sierra Leone (SCSL)   133, 195
state consent   36, 120, 215
state immunity   137, 198–9, 236–7
   comfort women and   198–9
   crimes against humanity   236–7
   customary international law   198–9
   human rights   199
   national courts   137, 198
state responsibility   9, 28–30, 37, 43, 76, 131, 135–6, 159, 181, 186, 209, 236, 239
state sovereignty   8, 134, 174, 199, 211, 215, 258
stereotypes   16, 73, 161, 164, 251

essentialism   16, 53, 74
   peaceful, women as   53, 92–3, 96, 245
   victims, women as   92, 96, 99, 186, 218
Street, Jessie   179
structural violence   9, 19, 99, 156, 249–50
suffrage   49, 102
Sustainable Development Goals (SDGs)   22, 46, 97, 113, 166
Suttner, Bertha von   49, 101, 218

Taliban   9, 28–9, 118–19, 134, 159
teaching international law   228, 244–58
Tehran Human Rights Conference 1968   60, 72, 94
Temple of Peace, Wales   2
Terrell, Mary Church   49
territorial jurisdiction   133–8
terrorism and violent extremism   157–9, 218
textbooks   56, 59
Thatcher, Margaret   65, 67
time
   arbitrariness of international law's time   156–7
   temporal jurisdiction   230, 235, 237
   time and space of international law   227–8
   women's time poverty   165
Toew, Miriam   152
Tokyo Women's Tribunal 2000   2, 185–6, 207–210
torture   11, 23, 137, 193, 216, 249
transitional justice   82, 230, 249, 254, 257
transnational/international/global feminist movement   2, 25, 31, 49–54, 58–64, 67–70, 71–2, 76, 77, 81, 83–4, 86–90, 98, 100–4, 105, 106, 107–8, 111–2, 245
Trust Fund for Victims (ICC)   26, 234–5
truth commissions   239, 242–3
truth, right to   173, 242
Tzouvala, Ntina   249

Ukraine, Russia's invasion of   10, 155, 161–2, 247
   arms, supply of   11, 56–7, 110, 188
   gendered effects   161–2
   hegemonic masculinities   110
   juridification of conflict   162
   National Action Plan   188
   networks   174
   political elites   161
   Ukrainian feminists   173–4
UN Commission on Human Rights   39, 59–60, 179
UN Decade for Women   6, 58–78
   capitalism, critique of   68
   class and economic privilege   67
   Cold War   56, 58, 65, 67–8, 78
   colonialism   61–3, 65, 69
   conceptualisation of peace   72–6
   disarmament   74, 108–9

education for peace   74
equality, development and peace objectives   40, 55, 63, 66–7, 70, 71, 76, 79
forerunners of the Decade   59–62
NIEO   40, 43, 66–7, 78, 118
NGOs/civil society   55, 63–4, 66–8, 70–1, 77
politicisation of peace   66–7, 70–2
soft law   76–7
UNESCO   228, 254
United Nations (UN) *see also*; General Assembly; Secretary-General; Security Council; UN Decade for Women
  Commission on Human Rights   39, 53, 59–60, 179
  Development Fund for Women (UNIFEM)   83, 86
  Guiding Principles on Business and Human Rights   149–50
  Human Rights Council (HRC)   25, 41–5, 124, 135, 183
  Human Rights Council Advisory Committee   41
  Office of the United Nations High Commissioner for Human Rights (OHCHR)   3, 25
  peacekeeping operations   6, 41, 82, 96, 137, 162–3
  Sustainable Development Goals (SDGs)   22, 46, 97, 113, 166
  War Crimes Commission   132
  UNIDIR   3
United Nations Charter
  Chapter VI   97
  Equality   179
  maintenance of international peace and security   105
  self-defence   122, 159
  use of force, prohibition of   35, 36, 42, 72, 78, 105, 118, 122, 134, 200, 211–212, 245
United States   86, 105, 106, 107, 193 *see also* **Afghanistan, conflict in; Cold War;**
  Alien Tort Claims Act   134
  anti-communism   62
  Covid-19   155–6
  Hague Congress 1915, US women attendees at   128
  Jim Crow laws   49
  Kellogg-Briand Pact 1928   7, 177
  Latin America, domination of   49–50
  peace societies, participation of women in   49
  September 11, 2001   158–9
  Vietnam War   111, 206
Universal Declaration of Human Rights (UDHR)   38, 179

Vanuatu   222–3
Vienna Conference on Human Rights 1993   21, 124, 181, 184
Vienna Declaration and Programme of Action   27
Vietnam War, Russell Tribunal during the   206
victims, women as   92, 96, 99, 186, 218
violence *see also* armed conflicts; sexual and gender-based violence (SGBV); violence against women and girls (VAWG)
  borders   43
  colonialism   61
  militarised   122, 128
  normalisation of   246, 258
  self-defence, use of force in   36, 122, 159
  structural violence of international law   9, 19, 99, 156, 249–50
  terrorism and violent extremism   157–9, 218
violence against women and girls (VAWG) *see also* **sexual and gender-based violence (SGBV)**
  armed conflicts in   92–3, 184
  Beijing Declaration and Platform for Action (PFA)   80, 82–3, 85, 92, 94–9, 217
  CEDAW Committee and   181
  crises and emergencies   156–7, 163–4
  Declaration on the Elimination of Violence against Women 1993   21, 60
  domestic violence and femicide during Covid-19, growth in   164–5
  due diligence   76, 150
  family, community and state, in the   75–6, 80
  GREVIO   143
  impunity   141
  International Tribunal on Crimes against Women, Brussels, 1976   75–6, 184
  Istanbul Convention   25, 143–6
  Nairobi Forward-Looking Strategies   75–6
  normalisation of   139
  on-line violence   144–50
  patriarchy   148–50
  prevention, prosecution and punishment   76
  reparations   230–4, 238, 241
  state responsibility   76
  stereotypes   251
von Suttner, Bertha   101, 218

war *see* armed conflicts
war crimes   95, 132, 186, 193–7, 207
war on terror   157
weapons *see also* disarmament; nuclear disarmament
  Arms Trade Treaty   22, 112, 188
  gendered impact   112
  small arms   114
  transfer of weapons   35–6

Weiler, Joseph   250, 252
welfarism   8, 65–6
Wilson, Woodrow   103
Women in Black   172–3, 175
Women, Peace and Security (WPS) agenda   3, 6, 41, 43–4, 46, 79, 198, 204, 245
   armed conflicts and   95–7, 217–18
   country-specific mandates, absence from   187
   disarmament   108–9, 111
   essentialism   160
   National Action Plans   98, 188
   NGOs/civil society   188, 217
   participation of women   204, 216–18
   peace processes   204
   reparations   232
   Resolution 1325   41, 44, 95, 96, 99, 108, 187, 217
   sexual and gender-based violence (SGBV) in armed conflicts   218
   sidelining peace   79
   terrorism and violent extremism, countering   218
   WILPF   96
Women Strike for Peace (WSP)   107
Women Talking (film)   152
Women's Active Museum on War and Peace (WAM), Tokyo   3
Women's Caucus for Gender Justice   185
women's courts and tribunals   206–10
   International Tribunal on Crimes against Women, Brussels, 1976   64, 75–6, 184
   World Courts of Women   207
Women's Encampment for a Future of Peace and Justice, Seneca Falls, 1983   71
Women's Initiatives for Gender Justice   190
Women's International Democratic Federation (WIDF)   61, 64, 69

Women's International League for Peace and Freedom (WILPF)   2, 53, 54, 60–1, 96, 177
   disarmament   102–3, 105–8
   ECOSOC consultative status   105
   Hague Women's Congress   50, 51, 92, 102, 128, 173, 177, 205, 211, 218
   nuclear disarmament   106–8
   peace caucuses   91
   triennial conferences   173
   Women, Peace and Security (WPS) agenda   96
Woolf, Virginia   203
workers' rights   49
World Courts of Women   207
World Disarmament Conference 1932   100–1, 104, 177
World War I   50–3 *see* Hague Women's Congress
   disarmament   102
   national, legal, and religious identities   122
   peace conferences   50, 52, 205
   reparations   132
   sexual and gender-based violence (SGBV)   132
   Versailles Treaty   52
World War II
   International Military Tribunal for the Far East (IMTFE)   132, 209, 236
   Nuremberg Military Tribunal (NMT)   132
   reparations   132

Yemen, conflict in
   Houthis   28, 123–4, 167
   Peace Track Initiative   205
Yugoslavia, conflicts in the former   56, 95, 122, 184 *see also* International Criminal Tribunal for the former Yugoslavia (ICTY)

Zurich Women's Congress   51, 52